Open distributed processing and multimedia

Gordon S Blair

Jean-Bernard Stefani

ADDISON-WESLEY

HARLOW, ENGLAND • READING, MASSACHUSETTS •
MENLO PARK, CALIFORNIA • NEW YORK • DON MILLS,
ONTARIO • AMSTERDAM • BONN • SYDNEY •
SINGAPORE • TOKYO • MADRID • SAN JUAN • MILAN •
MEXICO CITY • SEOUL • TAIPEI

© Addison Wesley Longman Ltd 1998

Addison Wesley Longman Limited
Edinburgh Gate
Harlow
Essex CM20 2JE
England

and associated companies throughout the World.

Cover designed by odB Design & Communication, Reading
Cover photograph by Steven Marks, Inc. © Image Bank
Text design by Sue Clarke
Typeset in 10/12 Baskerville by 32
Printed and bound in Great Britain
by Biddles Ltd, Guildford and King's Lynn

First printed 1997

Portions reprinted, with permission, from Blair (1996). © 1996 IEEE

ISBN 0–201–17794–3

British Library Cataloguing-in-Publication Data
A catalogue record for this book is available from the British Library

Library of Congress Cataloging-in-Publication Data
Blair, Gordon.
    Open distributed processing and multimedia/Gordon S. Blair, Jean-Bernard Stefani.
        p.   cm.
    Includes bibliographical references and index.
    ISBN 0–201–17794-3 (alk. paper)
    1. Electronic data processing–Distributed processing.
2. Multimedia systems.   I. Stefani, Jean-Bernard.   II. Tilte.
QA76.9.D5B53   1997
006.7′2–dc21   97-17905
                                                                                        CIP

Contents

CHAPTER 6
The multimedia examples revisited *143*

CHAPTER 7
Concurrent object-oriented programming within the new approach *183*

PART 3 Building distributed multimedia systems *223*

CHAPTER 8
Engineering support for multimedia *225*

CHAPTER 9
A technology approach based on microkernels *259*

PART 4 Analysis *391*

CHAPTER 12
Results, generalization and outstanding issues *393*

Trademark notice

The following are trademarks or registered trademarks of the company given in parentheses:
Unix (licensed through X/Open Company Ltd); Windows and Windows 95 (Microsoft Corporation); QuickTime (Apple Computer, Inc.); Java, Solaris and Ultra 1 (Sun Microsystems Inc.); Smalltalk (Xerox Corporation); VMS (Digital Equipment Corporation); Berkeley Unix (University of California); Chorus (Chorus Systèmes); Orbix (Iona Technologies).

Foreword

I t is a great pleasure to be asked by Jean-Bernard Stefani and Gordon Blair to write a foreword to this book on the design and implementation of distributed multimedia systems.

I had the privilege of working with Jean-Bernard as a co-rapporteur during the development of the ISO/ITU Reference Model for Open Distributed Processing. That work in turn built on France Telecom's sponsorship of the ANSA Programme, through cooperation in the ESPRIT Integrated Systems Architecture Project and more recently through the ACTS ReTINA project. I got to know Gordon and his colleagues at the University of Lancaster through their use of ANSAware in the early days of distributed systems research, and our friendship has continued through informal support for each other's work since that time. Both are well-known members of the distributed systems community.

This book is a *tour-de-force* in its field: it pulls together system modelling, formal methods, standards and practical engineering into a coherent whole. It will benefit both newcomers and established workers in the field as a point of reference and baseline for future work.

The foundations of the book are laid in the ISO/ITU Reference Model for Open Distributed Processing (RM-ODP). With its powerful concept of 'viewpoints', this standard gives the authors the means to separate key design concerns: overall system objectives, media description, functional partitioning, system implementation and technology choices.

System design is described in terms of the RM-ODP computational viewpoint. The book reveals the strong theoretical basis for the computational type system, binding, interaction and quality of service models. In this respect it is a valuable adjunct to the standard. Blair and Stefani show how these concepts can be used to capture a full range of distributed multimedia system structures and the expression of quality of service requirements in those systems.

Implementation issues are described in terms of both the RM-ODP engineering viewpoint and the OMG CORBA suite of specifications. The authors focus on the means by which resources can be managed to reach the quality of service requirements expressed in a computational design and practical protocols for managing connection models in support of complex bindings. The value of this material is threefold: an expansion and explanation of the RM-ODP engineering viewpoint beyond the bald narrative of the standard, a knitting together of RM-ODP and CORBA and a careful explanation of how to engineer time-constrained applications.

In counterpoint to the theory and modelling strand a strong practical grounding is given through outlines and examples of the real systems built by the authors during their research, exploring in detail the use of microkernels, real-time networks, C++ and distributed object technology.

I hope this foreword will encourage the reader to treat this book as one to read at many levels, and come back again and again for deeper insight and understanding. I congratulate Gordon and Jean-Bernard on a craftsman's job well-done in providing both a complete picture and describing it with clarity.

Bravo, mes amis!

Andrew Herbert
APM Ltd
Cambridge, UK
March 1997

Preface

About the book

Motivation for the book

Heterogeneity is arguably the most important problem facing the developers of distributed systems today. Many organizations suffer from problems caused by heterogeneity in hardware, in operating systems, in computer languages and in management policies. Consequently, there has been considerable interest in the field of *open distributed processing*. The goal of open distributed processing is to provide open access to distributed system services and to mask heterogeneity. An effective open distributed processing technology should also mask the difficulties of operating in a distributed environment, for example in locating objects or in dealing with component failures. Hence in using an open distributed processing technology it should not matter where the service runs, which workstation architecture or operating system has been used, which programming language has been used to develop the service, or which administrative domain is responsible for providing the service. Similarly, it should be straightforward to port services to a different hardware or software platform.

Major advances have been made in the area of open distributed processing and a number of standards and platforms are now available, including:

- the ISO Reference Model for Open Distributed Processing (RM-ODP)
- OMG's Common Object Request Broker Architecture (CORBA)
- the Open Group's Distributed Computing Environment (DCE)

There has been major interest in the application of open distributed processing to telecommunications. This is reflected in the work of the Telecommunication Information Networking Architecture (TINA) consortium.

It is crucially important, however, that such initiatives remain responsive to new end-user demands and the emergence of new technology. The major challenge at the present is the need to support *multimedia* in open distributed processing environments. This is motivated by the potential of applications such as desktop conferencing, multimedia email, virtual reality environments, distance learning and video-on-demand systems, and also because of the widespread deployment of high-speed multi-service networks such as ATM.

Multimedia applications impose considerable demands on the underlying distributed systems platforms. For example, it is necessary to deal with new continuous media types of information, such as audio and video. Multimedia applications also have stringent requirements in terms of quality of service and real-time synchronization. Finally, many distributed applications involve cooperative activities, and hence it is necessary to deal with communications between multiple participants.

Goals of the book

The overall goal of this book is to consider the impact of multimedia on open distributed processing. More specifically, the book has the following objectives:

1. to examine in detail the problem domain of open distributed processing and multimedia and to identify precise requirements for standards and platforms in this area;
2. to develop an object-oriented programming model to meet these requirements and hence to enable the development of multimedia applications in open distributed processing environments;
3. to consider systems support techniques which ensure that the real-time requirements expressed in the programming model are met by the underlying platform;
4. to generalize the results of the study to the range of open distributed processing standards and platforms.

The bias of the book is towards the ISO Reference Model for Open Distributed Processing. The concepts developed in this book have been influential in the development of RM-ODP and the majority of features we describe in the book appear in the standard. Consequently, we believe that the RM-ODP is at the forefront of the effort to incorporate multimedia in open distributed processing. Objective (4), though, ensures that the book is not specifically about RM-ODP but also addresses extending other standards and platforms to meet our requirements.

Note that, although the book is targeted towards multimedia, the ideas are also applicable to a broad spectrum of real-time applications.

Intended readership

The book is primarily aimed at researchers, developers and managers in the fields of distributed systems, telecommunications and multimedia information systems who are interested in the problems and solutions in open distributed processing and who would like to evaluate the potential impact of multimedia on this field.

The book is also of relevance to students of computer science or telecommunications. The book is particularly relevant for advanced courses, for example at a Masters level or as a supplement to PhD studies.

The book offers both audiences:

1. a detailed examination of the major developments in open distributed processing,
2. a concise description of the requirements of multimedia systems,
3. an in-depth description of a comprehensive approach to multimedia in an open distributed processing environment, in terms of both a programming model and associated systems support techniques.

Overview of the book

Structure of the book

The book is divided into four parts together with two appendices, as discussed below.

Part 1: The problem domain

This part addresses the problem domain of open distributed processing and multimedia and is divided into three chapters:

Chapter 1: Introduction to distributed multimedia
   Chapter 1 provides an initial introduction to the problem domain by charting the emergence of distributed systems and open distributed processing and then considering the particular requirements of multimedia and the consequent challenge for open distributed processing.

Chapter 2: Standards and platforms for open distributed processing
   Chapter 2 examines the field of open distributed processing in depth. The main part of the chapter is devoted to the three major players in the field, namely ISO/ITU's Reference Model for Open Distributed Processing (RM-ODP), OMG's Common Object Request Broker Architecture (CORBA) and the Open Group's Distributed Computing Environment (DCE). Other related activities are also considered: TINA and IMA's Multimedia System Services. A comparison of the various activities is also given.

Chapter 3: Requirements of distributed multimedia applications
   Chapter 3 presents an analysis of the requirements of distributed multimedia applications. Four key areas are examined: support for continuous media, quality of service management, real-time synchronization and multiparty communications. The keystone of the chapter is a checklist of requirements for multimedia. An assessment is also given of the standards and platforms introduced in Chapter 2 against this checklist.

Part 2: Designing distributed multimedia systems

This part examines the impact of multimedia on models for the design of distributed applications. The major contribution from this part is a comprehensive programming model for distributed multimedia applications. The part is divided into four chapters.

Chapter 4: A programming model for multimedia

Chapter 4 presents a programming model offering explicit support for distributed multimedia programming. An object-oriented approach is adopted. The chapter initially describes the basic object model and then the key extensions for multimedia, including stream and signal interfaces, quality of service annotations, explicit binding and reactive objects. The chapter then introduces three examples to illustrate how the programming model can be used to support the design of applications. In each case, a high-level object-oriented design is developed. Note that the programming model corresponds to the RM-ODP Computational Viewpoint (see later).

Chapter 5: An approach based on the programming model

Chapter 5 describes one particular approach based on the framework developed in the previous chapter. In particular, the chapter introduces specific languages for the expression of interface type signatures, quality of service annotations and real-time synchronization. The first language is based on CORBA's Interface Definition Language, but with extensions to support stream and signal interfaces. The second language is a real-time logic called QL. Finally, the third language is a real-time synchronous language called Esterel.

Chapter 6: The multimedia examples revisited

This chapter revisits the examples first introduced in Chapter 4. These examples are a QoS-managed stream binding, lip synchronization between an audio and a video stream, and a multimedia presentation. In each case, we revisit the high-level object-oriented design and then populate this with descriptions of the object interfaces (written in the extended IDL), the required QoS annotations on the interfaces (written in QL) and then the implementation of real-time synchronization (written in Esterel).

Chapter 7: Concurrent object-oriented programming within the new approach

Chapter 7 combines the ideas developed in the previous three chapters with concepts emerging from concurrent object-oriented programming. In particular, we introduce the concept of an active object as an encapsulation of arbitrary media processing. Active objects also feature abstract states (providing an abstract representation of the current state of the object) and state notification (enabling other objects to synchronize on particular abstract states). A hierarchy of active objects for multimedia is also developed. The approach is evaluated through a number of worked examples.

Part 3: Building distributed multimedia systems

Part 3 examines systems techniques to support the development of distributed multimedia systems. The part is divided into four chapters.

Chapter 8: Engineering support for multimedia

Chapter 8 presents an engineering model for the development of distributed multimedia platforms (corresponding to the Engineering Viewpoint in RM-ODP). The chapter reviews the engineering model developed in RM-ODP. The chapter then highlights the extensions required for multimedia. The resultant framework is technology-independent but prescribes an approach to crucial aspects of systems support including explicit binding and quality of service management.

Chapter 9: A technology approach based on microkernels

The next chapter then examines a particular approach based on the use of microkernels (corresponding to the selection of a particular technology in the Technology Viewpoint of RM-ODP). The rationale for this approach is described and a particular microkernel technology introduced (the Chorus microkernel). An architecture for the development of distributed multimedia platforms is also outlined. This architecture exploits the concept of subsystems in microkernels to enable multimedia services to coexist with other system services.

Chapter 10: Sumo-CORE: a specialized microkernel-based operating system for multimedia

Chapter 10 describes a set of extensions to Chorus to enable the microkernel to support multimedia services and applications. The resultant system is intended to operate over a wider range of network environments (including networks that do not offer absolute guarantees). The implementation supports the concept of active binding and also features a split level approach to resource management. These features together provide more lightweight and tailorable support for real-time traffic. This implementation also features a comprehensive QoS management framework with both static and dynamic QoS functions. A set of performance figures are presented for the platform.

Chapter 11: Sumo-ORB: an ODP subsystem for multimedia

Chapter 11 describes the design and implementation of an open distributed processing subsystem using the Chorus microkernel. This subsystem is based on CORBA but with significant extensions to reflect the programming and engineering models developed in Parts 2 and 3. This subsystem is designed to operate over an FDDI network and to exploit the characteristics of this network to give deterministic guarantees on quality of service. The chapter also describes static QoS management functions to achieve end-to-end guarantees in such an environment. Performance figures for the platform are also given.

Part 4: Analysis
The final part consists of one chapter:

Chapter 12: Results, generalization and outstanding issues
> Chapter 12 presents an analysis of the contributions of the book. Firstly, the chapter reviews the major results included in the book. Following this, the chapter considers the relationship to important standards and platforms including CORBA and DCE. Finally, the chapter highlights a number of outstanding research issues.

Appendices
The book also features two appendices:

Appendix A: Useful WWW addresses
> The first appendix contains a number of useful World Wide Web addresses pertaining to the book. Most importantly, the appendix contains pointers to web pages for the various standards described in the book. This is particularly important given the evolving nature of many of the standards. The appendix also contains pointers to other pages in the general areas of multimedia and open distributed processing.

Appendix B: An admission control test for jitter-constrained periodic threads
> This appendix contains the derivation of an admission control test for jitter-constrained periodic threads as required by the Sumo-CORE platform (described in Chapter 10).

Tips on how to read the book

The overall structure of the book is illustrated in Figure P.1. This structure is designed to be traversed in a number of different ways depending on the interests of the reader.

Firstly, as stated above, Parts 2 and 3 correspond to the RM-ODP Computational and Engineering/Technology Viewpoints respectively; this use of viewpoints in structuring the book means that readers with particular interests can focus on selected parts. It is recommended that all readers should read Part 1. After this, readers interested in design or programming of multimedia applications can concentrate on Part 2. Similarly, readers interested in systems support for multimedia can focus on Part 3. Part 4 can be read by people interested in seeing how the results can be applied to other standards and platforms.

Secondly, the book can be read to a number of different depths. Part 1 is structured so that Chapter 1 provides an initial overview of open distributed processing and multimedia. Chapters 2 and 3 then expand on the main points raised in the initial chapter. Similarly, the first chapter of Part 2 describes a complete object-oriented approach for programming multimedia applications. Readers interested in more details of specific notations or how this approach can be used with object-oriented programming languages can then read the remaining three chapters. Finally, in Part 3, the first two chapters provide an

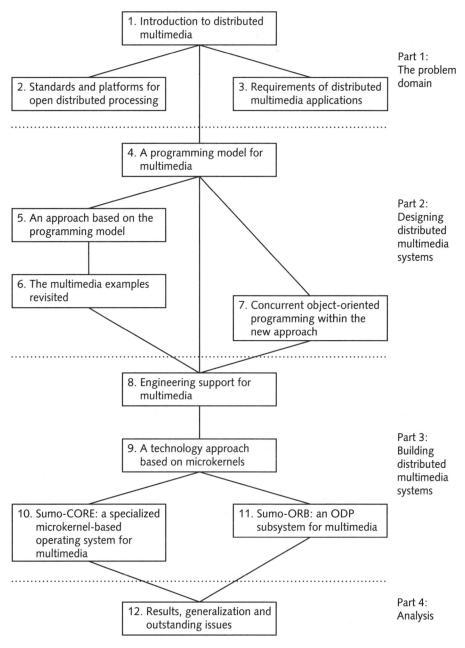

Figure P1 The structure of the book.

overview of the engineering model and a particular technology approach. The remaining two chapters then provide implementation details of specific platforms based on the general approaches.

The use of viewpoints together with the different levels of detail provides great flexibility to the reader. As a further illustration of this, a number of paths through the book are listed below:

1. Chapters 1, 4, 8 and 9 can be read by someone wanting an initial introduction to multimedia in open distributed processing from various perspectives.
2. Chapters 1, 2, 3, 4, 5, 6, 7, and 12 can be read by someone who is interested in obtaining detailed information about multimedia and its impact on the programming of open distributed processing.
3. Chapters 1, 2, 3, 4, 8, 9, 10, 11 should be read by someone more interested in obtaining information on the impact of underlying systems (Chapter 4 is included in the above list as it is important to have some appreciation of the overall programming model).

Acknowledgements

The authors would like to thank the many people who have contributed to the development of this book. Phil Adcock and Dan Waddington provided useful input in the areas of DCE and CORBA. Elie Najm and Kathleen Milsted provided invaluable assistance in the formalization of the programming model. Particular thanks are due to our technical reviewers, Andrew Herbert and Sacha Krakoviak, for their intelligent and helpful comments on the first draft of the book.

Jean-Bernard Stefani would like to thank collectively the members of the ISO WG7 group and the ISA consortium for many long, often arduous, but always stimulating discussions on the topic of open distributed processing. A special mention is due to Peter Linington for his insights on this topic. Thanks also to the above groups of people for the nightly entertainment.

Gordon Blair would like to thank CNET for supporting his stay in Paris during his sabbatical. Without this support, the book would not have been possible. He would also like to thank the members of the Arcade Group at CNET for making him so welcome. A special thanks to his wife, Lynne, and young son, Alistair, for their wonderful support during the time in Paris while the book was being written. Thanks also to his daughter, Kirsty, who was born as the book was nearing completion and who provided a welcome distraction during this time.

Major parts of the work described in this book were developed as part of the Sumo Project, a collaboration between CNET, France Telecom and Lancaster University. This work was funded under France Telecom grant number 93-5B-067. Funding for aspects of the systems support was also provided by the UK EPSRC under grant number GR/J16541. Finally, the contributions of Michael Papathomas were supported by the Swiss FNRS through grant number 8220-037225.

The participants in Sumo all played important roles in developing the ideas described in this book; their individual contributions are documented below.

Participants in Sumo

This book has been written in its entirety by the two authors to ensure a consistency in the style of writing. Nevertheless, major contributions have been made to the material in the book by the various participants in the Sumo Project. These contributions are acknowledged and recorded below. We initially look at the participants from CNET, and then from Lancaster University. In all cases, email addresses are provided.

CNET, France Telecom

The participants in the Sumo Project at CNET are as follows:

Jean-Bernard Stefani

Jean-Bernard Stefani is currently the head of the Distributed Systems Research Department of the Centre National d'Etudes des Télécommunications (CNET), Issy les Moulineaux, France. He is chairman of the Working Party in charge of the development of the Open Distributed Processing (ODP) framework in ITU-T Study Group 7. His current research interests cover open distributed systems, real-time distributed operating systems, synchronous programming and the formal semantics of concurrent object-based languages. He was responsible for the Sumo project in CNET.

Email: jean-bernard.stefani@issy.cnet.fr

François Horn

François Horn is a senior research engineer in the Distributed Systems Research Department of CNET, Issy Les Moulineaux, where he is in charge of the Open Systems research group. His current research interests include distributed real-time and multimedia systems, open distributed processing and distributed operating systems. He made major contributions to the Sumo programming model and to the design and development of the Sumo-ORB.

Email: francois.horn@issy.cnet.fr

Laurent Leboucher

Laurent Leboucher is a research engineer in the Distributed Systems Research Department in CNET, Issy Les Moulineaux, where he is in charge of the Information Network Architecture research group. He is active in OMG, ISO and ITU-T. His current research interests cover open distributed systems, information networks, real-time distributed operating systems, scheduling theory, formalization of temporal quality of service, cooperative multimedia applications, evolution of intelligent networks and telecommunication management networks. He joined Sumo in 1994 and developed the admission control scheme for binding objects.

Email: lebouche@issy.cnet.fr

Frédéric Dang Tran

Frédéric Dang Tran is a research engineer in the Distributed Systems Research Department of CNET, Issy les Moulineaux. His current research interests include open distributed systems, real-time distributed operating systems and multimedia systems. He was the main designer and developer of the Sumo-ORB and contributed also to the development of the Sumo-CORE.

Email: dangtran@issy.cnet.fr

Victor Pérébaskine

Victor Pérébaskine is a research engineer in CNET. He joined Sumo in 1994 when he started working in the Distributed Systems Research Department of CNET, Issy les Moulineaux. He is currently with the Information Networking Department in Lannion. His current research interests include open distributed systems, information networks, telecommunication service and management frameworks. He made major contributions to the design and development of the Sumo-ORB.

Email: victor.perebaskine@lannion.cnet.fr

Laurent Hazard

Laurent Hazard is a research engineer at Télis. He has been involved in Sumo since its inception. His research interests include open distributed systems, synchronous and reactive programming and multimedia systems. He made major contributions to the Sumo hybrid (synchronous/ asynchronous) programming model and was its prime implementor. He was also the main developer of several demonstration applications on the Sumo infrastructure.

Email: laurent.hazard@issy.cnet.fr

Lancaster University

The corresponding participants at Lancaster University are:

Gordon Blair

Gordon Blair is a Professor in the Computing Department at Lancaster University with research interests in the areas of distributed multimedia computing, operating system support for continuous media, the impact of mobility on distributed systems and the use of formal methods in distributed system development. He was jointly responsible (with Geoff Coulson) for managing the Sumo Project at Lancaster. Gordon also contributed significantly to the overall design of the extended Chorus platform.

Email: gordon@comp.lancs.ac.uk

Geoff Coulson

Geoff Coulson is a lecturer in the Computing Department at Lancaster University with research interests in operating system support for continuous media, distributed systems architectures and high-speed networking. He managed the Sumo Project along with Gordon Blair. Geoff also made major contributions to the design of the extended Chorus platform and also to the resource management framework in Sumo.

Email: geoff@comp.lancs.ac.uk

John Iball

John Iball joined the Sumo project as a Research Assistant in 1994, after a period working with VSO as a Lecturer in Computer Science at the University of Moratuwa, Sri Lanka. His main responsibility in Sumo was the implementation of the communications architecture in Chorus. He has now returned to industry to work as a software engineer with Mobile Systems International Ltd.

Email: johni@msi-uk.com

Michael Papathomas

Michael Papathomas joined the Sumo Project in 1994 as a Visiting Research Fellow. His research interests are concurrent object-oriented programming and multimedia applications. His contributions to Sumo were in the general area of real-time synchronization. In particular, he developed the active object concept described in Chapter 7. On completion of this research, Michael worked as a CaberNet funded Visiting Research Fellow at IMAG, Grenoble, before returning to Lancaster in early 1997 to work on the Sumo II Project.

Email: michael@comp.lancs.ac.uk

Philippe Robin

Philippe Robin joined the Sumo Project as a research assistant in 1993. Previously, he worked at Chorus Systèmes in the development of the Chorus/MiX Operating System and with Tolérance Computers on the development of fault-tolerant machines based on the Chorus technology. His main area of research is operating system support and quality of service management for continuous media applications. His particular responsibility in Sumo is for the design and implementation of the scheduling framework in Chorus.

Email: pr@comp.lancs.ac.uk

In addition, important contributions were made by the following:

Andrew Campbell

Andrew Campbell joined the E.E. faculty at Columbia University in January 1996. Previously, he was a BT research lecturer in the Computing Department at Lancaster University. His research interests are in quality of service management and B-ISDN networks. Andrew's research on quality of service architectures provided a major input to the specific approach to QoS management described in Chapter 11.

Email: campbell@ctr.columbia.edu

Andreas Mauthe

Andreas Mauthe is currently a research assistant at Lancaster University working on group services for multimedia architecture. He previously worked at IBM's European Networking Center where he specialized in scheduling for multimedia applications. His contribution to Sumo was in the development of an admission control test for earliest deadline first scheduling which makes allowance for jitter on periodic threads.

Email: andreas@comp.lancs.ac.uk

PART 1
The problem domain

Chapter 1   Introduction to distributed multimedia

Chapter 2   Standards and platforms for open distributed processing

Chapter 3   Requirements of distributed multimedia applications

1 Introduction to distributed multimedia

1.1 Introduction

Distributed systems built using commercially available software are becoming widely accepted. Furthermore, work is well advanced on the development of standards to enable open distributed processing. Considerable progress was made towards this goal with the ISO/ITU-T standard for a Reference Model for Open Distributed Processing (ISO/ITU-T RM-ODP). Specific technologies such as the Open Group's Distributed Computing Environment (DCE) and OMG's Common Object Request Broker Architecture (OMG CORBA) have also been developed. This work is also having an impact in the telecommunications arena through initiatives such as the Telecommunication Information Networking Architecture (TINA) consortium.

It is important that such standards and technologies remain responsive to new challenges. This book is particularly interested in the demands imposed by multimedia computing. More specifically, the book evaluates the requirements imposed by multimedia computing and proposes an approach to open distributed processing which meets these requirements. This initial chapter introduces the field by considering the emergence of distributed systems and open distributed processing (Section 1.2) and then considering the particular requirements of multimedia and the consequent challenge for open distributed processing (Section 1.3). The key points of the chapter are then summarized in Section 1.4.

1.2 Open distributed processing

1.2.1 Introduction to distributed systems

We introduce the field by first providing a definition of distributed systems and then examining the motivation for distributed computing. The section then looks at various problems introduced by distributed systems before concluding by highlighting major recent trends leading to the current interest in open distributed processing.

What is a distributed system?

Distributed processing is now one of the most important topics in computing. With the proliferation of both local and wide area networking, it is crucially important to have distributed systems technologies which can exploit such networked environments. It is notoriously difficult to provide a comprehensive definition of a distributed system; for the purposes of this book, however, we define a distributed system as follows:

> **Definition** *Distributed system*
> A distributed system is a system designed to support the development of applications and services which can exploit a physical architecture consisting of multiple, autonomous processing elements that do not share primary memory but cooperate by sending asynchronous messages over a communications network.

(Readers familiar with badly designed distributed systems might prefer the following definition, attributed to Leslie Lamport: 'A distributed system is one that stops you getting any work done when a machine you've never even heard of crashes!'.) The term *autonomous* is crucial to our definition. In a general distributed processing environment there is inevitably a question of ownership of resources. Resources may be shared, but at the discretion of the owner. This distinguishes distributed systems from more tightly coupled and specialized *parallel* architectures. The fact that communication is *asynchronous* is also important; the delay inherent in message-passing is a central characteristic of a distributed environment.

As mentioned above, a wide range of distributed systems technologies are now available, including distributed operating systems, distributed file systems and tools to support distributed programming. The rationale for this growth of distributed systems is examined in more detail below.

Why distributed systems?

Distributed systems have a number of benefits over more centralized architectures. The most important include the ability to share resources, the potential for increased availability, the ability to incrementally extend distributed systems to meet rising user demands, the improved performance from the availability of a parallel machine and, finally, the correspondence with modern organizational structures. These advantages are discussed in more detail below.

1. *Resource sharing*
   Resource sharing is often the primary motivation for evolving towards a distributed environment. In a distributed system, resources such as printers, magnetic disks, processors and cameras can be accessed remotely and shared between multiple users. Similarly, at a more abstract level, application services such as databases can be shared. Such resource sharing

means that resources do not have to be duplicated on every workstation. Rather, a smaller number of more sophisticated and more robust resources can be provided. This may also be more economical because overhead costs (administration, power supplies and so on) are shared.

2. *Availability*

   Distributed systems have the potential to have higher levels of availability than centralized equivalents (in spite of Lamport's definition!). This potential stems from the intrinsic redundancy in distributed configurations. For example, a typical distributed architecture will have a large number of processors, a number of independent disks and several different printers. Hence the loss of a particular resource need not be catastrophic; the system should be able to continue, albeit in a degraded way with depleted resources.

3. *Extensibility*

   A further benefit of a distributed environment is that it can readily be extended with new resources. For example, if the number of users of a system increases significantly, extra workstations can be connected and an extra storage server introduced. Similarly, if a new resource, such as a multimedia storage server, is required, it can readily be incorporated into the architecture.

4. *Performance*

   A distributed configuration is a powerful parallel machine exhibiting a large numbers of processors often interconnected by a high-speed network (although message latencies may be greater than in parallel architectures). Thus, there is potential in a distributed environment to parallelize applications and gain a consequent increase in performance.

5. *Distributed organizations*

   Finally, a critical factor in considering distributed technologies is that most modern organizations are highly distributed, with computer equipment, resources and personnel being geographically dispersed across a single site, between different sites in a given country and also often between sites internationally. There is therefore a strong correspondence between distributed systems technologies and such organizational structures.

It should be stressed, however, that the above are potential advantages and that realizing this potential can often be quite difficult. In particular, distributed systems also introduce a number of problems which must be overcome. These problems are discussed in some detail below.

Problems introduced by a distributed environment

In the following discussion we assume a simple client–server model (Figure 1.1) and briefly consider the potential difficulties introduced by the distributed nature of the system (further discussion of these often subtle issues can be found in Coulouris *et al.* (1994), Mullender (1993) and Bacon (1993)).

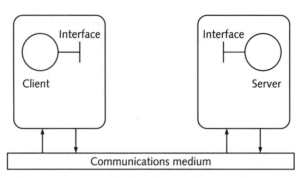

Figure 1.1 A simple client–server interaction.

Firstly, services can be accessed *concurrently* by a number of different client applications. With such concurrent access, it is possible for client requests to conflict. For example, two clients could concurrently attempt to write to the same field in a database. This would result in one of the writes being lost.

Further problems are introduced by the failure of components. Distributed systems are quite different from standalone machines in that *partial failure* can occur: parts of the system will fail but the system as a whole will keep running. In many ways, this is more difficult to deal with than a total system failure. One of the main problems is the lack of information on the cause of a failure. For example, if the client does not get a response from a server, the client will not necessarily know whether the server has crashed, the network is down or the network is partitioned. The actions in each case would be quite different.

Difficulties also exist in *locating* the right server in a distributed environment. A typical environment might offer very large numbers of servers. In such an environment, it is necessary to identify the correct server and then determine precisely where this server resides. The latter problem can be particularly difficult in systems which support server *migration* (for reasons of availability or performance). Once the server is located, it is then necessary to understand the correct method of *access* to this service; that is, what service the server offers and what protocol should be used to access the service.

Finally, servers might be *replicated* to enhance availability. In such environments difficulties exist in maintaining consistency of the copies of the server. This can be particularly difficult given the problems of partial failure as discussed above.

It would be undesirable if the application programmer had to deal with each of these problems when developing distributed programs. Hence, most systems will provide a level of *distribution transparency* to the programmer: the system will mask out the problems introduced by a distributed environment. Full distribution transparency would imply that all the problems associated with distribution are handled by the system, and the application programmer would not necessarily be aware of the distributed nature of the system. This would, however, inevitably carry a performance overhead in accessing servers. The other extreme of having no transparency would be much more lightweight but would add considerably to the complexity of the application program. Modern thinking is to provide *selective transparency*, where the application programmer can specify the required level of transparency for a given interaction.

Important trends in distributed processing

Distributed systems research has made considerable progress towards providing distributed systems platforms which offer solutions to all the above problems. Additionally, however, there have been some important technology trends that have moved distributed systems from the research laboratory to the global market-place and created a need for international standards.

Firstly, modern distributed systems are likely to be very *large*, consisting of potentially millions of machines interconnected by a complex network (such as the Internet). Given this trend, it is crucial that the techniques adopted in distributed systems platforms *scale* to larger configurations. It is also important that techniques are available to *manage* such large systems. This is made more difficult, however, by the fact that distributed environments will typically span many *administrative domains*. Hence the management of distributed systems is inevitably a highly complex and cooperative task involving many sub-domains of responsibility.

Secondly, as distributed systems become more global in scope, there is growing pressure for a *convergence* between distributed systems and telecommunications architectures. Telecommunications providers are increasingly looking towards distributed system technologies to address the problems of the construction and subsequent management of large-scale telecommunications networks. This is becoming even more important as the telecommunications industry extends the range of services offered by their networks. In addition, as distributed systems become more global, they are increasingly relying on telecommunication providers for large parts of their connectivity. This implies that distributed systems concepts must map on to available telecommunications services.

Finally, and centrally for this book, all the above developments imply that distributed systems are becoming more *heterogeneous* in that the individual components are likely to vary greatly across the global system. Heterogeneity is the principal motivating factor for the development of open distributed processing, and hence the topic is considered in more detail below.

1.2.2 Focus on heterogeneity

The *Oxford English Dictionary* defines heterogeneity as 'diverse in character'. A modern distributed system exhibits heterogeneity at a number of different levels:

1. *Heterogeneous hardware*
   Distributed systems will typically feature a variety of computer architectures interconnected by a range of network types. For example, a configuration might feature IBM-compatible PCs together with a range of workstations

developed by different manufacturers. The various machines in such a configuration will inevitably feature differences in memory sizes, byte order and instruction sets. Similarly, networks may vary from high-performance multi-service networks, such as ATM, through medium performance networks, such as Ethernet, to lower bandwidth services, such as X.25 networks, or mobile radio networks, such as GSM.

2. *Heterogeneous platforms*
   Secondly, the operating system platforms provided on each machine are likely to vary considerably. For example, a typical configuration will feature a mixture of Unix systems and Microsoft Windows environments. Each operating system has its own file formats, process layouts and so on. They will also have their own choice of protocol for communication.

3. *Heterogeneous languages*
   Thirdly, the various services in a distributed environment are potentially developed using different programming languages. For example, some may be developed using C or C++, while others could be developed using Ada or Pascal. The problem with heterogeneous languages is that each language will define its own model of communications (if any), rules for type checking and so on, making it difficult to achieve interoperability.

4. *Heterogeneous management policies*
   Finally, the approaches and policies used to manage a distributed system are likely to vary from domain to domain. For example, one cluster of machines might have very stringent security requirements, such as a confidentiality policy, whereas another cluster could be quite relaxed about security. Different policies could also coexist for other aspects of management, including user administration, accounting, naming and configuration control.

It is becoming increasingly important to tackle problems of heterogeneity in distributed systems. Heterogeneity is very much the general case in realistic distributed configurations. Even if an initial system configuration is homogeneous, this will inevitably change as the system evolves. For example, specialized computer equipment may be introduced into a distributed system, for example to provide high-quality graphics capabilities. Furthermore, as systems evolve, machines will be replaced over time by different people making purchasing decisions, each with their own preferences and requirements.

1.2.3 The goal of open distributed processing

Openness and distributed processing
In simple terms, the goal of open distributed processing is to enable interaction with services from anywhere in the distributed environment without concern for the underlying environment. Technically, this level of openness requires that systems *conform to well-defined interfaces*. An open system is then one that can guarantee conformance to the interface definitions. In contrast, a closed

system is one that exhibits private or proprietary interfaces. The primary goal for open distributed processing standardization is then to develop interfaces against which conformance can be tested.

A crucial part of this process is the definition of *conformance testing* procedures to ensure that different implementations by different manufacturers adhere to the standardized interfaces. A comprehensive conformance testing procedure should ensure two crucial benefits of open distributed processing:

1. *Interoperability*
   An implementation of an open distributed processing platform developed by one manufacturer should be able to interwork with a different platform implemented by a potentially different manufacturer.
2. *Portability*
   An application running on an open distributed platform developed by one manufacturer should be able to be ported directly to a different platform implemented by a potentially different manufacturer.

Open distributed processing has an additional goal: to develop systems architectures which are themselves open. More specifically, the goal of open distributed processing is not only to standardize the highest level interfaces; it is also seen as crucial to have a complete architecture where the individual components are themselves open. This approach has a number of important advantages:

1. the benefits of interoperability and portability extend to all components in the architecture,
2. the architecture can be specialized or can evolve by changing the implementation of individual components, and
3. the architecture can be extended by introducing new components at a later date.

The different levels of openness are contrasted in Figure 1.2.

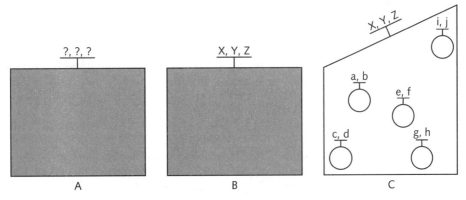

Figure 1.2 Different levels of openness.

Architecture A is a completely closed system. The interface is private and hence unknown in the global environment. In addition the internal structure is completely hidden (this can be viewed as a black box). Architecture B is a more open architecture in that the interface is published and conforms to a recognized standard. However, the internal details of the system are unknown. Architecture C exhibits the properties required of an open distributed processing architecture. The system is composed of a series of components, each offering its own published interface conforming to a recognized standard. Note, however, that such a system must also embody rules for the composition of such components into a coherent overall architecture.

Achieving open distributed processing

The main problem in achieving the goal of open distributed processing is the heterogeneity in the underlying environment (although the additional issues of scale and spanning multiple administrative domains should not be overlooked). To solve this problem, it is necessary to provide a level of *independence* from the heterogeneous infrastructure. The various types of independence are summarized in Table 1.1.

Network and machine independence is achieved by providing abstractions over the characteristics of the underlying physical environment. This aspect of heterogeneity is well understood and is solved, for example, by network protocols and standard interchange formats between different machine architectures. Platform independence implies providing abstractions over the underlying systems platforms. This is more difficult given the diversity of operating systems in use today. To achieve this goal, it is necessary to have a set of agreed abstractions over system resources such as virtual memory, file storage and processing. To achieve language independence, it is necessary to provide abstractions over the interfaces offered by different languages so that they can interwork. The key to this is to provide a language-independent type system which can then be translated into individual languages. Finally, to overcome heterogeneous management policies, it is necessary to provide a meta-architecture for management which can accommodate specific approaches and policies. Software which offers the various levels of abstraction is often referred to as *middleware*.

In providing such levels of abstraction it is crucial to achieve *neutrality*; that is, the abstractions should not prescribe a particular implementation. This is important to cope with the variety of components which may need to be

Table 1.1 Solving the problem of heterogeneity

Style of heterogeneity	Solution
Heterogeneous hardware	Network and machine independence
Heterogeneous platforms	Platform independence
Heterogeneous languages	Language independence
Heterogeneous management	Management independence

integrated into an open distributed processing environment. Such an approach will also help accommodate new hardware architectures, platforms and languages.

Achieving openness is not simply a matter of understanding the syntax of communication. It is also important to understand the underlying *semantics*. This applies at a number of different levels in a distributed interaction. For example, at one level it is necessary to know that a given message contains a request to carry out an operation. At a higher level, it is necessary to know the *intention* of this operation, for example to open a particular file. Furthermore, this intention must be interpreted unambiguously at any appropriate location in the open distributed environment. Clearly, in a distributed processing environment, there can be a spectrum of solutions offering different levels of understanding (ranging from no understanding through to full understanding of intentions in terms of, for example, speech act theory). One of the crucial challenges of open distributed processing standardization is to select the appropriate point in this spectrum to enable open access to services and subsequent management of the distributed services.

The role of standards
Standards organizations have a particularly important role to play in achieving open distributed processing. To achieve this goal, it is necessary to have *international agreement* on the abstractions to be provided. Furthermore, it is important that distributed systems manufacturers have a high level of *confidence* in the agreed abstractions to ensure uptake. Standards organizations are supportive of both these processes by providing the necessary mechanisms and infrastructure for reaching international consensus and by having the necessary international status to ensure acceptance of the results.

There are two styles of standards organization, both of which feature strongly in the quest for open distributed processing. Firstly, there are a number of international treaty-based standards organizations whose task it is to develop standards to enable international trade. Examples of such organizations are the International Organization for Standardization (ISO) and the International Telecommunication Union (ITU). Secondly, it is common in computing for industrial consortia to be formed to develop and promote particular standards. Examples of this style of organization are the Open Group (formed in 1996 following a merger of the Open Software Foundation (OSF) and X/Open), which promotes a range of standards from operating systems to windowing systems, and the Object Management Group (OMG), which is devoted to object-oriented technologies. Alternatively, it is often possible for standards to emerge from the market-place through achieving a certain level of market penetration, for example the IBM-compatible personal computer. Sun NFS or Java are other examples of vendor-initiated standards.

Standards produced by recognized standards organizations are referred to as *de jure* because their status is defined by law makers (via treaties). In contrast, standards which emerge from the market-place are referred to as *de facto* standards. Standards produced by consortia such as Open Group and OMG are also classed as *de facto*, in spite of the often widespread membership of such organizations, to reflect the fact that they have no international status as standards organizations.

Standards organizations and open distributed processing

A number of standardization activities are addressing the issues of open distributed processing. These are:

1. *ISO/ITU-T Reference Model for Open Distributed Processing*
   The Reference Model for Open Distributed Processing (RM-ODP) is a joint standardization activity by both ISO and ITU-T. The standard provides an object-oriented system specification methodology based on the concept of viewpoints together with a vocabulary and grammar for describing a distributed system from each viewpoint.
2. *OMG Common Object Request Broker Architecture*
   The Common Object Request Broker Architecture (CORBA) is a standardization activity promoted by the OMG. OMG is a non-profit organization sponsored by a number of IT and telecommunications companies with the specific aim of promoting an open object-oriented framework for distributed computing. The particular goal of CORBA is to provide the mechanisms by which objects transparently interact in a distributed environment.
3. *The Open Group's Distributed Computing Environment*
   The Distributed Computing Environment (DCE) is a standardization activity sponsored by the Open Group. The Open Group, like OMG, is a non-profit organization sponsored by a number of IT and telecommunications companies with the aim of promoting computing standards. DCE is an operating system-independent and network-independent software platform to achieve open distributed processing. In contrast to RM-ODP and CORBA, DCE supports a simple client–server architecture; it does not support object-oriented abstractions.

There are also a number of other activities which can be viewed as specializations of the above architectures. For example, the Telecommunication Information Networking Architecture (TINA) is currently being developed by the TINA consortium (TINA-C) consisting of a number of leading telecommunications companies. TINA is intended to provide a framework for the development of future telecommunications networks. The architecture exploits recent developments in open distributed processing (see discussion in Section 1.2.1). In particular, the architecture is based closely on RM-ODP, but with specializations to meet the particular demands of the telecommunications industry. Similarly, a further non-profit organization, the International Multimedia Association (or IMA), have developed an architecture for Multimedia System Services (*IMA MSS*). MSS is intended to provide an open approach to accessing a range of multimedia services. The approach is based on CORBA. MSS has also been adopted as the platform for the ISO graphics standard, PREMO. Note that in both TINA and MSS specialization is naturally supported by the object-oriented approaches of RM-ODP and CORBA respectively.

All the above activities share one common attribute. They are all *integrative standards*, in that their role is to bring together a set of components which might themselves be standardized into an overall framework. Examples of such components include TCP/IP, the Kerberos security service or an MPEG video source.

Note also that, to avoid confusion in the rest of the book, the term *open distributed processing* (with lower-case letters) will be used as a general term for all the activities discussed in this section; the term *Open Distributed Processing* (with initial capital letters) will be used for the specific ISO Reference Model.

1.3 The emergence of multimedia

1.3.1 Introducing multimedia

We introduce multimedia by firstly considering a definition of the term and then considering the motivation for multimedia systems. The section then examines in depth the characteristics of a multimedia system.

A definition
As with distributed systems, it is difficult to provide a precise definition of the term 'multimedia'. To do so, it is first necessary to consider the use of the term 'media'.

Definition *Media*
The term *media* refers to the storage, transmission, interchange, presentation, representation and perception of different information types (data types) such as text, graphics, voice, audio and video.

Table 1.2 clarifies the different usages of the word 'media' (Kretz, 1990). Because of these different aspects of media, it is important not to use the word in isolation. Rather, it is more correct to use terms such as *interchange media* for storage and transmission, *representation media* for an abstract description of the media, and so on.

Definition *Multimedia*
We use the term *multimedia* to denote the property of handling a *variety* of *representation media* in an *integrated* manner.

We stress the use of the phrase *representation media* because we believe the most fundamental aspect of multimedia systems is the support for different representation types. The terms variety and integration are also important in

Table 1.2 Usage of the term media

Term	Usage
Storage	The term 'storage media' refers to the type of physical means to store data (magnetic tape, hard disk, optical disk and so on).
Transmission	The term 'transmission media' refers to the type of physical means to transmit data (coaxial cable, twisted pair, fibre and so on).
Interchange	The term 'interchange media' refers to the means of interchanging data; this can be by storage media, transmission media or a combination of both.
Presentation	The term 'presentation media' is used to describe the type of physical means to reproduce information to the user or to acquire information from the user; for example, speakers, video windows, keyboard or mouse.
Representation	The term 'representation media' is related to how information is described (*represented*) in an abstract form, for use within an electronic system. For example, to *present* text to the user, the text can be coded (represented) in raster graphics, in graphics primitives or in simple ASCII characters. Thus, the presentation can be the same but with different representations. Other examples of representation media are ASN.1 and SGML.
Perception	The term 'perception media' is used to describe the nature of information as perceived by the user; for example, speech, music and film.

the above definition. It is *necessary* for a multimedia system to support a *variety* of representation media types (from now on referred to as media types for brevity). The range of media types could be as modest as text and graphics or as rich as animation, audio and video. However, this alone is not *sufficient* for a multimedia environment. It is also important that the various sources of media types are *integrated* into a single system framework.

Note that it is important to draw a distinction between multimedia systems which operate on a single computer workstation and those which can span a networked environment. The term *distributed multimedia system* is introduced to describe the general case of a number of multimedia workstations inter-connected by one or more multi-service networks. In addition, a *distributed multimedia application* is defined as an application which runs over a distributed multimedia system. The problems of managing multimedia in a distributed system are great and introduce a number of unresolved research problems. In contrast, the technological problems of standalone multimedia workstations are much better understood.

Motivation
The emergence of multimedia, and more precisely distributed multimedia systems, can be attributed to two factors. Firstly, there is an end user demand for systems which achieve better integration of a wide variety of media types.

Secondly, the technology is emerging to support multimedia computing. We examine each of these points in more detail below.

End user pull

In recent years, there has been a dramatic increase in the range of media used to convey information. A modern information system will have to deal with a wide range of media types including text, voice, fax, video and animation. Such advances provide a great opportunity for new developments in a range of areas such as education and commerce. However, there are also a number of problems associated with the growth of information in society. In particular, there is a great danger of creating *information overload*. This problem can be seen, for example, in business, where executives are required to make decisions based on an ever-increasing variety and volume of information. It is possible that decision makers will have difficulty finding the right information. Similar problems are also occurring in areas such as government, health care and education.

The other great trend in information technology, from a user perspective, is the decentralization of information. Most modern-day organizations are very large and tend to consist of a number of separate institutions spread across a wide geographical area. These institutions typically cooperate through the sharing and exchange of information. Thus, communication is a vital concern for most organizations. Efficient communications can make the difference between successful operation and failure. Without appropriate forms of communication, there is a danger of *information starvation*: decision makers do not have sufficient information to make the correct decisions.

End users are therefore faced with the two problems of information overload and information starvation. They may either have too much information or may not have sufficient information. There is therefore a need to help the end user to *manage* information to ease the burden created by the increasing importance of information. Essentially, the end user needs support in order to get the right information to the right people at the right time and in the right form. This clearly cannot be achieved by manual systems. Thus, there is a requirement for automation in the process of (multimedia) information management.

Technology push

The most noticeable trend in information technology from a technology perspective has been the increasing *integration* of media. For example, consider the state of the art in communications networks. Early networks were specialized to carry one type of service only; for example, the Public Switched Telephone Network supporting voice traffic or the X.25 network supporting computer data. The major trend in networking now though is towards multi-service networks.

In the local/metropolitan area, the central technologies are the Fibre Digital Data Interface (FDDI) and Distributed Queues Dual Bus (DQDB) networks. In the wide area, the Integrated Services Digital Network (ISDN) is becoming widely supported by telecommunications providers. Basic rate ISDN, intended for domestic use, provides a pair of 64 kbps channels for data and a 16 or 64 kbps channel intended for control traffic. Primary rate ISDN is intended for consumers with heavier requirements and specifies either 30×64 kbps channels (Europe) or 23×64 kbps channels (USA) together with a signalling channel. Broadband ISDN (B-ISDN) is a development of ISDN which offers far higher data rates (155 Mbps or 622 Mbps). B-ISDN is implemented with Asynchronous Transfer Mode (ATM) packet switching which uses small fixed sized packets (or *cells*) and allows variable numbers and capacities of connection, each with varying QoS properties (de Prycker, 1991). Finally, SMDS (Switched Multimegabit Data Service) is a network service being developed by Bellcore in the USA which has caused strong interest among the European telecommunications operators.

Significant developments are also taking place in the field of mobile communications. In wide area mobile communications, *cellular* radio-based systems are becoming prevalent. The most important cellular-based network at the present time is the second generation pan-European digital service commonly referred to as GSM (Groupe Spécial Mobile). This is intended to provide continent-wide mobile communications, mainly for voice but also increasingly for data communications. Third generation mobile communications services are also now envisaged. For example, it is expected that Mobile Broadband Systems (or MBS) will be available by the year 2000. Such systems will provide a full range of multimedia services over radio networks.

The capabilities of the various networks discussed above are given in Table 1.3 below (a good overview of such technologies can also be found in Fluckiger(1995) or Partridge (1994)).

Significant advances are also being made in computer support for multimedia. Workstations and computers are now available which support a wide range of media types, including audio and video. This is partially enabled by advances in data compression, but also by the availability of large capacity, high-bandwidth storage technologies. As a further indication of the advances in computer technology, we summarize the range of storage technologies available today (Table 1.4).

Table 1.3 An overview of multi-service networking technologies

Network	Service	Bandwidth (Mbits/s)
FDDI	Multi-service LAN	100
DQDB	Multi-service MAN	150
Basic rate ISDN	Multi-service WAN	0.128
Primary rate ISDN	Multi-service WAN	1.9
SMDS	Multi-service WAN	1–45
Broadband ISDN	Multi-service WAN	150–1200
GSM	Data+voice	0.01
MBS	Multi-service mobile	2–150

Table 1.4 An overview of current digital storage technologies

Technology	Technique	Attributes	Bandwidth (Mbytes/s)	Capacity (Mbytes)
Magnetic disks	Magnetic	Read/write	1.0–5.0	100–4000
RAID	Magnetic	Read/write	100	1 000 000
CD ROM	Optical	Read only	0.15–0.6	650
CD ROM/XA	Optical	Read only	0.15–0.6	650
WORM	Optical	Write once, read many	0.15–0.6	10 000
MO	Magneto-optical	Read/write	0.2–0.2	500–5000
Jukeboxes	Optical	Read	0.1–0.6	10 × 650

With the technology available today, it is therefore feasible to support a wide range of distributed multimedia applications such as multimedia desktop conferencing, multimedia email, virtual reality environments, distance learning and video-on-demand systems.

Characteristics of multimedia

Multimedia imposes considerable demands on the underlying infrastructure. In this section, we evaluate these demands. Firstly, however, it is necessary to distinguish between continuous and discrete media types. It is the former that poses the most problems for a system infrastructure.

Continuous and discrete media types

Two broad classes of (representation) media can be identified: *continuous media* and *discrete media*. Continuous media types are those with an implied temporal dimension: items of data must be presented according to particular real-time constraints for a particular length of time. Examples of continuous media types are audio, video and animation. In contrast, discrete media types have no temporal dimension. Examples of discrete media types include text and graphics. A selection of the media types in these two categories is provided in Table 1.5.

Continuous media types may be represented in either digital or analogue format. In the rest of this book, however, we assume a digital representation. From a multimedia computing perspective, there is a significant reason for promoting the use of such representations of all media types: it enables all media types to be fully integrated. However, as we shall show in the next section, the support of digital representations of continuous media places considerable demands on the underlying technologies.

Assessment of the demands of digital media

Given the range of media types, it is possible to calculate each of their basic data requirements for storage or transmission. Calculations for a cross-section of continuous media types are presented in Table 1.6. It is important to realize,

Table 1.5 Discrete and continuous media types

Discrete media types	Continuous media types
Plain data (data without any structure such as binary files)	Audio data (digitized speech and high-quality audio)
Raw ASCII	Formatted audio data (for example MIDI)
Numerical (data units of fixed length, such as integer or real)	Video data (digitized video information)
Encoded text (character strings of arbitrary length with embedded font control)	Formatted video data (for example compressed video)
Vector graphics	Animation data (sequences of vector graphics primitives)
Bitmap images	High-definition television (HDTV)

Table 1.6 Demands of digital continuous media

Media type	Average bandwidth (Mbits/s)
Voice	0.064
High-fidelity audio	1.0
Slow scan video	80
High-quality video	200

however, that, for a given media type, bandwidth requirements can vary dramatically depending on the precise parameters associated with the encoding (such as the frame rate or resolution for video). Hence, the figures in Table 1.6 are for general illustration only. These figures can be reduced considerably by the use of appropriate compression techniques. For example, depending on the compression technique adopted, video can be compressed by a factor of between 10 and 200.

The key objective of compression is to reduce the quantity of data by removing *redundancy*. The success of this process can be measured by the *compression ratio* achieved. One of the drawbacks of compression, however, is that it can transform a constant bit rate stream (CBR) into a variable bit rate stream (VBR). The burstiness and unpredictability of VBR streams can be difficult to handle in the underlying network.

The three most important compression techniques for image and video are JPEG, MPEG and H.261:

- *JPEG*
  JPEG (Joint Photographic Experts Group) is a collaboration between ISO and CCITT which resulted in the publication of the JPEG standard for image information in 1991. As JPEG is designed for still images, it employs an intra-frame compression technique. The technique can also be used for video by applying the compression algorithm on successive frames (Motion

JPEG). The compression ratio for both images and video is up to 70:1. JPEG is a symmetrical compression technique (compression and decompression are of similar complexity). It also has the attractive feature that the degree of loss can be traded off against the compression ratio achieved.

- *MPEG*

  MPEG (Motion Pictures Expert Group) has developed a compression standard within ISO specifically designed for the compression of video and its associated audio track. MPEG-I was standardized in 1992 and uses both intra- and inter-frame techniques. It is designed specifically for data streams of 1.5 Mbits per second (intended to support data from a CD-ROM device) and can achieve compression ratios of up to 200:1. MPEG-II is also currently under development. This is designed for the high-quality coding of either standard or High-Definition Television (HDTV) and is targeted towards high performance networks such as ATM. MPEG-II also offers a compression ratio of up to 200:1. Both techniques are asymmetrical and (as with JPEG) allow the degree of loss to be controlled.

- *H.261*

  The H.261 standard, or $p \times 64$, was adopted by CCITT in 1990. It is designed specifically for videophones and video-conferencing over digital networks offering between 64 kbits and 2Mbits per second. It uses both intra- and inter-frame coding techniques to achieve compression ratios sufficient to map to ISDN networks offering $p \times 64$ kbits/s channels, where $p = 1, 2, \ldots, 30$ (hence the alternative name). This technique is also asymmetrical. To enable interoperability across different networks, the standard also specifies an intermediate video format known as the Common Intermediate Format or CIF, with 352×288 pixels per frame and 30 frames per second. A special intermediate format for videophones has also been specified as Quarter CIF (QCIF), which offers a lower quality and frame rate.

The characteristics of the various compression standards are summarized in Table 1.7. Again, these figures are intended to provide only a general illustration of compression ratios. The figures can vary dramatically depending on the particular parameters given to the compression scheme.

Table 1.7 Characteristics of the major compression techniques

Standard	Standardization	Symmetry	Coding	Compression ratio
JPEG	ISO/CCITT, 1990	Symmetrical	Intra-frame	<70:1
MPEG-I	ISO, 1992	Asymmetrical	Intra- and inter-frame	<200:1
MPEG-II	ISO Work Item	Asymmetrical	Intra- and inter-frame	<200:1
H.261	CCITT, 1990	Asymmetrical	Intra- and inter-frame	100:1–2000:1

There are also a number of proprietary compression techniques such as Intel's Digital Video Interactive (DVI) or Apple's RPZ-RPZ, used with their QuickTime software. An excellent and comprehensive discussion on compression technologies can be found in Steinmetz (1994).

1.3.2 The challenge of multimedia for open distributed processing

The introduction of multimedia adds some significant challenges to the developers of (open) distributed systems platforms. The most fundamental challenges are briefly discussed below.

Support for continuous media
As mentioned above, one of the most fundamental characteristics of multimedia systems is that they incorporate continuous media, such as voice, video and animated graphics. The use of such media in distributed systems implies the need for *continuous data transfers* over relatively long periods of time; for example, playout of video from a remote surveillance camera. Furthermore, the timeliness of such media transmissions must be maintained as an ongoing commitment for the duration of the continuous media presentation.

A further problem arising from the consideration of continuous media is that traditional forms of interaction, such as synchronous or asynchronous communication or remote procedure calls, are inadequate to model the concept of the ongoing transmission of data. Consequently, new communication models must be developed for multimedia systems employing continuous media types.

Quality of service management
The second requirement of distributed multimedia applications (in common with other real-time and safety critical applications) is the need for sophisticated quality of service (QoS) management. In most traditional computing environments, requests for a particular service are either met or ignored. In a multimedia system, however, the quality of the service achieved is central to the acceptability of the application.

Quality of service management encompasses a number of different functions, including static aspects such as quality of service specification, negotiation, resource reservation and admission control, and more dynamic aspects such as quality of service monitoring and renegotiation. Furthermore, this management will be required at a number of different levels of the system (such as network, transport and operating system) with appropriate mappings between the various layers. At the highest level, quality of service is typically more user-oriented and declarative (for instance a high-definition video display), whereas at lower levels the descriptions are more system-oriented and prescriptive (for example 10 ms maximum delay). Finally, it is important to stress that, in distributed systems, quality of service should be *end-to-end* from the information source to the information sink. In order to achieve this, coordination is necessary between the end system and the network infrastructure.

Real-time synchronization

A further characteristic of distributed multimedia applications is the need for a rich set of real-time synchronization mechanisms covering both *intra-* and *inter-media* synchronization. Intra-media synchronization refers to the maintenance of real-time constraints across a single continuous media connection, for example to ensure that audio is presented with the required throughput, jitter and latency characteristics. In contrast, inter-media synchronization refers to the maintenance of real-time constraints across more than one media type. Examples of inter-media synchronization include lip synchronization between audio and video channels or synchronization of text subtitles and video sequences. Synchronization mechanisms must operate correctly in a *distributed* environment, potentially involving both local and wide area networks irrespective of the location of the objects involved in the interaction. They must also enable the user to specify *arbitrary* synchronization policies for objects and to be able to react to change at run-time.

Multiparty communications

Many distributed multimedia applications are concerned with interactions between dispersed groups of users. It is now recognized that this requires explicit support from the underlying distributed systems platform. There are several aspects to group support for multimedia. Firstly, it is necessary to provide a *programming model* for multiparty communications (supporting both discrete and continuous media types). Facilities should also be provided to enable management of such groups; for example, providing support for joining and leaving of groups at run-time. Secondly, it is important to ensure that the underlying system provides the right level of *support* for such communications, particularly for continuous media types. Thirdly, with multimedia, it is necessary to cater for multicast communications where receivers may require different *qualities of service*. This adds some complexity to quality of service management. Fourthly, it is important to be able to support a variety of *policies* for ordering and reliability of data delivery. For multimedia, real-time orderings may also be important.

1.4 Summary

The topic of this book is the impact of multimedia on the field of open distributed processing. This chapter has provided an initial introduction of this problem domain.

The first part of the chapter considered the topic of open distributed processing. The rationale for distributed systems was examined and the important problem of heterogeneity highlighted. The chapter then continued by considering the topic of openness and its relationship to distributed processing. A number of open distributed processing standards activities were then introduced, namely RM-ODP, CORBA, DCE, TINA and MSS.

The second part of the chapter then charted the emergence of multimedia. A number of fundamental requirements were highlighted, specifically support for continuous media, quality of service management, real-time synchronization and multiparty communications.

Part 1 now continues by looking at this problem domain in more depth. Chapter 2 examines in detail the area of open distributed processing standards and platforms. The five activities mentioned above are fully discussed. Chapter 3 then presents a more complete discussion of the fundamental requirements of multimedia culminating in the production of a checklist for open distributed processing technologies. A series of typical multimedia scenarios are also identified. These scenarios will provide the basis for examples throughout the book.

2 Standards and platforms for open distributed processing

2.1 Introduction

In this chapter we examine in more detail the major standards and platforms in the field of open distributed processing. The main part of the chapter is devoted to the three major initiatives in the field, namely ISO's Reference Model for Open Distributed Processing (RM-ODP), OMG's Common Object Request Broker Architecture (CORBA) and the Open Group's Distributed Computing Environment (DCE). These topics are covered in Sections 2.2, 2.3 and 2.4 respectively. Section 2.5 then examines other related activities: TINA and IMA's Multimedia System Services. (Note that these should not be viewed as lesser activities, but are included in this section as refinements of the above three technologies.) Following this, Section 2.6 presents a comparison of the various standards and platforms. It should be stressed, however, that a direct comparison is not possible as each of the initiatives is addressing different concerns. Indeed, the various activities can be viewed as quite complementary. This should become apparent as the discussion progresses. Finally, Section 2.7 summarizes the chapter.

2.2 ISO RM-ODP

2.2.1 Introducing RM-ODP

The Reference Model for Open Distributed Processing (RM-ODP) is a joint standardization activity by both ISO and ITU-T. It is therefore a *de jure* standard (see Chapter 1 for terminology) produced following a period of international consultation to reach a technical consensus. This consultation involves a number of national standards bodies such as AFNOR in France and the British Standards Institute (BSI) in the UK.

The aim of RM-ODP is to enable 'the development of standards that allow the benefits of distribution of information processing services to be realized in an environment of heterogeneous IT resources and multiple organisational domains' (ISO/IEC, 19T95a). It is important to stress, though, that RM-ODP does not itself prescribe particular standards for open distributed processing.

Rather, it provides a framework (in terms of architectural concepts and terminology) to enable specific standards to emerge. RM-ODP should thus be considered a *meta-standard* for open distributed processing. It is therefore essential in the definition of RM-ODP to be sufficiently generic to enable a range of standards to be accommodated within this framework. The main value of RM-ODP is then in providing a common set of concepts for the broader field of open distributed processing.

The standard consists of four parts. The heart of the standard is Foundations (Part 2) (ISO/IEC, 1995b), which defines basic modelling concepts for distributed systems followed by the Architecture (Part 3) (ISO/IEC, 1995c), which then constrains the basic model by introducing concepts which a conformant RM-ODP system should possess. The standard also includes an Overview (Part 1) (ISO/IEC, 1995a), providing motivation and a tutorial introduction to the main concepts, and an Architectural Semantics (Part 4) (ISO/IEC, 1995d), providing a formalization of the concepts behind RM-ODP.

An introduction to the major components of the standard is given below. This introduction covers the object-oriented modelling approach behind RM-ODP, the concept of viewpoints and the five particular viewpoints defined in RM-ODP, distribution transparency and, finally, the concept of functions in RM-ODP. The overview also includes a section on conformance and interoperability in RM-ODP (see Chapter 1 for definitions of these key concepts). Topics not covered in any depth include distributed systems management, security and federation. The interested reader is referred to a number of tutorials in the literature for more detailed introductions (Raymond, 1993; Linington, 1991).

Note that many of the ideas described below were initially developed in the ANSA/ISA project (van der Linden, 1993). This work also produced a prototype platform, ANSAware (APM, 1993), as a partial implementation of the ANSA architecture.

2.2.2 Major concepts in RM-ODP

An object-oriented approach
RM-ODP adopts an object-oriented approach for the specification of distributed systems. In this section, we examine the particular object model described in RM-ODP (taken from Part 2 of the standard). Firstly, however, it is necessary to consider the motivations for the deployment of such an approach.

Motivation for an object-oriented approach
The benefits of object-oriented computing are now well recognized in the distributed systems community. The arguments in favour of this approach are summarized below:

- *Encapsulation* is the natural approach to developing distributed applications.
- *Data abstraction* provides a complete separation between specification and implementation of objects, thus enabling design in terms of interfaces.

- The separation between specification and implementation also enables the system to *evolve* naturally by allowing an object to be replaced by an alternative implementation (as long as the interface remains the same).
- Object-oriented systems are completely *extensible* in that new classes and objects can be added at any time.
- The concepts of *implementation* and *interface inheritance* support the *reuse* of code and interfaces respectively.
- The concept of *subtyping* provides *flexibility* in selecting services in a distributed environment.

Equally importantly, the adoption of an object-oriented approach provides a potential design methodology for distributed programming. In particular, it is then possible to adopt techniques and tools developed by the object-oriented analysis and design community. Similarly, it is possible to exploit object-oriented programming languages in the development of distributed applications.

The RM-ODP object model
The goal of the RM-ODP object model is to define a precise and unambiguous object model tailored towards the needs of open distributed processing. This contrasts with the rather incomplete and muddled terminology often found in object-oriented computing. The RM-ODP object model centres on the concept of *objects*, which encapsulate details of their implementation and provide an abstract view of the behaviour of the object. (This is similar to the classical view of objects as found in languages such as Smalltalk or Java.) Objects are accessed through one or more *interfaces*, where a given interface provides one abstract view of the object. The fact that *multiple interfaces* can be supported by an object is an original and important feature in RM-ODP. With this approach, the behaviour offered by an object can be partitioned into a number of separate services (referred to as *roles*) each visible at a distinct interface. For example, one interface could provide the basic operations defined on an object, whereas a second could be responsible for management of the object.

Objects are defined in terms of *templates*; a given template contains a complete description of an object at a given level of abstraction. They can then be used to instantiate objects (add new objects to the environment). Note that this is a rather general definition of the term. This is quite deliberate. RM-ODP adopts this approach to enable a number of realizations of the template concept. For example, in one realization, a Smalltalk class could act as a template, detailing the data structures and algorithms required to implement a (distributed) Smalltalk object. In a second realization, a much more abstract style of template could be used, specifying, for example, an audio storage object which should support a given throughput and maximum delay for retrieval. In other words, the detail of a template can vary from a complete implementation to an abstract specification.

RM-ODP also defines the concepts of type and class. Again, general definitions are given. A *type* is a predicate defined over the environment of objects. In other words, a type is a property that a set of objects should possess, such as the set of all objects owned by a particular user. *Class* is then defined as the set of objects which adhere to this predicate. Type is therefore the *intention* (the predicate) whereas class is the *extension* (the set of objects satisfying this predicate at a given time). One particular type of interest is the *template type*. A template type is a predicate which is true for all objects instantiated from a particular template. This set of objects is then defined by the corresponding class.

Corresponding to type and class, RM-ODP also defines the notions of *subtype* and *subclass*. In RM-ODP, a type T_1 is a subtype of a type T_2 if and only if the corresponding predicate for T_1 implies the predicate for T_2. Similarly, subclassing in RM-ODP can be defined in intuitive set-theoretic terms as follows: a class C_1 is a subclass of a class C_2 if and only if C_1 is a subset of C_2.

Note that there is a strong relationship between these two concepts. Every type has an associated class which is the extension of this type. Suppose that T_1 has class C_1 and T_2 has subclass C_2. Then it is also true to say that type T_1 is a subtype of a type T_2 if class C_1 is a subset of class C_2.

The relationship between template, type and class is summarized in Figure 2.1 (taken from Rudkin (1993)).

The concepts of subtyping and subclassing lead to the creation of subtype and subclass *hierarchies* respectively. RM-ODP also defines the concept of *incremental inheritance* which allows a *derived class* to be created by the modification of the template associated with the original class. Again, though, RM-ODP is careful to avoid too rigid a definition of incremental inheritance. In particular, this concept does not necessarily equate to implementation inheritance as featured, for example, in Smalltalk. Indeed, it is now recognized that this style of inheritance can lead to major difficulties for general distributed systems (in resolving behaviour at run-time) (Wegner, 1987). It is also important to

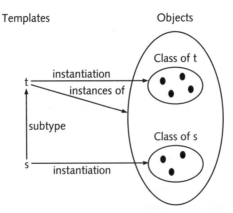

Figure 2.1 Templates, types and classes in RM-ODP.

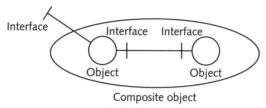

Composite object

Figure 2.2 A simple composite object in RM-ODP.

emphasize that a derived class may not be a subclass. This situation can arise if the template is altered in such a way that the associated type predicate no longer holds.

Finally, the object model supports the concept of a *composite object*. A composite object is a configuration of interacting objects which offer a composite behaviour; that is, through one or more interfaces on to the composite object. This concept is illustrated in Figure 2.2.

Note that the definitions above must be able to describe any distributed object-oriented computation. Hence, apart from the basic modelling concepts, there are no further assumptions about the application of the model. In particular, the following statements hold:

- There are no assumptions about the granularity of objects; for example, objects can be as small as an integer or as large as a film sequence.
- Objects can exhibit arbitrary encapsulated behaviour; for example, the underlying algorithms and data structures can be very simple or highly complex and can feature arbitrary amounts of internal parallelism.
- Interactions between objects are not constrained; they can be asynchronous, synchronous or isochronous.

An excellent overview of the object model can be found in Rudkin (1993).

Viewpoints and viewpoint models

One of the major problems in open distributed processing is the wide scope and inherent complexity of the domain. This is reflected in the large amount of information required to produce a complete specification of a distributed system. For example, such a specification must address (among other things) how to model information flowing around a (distributed) organization, how to design distributed systems to support this process, how to then build supportive applications and what technologies to employ in this process. Without assistance this would quickly become unmanageable. RM-ODP addresses this problem by introducing the concept of *viewpoints*.

Viewpoints are used to partition a system specification into a number of different components. Each component (viewpoint) is a complete and self-contained description of the required distributed system targeted towards a particular audience. The terminology (language) used for this description is therefore tailored towards this target audience.

Example *Viewpoints analogy*
To illustrate the concept of viewpoints further we consider a non-computing example: different viewpoints on a civilian aircraft. One viewpoint is that of the manager responsible for the operation of the aircraft. This manager views the aircraft as an artefact with a given lifetime, requiring maintenance at certain intervals at a certain cost and capable of carrying passengers on certain routes at a given profit margin. The maintenance engineer, on the other hand, views the aircraft as a set of interconnected components with given technical specifications and testing regimes. Finally, an air traffic controller will view an aircraft as occupying a particular location in space at a given time and flying on a predetermined route. Each participant will have a terminology for discussing the aircraft with colleagues in an unambiguous manner.

Viewpoints are as central to RM-ODP as the seven-layer model is to the ISO standard for Open Systems Interconnection (OSI). It should be stressed, however, that viewpoints are not layers. Rather, they are projections on to the underlying system. This distinction is illustrated in Figure 2.3.

RM-ODP defines five viewpoints, namely the Enterprise, Information, Computational, Engineering and Technology Viewpoints. Each viewpoint has a corresponding viewpoint model. The models all share the general object modelling concepts described above; each model can be thought of as a specialization of this general model for the particular target domain.

The RM-ODP standard actually uses the phrase 'viewpoint language'. Note, however, that the various languages do not prescribe a particular syntax and semantics. Rather, they provide a basic terminology required to model the concerns of a given viewpoint. In this sense, the viewpoint languages can be considered to be meta-languages which can then be instantiated with particular notations in a given usage (see the discussion on standards and meta-standards in Section 2.2.1). To avoid this potential confusion over the usage of the term language, we prefer to use the phrase 'viewpoint model' throughout the remainder of the book. In particular, we will refer to the Computational Model, the Engineering Model and so on.

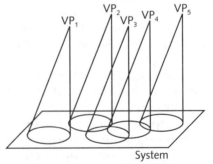

Figure 2.3 (a) Layering and OSI; (b) viewpoints and RM-ODP.

More detail on the five viewpoints and associated models is given below.

1. *Enterprise Viewpoint*

   The Enterprise Viewpoint considers the role of the distributed system in the operation of an enterprise. The aim of the corresponding specification is to model the scope and objectives of the system. The main concept behind the Enterprise Viewpoint is that of a *contract* expressing the obligations of the various participants in the distributed enterprise. The Enterprise Model then supports the specification of such contracts. Key concepts in the Enterprise Model include *agents, artefacts, roles, communities* and *federation*.

2. *Information Viewpoint*

   The Information Viewpoint considers a distributed system from the perspective of the information content. More specifically, it considers the various information elements in an organization, the flow of this information around the organization and processes for manipulating this information. The corresponding model defines the basic concepts of objects and composite objects; it then enables the specification of information schemata over these objects. Three styles of schemata are defined: *invariant schemata*, which describe relationships which must always be true in the specification, *static schemata*, which describe assertions which must be true at a single point in time, and *dynamic schemata*, which define how the system should evolve in terms of changes to the environment and to individual objects.

3. *Computational Viewpoint*

   The Computational Viewpoint considers the logical partitioning of the distributed system into a series of interacting entities. This partitioning is logical in that it does not imply any particular realization in a distributed environment, such as mapping to nodes or address spaces. The corresponding model adopts an object-oriented approach (a specialization of the model presented earlier). An application is decomposed into a number of interacting *objects* with each object offering one or more *interfaces*. All interaction is via these interfaces. In order to interact, it is necessary to have a *binding* to the target object(s). Three styles of binding are supported: *operational* binding (supporting the invocation of operations), *stream* binding (supporting continuous media interactions) and *signal* binding (supporting real-time processing). The application developer can also specify a set of constraints on the underlying implementation of the object through an *environmental contract*. This contract includes specification of the required level of *distribution transparency* and the *quality of service* offered by the interface. Such specifications are declarative in that they say *what* is required rather than *how* it is to be achieved. The latter issue is the concern of the Engineering Viewpoint, as discussed below.

4. *Engineering Viewpoint*

   The Engineering Viewpoint considers the infrastructure required to support the physical realization of a distributed application in terms of both communications and end systems technologies. The Engineering

Model defines a basic set of abstract concepts required to model communications and end system resources. In terms of communications, the model defines the concept of a *channel*, which consists of a configuration of *stubs*, *binders* and *protocol objects*. In terms of end system resources, the model defines the concepts of *nodes* (as physical machines), *capsules* (as an execution environment for objects) and *clusters* (as a migratable set of objects). In addition, the model defines *transparency functions* as a means of achieving a given level of distribution transparency; there is a direct translation between the requirements specified in the environmental contract (see above) and the set of transparency functions provided.

5. *Technology Viewpoint*

   The Technology Viewpoint considers the development of a distributed system from the perspective of the identification, procurement and installation of particular hardware or software technologies. This viewpoint effectively grounds the overall design in terms of realizable technologies. The corresponding model is used to justify rather than to describe the selection of particular technology artefacts. In particular, the Technology Model enables the technology provider to provide a declaration that a particular technology will meet its requirements in terms of Implementation eXtra Information for Testing (or IXIT).

A summary of the various viewpoints and models is given in Table 2.1.

The different viewpoints outlined above effectively create a *separation of concerns* in the specification of a distributed system. The five viewpoints collectively provide a complete specification of the system which would enable an RM-ODP compliant implementation to be developed. Note, however, that some issues will appear in a number of different viewpoints. For example,

Table 2.1 RM-ODP viewpoints and models

Viewpoint	What it addresses	Modelling concepts
Enterprise	Business concerns	Contracts, agents, artefacts, roles and so on
Information	Information, information flows and associated processes	Objects, composite objects, schemata (static, dynamic, invariant)
Computational	Logical partitioning of distributed applications	Object, interface, environmental contract and so on
Engineering	Distributed infrastructure to support applications	Stubs, binders, protocol objects, nodes, capsules, clusters and so on
Technology	Technology procurement and installation	Implementation, conformance point, IXIT

consider the provision of security in a distributed system. In the Enterprise Viewpoint, the specification might state that a particular project should operate with a 'need to know' policy: each project manager should know the minimal amount of information for the goals of the project to be met; in the Information Viewpoint, this would translate into constraints on the schema offered to different participants; at the Technology Viewpoint, a decision could be taken to adopt the Kerberos security service (see Section 2.4.2) to implement the desired policy.

The one added difficulty of introducing such viewpoints is that of ensuring consistency between the different specifications. This is a difficult problem and comprehensive solutions are currently beyond the state of the art. One approach is to consider the use of appropriate formal specification techniques for each viewpoint and then employ mathematical analysis to ascertain consistency (Bowman *et al.*, 1996). This issue is not considered further in this book.

Distribution transparency

The concept of distribution transparency was introduced in Chapter 1 as the ability to mask out problems occurring in the distributed environment. A high level of distribution transparency therefore implies that the programmer need not be aware of the distributed nature of the system. This can be highly beneficial by reducing the complexity of distributed programming. It is worth mentioning, though, that transparency can also have its problems, as programmers may sometimes have to be aware of the distribution of the system, for example if they are concerned with the real-time behaviour of the system or in mobile environments.

The approach in RM-ODP is to support *selective* transparency whereby the programmer can elect for a given level of transparency. As mentioned above, the requirements for distribution transparency are expressed in the Computational Model as part of the environmental contract. The Engineering Model is then responsible for meeting the desired level of transparency by employing the required number of transparency functions.

A number of distribution transparencies are defined in RM-ODP. The two most basic are access and location transparency, as defined below.

Access transparency
This transparency masks differences in access methods when interworking between objects. To solve this problem, it is necessary to deal with potentially different data representations and different invocation mechanisms.

Location transparency
This transparency hides the physical location of the object in the distributed environment. A logical name (or unique identifier) can be used for the object in place of a physical address.

Access and location transparency together enable objects to interact (for example, one object invoking an operation on another object) without needing to be aware of the location of the object or the particular means of access to that object. This combined effect provides a major step towards solving problems of heterogeneity in an open distributed processing environment. Further levels of transparency are then defined which offer added value to the programmer:

Failure transparency
This transparency hides the occurrence of failure from other objects. In order to achieve this effect, it is necessary to implement a suitable recovery scheme.

Migration transparency
This transparency hides the fact that a system might decide to move an object to another location. Such a decision might be made for reasons of load balancing or to reduce latency in accessing the object.

Relocation transparency
Relocation transparency hides the fact that an object which is currently involved in an interaction (through established bindings) has moved. Migration transparency does not deal with this case (the binding would appear to fail). To hide relocation, it will be necessary to alter the binding or perhaps create a new binding.

Replication transparency
This transparency hides the fact that a given object is replicated at several locations in a distributed system; for example, to increase availability or improve performance. To realize this transparency, it is necessary to ensure that the replicated objects are kept consistent.

Persistence transparency
Objects in RM-ODP can be persistent: their state should survive over a number of different interactions. This transparency masks persistency from the programmer by dealing with the necessary activation and deactivation of objects.

Transaction transparency
In a distributed environment, it is often necessary to maintain consistency across a configuration of objects in spite of concurrent access and failure. This transparency will mask out the mechanisms required to achieve this consistency.

A summary of the distribution transparencies defined in RM-ODP is given in Table 2.2. Note that this list is not intended to be exhaustive; further transparencies can be introduced for a particular application domain.

Table 2.2 Distribution transparencies in RM-ODP

Transparency	Concern	Effect
Access	Means of access to objects	To mask out differences in data representation or invocation mechanism
Location	The physical location of objects	To enable objects to be accessed by a logical name
Failure	The failure of an object	To mask out this failure from the user through an appropriate recovery scheme
Migration	The movement of objects	To mask out the fact that an object has moved
Relocation	The movement of objects involved in existing interactions	To mask out the fact that an object has moved from the other interacting objects
Replication	Maintaining replicas of objects	To hide the mechanisms required to maintain consistency of replicas
Persistence	To maintain persistency of data across interactions	To mask out the mechanisms required to maintain the persistency of the data
Transaction	Maintaining consistency of configurations of objects	To hide the mechanisms required to maintain consistency of configurations

RM-ODP functions

RM-ODP defines a number of *functions* which are necessary to support a comprehensive RM-ODP platform. Functions fulfil a number of different purposes in RM-ODP. For example, a group of functions provides *management* in the *engineering viewpoint*. Examples of such functions include node management functions (to create and manage threads, to provide access to clocks and timers, to enable the creation of communication channels and to instantiate and delete capsules), capsule management functions (to instantiate and delete clusters), cluster management functions (to support the checkpointing, activation and deactivation and migration of objects). A further set of functions support the implementation of security (including the functions of access control, authentication, key management and security auditing). Some functions, including a number of those introduced above, are required for the specific task of realizing distribution transparency (see previous section).

The standard also defines a *trading function* to act as a broker for services in the distributed environment. This service is viewed as central to RM-ODP (and to the Computational Model in particular) and hence the trading function merits a separate document in the standardization of RM-ODP (ISO/IEC, 1997). Briefly, the trading function enables objects to make interfaces available by exporting a service offer to the trader. An object wishing to interact with a service interface must *import* the interface by specifying a set of requirements in terms of service type and related constraints. This will be matched against the available services and a suitable candidate selected. Note also that any number of traders can exist in a given distributed system and these may be *linked* to allow access to services in different domains.

The complete set of functions defined in RM-ODP is summarized in Table 2.3.

2.2.3 Conformance in RM-ODP

As mentioned earlier, conformance is essential in the provision of open distributed processing systems. The role of conformance is to ensure that platforms developed by different manufacturers conform to the standard, hence guaranteeing the crucial properties of interoperability and portability.

Conformance in RM-ODP is defined as follows:

Definition *Conformance*
Conformance is a relationship between specifications and the implementation. The relationship holds when specific requirements in the specification are met by the implementation.

Being a meta-standard, RM-ODP does not define the conformance relationship or the particular requirements that should be met. Rather, RM-ODP provides a framework to enable such conformance to take place. This framework is defined in terms of *conformance points*: the points at which an implementation should be *tested* by delivering stimuli and monitoring the resultant behaviour. A particular open distributed processing standard must then define the particular conformance points for that architecture.

Conformance in RM-ODP is complicated by the existence of viewpoints. In particular, it is necessary to ensure that the implementation of the platform conforms to the requirements specified in each of the viewpoint models. A further discussion of this issue can be found in the literature (Cowen *et al.*, 1993; Linington *et al.*, 1996).

2.3 OMG CORBA

2.3.1 Introducing CORBA

The Common Object Request Broker Architecture (CORBA) is supported by the Object Management Group (OMG) as part of an initiative to develop a comprehensive Object Management Architecture (OMA) for object-oriented computing. OMG is a non-profit organization sponsored by over 500 organizations including computer manufacturers, software companies, telecommunications companies and end users. The overall objective of OMG is

Table 2.3 Functions in RM-ODP

Area	Specific function	Concern
Management	Node management	Manages resources of a node, including threads and clocks
	Object management	Checkpointing and deletion of objects
	Cluster management	Checkpoints, recovers, migrates, deactivates or deletes clusters
	Capsule management	Instantiates, checkpoints or deactivates associated clusters and deletes capsules
Coordination	Event notification	Records and makes available event histories
	Checkpointing and recovery	Overall coordination for checkpointing and recovery of clusters
	Deactivation and reactivation	Overall coordination for deactivation and reactivation of clusters
	Groups	Coordinate the interaction of objects in multiparty binding
	Replication	Coordinates interaction in a replica group
	Migration	Coordinates the migration of clusters between capsules
	Interface reference tracking	Maintains information on interface references
	Transaction	Coordinates set of operations to ensure a level of visibility, recoverability and permanence
Repository	Storage	Provides the storage for data
	Information organization	Supports modification of information schema, querying, and modification of the data
	Relocation	Supports relocation transparency through a relocator object
	Type repository	Maintains a repository of type specifications and relationships
	Trading	Supports advertising and discovery of interfaces
Security	Access control	Prevents unauthorized interaction on interfaces
	Security audit	Monitors and collects security information
	Authentication	Confirms identity of an object
	Integrity	Prevents unauthorized creation, alteration or deletion of data
	Confidentiality	Prevents unauthorized disclosure of information
	Non-repudiation	Prevents the denial of an object from having participated in an interaction
	Key management	Manages cryptographic keys

to 'promote the theory and practice of object technology (OT) for the development of distributed computing systems'. The approach adopted by OMG to achieve this goal is 'to provide a common architectural framework for object-oriented applications based on widely available interface specifications ... conformance to these specifications will then make it possible to develop a heterogeneous applications environment across all major hardware platforms and operating systems'.

The OMG approach to standardization is to issue Requests for Proposals in given areas. Particular vendors can then submit proposals meeting a predefined set of requirements. The membership then selects between revised proposals following a period of evaluation. In practice, vendors often cooperate to produce a combined, revised proposal. CORBA was the result of such a process; the initial specification was produced from proposals submitted by DEC, HyperDesk, Hewlett-Packard, SunSoft, NCR and Object Design.

The particular goal of CORBA is to provide the mechanisms by which objects transparently make requests and receive responses. The heart of the architecture is an Object Request Broker (ORB) which fulfils this function. This section provides an introduction to CORBA and the Object Request Broker. Section 2.3.2 introduces the key features of CORBA, focusing initially on the CORBA object model and the overall architecture and then considering the individual components of CORBA, namely the Object Request Broker, Object Services, Common Facilities and Application Objects. Following this, Section 2.3.3 introduces the approach to conformance and interoperability adopted by CORBA.

Further details of CORBA can be found in the literature (Object Management Group, 1995a; Mowbray and Zahavi, 1995; Yang and Duddy, 1996).

2.3.2 Major concepts in CORBA

An object-oriented approach
CORBA adopts an object-oriented approach for precisely the same reasons as given above for RM-ODP. In this section, we present an overview of the particular object model adopted in CORBA. We then look in more detail at the particular Interface Definition Language (IDL) adopted by CORBA.

The CORBA object model
The CORBA object model defines an *object* as 'an identifiable, encapsulated entity that provides one or more services that can be requested by a client'. In order to access the service, clients issue a *request* for a service. Requests consist of the target object, the required operation name, zero or more actual parameters and an optional *request context*. The request context is used to define additional information about the interaction. This information, in the form of name/value pairs, can convey information about the client or about the environment. For example, the context can be used to define a user's preferences. Should a request fail, an *exception* is raised in the client object.

Objects in CORBA support interfaces where each interface can be defined in terms of an interface type. As with RM-ODP, types are defined as predicates (defined over the domain of possible values). CORBA also defines the extension of a type as all values that satisfy that type at a given point in time (class in RM-ODP). CORBA supports inheritance at the level of interfaces (*interface inheritance*). This process creates a *derived interface* from a *base interface*. The rules for interface inheritance are quite strict: a derived interface can only be extended; that is, through the addition of new operations. This implies that a derived interface is always a subtype (in RM-ODP terminology) of the base interface. CORBA also supports *multiple inheritance*. This can be used, for example, to inherit a functional interface and a management interface giving a similar expressive capability as multiple interfaces in RM-ODP. Note, however, that this is not the same as multiple interfaces; the two interfaces are merged in the derived interface.

The CORBA object model also defines a number of concepts but leaves the implementation detail open. For example, the creation and deletion of objects is mentioned, but is expected to be supported by sending requests to particular types of objects, such as objects supporting a new operation. Similarly, CORBA mentions implementation inheritance as the inheritance of the code and data structures encapsulated in the object (compare interface inheritance). Again, it is (deliberately) not specified how this should be accomplished.

Introducing IDL

Interfaces are described in terms of an Interface Definition Language (IDL). IDL is a language-independent, declarative definition of an object's interface. It is not expected that the object implementation shares the typing model of IDL. Rather, a mapping must be provided between IDL and the host language. IDL closely resembles C++, but with added features to support distribution.

A particular IDL specification consists of one or more *interface declarations* along with associated type and constant declarations and a set of possible exceptions. In addition it is possible to declare *modules* which are used to provide an element of scoping in large specifications. An interface declaration then consists of an *interface header* and a *body*. The header specifies the *interface name* together with an optional set of *inherited interface specifications*. The body consists of constant, type and exception declarations exported by the interface, together with the operation declarations. Individual operations are defined in terms of the operation name, the parameters and the expected results, together with the exceptions that can be raised as a result of requesting this operation.

By default, an operation is carried out with at-most-once semantics, guaranteeing that if a result is obtained, the operation was carried out exactly once; otherwise, if an exception is raised, it was carried out *at-most-once* (that is, the operation is never duplicated). This semantic can be overridden with an optional oneway tag implying that the request is sent with *best-effort* semantics.

The sender does not receive a result in this case and does not synchronize with the receiver. The body also allows the user to specify *attributes* of the interface. Attributes are arbitrary (typed) properties of the interface. Attributes are logically equivalent to having additional get and set operations to access a particular value.

Types in IDL can be either basic values (short, long, char, string and so on), constructed values (struct, array, union and so on) or references to other objects. The complete set of types is depicted in Figure 2.4.

The features of IDL are best illustrated by example. The following IDL specification defines a simple stock control system:

```
// OMG IDL definition

interface inventory
{
  // attributes and type definitions

  const long MAX_STRING = 30;

  typedef long part_num;
  typedef long part_price;
  typedef long part_quantity;
  typedef string part_name<MAX_STRING+1>;

  struct part_stock {
    part_quantity max_threshold;
    part_quantity min_threshold;
    part_quantity actual;
  };

  // operations

  boolean is_part_available (in part_num number);
  void get_name (in part_num number, out part_name name);
  void get_price (in part_num number, out part_price price);
  void get_stock (in part_num number, out part_quantity
                   quantity);
  long order_part (in part_num number, inout part_quantity
                   quantity, in account_num account);
};
```

Note that the in, out or inout annotations define whether the associated parameter carries data into the object, returns results from the object or a combination of both. The remainder of the IDL is relatively straightforward and is not described further.

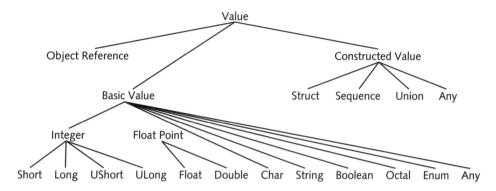

Figure 2.4 Valid types in CORBA IDL.

The overall CORBA architecture

The overall architecture of CORBA is illustrated in Figure 2.5. This diagram shows four main components of CORBA, namely the *Object Request Broker*, the *Object Services*, the *Common Facilities* and the *Application Objects*. The Object Request Broker is the logical heart of the architecture and provides the means for objects to interact in a heterogeneous environment. The Object Services are then a set of objects offering basic services to the platform. These services include naming and concurrency control. The Common Facilities are again a particular set of objects offering higher level services, including management aspects of the platform. Finally, the architecture features a number of application objects which are objects developed by outside vendors. The interfaces of such objects are therefore not under the control of the CORBA architecture. We look at each of these in more detail below, with particular emphasis on the Object Request Broker and the Object Services.

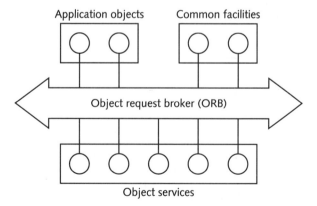

Figure 2.5 The CORBA architecture.

The Object Request Broker

The role of the Object Request Broker (ORB) is to enable requests to be carried out in a heterogeneous distributed environment. Clients can therefore issue requests on object implementations and the ORB will deal with finding the objects, sending the requests to the appropriate objects and preparing the objects to receive and process the requests and return the results back to the clients. The ORB therefore implements a level of distribution transparency (actually location and access transparency).

ORB interfaces

An ORB offers a number of different interfaces to the object developer. These interfaces are depicted in Figure 2.6. In this diagram, arrows from the ORB to the client or object implementation are referred to as upcalls and arrows in the opposite direction are more traditional (down) calls.

The *ORB Core* is the lowest level in the ORB architecture. This level supports the basic representation of objects and the means of communicating between objects. An application programmer will typically not access this interface directly, but will access the higher level interfaces indicated in the diagram. Indeed, this interface is not open, as the precise functionality is not given in the CORBA specification. We discuss each of the higher level interfaces below.

Consider initially the most straightforward case of a client accessing an object implementation using the interfaces offered by the *IDL Stubs* and the *IDL Skeleton*. IDL Stubs provide the mechanisms for clients to be able to issue requests transparently. In particular, they deal with the marshalling of parameters and the unmarshalling of results (mapping typed parameters on to a flat message format and vice versa). The stubs are normally pre-compiled from the IDL definitions of the required object implementations. Hence, the set of stubs is *static*. The IDL Skeleton interface offers the same service at the receiving end of the request. It identifies the required procedure, unmarshalls the parameters, upcalls the object implementation to request that the operation be carried out and then deals with marshalling the results and returning them to the client. Again, the object types that this interface can deal with are static.

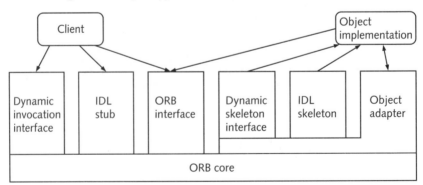

Figure 2.6 The Object Request Broker.

It is sometimes the case that an application object will dynamically locate an object and not have the appropriate stub accessible through the Stubs interface, for example when browsing an object-oriented database. In this case, the client can use the *Dynamic Invocation Interface*. Using this interface, the client must manually construct a request indicating the required operation, the parameters and so on. This is obviously more difficult, but the flexibility is sometimes required in object-oriented applications. CORBA also now supports an analogous Dynamic Skeleton Interface on the implementation side.

Finally, objects have access to an *Object Adapter* interface. This interface provides access to a range of services including the generation and interpretation of object references, the registering of implementations with object references and the activation and deactivation of objects. Different object adapters can be provided to support different styles of object. It is important, though, that every implementation supports a *Basic Object Adapter* offering a core set of services to the object developer.

Interface and implementation repositories

The ORB provides two services offering persistent storage of information concerning objects: the *interface repository* and the *implementation repository*. The former manages and provides access to a collection of object definitions specified in IDL. Each object definition is itself stored as an object and provides access to the interface definition at run-time. This can be used, for example, when an object with an unknown type is encountered and hence the dynamic invocation interface has to be used (see above). The information from the interface repository can be used to determine precisely which operations can be carried out and what parameters the operation expects. The implementation repository performs a similar function, but for the implementations of objects. This information is used by the ORB when a particular instance of a given object type must be activated.

The respective role of the two services is summarized in Figure 2.7.

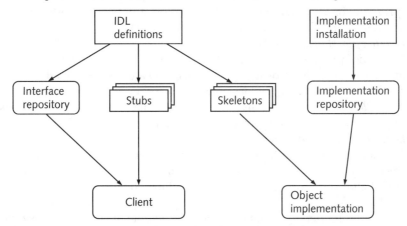

Figure 2.7 Interface and implementation repositories.

Object Services

The Object Services in CORBA are a set of services offering basic functionality to enhance the underlying ORB. They are defined in the Common Object Services Specification (COSS) (Object Management Group, 1995b). Each service is a CORBA object type and is defined by IDL. The existing object services are described below.

- *The Naming Service*
  This is a directory service which is interoperable with existing directory services such as X.500. This therefore enables interoperability with DCE (see Section 2.4).
- *The Event Service*
  Using this service, objects can register interest in one or more *events* and can then be notified if these events occur. Events are notified through an *event channel*.
- *The Persistence Service*
  This service enables objects to be made persistent; to outlive the creating thread or process. This service is more general than the basic persistence mechanisms offered by the Object Adapter mechanism.
- *The Transaction Service*
  This service enables configurations of objects to be updated consistently using a *two-phase commit* transaction protocol. The service also supports *nested transactions*.
- *The Relationships Service*
  This service allows links to be created between CORBA objects. Links can have associated type and cardinality. Clients can then navigate the resultant structure created by the links.
- *The Externalization Service*
  This service is used to externalize an object; to record the state of the object as a stream of data in a file (or other means of storage). This representation can then be transported across a network or other medium and later internalized to recreate the initial object.
- *The Life-cycle Management Service*
  This service provides support for the lifetime of the object including its initial creation, copying or moving of the object and its eventual deletion. Creation is supported by factory objects. The other aspects are governed by a *LifeCycleObject* interface. This service can also manage compound objects, relying on the relationship service to maintain the compound structure.
- *The Concurrency Control Service*
  This service enables multiple clients to coordinate their access to shared objects. This is provided by a lock mechanism; various lock modes are defined allowing more flexibility in controlling concurrency.

This list is not intended to be static. Indeed, at the time of writing, five additional services are being defined: querying, licensing, security, properties and time.

Common Facilities and Application Objects

The CORBA *Common Facilities* are additional services which an application might require but which are not as fundamental as the Object Services defined above. Again, the services are CORBA objects and are defined in terms of IDL. At the time of writing, the Common Facilities are not fully developed and hence are not covered in any great depth in this book. Briefly, however, the Common Facilities have been divided into two categories: the *horizontal category* and the *vertical category*. This division is illustrated in Figure 2.8.

The horizontal services are generic to all application objects and concern user interfaces and management aspects of the system. The vertical services are specific to a particular application domain and define conventions for services in areas such as health, retail or finance.

Finally, *Application Objects* are CORBA objects which are developed by outside vendors. They are therefore not under the control of the CORBA architecture apart from offering CORBA interfaces. They will, however, use the ORB for communication and may rely on the Object Services or Common Facilities of CORBA.

2.3.3 Conformance in CORBA

In the first version of CORBA (CORBA 1.0), conformance was met as long as a given implementation offered the correct interfaces. This is, however, a rather weak relation. Firstly, such an approach provides no guarantees in terms of portability. For example, implementors are given too much freedom in developing their own (proprietary) strategies in areas such as security or threads management. Secondly, there are no guarantees in terms of

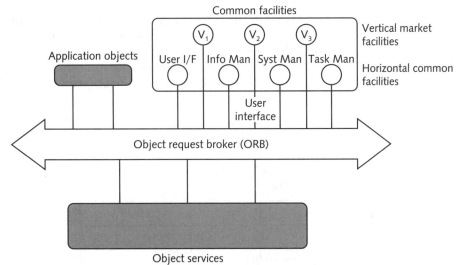

Figure 2.8 Common facilities in CORBA.

interoperability. Again, implementors can develop their own protocols for communication within the ORB.

In response to these problems, CORBA 2.0 has introduced a more rigorous approach to conformance. The main aim of this work is to improve interoperability between ORBs. To tackle this problem, the OMG have defined an ORB *Interoperability Architecture* which enables different ORBs to interwork and also allows ORB implementations to interwork with other distributed system platforms. In this architecture, each ORB is assumed to run in a particular *domain*, with the domain defining a number of characteristics of the implementation including the approaches to naming and security and the particular protocols used in that domain. The mapping from domains to ORBs may be one-to-one, one-to-many or many-to-one. Interoperability is then concerned with crossing domain boundaries. This involves techniques for mapping the characteristics of one domain on to the characteristics of another.

CORBA defines several protocols which will allow interoperability, as illustrated in Figure 2.9. The central part of the architecture is the *General Inter-ORB Protocol* (GIOP). This protocol is a minimal and generic connection-oriented protocol which can be mapped on to a number of underlying transport services. For example, GIOP can use the *Internet Inter-ORB Protocol* (IIOP) which defines how GIOP messages are exchanged across the Internet (using the TCP transport service). GIOP could similarly be implemented in an OSI environment. The implementations would not be able to communicate directly, but the common conventions defined by GIOP would mean that the translation would be minimal (see below). Note that both GIOP and IIOP are compulsory for any implementation to be CORBA-compliant. Indeed, as will be seen below, IIOP is the preferred inter-domain protocol in the architecture.

The interoperability architecture also defines a family of *Environment-Specific Inter-ORB Protocols* (ESIOP). These protocols allow an ORB to communicate directly with other distributed system platforms. One such protocol is the *DCE Common Inter-ORB Protocol* (DCE-CIOP) which enables ORBs to communicate directly with a DCE platform. Such protocols are optional; they are only

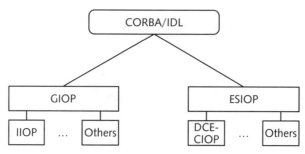

Figure 2.9 Interoperability protocols in the ORB.

required in ORBs where there is a requirement to communicate with other platforms.

The concept of *bridges* allows ORBs in different domains, running different protocols, to interact. Bridging in CORBA can either be *mediated* or *immediate*. In the former case, the two ORBs agree on a common form for communication. Interactions are then mapped to the common form at the boundary of the originating domain and subsequently mapped back at the boundary of the receiving domain (in the respective bridges). In the immediate case, a direct mapping takes place at the boundary of each domain between the representation used in the originating domain and the representation in the receiving domain – there is no third-party representation involved. Mediated bridging is more general and flexible, but carries a significant performance overhead when compared with immediate bridging. The two cases are summarized in Figure 2.10. Note that, in both cases, the common representations can be private between two specific domains or can have more general applicability across a set of domains.

CORBA defines two styles of bridges, namely *half-bridges* and *full bridges*. Half-bridges are mediated bridges where the two parties agree to use IIOP as the common form for communication. To achieve interoperability, it is then required to provide a half-bridge which translates between the internal protocol used in a domain and IIOP. In contrast, full bridges are examples of immediate bridging where the bridge translates directly between one protocol and another without using the intermediary IIOP. This is of course a less general solution, as the bridge can only be used in this context.

The following example provides an illustration of the use of bridges in the CORBA Interoperability Architecture.

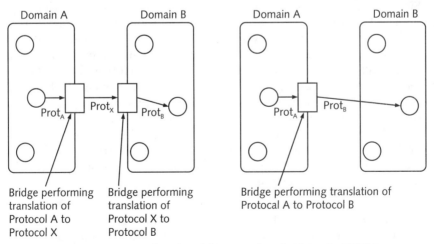

Figure 2.10 (a) Mediated and (b) immediate bridging in CORBA.

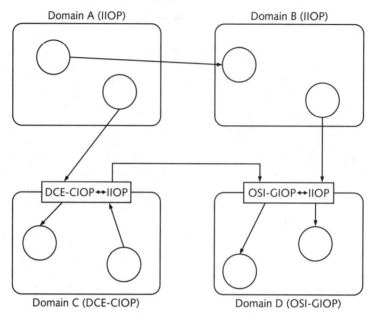

Figure 2.11 Examples of interoperability in CORBA.

Example *Bridging in a typical CORBA configuration*
Figure 2.11 illustrates a typical CORBA configuration featuring four
different domains, A, B, C and D. Domains A and B use IIOP directly as
their internal protocols, domain C uses DCE-CIOP and domain D uses an
OSI implementation of GIOP. Domains A and B can communicate directly
without bridging support. For either domain to interact with domain C,
however, it is necessary to provide a half-bridge from IIOP to DCE-CIOP.
Similarly, a half-bridge is required for A or B to communicate with
domain D. In this case however, the translation should be minimal, as
both IIOP and the OSI equivalent share the GIOP conventions (as
discussed above). Communication between domains C and D is achieved
by the half-bridge translating from DCE-CIOP to IIOP and then the
second bridge translating to the OSI implementation of GIOP. This
illustrates the flexibility of half-bridges, in that the half-bridges at the
interfaces of domains C and D can be reused in different ways to achieve
interoperability with a range of different domains. Alternatively, a full
bridge could be provided between domains C and D, translating between
DCE CIOP and the OSI implementation of GIOP. This bridge can only be
used for this specific purpose, however.

Note that the new approach still does not provide guarantees in terms of
portability. However, at the time of writing, OMG are planning to extend the
approach to conformance by, firstly, defining an associated portability

architecture for ORBs and, secondly, providing conformance tests based on the CORBA specification.

2.4 The Open Group's DCE

2.4.1 Introducing DCE

The Distributed Computing Environment (DCE) is a standardization activity sponsored by the Open Group. The Open Group (like OMG) is a non-profit organization sponsored by a number of IT and telecommunications companies including AT&T, Bull, Digital, Fujitsu, Hewlett-Packard, Hitachi, IBM, Siemens Nixdorf, Silicon Graphics, SunSoft and Sony. The role of the Open Group is to 'assist the information technology industry in research, development, and delivery of key vendor-neutral technology (software source code) to make open systems possible'.

The organization supports openness through a process of 'selection, certification and integration of software technologies which guarantee stability and continuity to customers'. The Open Group defines two approaches based on this general process. The first approach is based on the concept of a Request for Technology (RFT). With this approach, the Open Group identifies a particular area requiring an open systems solution. They then publish an RFT as part of an industry-wide search for possible solutions. They then collect the inputs, analyze them and produce a specification which integrates the best elements of the various submissions. The Open Group have also added a second approach, the Pre-Structured Technology, or PST, process. With this process, potential technology projects are identified directly by industrial consortia (rather than by the Open Group). They are then approved by the Open Group Board and are subsequently managed by the Open Group together with industrial representatives until a system specification is delivered.

DCE was the result of an RFT process and is an operating system-independent and network-independent software platform to achieve open distributed processing. Unlike RM-ODP and CORBA, DCE does not feature an object-oriented approach. Instead, DCE has a classic client–server architecture. Indeed, DCE is best viewed as an integrated set of services offering a distributed programming environment. It does not support object-oriented features such as class, type, subclass, subtype, object instantiation or derived classes (inheritance).

An introduction to the main features of DCE is given below. The approach taken is firstly to introduce the overall service architecture and then to examine each component service in turn. The discussion then concludes with a consideration of conformance and interoperability in DCE.

Further details on DCE can be found in the literature (Open Group, 1990a, 1994a).

2.4.2 Major concepts in DCE

The overall architecture

The overall architecture for DCE is illustrated in Figure 2.12. This diagram shows a configuration of service layered on top of an existing operating system and communication service. DCE therefore sits between the operating system and applications, offering a set of platform-independent abstractions to the programmer.

The services can be divided into two classes, namely the *fundamental services* (or secure core) and the *data sharing services*. There is also provision for *management* of these services. The fundamental services are the threads service, the RPC service, the time service, the naming service and, finally, the security service. The data-sharing services are then the distributed file system and the associated diskless support service. DCE also provides a limited number of management tools for some of the services, including the security and time services. Distributed systems management can also make use of a separate Open Group development, namely the Distributed Management Environment (or DME) (Open Group, 1994b).

The remainder of this section provides an overview of the fundamental services and data sharing services (management services are not considered further).

The fundamental services

As mentioned above, the fundamental services are the threads, RPC, time, naming and security services. Together, they provide a hardware-, platform- and language-independent view of the distributed environment, enabling open applications to be developed. We consider each service in turn below.

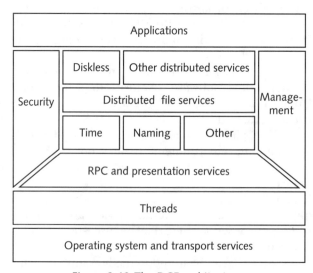

Figure 2.12 The DCE architecture.

The threads service

The threads service supports the creation and management of threads (or lightweight processes) in the DCE environment. Threads are sequential flows of control within an address space. Using this service, a client or server can then have multiple flows of control providing a level of internal concurrency. The term 'lightweight processes' highlights the relatively low cost of this approach to concurrency. A lightweight process can be around ten times cheaper than normal processes in terms of creation and context switching. This service is the lowest level of the DCE architecture and is used by many of the other services to enable concurrent programming.

The threads service is based on Digital's Concert Multithreaded Architecture. This architecture implements the IEEE POSIX 1003.4a *pthreads* standard, thus ensuring an additional level of openness in the system. This package is implemented at the *user level*. The underlying operating system kernel is responsible for scheduling the encapsulating process; the threads package then schedules threads within this process. Note that there is no communication between the user level and the kernel and hence there is no guarantee on the scheduling of threads (this point is revisited in Chapter 10).

Three classes of scheduling policy are provided: *prioritized FIFO, prioritized round robin* and a default *timesliced* policy. The prioritized FIFO policy involves multiple first in, first out queues of threads ordered by priority. The scheduler will service the highest priority queue in order, then the next priority queue and so on. Each thread runs until completion. The prioritized round robin policy in contrast simply selects the highest priority thread; if several threads have this priority then they are timesliced (after a quantum of time they will be preempted). The default policy treats all threads as having equal priority and then implements a timeslice policy. Note that the three policies can coexist in an implementation with the scheduling policy being determined on a per thread basis.

Finally, threads introduce the potential for concurrent access to shared data structures. To overcome this problem, the DCE threads service offers both mutual exclusion primitives and condition variables.

The RPC service

The Remote Procedure Call (RPC) service provides the means of interprocess communication in DCE and is based on the Network Computing System by Digital and Hewlett-Packard. The service supports the invocation of operations on potentially remote servers. The associated presentation service provides a uniform view of data types hiding details of byte ordering or the type system of the languages involved. Together, the RPC and presentation services thus realize access and location transparency.

A given server can offer one or more interfaces (compare RM-ODP), with each interface being described in terms of an Interface Definition Language (or IDL) definition. This IDL consists of two parts:

- *The IDL header*
  This part features a *universal unique identifier* (UUID) for the service which is guaranteed to be unique in a global distributed environment. Such UUIDs can be generated by a DCE utility called *uuidgen*. The header also includes a version number consisting of a major and minor number (such as version 4.1).
- *The IDL body*
  The IDL body defines each operation on an interface in terms of operation name and the name and type of the parameters and results. Data types can have associated *in, out* or *in,out* denotations to indicate whether the associated parameter carries data into the server, returns results from the server or a combination of both (as with CORBA IDL). The IDL body may also contain additional attributes about the interface, for example if certain operations are idempotent (capable of being repeated).

As an example, we present a DCE IDL version of the stock control interface presented above for CORBA IDL.

```
/* DCE IDL definition */


[
  uuid (007A3B76-94A5-11C7-67B0-08001A146B53)
  version (2.1)
] interface stock_control
{
  /* type definitions */

  const long MAX_STRING = 30;

  typedef long part_num;
  typedef long part_price;
  typedef long part_quantity;
  typedef [string] part_name<MAX_STRING+1>;

  typedef struct part_stock {
    part_quantity max_threshold;
    part_quantity min_threshold;
    part_quantity actual;
  } part_stock;

  // operations

  boolean is_part_available ([in] part_num number);
  void get_name ([in] part_num number, [out] part_name name);
```

```
       void get_price ([in] part_num number, [out] part_price price);
       void get_stock ([in] part_num number, [out] part_stock
                   *stock);
   long order_part ([in] part_num number, [in,out] part_quantity
                quantity, [in] account_num account);
};
```

Again, this is relatively straightforward and should not require further explanation. Note, however, that the syntax does look rather similar to the syntax for CORBA. There are, however, important differences between the two systems (not shown by this example). Most importantly, CORBA features object references as first-class data items (reflecting the object-oriented approach of CORBA). This allows object references to be passed around as arguments in a request. In contrast, DCE has the concept of binding handles which are not included as first-class data items. Binding handles are therefore managed externally to DCE.

As with RM-ODP, it is necessary to have a *binding* to an interface before invocations can proceed. The establishment of a binding can be controlled by an *attribute configuration file* (ACF). Clients and servers can each have their own attribute configuration file. This file enables control over a large number of aspects of the implementation of a binding. For example, it is possible to control the means of handling exceptions (either by generating an exception or by receiving status codes). In addition, it is possible to bypass normal marshalling or unmarshalling code (see below) for procedures and provide your own. This might be useful, for example, for multimedia data. Most importantly, the attribute configuration file enables the programmer to select the *binding method* to be used. The methods vary in the level of transparency (and conversely the level of flexibility) offered to programmers. Three methods are supported: *automatic*, *implicit* and *explicit*. The automatic method is the most transparent. The infrastructure selects which server should provide the required service, and should this fail then a replacement is selected. The implicit method enables the client to select a server at the start of a binding. A binding handle is returned to the client. This is then included implicitly in subsequent calls to the server. The binding must be managed by the application, for example if the server crashes. The explicit method is similar to the implicit method apart from binding is on a per-invocation basis.

The implementation of DCE RPC is shown in Figure 2.13. The RPC *stubs* are created from an IDL definition by an IDL compiler provided with DCE. The role of stubs is to marshall and unmarshall data for the procedure calls; that is, flatten the parameters into a message buffer for transmission to the server and carry out the opposite process on reception. The RPC runtime provides the implementation of the remote procedure call protocol and supporting protocol stack. Transmissions are encoded using the Network Data Representation (NDR) transfer syntax. Note that the protocol profile selected can be controlled by the programmer. For example, if operations are marked

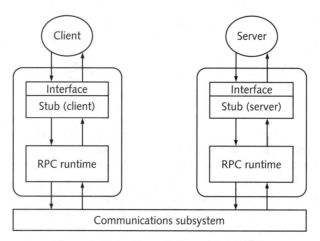

Figure 2.13 Implementation of DCE RPC.

as idempotent (see above), then an at-least-once implementation of RPC will be selected, otherwise the more expensive at-most-once semantics will be employed (see Coulouris *et al.* (1994) for a discussion of the different semantics for a remote procedure call).

The time service

The time service provides a system-wide measure of time synchronized to Coordinated Universal Time (UTC). The service is based on Digital's Distributed Time Service product. Interoperability is also provided with the Internet Network Time Protocol (NTP). The accuracy of the service is of the order of 10 milliseconds.

The service provides access to *timestamps* representing the current global time. The service also supports conversion between different timestamp structures, comparison of timestamps, calculation of time zone information and conversion between local time and UTC.

The implementation of the service consists of a number of clerks (clients) and associated time servers. Four different types of time server exist:

*   *local servers*, which maintain synchronization between each other in a local area network environment,
*   *global servers*, which maintain synchronization across a wide area network environment,
*   *courier servers*, which synchronize local servers and global servers, and
*   *time provider servers*, which inject accurate measurements from an external UTC source (such as a satellite).

The latter servers are not necessary but can increase the accuracy of the timestamp information by correcting global skew.

The naming service

The naming service allows servers to advertise services and clients to locate services in the global distributed environment. The service therefore fulfils the role of the trader in RM-ODP. (A comparison of the DCE naming service and trading can be found in Beitz (1993)). The implementation consists of two separate components:

- *The Cell Directory Service (CDS)*
  The Cell Directory Service provides a hierarchical name space for a logical grouping of local machines (the *cell*). This technology is based on Digital's Distributed Naming Service (DNS). The CDS maintains a replicated database mapping names to UUIDs (the Clearinghouse). A clerk is then created for each client of the Clearinghouse. Clerks on the same machine maintain a cache of recently accessed names to speed up query processing. This introduces the problem of cache inconsistency; for example, if the required server has moved or failed. This will be detected the next time the client accesses the server. At this point, the clerk will perform a remote CDS lookup and then update its cache.
- *The Global Directory Service (GDS)*
  The Global Directory Service extends the hierarchical name space between cells, thus providing a world-wide naming service. The technology is based on the ISO/ITU-T X.500 series of standards. Interoperability is also supported with the Internet's Domain Name System (DNS). GDS also features a replicated distributed database known as the Directory Information Base.

This overall structure is summarized in Figure 2.14. Interoperability between the two levels is managed by a Global Directory Agent (GDA). This provides a naming gateway between a CDS and a GDS. Whenever a CDS is passed a global name, the query is passed on to the GDA. This will then forward the request to the appropriate GDS. Note that the GDA is also used to achieve interoperability with the Internet DNS. GDA can recognize DNS requests and pass them on to a DNS server rather than a GDS server. To an end user, a DCE name has the following format:

```
/.../C=UK/O=LANCS/OU=COMP/users/gordon/ODP.book
```

The first component, /. . ., refers to the root of the global naming structure. The next component is a standards X.500 name, /C=UK/O=LANCS/ OU=COMP. This identifies the country (C=), the organization (O=) and the organizational unit (OU=). Finally, the latter part of the name is a Cell Directory Service name: /users/gordon/ODP.book. This follows the standard Unix naming convention.

From within a given cell, the above name can be shortened to:

```
/.:/users/gordon/ODP.book
```

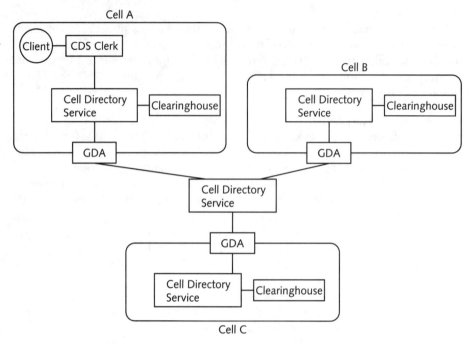

Figure 2.14 The naming service in DCE.

The boundary between the CDS and GDS services is transparent to the user of the system. However, access to the GDS level is inevitably slower because of the increased latency of messages.

The security service
The security service enables secure access to servers in a DCE environment. More specifically, the service implements the following security functions:

- *authenication* to ensure that principals (users or applications) are who they claim to be,
- *authorization* to check whether the requesting principal has rights to access a service in a given way,
- *verification* to ensure that data is not corrupted or subject to unauthorized tampering,
- *data privacy* to enable data to be sent privately between clients and servers (by using appropriate encryption methods).

This functionality is achieved using a combination of the Kerberos authentication server from MIT, the IEEE POSIX standard 1003.6 for Access Control Lists and the Data Encryption Standard (DES).

To illustrate the use of the security service, consider the secure invocation of a remote operation using DCE RPC. We assume that the associated user will already have logged on to the DCE machine and gone through authentication with the *authentication service*. At this stage the user will have received an encrypted *ticket granting ticket* (TGT). The encryption key is based on the user's password and hence the TGT can be decrypted when received. This TGT is used to interact with a privilege service to determine the level of privileges offered to that user. The interaction then proceeds as follows:

1. The client must firstly carry out a handshake with the privilege server to ascertain that the client is a trusted principal; this is achieved by sending the decrypted TGT to the privilege server. The privilege server then returns a privilege access certificate (PAC) which must be quoted on all subsequent interactions.
2. When the client wishes to invoke a particular operation on a server, it requests a ticket from the privilege server quoting the PAC. The server will then return the appropriate ticket to the client. This has a particular lifetime; after this time has expired another ticket must be requested.
3. The client invokes the required operation quoting the ticket. This ticket is checked against the server's access control list to determine whether the operation is allowed for that given client. If it is, the operation is carried out; otherwise it is aborted. Note that access control list entries in DCE can be defined at the granularity of individual operations (compare Unix).

The above protocol is further complicated if encryption is considered. Nevertheless, it serves to illustrate the basic operation of the security service. Further details can be found in Open Group (1990b).

The data-sharing services
The data-sharing services consist of two main components, namely the *distributed file service* and *diskless support*.

The distributed file service
The distributed file service provides location and access transparency when accessing files over local and remote systems. It relies on the naming service, described above, to provide a hierarchical name space. The service is based on the Andrew File System (AFS) from CMU (Levy and Silbershatz, 1990) and offers IEEE POSIX 1003.1 file system semantics. The file system can also interoperate with the alternative NFS technology (Levy and Silbershatz, 1990).

The file system is designed with the primary goal of extensibility: it should provide good performance in an environment with very large numbers of clients and servers. This is largely achieved by adopting the AFS strategy of whole file caching (Levy and Silbershatz, 1990). In addition, servers take responsibility for issuing call-backs to clients to deal with cache updates. This prevents the client from having to poll the server, which in turn reduces the loading on the server and hence improves extensibility.

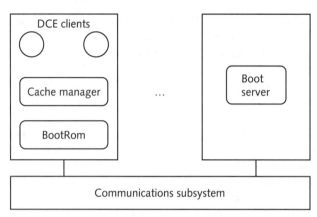

Figure 2.15 The diskless support service in DCE.

The distributed file service uses a particular file server called Episode. Episode is a high-performance, highly reliable file server featuring the use of *logs*. In particular, Episode logs all operations on meta-data. This log can then be replayed on restart after failure to return the file system to a consistent state. This approach has the added advantage that it provides fast restarting after failure. Episode also provides high availability through replication and strong security guarantees through integration with the DCE security service (described above). Note that an alternative file server such as a Unix file server can be used in place of Episode, but the system will no longer provide the same level of performance, recoverability, availability or security.

Diskless support

The diskless support service is used to extend the distributed file service to diskless workstations. This service is based on Hewlett-Packard's diskless support technology, which in turn uses the Internet *de facto* standards, the Boot Protocol (BOOTP) and the Trivial File Transfer Protocol (TFTP). The overall architecture of the service is shown in Figure 2.15. The BootRom component must be in the ROM of the client machine. This component is responsible for bootstrapping the client on restart by broadcasting a message in the local cell requesting a boot server. A suitable boot server then returns the required information for restart (the boot file of the client, its network address, the address of the Cell Directory Service and Distributed File Service and so on). Once started, the diskless client has a *cache manager* that interacts with the distributed file server and caches files locally.

2.4.3 Conformance in DCE

The Open Group have developed a framework for achieving open systems which includes a specification and branding process. The Open Group relies on this process to check conformance of DCE implementations. More specifically, the Open Group have developed a system specification and associated conformance test suites for DCE and will only award its brand if a product meets the specification and passes the conformance tests. This process is intended to ensure both interoperability and portability.

2.5 Others

2.5.1 TINA

The *Telecommunication Information Networking Architecture* (TINA) is a development by the TINA consortium (TINA-C) (Dupuy *et al.*, 1995). This consortium features many of the world's leading telecommunications companies and is centred on a core team located at Bellcore in New Jersey. TINA is intended to provide a framework for the development of future telecommunications networks. The aim is to have an architecture which supports improved interoperability, to be able to reuse both software and technical specifications and to have more flexibility in the design and deployment of distributed applications that comprise a telecommunications network. A further aim is to provide a path of evolution and integration from existing telecommunications architectures such as IN (Abernethy and Munday, 1995) and TMN (ITU-T, 1991). The architecture is based closely on the RM-ODP, but is specialized to meet the particular demands of the telecommunications industry.

The overall architecture is illustrated in Figure 2.16. TINA places a distributed processing environment (DPE) at the heart of an information network architecture. This DPE adopts the RM-ODP Computational Model (with its notions of objects, interfaces and so on) and is also organized along the lines of the RM-ODP Engineering Model. The TINA consortium has identified CORBA as the technology of choice to serve as a basis for the TINA DPE. A particular notation has been developed for the description of objects and their associated interfaces. This notation is referred to as the TINA *Object Definition Language* (ODL) and is an extension of the OMG IDL described earlier. The main extensions are the ability to describe an object as a collection of interfaces and the association of attributes with objects.

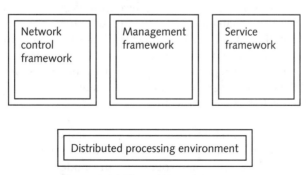

Figure 2.16 The TINA Architecture.

The DPE in TINA provides a uniform platform for the execution and deployment of the different distributed applications that can be found in a telecommunications network. TINA has identified three broad classes of applications. Software frameworks for these classes then complete the TINA-C architecture. We look at each of these frameworks in turn below:

- *The network control framework*
  This framework defines a generic set of concepts for describing and controlling transport networks. It comprises a network resource information model and a connection management framework. The network resource information model is inspired by ITU-T Recommendation G.803 and defines a generic network architecture, organized around transmission and switching technology independent notions of network elements and connections. The model describes the individual elements in a network, how they are related (aggregations) and topologically interconnected, and how they can be configured to provide an end-to-end path. The connection management framework describes generic components for the control of end-to-end communication paths in a network. The framework is organized around notions of connection graphs that describe logical and physical topologies of network connections.
- *The service framework*
  This framework defines principles, concepts, and basic classes necessary for the design, deployment, operation and management of information services in a TINA environment. It includes notions such as user agents, service and communication sessions, access management, and mediation services.
- *The management framework*
  The management framework defines a set of principles for the management of the components in the distributed computing infrastructure, and in the network control and service frameworks described above. The framework covers two main areas. The first, referred to as computing management, is responsible for the management of computers, the DPE and related software. The second, referred to as telecommunications management, is concerned with the management of information network services and software related to the underlying network. The latter is further divided into service, network and element management in a similar manner to TMN. Finally, the architecture partitions management into a number of functions including the OSI management functions of fault, configuration, accounting, performance and security.

The breadth of the architecture should be apparent from the above description of the main components in TINA. This illustrates the level of complexity of dealing with heterogeneity in modern telecommunications environments.

(The TINA-C documents use the term 'architecture' where we have employed the term 'framework'. We have reserved the use of the term 'architecture' for the open distributed system architecture provided by the RM-ODP standard. We use the term 'framework' to make an explicit reference to the notion of object-oriented software frameworks.)

2.5.2 IMA MSS

Multimedia System Services (or MSS) is an open distributed processing architecture specifically designed to support multimedia. The architecture is developed by the International Multimedia Association (IMA), a trade organization tackling issues including 'application portability and inter-operability, intellectual property rights, and technology convergence'. The specific goals of the IMA are, firstly, to 'promote the successful application of interactive multimedia in business and consumer markets', and, secondly, to 'reduce key barriers to the widespread use of interactive multimedia technologies and applications'. The IMA organizes a number of activities including several Interactive Media Forums. MSS is one such forum (others deal with multimedia data exchange, CD formats, video disk formats, digital audio formats and so on). The MSS initiative is attracting considerable attention. For example, MSS has been adopted as the underlying platform for the ISO graphics standard, PREMO (ISO/IEC, 1996).

MSS is based directly on CORBA. In particular, the architecture specializes CORBA by defining new object classes for multimedia. It should be stressed that the specifications are highly detailed, for example in comparison with RM-ODP. Each class is specified completely in terms of the methods and parameters to be used. The major components in MSS are illustrated in Figure 2.17. The three main object types are virtual devices, virtual connections and groups.

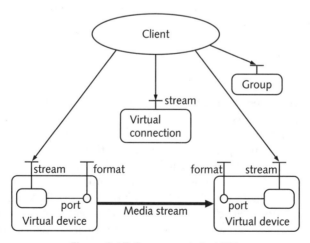

Figure 2.17 Components in MSS.

A *virtual device* is an abstraction over a physical device and can be, for example, a CD player, a file, a microphone, a speaker or a video window. Virtual devices offer a *stream interface* which enables the user to observe media stream positions and optionally to control this positioning; the latter is achieved by using a subclass of stream referred to as *ControlledStream*. This interface provides methods such as `pause`, `resume`, `prime` and `mute`. Virtual devices also feature one or more *format interfaces* providing an abstract representation of the details of media formatting, such as whether it is MPEG encoding. This interface also enables users to control aspects of the encoding, such as the frame mix for MPEG. Finally, virtual devices feature one or more *ports* as input or output mechanisms for virtual devices.

Virtual devices are subclasses of a *virtual resource* class. The importance of the virtual resource class is in managing resource allocation and deallocation. For example, this class supports an `acquire_resource` method which will attempt to allocate resources according to a specified quality of service. Quality of service for multimedia objects is normally specified in terms of reliability, maximum and minimum delay, maximum and minimum bandwidth, maximum and minimum jitter and whether these parameters should be guaranteed, best effort or with no guarantee. This can be specialized, however, for a particular class of objects.

A *virtual connection* is an object representing an abstract view of media transport from the output port of one virtual device and the input port of another. This object is responsible for negotiating the connection. In reaching agreement, the following parameters are considered:

- the *media type* to be transported, as given by the format interfaces of the ports involved,
- the *type of connection*; for example a direct hardware transfer from a DMA device or a communication across a network,
- the *quality of service* required, specified using the same parameters as given above for virtual resources, and
- the *stream and synchronization capabilities*, defining for example the required data exchange mechanisms and synchronization mechanisms and policy to be used.

Note that if the type of connection field specifies a network connection, additional engineering is required. In particular, virtual connection adapters are created at each port to manage the transfer of data. Part of the job of the adapters is to select an appropriate protocol for this communication. A number of protocols can be used but MSS specifically defines one protocol, the Media Stream Protocol (MSP), for this task. This protocol runs over a number of transport services, including TCP/IP, NETBIOS, SPX/IPX and RTP/ST-II. MSP defines a media packet consisting of media data together with a header, which includes such fields as a timestamp and a relative priority for the media processing.

Each virtual connection provides a stream interface (as above) which enables users to monitor and optionally control the connection. Virtual connections also enable the creation of multiparty communications, from one output port to one or more input ports. This capability is supported by a specialization of the virtual connection class which also offers `attach` and `detach` methods (to add or remove ports from the multiparty communication).

The *group* object supports the management of a particular configuration of objects. For example, in the diagram above, the group object can be used to support atomic resource allocation and end-to-end QoS management across the two virtual devices and the virtual connection. The group object offers a stream interface to enable the end-to-end communication to be monitored and potentially controlled.

In addition, MSS provides support for real-time synchronization by providing a subclass of the ControlledStream interface referred to as a *SyncStream*. This interface can be used in a number of different ways. For example, the interface enables one stream to be used as a reference point for another through the use of an `attach_master` method. Using this approach, an audio stream could be used to synchronize a video stream, for example. The user can specify the required granularity of this synchronization. Alternatively, two streams can be synchronized to a common clock.

To summarize the above discussion, the interface inheritance diagram for MSS objects is shown in Figure 2.18.

Finally, clients can monitor events in an underlying configuration of objects by using the COSS Event Service (described in Section 2.3.2). Using this service, clients can register for events, for example to see if a stream fails to deliver its required level of synchronization.

Further information on IMA MSS can be found in the literature (Interactive Multimedia Association, 1994a, b).

2.6 Comparison

It should be apparent from the discussion above that RM-ODP, CORBA, DCE, TINA and MSS are quite different. We revisit each in turn below.

- RM-ODP is a *meta-standard* defining a framework to enable the emergence of more specific object-oriented technologies for open distributed processing.
- CORBA is a *specific* object-oriented technology providing interoperability of objects in a heterogeneous environment by identifying an architecture with associated interfaces and IDL language.
- DCE is a *client–server architecture* (rather than an object-oriented architecture) achieving *integration* between a range of key services, including time, RPC, security and file services.

- TINA is a *specialization of RM-ODP* for the field of telecommunications featuring, for example, a specialized binding architecture reflecting the concerns of establishing and managing a connection in a complex telecommunications environment.
- MSS is a *specialization of CORBA* addressing the lack of *multimedia* support in CORBA by defining a particular class hierarchy for multimedia devices and connections.

The various initiatives can be viewed as complementary, with a potential path to convergence. RM-ODP is the most comprehensive and far-reaching of the initiatives, tackling issues such as object orientation, persistency, migration, security and transaction processing. It can therefore be viewed as a reference

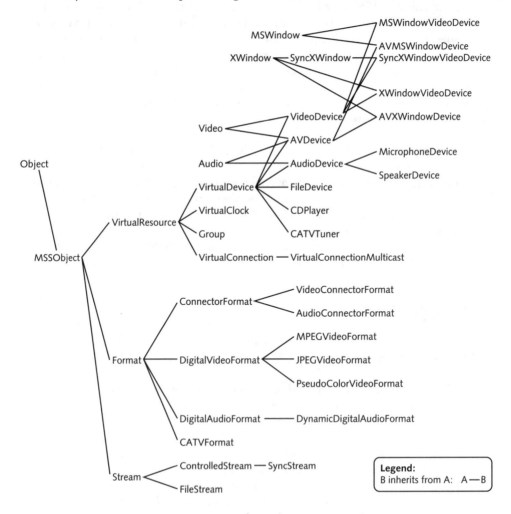

Figure 2.18 Interface inheritance in MSS.

point for the development of current and future open distributed processing solutions. In contrast, DCE and CORBA can be viewed as more immediate solutions to open distributed processing, with DCE identifying and integrating key services and CORBA offering object-oriented abstractions. One path to convergence is to offer a CORBA interface on top of DCE services and then for this architecture to evolve gradually towards a full RM-ODP architecture through the provision of additional facilities and through the definition of further viewpoint models. To a certain extent, this process has already happened, with DCE RPC now defined as one possible protocol within the CORBA Interoperability Architecture. The other initiatives, TINA and MSS, are more specialized but have interesting contributions to make in their own domains of interest. A number of problems remain, however, before full convergence can be achieved. For example, differences exist between the object models of RM-ODP and CORBA. Furthermore, the whole area is in a state of flux in reacting to the demands of multimedia. This issue will of course be discussed further in the remainder of the book.

2.7 Summary

This chapter has examined the important standards and platforms for open distributed processing. The chapter opened by examining the contribution of the ISO Reference Model for Open Distributed Processing. A number of major features of the standard were discussed, including the object-oriented approach, the use of viewpoints and the corresponding set of viewpoint models, distribution transparency, and the more specific topic of trading. It was stressed that RM-ODP offers a meta-standard allowing more specific standards to emerge.

Following this, the chapter considered OMG's CORBA specification. This is emerging as a *de facto* standard for open distributed processing. Key features of CORBA were discussed, including the CORBA object model, the Object Request Broker and the associated Object Services. The importance of CORBA is in defining an architecture with associated interfaces and an IDL language to enable interoperability between objects.

The next section considered the DCE architecture in some depth. The overall architecture was presented followed by an examination of each of the services offered by DCE. The important contribution of DCE is in achieving integration between the services required for a comprehensive client–server computing environment. However, DCE lacks an object-oriented interface.

The chapter then considered two more specific activities: TINA (a specialization of RM-ODP for the telecommunications industry) and MSS (a specialization of CORBA for multimedia applications). Both have very important contributions to make for their respective areas.

Finally, the chapter ended by comparing the different architectures. This discussion concluded that the architectures are complementary and a path to convergence can be foreseen. More work is required, however, before this can be achieved, for example in reaching consensus on tackling problems of multimedia. The next chapter looks in more depth at the problems of multimedia and derives a set of requirements that future open distributed processing standards and platforms should accommodate.

3 Requirements of distributed multimedia applications

3.1 Introduction

This final chapter in Part 1 examines in depth the requirements of distributed multimedia applications. The first chapter has already identified four key issues, namely:

- support for continuous media,
- quality of service management,
- real-time synchronization, and
- multiparty communication.

Section 3.2 examines each of these areas in more depth (in Sections 3.2.1–3.2.4 respectively). This discussion culminates (in Section 3.3) with a checklist of requirements for distributed multimedia applications. This checklist will be used as a reference point for the standards and platforms considered later in the book. Section 3.4 then reflects on the response to the challenge of multimedia in the open distributed processing community. The various standards and platforms introduced in Chapter 2 are considered with respect to the checklist. Finally, Section 3.5 summarizes the major contributions of the chapter.

Note that this chapter does not attempt to provide a full treatment of multimedia systems and the various associated media types, but rather focuses on the general requirements of such systems. For a more comprehensive treatment of multimedia, the interested reader is referred to Steinmetz and Nahrstedt (1995) or Fluckiger (1995).

3.2 The challenge of multimedia

3.2.1 Supporting continuous media

The first requirement of multimedia is the need to provide support for continuous media types, such as audio, video and animation. Such support is required in programming models for distributed computation and also in the underlying systems support. We consider each in turn before considering in more detail the styles of continuous media interaction found in distributed multimedia applications.

Programming models for continuous media

Existing programming models for distributed computing are generally based on one of the following paradigms:

- asynchronous or synchronous message passing
- remote procedure calls
- object invocation

The first two paradigms are associated with client–server computing and the latter paradigm with object-oriented models.

Such paradigms have one thing in common: they enable the programmer to model *discrete* interactions between client and server or between interacting objects. For example, a remote procedure call can be used to request a name lookup from a directory server. The paradigms however do not directly support the modelling of *continuous* interactions over a period of time. This crucial distinction is illustrated in Figure 3.1.

In the discrete interaction, there is a single exchange between A and node B. In the continuous interaction, however, a series of exchanges take place over a period of time. Furthermore, it is likely that there will be a temporal relationship between the various exchanges (for example one exchange every 10 ms).

In terms of multimedia, existing platforms therefore directly support discrete media types but not continuous media types. Of course, continuous media can be modelled by a sequence of discrete interactions. For example, each frame of a video sequence can be sent in an individual message. However, this solution is inadequate for a number of reasons. Firstly, this approach places an unnecessary burden on the programmer in terms of repeatedly initiating interaction. A more natural solution would be to establish the interaction and then perform a more distant role in terms of monitoring and controlling the interaction. Secondly, the programmer would have to specify requirements on each individual interaction; it is not possible to specify requirements over an ongoing sequence of interactions (see discussion on quality of service below). Finally, the solution prescribes one approach to the interaction and does not give the system the required

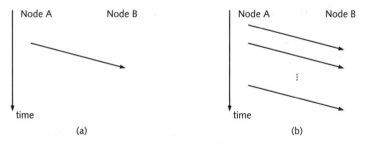

Figure 3.1 (a) Discrete vs. (b) continuous interactions.

level of freedom to make optimizations. For example, sending frames in individual messages precludes the use of compression techniques such as MPEG, where a mixture of frames and differences are sent.

It is also important that support for continuous media interaction is as comprehensive as for other styles of interaction. In particular, it should be possible to *access* and *manipulate* the media types at the interfaces of the interaction. It is now recognized that a class of multimedia applications require this ability to manipulate continuous media data types, such as those involving image or voice recognition.

In summary, there is therefore a requirement, from a programming perspective, to provide comprehensive support for interactions involving continuous media. For the rest of this chapter, we refer to this as *stream interactions*.

Systems support for continuous media

Systems support in existing platforms is generally tailored towards the support of discrete interactions. For example, sophisticated techniques now exist to provide efficient message passing in distributed environments. Similar techniques are also available for remote procedure calls or object invocations.

Systems support is even more crucial with respect to continuous media. A fundamental characteristic of continuous media types is the real-time relationship between individual components of that media type. For example, a given video type might have to be presented at 25 ± 5 frames per second for the integrity of the media type to be maintained. Systems support is then required to maintain such real-time relationships. Furthermore, the required level of support must be sustained for the duration of the interaction.

This requires careful support from the infrastructure in terms of areas such as scheduling, communications protocols and memory management. In many cases, novel techniques will be required to deal with continuous media types. For example, it is now recognized that existing transport protocols such as TCP have limitations when transporting continuous media, particularly over high-speed networks.

Again, from a system perspective, we can therefore identify a need to provide explicit support for stream interactions.

Styles of stream interaction

On closer examination, stream interaction is a general concept covering a number of different styles. In particular, it is possible to identify two broad classes of stream interaction:

- *Simple streams*
  A simple stream consists of a single flow of data where the data is of a single continuous media type, such as a single flow of audio or video data.
- *Complex streams*
  A complex stream consists of several flows of data where each flow has a

designated and potentially distinct media type. For example, a complex stream could consist of an audio flow and a video flow or two separate audio flows representing stereo sound.

In addition, both simple streams and complex streams can encapsulate *arbitrary behaviour*. For example, a simple stream could be implemented directly by a transport service. Alternatively, the stream might employ processing in the form of compression and decompression at either end of the transport service. The actual communication could be in digital form over a multi-service network. Alternatively, the stream could represent an analogue transmission. Even more complexity is introduced when considering complex streams. The individual flows of a complex stream could be transmitted down separate connections. Alternatively, they could be multiplexed down a single connection. Again, the flows could be subjected to arbitrary processing, such as for compression or decompression. This discussion also ignores the complexities introduced by multiparty interactions (see Section 3.2.4).

To summarize the above discussion, in supporting continuous media it is necessary *to provide support for both simple and complex streams where both styles of stream can encapsulate arbitrary behaviour*. Complex streams can, of course, be constructed out of individual streams. It could therefore be argued that it is unnecessary to provide this abstraction directly in open distributed processing standards and platforms. We disagree with this view, however. Complex streams provide a useful abstraction for the programmer to mask out the complexities of dealing with individual flows of data. Furthermore, in many cases, complex streams are provided directly by the infrastructure, and it is therefore crucial to be able to provide access to such services through open distributed processing platforms. This is the case, for example, in the telecommunications domain, where the telecommunications network can provide call services of arbitrary complexity (see the discussion on TINA in Chapter 2). A more general interpretation of streams enables a direct mapping to such services.

3.2.2 Quality of service management

Definitions and terminology

The second requirement of distributed multimedia applications (in common with other real-time and safety critical applications) is the need for sophisticated quality of service (QoS) management. In most traditional computing environments, requests for a particular service are either met or ignored. In a multimedia system, however, the quality of the service is central to the application.

A service in a distributed environment is normally defined in terms of a set of functions (such as operations) exported by the system and accessible to its clients. For example, a camera would be defined in terms of a set of functions such as play, pan, zoom and tilt. In order to provide a complete specification of a multimedia service, however, it is also necessary to consider the non-functional properties associated with the service. These properties are referred to as *quality of service* properties. Returning to the example, the quality of service of the camera would be defined in terms of the parameters such as the frame rate produced by the camera, the quality of the picture and the response times to pan, tilt and zoom the camera. *Quality of service management* is then defined as the necessary supervision and control to ensure that the desired quality of service properties are attained and, in the case of continuous media, sustained. Again, with respect to the camera, quality of service management would be required to ensure that the camera is producing the required frame rate and is responding quickly enough to pan, tilt and zoom operations.

Note that this example highlights that quality of service management applies both to continuous media interactions (managing the frame rate of the camera) and to discrete interactions (managing the response time for control operations on the camera).

We examine quality of service and quality of service management in more detail in the following two subsections.

Fundamentals of QoS
In this subsection we examine the fundamentals of quality of service under the headings of QoS categories, QoS dimensions, expressing QoS requirements, QoS dependencies and contracts, and QoS and viewpoints.

QoS categories
As stated above, quality of service is concerned with the non-functional requirements of a system. It is useful to group such requirements into a number of discrete categories. In terms of distributed multimedia systems the most important categories are:

- timeliness,
- volume, and
- reliability.

These are the main categories that will be considered in the book. Note, however, that this list is far from exhaustive. Other categories worthy of mention are *criticality*, which relates to the assignment of relative priority levels between activities, *quality of perception*, which is concerned with issues such as screen resolution or sound quality, and *logical time*, which is concerned with the degree to which all nodes in a distributed system see the same events in an identical order. *Cost* is another important category. This may contain parameters such as the rental cost of a network link per month, the cost of transmitting a single media frame in a flow, or the cost of a multiparty, multimedia conference call. A more complete selection of QoS categories can be found in ISO/IEC (1995e).

QoS dimensions

In order to quantify and measure quality of service, it is necessary to identify particular *dimensions* within each category. For multimedia the key dimensions for the three key categories are given below.

- *Timeliness dimensions*
  The timeliness category contains dimensions relating to the end-to-end delay of either continuous media or discrete interactions. For stream interactions, the key dimensions are *latency* (or *delay*), measured in milliseconds and defined as the time taken from the generation of a media frame to its eventual display, and *jitter* (sometimes referred to as *delay jitter*), also measured in milliseconds and defined as the variation in overall nominal latency suffered by individual messages on the same stream. For discrete interactions, the relevant dimension would simply be the desired *latency* of the individual interaction.
- *Volume dimensions*
  The volume category contains dimensions that refer to the *throughput* of data. For continuous media interactions, this would be measured in terms of the number of individual elements delivered per second. For example, for video this would be measured in term of frames delivered per second. For discrete interactions, the appropriate dimension would be the throughput achieved for the particular interaction measured in bytes per second.
- *Reliability dimensions*
  The reliability category is rather broad, covering a range of issues including the overall reliability of the system measured in terms of Mean Time Between Failure (MTBF) and Mean Time To Repair (MTTR). For multimedia, we focus on the reliability of interactions. For streams, this translates to the permitted percentage of loss of media frames and the bit error rates within a frame. For discrete interactions, we are only concerned with issues such as bit error rates in the individual interaction.

The full list of dimensions and categories is summarized in Table 3.1.

Table 3.1 Example categories and dimensions

QoS categories	Example dimensions for stream interactions	Example dimensions for discrete interactions
Timeliness	End-to-end latency of frames; permitted jitter on latency	End-to-end latency of interactions
Volume	Perceived throughput in frames per second	Perceived throughput in bytes per second
Reliability	% loss of frames; bit error rate within frames	Bit error rates in individual interactions

Expressing quality of service requirements

Having considered the range of QoS dimensions, it is now possible to focus on the specification of QoS requirements. Such requirements can be expressed over the above dimensions in a variety of different ways:

- deterministically,
- using probabilities, or
- in terms of stochastic distributions.

Deterministic requirements are expressed in terms of the precise value or range of values required. For example, with this approach, it would be possible to state that a given latency should be 50 ms or, more realistically, that the maximum and minimum bounds are 55 and 45 ms respectively. Probabilistic requirements allow more flexibility by enabling the user to specify the required probability of a quality of service target being achieved. For example, the user could specify that the probability of receiving a frame within 50 ms should be 0.95. This is clearly a generalization of the previous method. Deterministic statements correspond to a probability of 1. Finally, the user could specify that a set of events should conform to a particular stochastic distribution. For example, the user could specify that the arrival of video frames should follow a normal distribution with mean inter-arrival time of 40 ms and variance of 5 ms.

Different *classes* of quality of service can also be identified. For example, quality of service can be expressed in terms of whether the service should be *best effort* or *guaranteed*. With a best effort service, the system does its best to achieve the required level of service but may fail to achieve the required level under congestion. With a guaranteed service, the system guarantees to provide the desired quality of service even in overload conditions. This requires support from the system in terms of resource reservation and admission control (see below). Other classes can also be identified, including statistical, predictive and adaptive services.

In multimedia systems, the actual values and relative priorities for the different dimensions can vary considerably between the different media types. For example, video connections require consistently high throughput, but can tolerate reasonable levels of jitter and bit or packet errors. In contrast, audio does not require such high bandwidth, but places tight restrictions on jitter and error rates. A summary of media types and typical quality of service requirements is given in Table 3.2 (taken from Hehmann *et al.* (1990)).

QoS dependencies and contracts

So far, the discussion has ignored the structure of the system and the fact that quality of service at one part of the system will *depend* on quality of service in another part. The most obvious example of such dependencies is in terms of a *layered* system, where QoS at the higher layer will be dependent on QoS at a lower layer. For example, a timeliness requirement for end-to-end latency would map on to more specific latency requirements in terms of network

Table 3.2 Typical quality of service requirements

QoS	Maximum latency (s)	Maximum jitter (ms)	Average throughput (Mbit/s)	Acceptable bit error rate	Acceptable packet error rate
Voice	0.25	10	0.064	$< 10^{-3}$	$< 10^{-4}$
Video (TV quality)	0.25	100	100	10^{-2}	10^{-3}
Compressed video	0.25	100	2–10	10^{-6}	10^{-9}
Data (file transfer)	1	–	2–100	0	0
Real-time data	0.001–1	–	< 10	0	0
Image	1	–	2–10	10^{-4}	10^{-9}

transmission, protocol processing and possibly compression and decompression. Similarly, a throughput requirement specified in terms of video frames per second would be equivalent to *peak-rate* throughput and *statistical* throughput measured in cells per second in an ATM network. Finally, the error rates in a video frame would be dependent on the cell loss in an ATM network.

This layered view of a system is most commonly found in communications architectures (such as the OSI seven-layer model). A more general view of a system architecture is of an interacting set of objects. Such objects may be logically divided into layers corresponding to levels of abstraction in the system. In such an architecture, QoS dependencies will exist between arbitrary groupings of objects. More precisely, a QoS dependency is a relation between the object offering a service and one or more objects supporting this service. As an example, the quality of service of a multimedia presentation object could be dependent on the quality of service of a video storage service and an associated audio storage server service. This more general view of dependencies is illustrated in Figure 3.2. Clearly, a layered architecture can be expressed in terms of this more general view.

There is therefore a requirement to be able to specify not only the required quality of service but also any dependencies that this quality of service might have on other objects. Such a requirement can be expressed in terms of a QoS contract which, when agreed, will provide the basis of the QoS commitment.

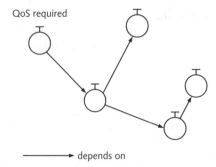

Figure 3.2 A general view of dependencies.

QoS and viewpoints

Finally, we consider the relationship between quality of service and the concept of viewpoints (as defined in RM-ODP). As stated in Chapter 2, viewpoints provide different perspectives on a system development. These different perspectives are also important when considering quality of service in a system. To demonstrate this further, we consider the interpretation of quality of service in each of the five RM-ODP viewpoints. This discussion is illustrated with examples taken from the development of a desktop conferencing system supporting medical diagnosis.

- *QoS and the Enterprise Viewpoint*
  The Enterprise Viewpoint is concerned with the business perspective. At this level, quality of service would be concerned with overall policies for service provision. Such policies would then direct the system development in the remaining viewpoints. For example, in the development of the desktop conferencing system, the management might express a policy that the system should improve the overall diagnosis rate and that every step should be taken to ensure that the system cannot be blamed for incorrect diagnosis.
- *QoS and the Information Viewpoint*
  The Information Viewpoint is concerned with the information types and their flows through the organization. Quality of service at this level is then used to state requirements in terms of the information types in a high-level manner. For example, in the desktop conferencing system, the associated Information Model would highlight access to live video recordings of, say, a heart scan and state that the quality of this information should be equivalent to HDTV to improve diagnostic rates.
- *QoS and the Computational Viewpoint*
  The Computational Viewpoint is concerned with the decomposition of the system into a number of interacting components (corresponding to an object-oriented design). At this level, quality of service is stated in terms of the non-functional requirements of each component. The requirements should be end-to-end; that is, expressed over the visible behaviour of objects. They should not be concerned with internal implementations of objects. In the conferencing example, access to the live video would be broken down into the required quality of service for the camera and the presentation device and the associated communications channel. At this level, quality of service would be more specific and expressed in terms of the QoS dimensions as expressed above.
- *QoS and the Engineering Viewpoint*
  The Engineering Viewpoint is concerned with the infrastructure supporting the (distributed) application. At this level, quality of service is concerned with the non-functional requirements imposed on the individual components in the infrastructure. In the desktop conferencing system, this would involve the translation of the desired quality of service

from the computational level into associated requirements in terms of scheduling, communications, device management and storage. It might also be decided that a particular compression technique should be used. The computational statement of quality of service would be used to place constraints on this compression process, such as determining that the technique should be lossless to achieve the desired picture quality.

- *QoS and the Technology Viewpoint*
  Finally, the Technology Viewpoint is concerned with the deployment of the individual technologies used to build the system. Quality of service at this level corresponds to non-functional requirements on these technologies. For example, in the desktop conferencing system, a quality of service requirement might be the overall reliability of the cameras being deployed.

It should be apparent from the above discussion how viewpoints can be used to express quality of service in a language suitable for a given audience. There are also strong relationships between the quality of service requirements expressed in different viewpoints. As already stated, the policies expressed in the Enterprise Viewpoint determine many of the non-functional aspects of the design. As a further illustration, there is a mapping from the QoS requirements in the Information Model to the QoS of individual objects in the Computational Model and then to infrastructure components in the Engineering Model.

Fundamentals of QoS management

Quality of service management encompasses a number of *different functions*, including static aspects applicable at service establishment time, and more dynamic aspects concerned with the ongoing provision of a service. We look at the functions associated with static and dynamic management in more detail below.

Static QoS management functions

Static QoS management functions are carried out when a given service is initially established. The role of these functions is to ensure that the appropriate steps are initially taken to attain the desired quality of service.

The first group of functions are concerned with the service establishment and are as follows:

- *QoS specification*
  The QoS specification function is concerned with the creation of a QoS contract using an appropriate means of expressing the QoS requirements as discussed above. For example, the QoS contract could state deterministic bounds on the appropriate dimensions in the timeliness, volume and reliability categories. Importantly, the specifications may include dependencies on other services and the quality of service they support.

- *QoS negotiation*
  QoS negotiation is required to reach agreement on the QoS contract
  between all parties involved (the objects in the contract and the associated
  dependencies). This process will involve establishing the precise quality of
  service for each of the components and ensuring that the overall quality of
  service is within the acceptable bounds defined in the contract. One
  possible outcome at this stage is for the contract to be rejected. The
  application must then decide on whether to abort the interaction or re-
  submit an amended contract.

The second grouping is then concerned with ensuring that the required level
of commitment is obtained.

- *Admission control*
  One crucial approach to ensuring that the desired QoS can be provided is
  to carry out an admission control test. This test will determine whether the
  system can at that precise moment in time deliver the required service. If
  the test is passed, the system will then guarantee that the quality of service
  can be met. Admission control tests are often defined for the different
  resources in a system, including the network and the processor.
- *Resource reservation*
  Admission control is often used in conjunction with resource reservation.
  The latter is used to guarantee the desired level of service by reserving
  resources to that interaction. Again this applies to each of the resources in
  a system including the network and the processor.

The second set of functions would not normally be applied for best effort
services.

Dynamic QoS management functions
Dynamic QoS management functions are concerned with the run-time
monitoring and control of services. The role of these functions is to ensure that
the appropriate steps are taken to ensure that the desired quality of service is
sustained.
  The first grouping of functions considered under this heading is concerned
with ongoing control of the service:

- *QoS monitoring*
  The QoS monitoring function is concerned with monitoring the level of
  service being offered by that object and reporting any problems to a higher
  level. The user should be able to specify the granularity of the monitoring, for
  example whether checks are made every 100 milliseconds or every second.
- *QoS policing*
  In contrast, QoS policing is concerned with ensuring the user of the
  service is adhering to the contract. For example, the user might agree to

send 25 frames per second to a communications service for transmission. It is important to police this aspect of the contract to prevent the service from being swamped by a burst of frames over this limit.

- *QoS maintenance*
  QoS maintenance is concerned with action that can be taken within a given service to ensure that the quality of service is sustained. For example, if changes in the quality of service are detected, then the service can ask for more resources.

The final QoS function is then concerned with actions should the above functions fail to sustain the desired level of QoS.

- *QoS renegotiation*
  QoS maintenance as described above attempts to take internal actions to recover from drops in the quality of service. Often this will be enough to deal with minor fluctuations. If, however, the contract is clearly broken, it becomes necessary to inform the user of the service and to initiate a renegotiation of the quality of service. The user may of course decide to abort the service at this stage.

Further discussion on quality of service management in distributed systems can be found in Hutchison *et al.* (1994).

3.2.3 Real-time synchronization

The third major requirement of distributed multimedia applications is the need to provide comprehensive support for real-time synchronization. Many existing distributed systems platforms provide extensive synchronization primitives in terms of, for example, semaphores, mutexes, condition variables or message passing services. It is less common to support real-time synchronization directly. This section looks in more detail at the precise requirements for real-time synchronization. We firstly consider the two main styles of synchronization that must be supported and then examine other considerations in the provision of such a service.

Two styles of real-time synchronization
Two styles of real-time synchronization can be identified in distributed multimedia applications. The first style is *intra-media* synchronization, referring to the maintenance of real-time constraints across a continuous media stream. The second style is *inter-media* synchronization, referring to the maintenance of real-time constraints across more than one media type.

Intra-media synchronization is required to ensure that the real-time integrity of a particular continuous media type is preserved in an interaction. For example, this style of synchronization would be required to ensure that a video stream is presented with the required throughput, jitter and latency

V_i = arrival of video frame *i*

Figure 3.3 Intra-media synchronization.

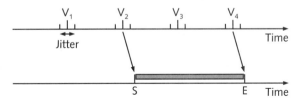

V_i = arrival of video frame *i*
S = start of caption display
E = end of caption display

Figure 3.4 Inter-media synchronization.

characteristics. This corresponds directly to quality of service requirements for continuous media as discussed above. Indeed, quality of service management can be viewed as a mechanism to achieve intra-media synchronization. Intra-media synchronization is illustrated in Figure 3.3.

Inter-media synchronization is more complex and is concerned with arbitrary real-time relationships between different interactions (discrete or continuous). Such relationships can either be expressed in absolute terms with respect to a global real-time clock (for example, two stream interactions should start at a given time) or in relative terms with respect to each other (for example, a particular video clip should start 100 milliseconds after the end of an animation). This style of synchronization is depicted in Figure 3.4.

Examples of inter-media synchronization include lip synchronization between audio and video channels, synchronization of stereo audio channels and synchronization of text subtitles and video sequences. Note that the first two inter-media examples refer to constraints between continuous media types; the third example illustrates inter-media synchronization between a continuous media type and a discrete type.

Other considerations
Both intra- and inter-media synchronization mechanisms must operate correctly in a *distributed environment*, potentially involving both local and wide area networks. This adds considerably to the complexity of providing such mechanisms. For example, it is necessary to ensure that intra-media synchronization is maintained between the producer and consumer of the media type when they are on different nodes. Similarly, in inter-media synchronization, real-time constraints must be met even when producers are on different nodes, such as audio and video transmitted from separate storage

servers. Finally, some applications demand that media presentations are synchronized even though each of many producers and each of many consumers are all on different nodes; for example, a coordinated multimedia presentation across multiple nodes.

In addition, it is required that the actions to maintain real-time synchronization can be determined *dynamically* – at run-time. There are two reasons for this. Firstly, multimedia applications are typically interactive, and hence the precise real-time requirements cannot be predicted in advance. Secondly, the quality of service offered by the network and underlying systems software may change, for example due to temporary overloading. For both these reasons, static schemes, such as those based on pre-allocated timestamps on media objects, are problematical. For a fully general solution, it is necessary to provide a general purpose language to enable *arbitrary* synchronization policies to be specified.

In summary, distributed multimedia applications require mechanisms to enable the expression of arbitrary intra- and inter-media real-time synchronization constraints. The supporting infrastructure must then provide the required level of service in the distributed environment.

3.2.4 Multiparty communications

The final requirement is the need to support multiparty communication. Many distributed multimedia applications are concerned with interactions between dispersed groups of users. For example, in desktop conferencing applications a group of users may be receiving audio and video inputs from each of the participants simultaneously. In addition, they may be viewing other information, such as a shared document or a film sequence. It is now recognized that such multiparty communication requires explicit support from the underlying distributed systems platform. The requirements generated by multiparty communications are discussed in more detail below.

Programming models and systems support
Firstly, it is necessary to have a *programming model* for multiparty communications supporting both discrete and stream interactions. This model should support a variety of styles of multicast including $1 \rightarrow N$, $N \rightarrow 1$ and $M \rightarrow N$. In addition, the programming model should enable the management of the resultant groups. Important management functionality includes the ability to create and destroy groups, the provision of an interface to enable participants to join or leave a group, and control of membership of the group.

Secondly, it is necessary to provide underlying *system support* for multiparty communications. This is particularly important for stream interactions; without systems support, the bandwidth requirements of multiparty stream interactions would be considerable. Such support should allow multicast graphs to be constructed using both splitting and merging functions. The latter is particularly complex with continuous media types requiring mixing in the

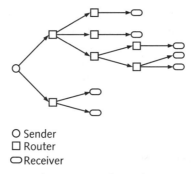

O Sender
□ Router
◯ Receiver

Figure 3.5 The concept of a multicast graphs.

case of audio and overlaying in the case of video. An example multicast graph is shown in Figure 3.5.

Impact on QoS management
Multiparty communication also adds considerably complexity to *quality of service management*. In particular, it is necessary to cater for multicast communications where receivers may require *different* qualities of service. This can happen, for example, where participants in a desktop conference have heterogeneous equipment. Some participants may have workstations and networks which can support high-quality colour video at 25 frames per second. Other participants might have more restricted facilities only allowing slow scan, grey-scale video. The underlying systems support should also be able to optimize the transmission of the multiparty communication through the appropriate use of *filtering* (Pasquale *et al.*, 1994; Yeadon *et al.*, 1996). For example, consider the multicast graph shown in Figure 3.6. The sender sends out data as full colour video at 25 frames per second. Filter F_1 reduces this to 10 frames per second (full colour). Filter F_2 then reduces this further to 10 frames per second (grey-scale). Hence the quality of service for the video received by each participant will be as follows:

- participant A receives video at 25 frames (full colour)
- participants B and C receive video at 10 frames (full colour)
- participant D receives video at 10 frames (grey-scale)

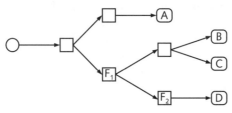

Figure 3.6 Example multicast communication.

Note that a number of applications might require the quality of service in parts of the multicast graph to be changed dynamically. This can happen, for example, if one user wants to increase the quality of the video presentation for a period of time. To achieve this, it could be necessary to renegotiate resources, re-route the connection or alter the operation of filters. Such an effect can also be supported through the use of dynamic media scaling (Delgrossi *et al.*, 1994b; Hoffman *et al.*, 1993).

Impact on synchronization

Multiparty communication also adds complexity to *synchronization* in general (not just real-time synchronization). In particular, it is important to be able to support a variety of policies for ordering data delivery. A number of *ordering* semantics are defined in the literature, such as total ordering, source (local) ordering, partial ordering, causal ordering, section ordering, attribute ordering and associated hybrid orderings (Hadzilacos and Toueg, 1994). This is further complicated by the real-time requirements of both discrete and stream interactions in multimedia systems. With the need to support such wide policies, the major requirement is to have a programming model which allows the specification of a variety of synchronization policies to be specified.

3.3 Checklist of requirements

To summarize the above discussion, we present a checklist of requirements for open distributed standards and platforms. This checklist is extracted from the discussions above, selecting the most important requirements.

   To fully support multimedia, we believe it is necessary to answer positively each of the following questions:

1. Does my standard or platform offer comprehensive support for continuous media interactions in terms of:
    (a) a programming model for stream interaction covering both simple and complex streams,
    (b) the ability to access and manipulate continuous media data, and
    (c) underlying system support for streams?
2. Does my standard or platform offer comprehensive support for quality of service management in terms of:
    (a) the ability to specify deterministic, probabilistic or stochastic QoS requirements over both discrete and stream interactions,
    (b) the ability to specify classes of service such as best effort and guaranteed,
    (c) the ability to specify QoS contracts featuring the identification of QoS dependencies,
    (d) support for the static QoS management functions of QoS specification, negotiation, admission control and resource reservation, and

    (e) support for the dynamic QoS management functions of QoS monitoring, policing, maintenance and renegotiation?

3. Does my standard or platform offer comprehensive support for real-time synchronization in terms of:
    (a) support for real-time intra-media synchronization,
    (b) support for real-time inter-media synchronization,
    (c) the ability to operate in an arbitrary distributed configuration, and
    (d) the ability to specify arbitrary actions potentially determined at run-time?

4. Does my standard or platform offer comprehensive support for multiparty communication in terms of:
    (a) a programming model for multiparty communications enabling the establishment and management of both discrete and stream group interactions,
    (b) systems support for the establishment and management of multiparty communications,
    (c) support for multiparty communications where the participants may have different and potentially changing quality of service requirements, and
    (d) the ability to specify a wide range of synchronization policies for multiparty communications?

This checklist will be used as a reference point throughout the remainder of this book.

3.4 Responses to the challenge

It should now be apparent that multimedia applications impose significant requirements on open distributed processing technologies. In this section, we consider the response to these challenges. In particular, we assess the open distributed processing standards and technologies identified in Chapter 2 against the requirements highlighted above. We look at the standards and platforms in the following order:

1. CORBA and MSS
2. DCE
3. RM-ODP and TINA

We leave the RM-ODP standard to last because of the special role that this standard has in the book.

3.4.1 CORBA and MSS

As mentioned in Chapter 2, CORBA is a specification which supports object interaction in a heterogeneous distributed environment. CORBA only supports discrete interaction through the ability to issue requests. Similarly, CORBA does not provide any explicit support in the areas of quality of service management, real-time synchronization or multiparty communications.

In fairness to CORBA, though, it was not within the terms of reference of the CORBA initiative to support multimedia. MSS is, however, an attempt to work within the CORBA framework and to develop a set of classes to support such applications. This raises the interesting and crucial question of whether such support can be developed simply through exploiting the object-oriented framework of CORBA (through the mechanisms of class and inheritance). An alternative way of wording this question is whether there is anything *missing from the basic CORBA object model* to prevent the development of distributed multimedia applications. This question is examined below through a more in depth examination of MSS. We look at each question in the checklist in turn.

1. *Does my standard or platform offer comprehensive support for continuous media interactions in terms of:*
   (a) *a programming model for stream interaction covering both simple and complex streams,*
   (b) *the ability to access and manipulate continuous media data, and*
   (c) *underlying system support for streams?*
   > MSS supports stream interaction through the concept of virtual connections. Virtual connections, however, correspond to simple streams; there is no support for complex stream interaction. With virtual connections, it is possible to access and manipulate continuous media data through the interface on port objects. The MSS document does state, however, that port objects are normally encapsulated and not directly accessed, so this is not an expected mode of interaction with an MSS platform. Finally, it is possible to provide tailored system support for stream interactions encapsulated in the implementation of the various object classes. However, MSS does not specify a particular approach to systems support or offer a framework for this activity.

2. *Does my standard or platform offer comprehensive support for quality of service management in terms of:*
   (a) *the ability to specify deterministic, probabilistic or stochastic QoS requirements over both discrete and stream interactions,*
   (b) *the ability to specify classes of service such as best effort and guaranteed,*
   (c) *the ability to specify QoS contracts featuring the identification of QoS dependencies,*
   (d) *support for the static QoS management functions of QoS specification, negotiation, admission control and resource reservation, and*
   (e) *support for the dynamic QoS management functions of QoS monitoring, policing, maintenance and renegotiation?*
   > QoS requirements in MSS are deterministic. They are specified in terms of a maximum and minimum value for delay, bandwidth and jitter. QoS can only be specified for devices and virtual connections.

It is not possible to specify QoS for standard CORBA requests (corresponding to discrete interactions). Note also that the QoS parameters are prescribed in MSS; it is not possible to define your own. MSS supports three classes of services: best_effort, guaranteed and no_guarantee. MSS, however, does not support the concept of dependencies though it does allow objects to be grouped and resources to be allocated atomically for this group. This is a less general mechanism than a contract, however. Finally, there is no explicit framework in MSS for either static or dynamic QoS management. Static functions, with the exception of admission control, are, however, implicitly present in the virtual resource classes. In terms of dynamic functions, virtual resources do support a get_qos operation but this is insufficient as a mechanism for monitoring. QoS policing and maintenance could be encapsulated in virtual resources, but this is not explicitly identified in the specification. Similarly, MSS fails to provide an interface for renegotiation. Presently, it would be necessary to close a virtual connection and create a replacement one.

3. *Does my standard or platform offer comprehensive support for real-time synchronization in terms of:*
    (a) *support for real-time intra-media synchronization,*
    (b) *support for real-time inter-media synchronization,*
    (c) *the ability to operate in an arbitrary distributed configuration, and*
    (d) *the ability to specify arbitrary actions potentially determined at run-time?*
    Intra-media synchronization is assumed to be encapsulated within virtual connections in MSS. The stream interface also enables users to monitor the position of a stream. Similarly, the controlled stream interface provides some rudimentary control. In terms of inter-media synchronization, the SyncStream class enables two stream interactions to be synchronized together or to a common clock. In addition, the COSS Event Service can be used to monitor particular events. In terms of distribution, arbitrary configurations are partially supported, although it is not clear how two presentations on different workstations would be synchronized together in the absence of a global clock. Finally, programmers have the freedom in MSS to develop their own object classes to monitor events and take arbitrary actions to maintain synchronization.

4. *Does my standard or platform offer comprehensive support for multiparty communication in terms of:*
    (a) *a programming model for multiparty communications enabling the establishment and management of both discrete and stream group interactions,*
    (b) *systems support for the establishment and management of multiparty communications,*
    (c) *support for multiparty communications where the participants may have different and potentially changing quality of service requirements, and*

(d) *the ability to specify a wide range of synchronization policies for multiparty communications?*

It is possible to establish and manage group stream interaction through virtual connections. However, there is no support for discrete groups. In terms of system support, the Media Stream Protocol in MSS can exploit the facilities offered by transport services such as ST-II for group establishment. Finally, it is not possible to support different levels of quality of service or different synchronization policies in MSS.

Overall, MSS provides many of the services required to support multimedia in open distributed processing. However, the MSS specification does have some weaknesses. The services focus on *stream interaction* and do not provide the same level of support for discrete interactions. This means that, for example, it is not possible to manage the quality of service on requests. The specification also concentrates on providing a programming model for multimedia. In other words, MSS is solely concerned with the Computational Viewpoint. Other issues, most notably concerned with the Engineering Viewpoint, are ignored or assumed to be encapsulated within objects. For example, there is no explicit framework for implementing QoS management functions. Indeed there is no requirement for many of the functions to be present. Consequently, some implementations of MSS could offer their own proprietary implementations of QoS management functions while others could provide little or no QoS management. This makes it impossible to guarantee interoperability in terms of QoS management functions. In general terms, there are no guidelines in MSS to ensure that the overall platform meets the desired real-time behaviour for multimedia applications. Finally, there are a number of *omissions* in the MSS specification including support for QoS dependencies, support for different qualities of service in multiparty communication and the ability to specify the required synchronization policy for multiparty communication.

3.4.2 DCE

DCE provides a traditional client–server programming model supported by the RPC, threads and security service. This model does not meet the needs of continuous media interaction. Similarly, the implementation is optimized for RPC traffic and not for continuous media. DCE also does not meet any of the requirements in the areas of quality of service management, real-time synchronization and multiparty communications. Again, though, it must be stressed that DCE was not intended to support multimedia applications.

Note that, as with CORBA/MSS, it is not straightforward to extend DCE for multimedia. Rather, we believe that such an extension requires fundamental changes to the architecture. We return to this issue in Chapter 12.

3.4.3 RM-ODP and TINA

The work behind this book was carried out within the framework of the RM-ODP. The reason for this is quite simple. As mentioned in Chapter 2, RM-ODP is a meta-standard for open distributed processing. Thus, by developing techniques in RM-ODP for multimedia, it should be possible to apply the same techniques to a specific distributed system technology. For example, it should be possible to use the analysis to extend CORBA with multimedia capabilities.

The techniques developed in this book provide comprehensive support for multimedia in that they address *all* the requirements identified above. The techniques are also now present in the RM-ODP. Hence we conclude that RM-ODP is at the forefront of supporting multimedia in open distributed processing. The standard provides a framework which enables more specific multimedia platforms to emerge.

TINA is one example of applying the RM-ODP principles in the telecommunications domain. TINA therefore provides a good illustration of the generality of the principles behind RM-ODP.

Clearly, these claims need considerably more justification. The remainder of the book will examine our approach to multimedia in more detail, identify the features incorporated in RM-ODP and demonstrate that the approach meets our requirements.

3.5 Summary

This chapter has examined the requirements of distributed multimedia applications in some depth. In particular, the following areas have been looked at in detail: support for continuous media, quality of service management, real-time synchronization and multiparty communication. This analysis culminated in the development of a checklist of requirements for open distributed processing standards and platforms. Key requirements identified included:

- the need to provide explicit programming models and systems support for stream interactions,
- the need to enable the specification of QoS requirements in terms of deterministic, probabilistic or stochastic properties, different classes of service and, importantly, dependencies on other services,
- the need to support a range of static and dynamic QoS management functions,
- the need to provide a dynamic and flexible approach to both intra- and inter-media real-time synchronization,
- the need to provide explicit programming models and systems support for multiparty interactions,
- the need to support QoS management and synchronization in multiparty interactions.

The chapter then examined the response to these challenges in the open distributed processing community. It was shown that many existing standards and platforms (such as CORBA and DCE) fail completely to address the requirements identified above. This is understandable as the majority of initiatives in this area did not explicitly seek to support multimedia. More importantly, it was argued that it is not straightforward to extend such technologies to address the requirements. In contrast, the approach developed in this book seeks to address all the requirements and hence provides comprehensive support for multimedia in open distributed processing. The approach is developed in the framework offered by RM-ODP; indeed, the techniques developed in this book are now included in the standard.

The remainder of the book will examine this new approach in depth. Part 2 will examine the programming model (Computational Viewpoint of RM-ODP) and Part 3 the systems support techniques (Engineering and Technology Viewpoints of RM-ODP). Part 4 will then demonstrate that the approach meets the above requirements and will then generalize the results to other standards and platforms.

PART 2
Designing distributed multimedia systems

●●●●●●●●●●●●●●●●●●●●●●●●●●●●

4 A programming model for multimedia

4.1 Introduction

In this chapter, we develop an extended object model with explicit support for multimedia (addressing the various requirements identified in the previous chapter). This model corresponds directly to the Computational Viewpoint of RM-ODP, addressing the concerns of application designers. Note that, as with RM-ODP, the model provides an overall framework in terms of defining general concepts and terms for the description of application designs. More specific notations can then be derived from this framework, for example based on C++. The chapter also develops a graphical notation for the extended object model; this will be used consistently throughout the remainder of the book.

The basic object model is described in Section 4.2. This model is based directly on RM-ODP and has been briefly described in Chapter 2. This chapter provides a more comprehensive and detailed description of the object-oriented approach. The multimedia extensions are then introduced in Section 4.3. The key features described include: the concept of streams and stream interfaces, explicit binding and quality of service, signals, and reactive objects. Following this, Section 4.4 presents some examples of using the model. Finally, Section 4.5 presents a summary of the chapter.

Note that a formalization of the programming model has been developed. Further details of this formalization can be found in the literature (Najm and Stefani, 1995a, b; Leboucher and Stefani, 1995b). In addition, copies of the latter two reports are available on the World Wide Web, on the web page for this book (see Appendix A, Section A.3.1).

4.2 The basic object model

4.2.1 Objects and operational interfaces

The proposed programming model is based on a location-independent object model where all interacting entities are treated uniformly as encapsulated *objects*. Objects can vary in terms of granularity and can encapsulate arbitrary behaviour. For example, objects can vary from an integer through to an audio-visual film. In addition, the object model does not prescribe the internal structure of objects. In particular, objects can be implemented using arbitrary programming languages and can exhibit an arbitrary level of internal concurrency (using threads plus semaphores or language-specific concurrency models).

Objects are accessed through one or more *interfaces*. The programming model also allows interfaces to be added or removed dynamically during the lifetime of an object. The ability to have multiple interfaces is important in the object model. This allows the external behaviour to be partitioned into logically distinct sets. For example, an object can offer a management interface and service interface. Interaction then occurs between *conformant* interfaces (where the precise meaning of conformant will be discussed in Section 4.2.2). To achieve interaction, however, it is necessary to have an *interface reference* for a given interface. Such an interface reference can be obtained through communication with other objects. For example, it is expected that most environments will provide a *trading service* (as discussed in Section 2.2.2). On receiving an interface reference an *implicit binding* is created to the appropriate object. Note that, in modelling interaction, we assume that the underlying communications medium is *asynchronous* and provides *no guarantees* in terms of ordering or correct delivery. We also assume that both objects and the underlying communications medium can fail.

In the basic object model, we consider one type of interface, namely *operational interfaces* (other styles, designed to support multimedia, will be introduced below). Operational interfaces support the invocation of operations on potentially remote objects. They are described in terms of named operations together with constraints on their invocation. An operation can be either an *interrogation* (a two-way operation, comprising an *invocation*, later followed by a *termination* carrying results or exceptions), or an *announcement* (a one-way operation, comprising an invocation only). The division of interrogations into invocations and terminations allows a variety of styles of operational interaction to be represented in the model, such as a remote procedure call (RPC) style interaction, where the termination immediately follows the invocation, or an asynchronous RPC, where the termination may be redeemed at a later date. Similarly, the inclusion of announcements increases the expressiveness of the model and enables the identification of interactions where a termination is not wanted or required (perhaps for reasons of performance).

Each operational interface is completely described by an operational interface signature which contains the following elements:

- a set of interrogation or announcement signatures, one for each operation in the interface, and
- a definition of the causality of the interface, (whether it acts as a client or server (or both) in interaction). (The causality is required in order to support third-party binding, where the binding is created by an object which is neither the client nor the server. We return to this issue in Chapters 8 and 11.)

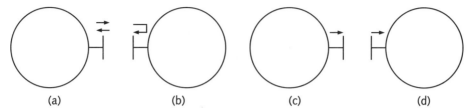

Figure 4.1 (a) Client operational interface; (b) server operational interface; (c) client announcement interface; (d) server announcement interface.

An interrogation signature is specified in terms of the *name* of the invocation, the number, name and associated types of the *parameters* to the invocation, and one or more *termination types* (defined in terms of the name of the termination together with the number, name and associated types of the results of the invocation). Similarly, an announcement signature is given by the *name* of the invocation and the number, name and associated types of the *parameters* to the invocation.

Finally, the proposed programming model assumes the existence of particular objects, referred to as *factory objects*, which have the task of adding new objects to the (distributed) environment. It is further assumed that a number of factories will coexist in a given distributed environment, enabling the creation of a variety of different types of objects. Further details on factory objects are given in Section 4.2.2 below.

We also introduce a simple graphical notation for the basic object model. Figures 4.1(a) and (b) illustrate an object offering a client operational interface and server operational interface respectively. Figures 4.1(c) and (d) then show the special cases where all operations are announcements. Note that, throughout the remainder of the book, in the absence of a graphical annotation, an interface is assumed to be an operational interface by default.

To illustrate the above concepts, we present a simple example of a temperature monitoring object.

Example *Temperature monitor*

Consider a temperature monitoring object which is part of a process control environment. This object offers three interfaces, namely a service interface, a management interface and an exception interface (Figure 4.2). The service interface offers a single interrogation, comprising a *request_temperature* invocation and a *current_temperature* termination. The management interface offers two interrogations to *enable* and *disable* the device. Each invocation has a corresponding confirmation termination (*enable_confirmed* and *disable_confirmed* respectively). Both the service and the management interface have a server causality: they provide this service to the environment. In contrast, the exception interface has a client causality. This interface offers one announcement, *alarm*. This is raised if the temperature rises above a threshold. Should this happen, a back-call is issued to the client program. In this case, the temperature monitor initiates the interaction, hence the causality.

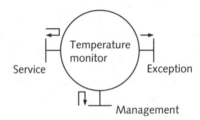

Figure 4.2 An example temperature monitoring object.

4.2.2 Types, subtypes and templates

Abstract syntax for operational interface types

The programming model defined in this chapter is strongly typed; interaction can only take place after type compatibility has been checked. This is important in an open distributed environment to ensure the integrity and safety of distributed applications. Note that, in the spirit of a framework, we do not prescribe a given syntax for the type system. Rather, we present an *abstract syntax* (a syntax where we do not define the nature of primitive types). It is possible to realize this abstract syntax using a variety of Interface Definition Notations (IDNs), such as defined in CORBA (see Section 2.3.2). In the case of CORBA, the primitive types would be the basic types in IDL, not including object references (short, long, float, string, struct, sequence and so on). Note that, although this abstract syntax is rather general, it is still sufficient to ensure that errors do not occur in communication due to type mismatches.

The abstract syntax for operational interface types is given in Figure 4.3. The abstract syntax defines a first-order type system with recursive types and is part of the formalization as discussed in Najm and Stefani (1995b) (available from the World Wide Web as discussed above).

In Figure 4.3, the following conventions are used:

- c denotes an interface type constant. An interface type constant either corresponds to some primitive type or to some recursively defined interface type. In the latter case we assume that there is a defining equation of the form: $c ::= IfType$ (actually *OpIfType* in the context of Figure 4.3);

$$
\begin{aligned}
&OpIfType ::= \quad c \quad | \quad \langle m_1 : Sig, \dots, m_q : Sig \rangle \\
&Sig ::= \quad Inter \quad | \quad Ann \\
&Inter ::= \quad Arg \rightarrow Term \\
&Ann ::= \quad Arg \rightarrow Nil \\
&Term ::= \quad [t_1 : Arg, \dots, t_p : Arg] \\
&Arg ::= \quad Nil \quad | \quad IfType_1 \times \dots \times IfType_n \\
&IfType ::= \quad OpIfType \quad | \quad StreamIfType \quad | \quad SignalIfType
\end{aligned}
$$

Figure 4.3 Abstract syntax for operational interface types.

- m_i denotes an operation name and t_j denotes a termination name;
- *Nil* is a special type constant that is used to denote the absence of parameters in an operation;
- operational interface types are given by the production *OpIfType* ::= ...;
- interface types are denoted by *IfType*; they correspond to the different sorts of interfaces (operational, stream and signal – see Section 4.3.1).

Note that the productions *OpIfType*, *Sig*, *Inter*, *Ann*, *Term* and *Arg* correspond to an operational interface type, a signature, an interrogation, an announcement, a termination and an argument respectively. Together, the rules provide the necessary conditions for a given IDN to conform to the programming model. For example, the productions imply that a given IDN must be able to express interrogations, taking arguments and returning terminations, and also announcements, taking arguments and returning nil. The concrete syntax is however left open.

Subtyping rules

To increase the flexibility of the programming model, the typing system is polymorphic; that is, interfaces can be considered to have more than one type. In particular, the type system supports subtyping, where one type (a subtype) can be substituted for another. This ability to substitute one type for another is important in a distributed system; it is crucial, though, that this added flexibility is not at the expense of type safety (we return to this point below).

In the programming model, a subtype is a relation between types where (informally) a subtype is a type which can be substituted for a given type. In terms of operational interfaces, this implies that a subtype must support at least the external behaviour of the given type (the subtype may have additional operations). This implies that the subtype will support any operation defined on the original type.

More specifically, we say that interface type I_1 is a subtype of interface type I_2 if the following rules are verified:

- all operation names that appear in I_2 also appear in I_1;
- for each operation name m that appears in I_2, its associated operation signature Sig_2 is a supertype of the operation signature Sig_1 associated with m in I_1;
- operation signature Sig_1 is a subtype of operation signature Sig_2 if the argument type Arg_1 of Sig_1 is a supertype of the arguments type Arg_2 of Sig_2 and if the terminations type Ter_1 of Sig_1 is a subtype of the terminations type Ter_2 of Sig2;
- arguments type Arg_2 is a subtype of arguments type Arg_1 if Arg_2 has the same number of arguments as Arg_1 and if each type of argument in Arg_2 is a subtype of the corresponding type of argument in Arg_1;
- terminations type Ter_1 is a subtype of terminations type Ter_2 if each termination name in Ter_1 also appears in Ter_2, and if for each termination

name t in Ter_1, its associated arguments type is a subtype of the arguments type associated with t in Ter_2.

Note that the rule for termination types is the opposite way round from the rule for argument types. This is referred to as *contravariance* in the literature and is required to ensure type safety. To appreciate this, it is important to realize that the main role of subtyping is to ensure substitutability. In order for a type I_1 to be substituted for a type I_2, the arguments of the operations in I_1 must be substitutable for the arguments in I_2 (the argument type from I_1 will be used as if it is an argument type from I_2). In contrast, a termination from I_2 must be substitutable for a termination from I_1 (the termination type from I_2 will be used as if it is of type I_1). Some researchers also propose that the rule for termination types should be the same way round as for argument types (*covariance*). This is *not* fully type safe, but is argued to be more natural, flexible and expressive. For open distributed systems, however, researchers agree that type safety is the dominant consideration, and hence contravariance is adopted. (An interesting discussion on the issue of contravariance and covariance can be found in Castagna (1995).)

The above rules are presented more formally in Figure 4.4 (again, these rules are extracted from the formalization given in Najm and Stefani (1995b)). The rules correspond to logical implications of judgements of the form: $\Sigma, E \vdash \alpha \leqslant \beta$. A judgement intuitively captures the assertion: '$\alpha \leqslant \beta$ holds in the context of typing context Σ and defining (interface type constant) equations E'. A typing context is just a set of the form $\{c_1 \leqslant d_1, \ldots, c_q \leqslant d_q\}$, that records typing relations between type constants.

Rules (*fun*), (*pro*), (*rcd*) and (*uni*) correspond directly to the informal rules above. Rule (*assmp*) indicates that a typing context records typing information. Rule (*var*) indicates that the subtype relation is reflexive. Rule (*rec*) deals with recursively defined interface types. Together, the rules in Figure 4.4 define a subtyping algorithm. The algorithm consists of applying the rules backwards, starting from an initial judgement $\Sigma, E \vdash \alpha \leqslant \beta$, with $Var(\Sigma) \cap dom(E) = \varnothing$. The algorithm succeeds if all the leaves of the execution tree thus constructed (through the application of the rules) correspond to an application of one of

(*assmp*)	$c \leqslant d \in \Sigma \Rightarrow \Sigma, E \vdash c \leqslant d$
(*var*)	$\Sigma, E \vdash c \leqslant c$
(*fun*)	$\Sigma, E \vdash \gamma \leqslant \alpha \land \Sigma, E > \beta \leqslant \delta \Rightarrow \Sigma, E \vdash \alpha \rightarrow \beta \leqslant \gamma \rightarrow \delta$
(*pro*)	$\forall i \in \{1, \ldots, q\} \Sigma, E > \alpha_i \leqslant \beta_i \Rightarrow \Sigma, E \vdash \alpha_1 \times \ldots \times \alpha_q \leqslant \beta_1 \times \ldots \times \beta_q$
(*rcd*)	$\forall i \in \{1, \ldots, q\} \Sigma, E > \alpha_i \leqslant \beta_i \land q \leqslant p$
	$\qquad \Rightarrow \Sigma, E \vdash \langle m_1 : \alpha 1, \ldots, m_p : \alpha_p \rangle \leqslant \langle m_1 : \beta_1, \ldots, m_p : \beta_q \rangle$
(*uni*)	$\forall i \in \{1, \ldots, q\} \Sigma, E > \alpha_i \leqslant \beta_i \land q \leqslant p$
	$\qquad \Rightarrow \Sigma, E \vdash [m_1 : \alpha 1, \ldots, m_p : \alpha_q] \leqslant [m_1 : \beta_1, \ldots, m_p : \beta_p]$
(*rec*)	$c, d \in dom(E) \land \Sigma \cup \{c \leqslant d\}, E \vdash E(c) \leqslant E(d) \Rightarrow \Sigma, E \vdash c \leqslant d$

Figure 4.4 Subtyping rules for operational interfaces.

the rules (*assmp*), or (*var*). It fails if at least one leaf of an execution tree is an unfulfilled goal (if no rule can be applied to it).

As stated above, the type system described here is a first-order type system in that it does not allow the definition of generic types such as List<T>. In other words, we do not allow types that are dependent on an explicit type parameter such as T and that can yield numerous type instances such as List<Int>, List<List<Int>> and so on. Introducing generic types would require adopting a second-order type system. Unfortunately, the subtyping problem for second-order type systems is in general undecidable (Pierce, 1994; Tiuryn and Urzyczyn, 1996), which means that there is no algorithm to check for type compatibility in these systems. Finding an appropriate (practical) type system for higher-order types thus remains an active area of research.

Templates

The role of a template in the programming model is to provide a complete description of a given object. This template can then be used by an appropriate factory in the process of instantiation. In particular, factory objects rely on the information contained in templates in order to create an object with the required interfaces and properties.

More specifically, a template contains the following information:

- a set of interface templates which fully define each interface offered by the object,
- a behaviour specification giving sufficient detail of the encapsulated behaviour to enable instantiation (see discussion in Section 2.2.2), and
- an environmental contract placing constraints on the distributed implementation.

Each interface template in turn is defined by the interface signature defined with respect to the type system above, a behavioural specification and an environmental contract. This provides a flexible model where, for example, constraints can be expressed on individual interfaces or on the whole object.

The environmental contract is crucial in the programming model. The model considers applications or services as consisting of a number of interacting objects. No direct consideration is given to the distribution of these objects, such as where they are located or whether they are replicated for increased availability. The environmental contract enables the designer, however, to place constraints on the eventual (distributed) implementation. Such constraints specify, for example, the level of distribution of transparency requested for that object. Further information on the environmental contract will be given below when we consider support for multimedia.

Note that the concepts of type, subtype and template described above are compatible with type, subtype and template as defined in the (descriptive) object model for RM-ODP (see Section 2.2). The concepts above are, however, more specialized to reflect the interests of the Computational Viewpoint: they define interface types, relationships between interface types and templates for computational objects respectively.

4.3 Extensions for multimedia

4.3.1 Two additional styles of interface

The first extension to the object model presented above is the introduction of the two new styles of interface, namely stream interfaces and signal interfaces. Stream interfaces model the production and consumption of continuous media data, whereas signal interfaces provide access to real-time events. Further details of each style of interface are given below.

Stream interfaces
Stream interfaces provide direct support for continuous media interactions. They are defined in terms of one or more component *flows*, where a flow is the point of production or consumption of a single continuous media type. Each flow is represented by a flow name, the type of the continuous media it handles (such as MPEG encoding of video) and the direction of the flow (either producer or consumer). Example stream interfaces include:

- a single uncompressed audio flow produced by the interface,
- a single variable bit rate video flow resulting from MPEG compression produced by the interface,
- a consumed audio flow and a produced audio flow representing a telephone object,
- a produced video flow together with an associated outgoing audio flow representing the output of a video-on-demand server.

Figure 4.5 shows the diagrammatic representations that will be used to represent stream interfaces throughout the book.

Note that it is likely for an object to have both stream interfaces and operational interfaces. For example, a camera may provide a stream interface containing a source video data flow and an operational interface with control options such as zoom, pan and tilt.

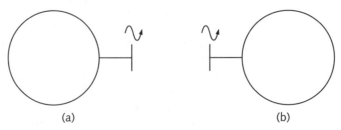

(a)   (b)

Figure 4.5 (a) A producer stream interface; (b) a consumer stream interface.

$$StreamIfType ::= \quad c \quad | \quad \langle m_1 : Sig, \ldots, m_q : Sig \rangle \rightarrow \langle n_1 : Sig, \ldots, n_p : Sig \rangle$$
$$Sig ::= \quad Arg \rightarrow Nil$$
$$Arg ::= \quad Nil \quad | \quad IfType_1 \times \ldots \times IfType_n$$

Figure 4.6 Abstract syntax for stream interface types.

Stream interfaces are described in terms of a *stream interface type*. Again, this is given by an abstract syntax (see rationale in Section 4.2.1). The abstract syntax for stream interface types is shown in Figure 4.6. We follow the same conventions as in Section 4.2.1. Here, m_i and n_j denote flow names. Flows n_j correspond to input flows or flows with a consumer causality, whereas flows m_i correspond to output flows or flows with a producer causality.

Subtyping rules are also defined for stream interface types. Informally, a stream interface S_1 is a subtype of another stream interface S_2 if the following conditions are met by each flow with identical names:

- if the causality is producer, then the associated arguments type in S_1 is a subtype of the associated arguments type in S_2;
- if the causality is consumer, then the associated arguments type in S_1 is a supertype of the associated arguments type in S_2.

Note that a formal statement of this subtyping relation is again given by the rules in Figure 4.4 (bearing in mind the different syntax for stream interfaces). Again, further details of the formalization of the abstract syntax and subtyping rules can be found in Najm and Stefani (1995b).

A more precise specification of the semantics of streams and flows is deliberately not given in the programming model. In fact, there can be many different semantics, depending on the application domain. For example, an individual flow could represent a digital transmission of continuous media over an ATM network or could be an abstract representation of an analogue communication. Similarly, the concept of subtyping is rather minimal; it is possible though for particular classes of objects to have stronger rules for compatibility.

Signal interfaces

To facilitate real-time programming, we introduce the primitive concept of *signals*. Signals correspond to real-time events and provide the necessary low-level support for implementation of a range of real-time synchronization and quality of service management functions. For example, captions could be displayed on the reception of certain signals. In addition, the arrival distribution of signals could be monitored to receive an indication of the provided quality of service. Two styles of signals are defined: pure signals, which convey the occurrence of an event, and valued signals, which additionally have associated data values. For example, a pure signal could denote the arrival of a particular video frame; a valued signal could convey the

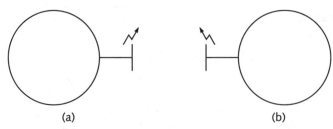

(a)   (b)

Figure 4.7 (a) A producer signal interface; (b) a consumer signal interface.

same information but also provide access to a data structure representing the frame.

All signal interactions take place at signal interfaces. In particular, signal interfaces support the production and consumption of signals. Each signal in an interface is represented by a signal name, the name and type of any associated values and the causality of the signal (either *initiating* for the production of signals or *responding* for the consumption of signals). The diagrammatic notation for signal interfaces is shown in Figure 4.7.

The programmer can define arbitrary signals for a given class of object. One particular use of signals, though, is to access events associated with either operational or stream interactions. In both cases, signals would represent the emission or reception of individual data items to/from an interface. For operational interactions, signal emissions would correspond to invocation emissions or termination emissions, and signal receptions to invocation receptions or termination receptions. Similarly, stream interactions could provide either flow emissions of continuous media data items or flow receptions of continuous media data items. The two styles of communication and associated signals are illustrated in Figure 4.8.

Signal interfaces are defined in terms of a signal interface type. The abstract syntax for signal interface types is shown in Figure 4.9 (again extracted from Najm and Stefani (1995b)). We adopt the same conventions as above. In particular, signals n_j correspond to input signals or signals with a consumer causality, whereas signals m_i correspond to output signals or signals with a

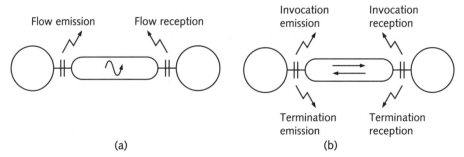

(a)   (b)

Figure 4.8 Signals corresponding to (a) stream interaction and (b) operational interaction.

SignalIfType ::= c | $\langle m_1 : Sig, \ldots, m_q : Sig \rangle \rightarrow \langle n_1 : Sig, \ldots, n_p : Sig \rangle$
Sig ::= Arg → Nil
Arg ::= Nil | $IfType_1 \times \ldots \times IfType_n$

Figure 4.9 Abstract syntax for signal interface types.

producer causality. Note that the abstract syntax for signal interface types is similar to that for stream interface types.

In addition, subtyping rules are defined. Informally, a signal interface S_1 is a subtype of another signal interface S_2 if the following conditions are met by each signal with identical names:

- if the causality is producer, then the associated arguments type in S_1 is a subtype of the associated arguments type in S_2;
- if the causality is consumer, then the associated arguments type in S_1 is a supertype of the associated arguments type in S_2.

A formal presentation of these rules is again given by the rules in Figure 4.4.

4.3.2 QoS annotations

The second extension is the association of *quality of service* annotations with interfaces. A *contractual* approach to quality of service is adopted (see Section 3.2.2). In particular, QoS annotations enable the expression of two clauses:

- the quality of service *provided* to the environment, and
- the quality of service *required* from other objects and the environment (the dependencies).

An object will provide a given level of quality of service if and only if it receives the desired quality of service from the set of dependent objects (the environment is also assumed to be modelled as objects). For example, a storage server can provide a certain level of service (as specified in the provided clause), but only if it receives a certain quality of service from the underlying file system and also the scheduling subsystem (as specified in the required clause). This approach enables arbitrary dependency graphs to be constructed representing the QoS dependencies in a given environment.

More formally, we propose that quality of service constraints should take the following form:

Req(A) → Prov(A)

where:

- Req(A) is a specification of the QoS required by A from its environment,
- Prov(A) is a specification of the QoS provided by A, and

- → is a form of logical implication that can informally be read as 'constraint Prov(A) is met at least as long as constraint Req(A) is met'. (Note that the operator → is stronger than the implication operator ⇒ in classical logic. A more formal interpretation of the → operator can be found in Leboucher and Stefani (1995b).)

Both Req(A) and Prov(A) can be *boolean combinations* of individual constraints where an individual constraint can express a deterministic, probabilistic or stochastic property expressed in terms of underlying *signals* (see requirements in Section 3.3). In addition, it is possible to specify the *class of commitment* associated with the overall contract (such as best effort or guaranteed).

In terms of the programming model, the QoS annotations form part of the environmental contract (see Section 4.2.2). This contract therefore expresses all constraints on the underlying distributed infrastructure, including constraints on the desired quality of service.

4.3.3 Explicit binding

Explicit binding and QoS management
As mentioned above, binding is *implicit* in the basic object model. However, in order to support multimedia, we believe it is necessary to introduce explicit binding. In particular, explicit binding is required to support both static and dynamic QoS management. This relationship between explicit binding and QoS management is explored in more depth below.

- *Static QoS management*
  The fundamental aspect of explicit binding is that bindings are objects. Bindings are therefore created in the same way as other objects, by using factory objects. In particular, it would be possible to request a binding between a number of participant interfaces. With this approach, it is possible to *specify* the desired quality of service of the binding by associating an appropriate environmental contract with the object template. A process of *negotiation* must then take place to resolve the QoS specified for the binding with the QoS of each of the participant interfaces. QoS dependencies must also be considered at this point. A binding can then only be created if the negotiation is successful *and* if the types of the interfaces involved are compatible. Finally, the creation of a binding provides a placeholder for *admission control* and *resource reservation* (if required).
- *Dynamic QoS management*
  As bindings are objects, their behaviour can be represented by one or more interfaces. We exploit this feature of the programming model by offering an (operational) interface on binding objects supporting dynamic QoS management functions. Different classes of binding objects can support different levels of QoS management. For example, one object class might only offer operations to enable monitoring of the QoS achieved by the

object. Other classes might support QoS monitoring and renegotiation. Other aspects of dynamic QoS management are encapsulated within binding objects: QoS policing and QoS maintenance. Again, however, it is possible to provide operational interfaces to constrain this functionality, for example to define particular policies for maintenance.

Note that we obtain considerable flexibility by modelling bindings as first-class objects. In particular, it is possible to provide a range of different factories providing a variety of binding implementations. This point was already illustrated above by the differing levels of QoS management that can be supported. This approach can also be used to model both unicast and multicast bindings. Similarly, it is possible to encapsulate arbitrary behaviour within objects, such as an intelligent caching strategy or a particular approach to compression. More specific examples of this flexibility will be given in the discussion below when particular styles of binding are considered.

Styles of explicit binding

Explicit bindings can be created between operational interfaces, stream interfaces or signal interfaces. In general, an explicit bind action will succeed if the interface to be bound is of the required kind (operational, stream or signal), if the causality is correct, and if the interface is a subtype of that expected by the binding.

We look at each style of explicit binding in more detail below.

Explicit operational bindings
As mentioned earlier, the basic object model supports operational interaction over implicit bindings. With the extended object model, it is also possible to have operational interactions over explicit bindings. Such an approach enables quality of service management of such interactions. In this case, quality of service will be expressed in terms of properties such as the latency of announcements or the round-trip time of interrogations.

The graphical representation of operational bindings is shown in Figure 4.10. This diagram shows an operational binding between two operational interfaces. The operational binding also supports an (operational) interface providing QoS management functions. This binding is point-to-point, but it

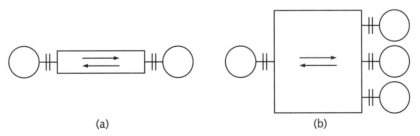

(a)   (b)

Figure 4.10 (a) Operational bindings; (b) multiparty operational bindings.

is also possible to have multiparty operational bindings where an operation is sent to several server interfaces (Figure 4.10(b)). The precise semantics of this multicast will be controlled by the environmental contract of the binding. Note that in both cases we omit the graphical annotation on the interfaces for simplicity.

Explicit stream bindings
Before stream interaction can take place, it is necessary to establish a stream binding between stream interfaces. Stream bindings provide an abstraction over the engineering infrastructure required to support one or more flows of continuous media data. This concept of stream binding is illustrated in Figure 4.11(a). Again, multiparty bindings can also be created (Figure 4.11(b)).

A wide range of stream bindings can be supported. For example, one class of binding might encapsulate MPEG compression and decompression and hide this from the application programmer. A second class of binding might send uncompressed video frames between the producer and consumer interfaces. Bindings can also encapsulate one or more flows. Some bindings might support real-time synchronization between the component flows and others might leave this to higher levels of the architecture.

Note that the rules for subtyping for streams (as defined in Section 4.3.1) allow a binding to accept interfaces with additional flows (dangling flows). However, dangling flows are restricted to the input side: the rules state that a subtype must provide *at least* input flows with the same names as those of its supertype, and may provide *no more* output flows than those provided by its supertype. This is yet another instance of the *no-surprise* rule that lies behind the notion of subtyping: a producer in the environment of a stream interface A must not see its outputs dangling if A is replaced by a compatible stream interface B (that is, where B is a subtype of A); a consumer in the environment of stream interface A may only receive inputs on flows with the same name as those of A (it need not receive inputs on all its flows). The constraint that no output flow be dangling may be seen as overly restrictive, preventing, for example, a videophone interface supporting audioOut and videoOut to be connected to an interface supporting only audioIn. However, this is not really a restriction, for a binding can be created that conforms to the videophone interface on one side and to the audio interface on the other

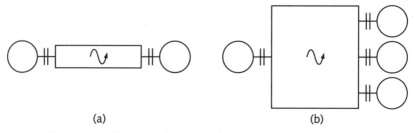

(a)   (b)

Figure 4.11 (a) Stream bindings; (b) multiparty stream bindings.

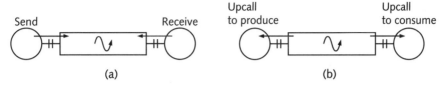

Figure 4.12 (a) Passive and (b) active stream bindings.

side but transmits only audio frames. We return to this issue of dangling flows in Chapter 11 (Section 11.3.1).

One interesting feature of stream bindings is that they enable programmers, if they want, to access and manipulate the incoming continuous media data; that is, to touch the bits. We envisage two different styles of stream binding supporting such access, namely passive and active bindings. In *passive bindings*, the producer sends data to the binding and the consumer receives data from the binding (the producer and the consumer are hence the active parties in initiating interaction). In *active bindings*, however, the binding is responsible for initiating interaction. At the producer end, the binding signals the producer requesting data. Similarly, at the consumer end, the binding signals the consumer when data is available. The producer/consumer must then provide handlers to deal with the data in each case. This distinction is illustrated in Figure 4.12.

Explicit signal bindings
Signal bindings enable signals to be communicated between signal interfaces. In particular, they enable signals emitted at one interface to be received at one or more target interfaces. In this case, quality of service statements enforce constraints over the signal emissions and receptions; for example, to constrain the latency between a signal emission and its eventual reception or to constrain the rate of signal arrival.

Again, two styles can be identified, namely point-to-point (Figure 4.13(a)) and multiparty (Figure 4.13(b)).

As with streams, few restrictions are placed on signal bindings. Again, they can be point-to-point or multicast and can have varying levels of guarantees. In addition, the programming model for emitting and receiving signals is not prescribed. For example, this could be based on an exception model, a

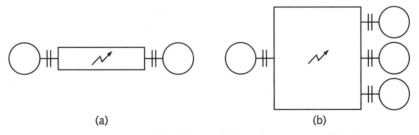

Figure 4.13 (a) Signal binding and (b) multiparty signal binding.

guarded command notation, or a polling based approach (compare active and passive stream bindings above).

4.3.4 Reactive objects

The object model presented so far is entirely *asynchronous*. In other words, all objects take a certain and often unpredictable amount of time to carry out actions. For example, binding objects take a certain amount of time to deliver data (in the form of operations, streams or signals) to the destination. Similarly, other objects will take a certain amount of time to process incoming data or to generate new data. The role of real-time QoS annotations is then to place constraints on this asynchronous behaviour and to demand a level of commitment from the engineering infrastructure. Difficulties emerge, however, when you introduce control into this model, for example to undertake QoS management or to implement real-time synchronization policies. In particular, objects implementing the control are themselves asynchronous and hence their real-time behaviour must also be constrained and potentially monitored. The end result is a recursive management structure where it is necessary to control the controllers, and so on *ad infinitum*.

To overcome this difficulty, we introduce the concept of *reactive objects*. Reactive objects are effectively real-time controllers which maintain a permanent interaction with their environment, accepting signals from the environment, reacting, and consequently emitting signals to the environment. (This follows the use of the term 'reactive' by Harel and Pnueli (1985).) Crucially, we require reactive objects to be synchronous: to adhere to the synchrony hypothesis (Berry and Gonthier, 1988; Halbwachs, 1993).

Synchrony hypothesis
The synchrony hypothesis states that reactions should be instantaneous; that is, atomic with respect to the environment (the environment should remain invariant during execution).

This implies that the reaction to incoming signals and the subsequent generation of new signals takes zero time. One class of language capable of meeting the synchrony hypothesis is the class of *synchronous languages* (Berry, 1989). These languages compile into table-driven finite state automata, and uphold the synchrony hypothesis as long as the transitions are an *order of magnitude faster* than the inter-arrival gap between external events. It is possible to verify this condition statically as there are a fixed and known number of machine instructions executed for each transition. This makes it feasible to realize the synchrony hypothesis in practice.

The concept of reactive objects is illustrated in Figure 4.14. Reactive objects are used in the programming model to implement all aspects of real-time control, including the realization of dynamic QoS management functions for monitoring and potentially renegotiating quality of service and also to

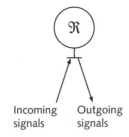

Figure 4.14 Reactive objects.

realize real-time synchronization (Blair *et al.*, 1994, 1996). Examples of the use of reactive objects will be given in Section 4.4.

4.3.5 Discussion

The programming model we propose features a *hybrid* object model where an activity consists of a number of interacting objects some of which are reactive, and take zero time, and others of which are non-reactive, and take a finite amount of time (perhaps constrained by QoS annotations). This hybrid object model offers a clean *separation of concerns* between the synchronous world, where execution can be considered to be instantaneous, and the asynchronous world, where object execution and interaction take a finite amount of time. This approach is encapsulated in the following equation:

$$REAL\text{-}TIME = QUALITY\ OF\ SERVICE + CONTROL$$

In other words, a real-time program consists of synchronous objects implementing control and quality of service constrained asynchronous objects representing the main behaviour of the program (including bindings between objects).

This clean separation has a number of important benefits for the development of multimedia applications:

1. All timing assumptions are *explicitly* recorded as quality of service annotations; there are no hidden assumptions embedded in objects.
2. The programmer can develop reactive objects implementing synchronization algorithms *without concern* for the real-time behaviour of the algorithm; the quality of service controlled bindings to and from the reactive object anchor the (abstract) algorithm in the asynchronous environment.
3. *Portability* for real-time distributed multimedia applications is enhanced because only the quality of service declarations need be changed on moving to a different environment, such as a different topology, a faster processor or a lower speed network.

4. No special mechanism is required to represent *time* in the development of reactive objects. Rather, reactive objects receive an event from the external environment which happens to derive from an external clock. The clock event is treated like any other event. This permits various time granularities and accuracies to be freely chosen; the quality of the clock is expressed as a quality of service statement.

5. The synchrony hypothesis allows *rigorous formal reasoning* about time because the fact that statement execution takes no time allows us to assume that dates of clock events can be manipulated arithmetically. For example, given a statement *sleep()* which is driven by clock events as described above, it can be asserted that *sleep(1)* executed 100 times in sequence is precisely equivalent to *sleep(100)*. This desirable formal property does not hold with conventional environments such as Unix.

To illustrate the points raised above, we revisit the temperature monitoring object introduced in Section 4.2.1. In particular, we consider the implementation of the alarm functionality defined at the exception interface.

Example *The temperature monitor revisited*

The exception interface of the temperature monitoring object raised an alarm at the exception interface if the temperature exceeded a certain threshold. For the purposes of this example, we introduce an added quality of service requirement that this alarm should be raised within 50 ms of the temperature exceeding the threshold. This functionality could be implemented by decomposing the monitoring object into a number of interacting objects as shown in Figure 4.15. All real-time assumptions would then be explicitly stated as QoS constraints on bindings (point 1). For example, the following QoS assumptions could be requested: the binding between the clock and the monitor delivers a tick signal every millisecond with an accuracy of ±10 microseconds; signals sent to and from the temperature sensor take 10 milliseconds ± 1 millisecond; it takes a similar amount of time to send a message to raise the alarm. The behaviour of the reactive object can then be implemented without mention of these real-time parameters: on receiving a tick, poll the sensor and on receiving the temperature, check the value and if necessary raise the alarm (point 2). Crucially, this implementation could be ported to another environment where the requirements are different simply by changing the quality of service annotations, for example by altering the granularity of the clock signal (point 3). There is no special semantics associated with the clock in this example; it is simply another input signal (point 4). Finally, it is possible to formally reason about the overall system behaviour; by assuming the reactive object takes zero time it can easily be seen that the requirement to raise the alarm within 50 ms can be met (point 5).

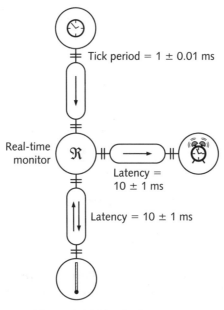

Real-time monitor

Tick period = 1 ± 0.01 ms

Latency =
10 ± 1 ms

Latency = 10 ± 1 ms

Figure 4.15 Monitoring process.

Further, multimedia oriented, examples are given in the section below.

4.4 Multimedia examples

In this section, we demonstrate the flexibility of the programming model by discussing three contrasting examples. The first example is concerned with managing a continuous media binding. This illustrates how intra-media synchronization can be programmed using our approach. The second example then shows how lip synchronization can be achieved between an audio and a video stream, illustrating inter-media synchronization. Finally, the third example demonstrates how a more general multimedia presentation can be programmed using reactive objects.

In each case, we present a high-level object-oriented design in terms of objects, interface, QoS annotations, bindings and reactive objects. At this stage we avoid the use of any particular notation for interface types, QoS annotations or the implementation of objects and merely present an informal and abstract description of the behaviour. The examples will be revisited in Chapter 6 after specific notations have been introduced in Chapter 5.

4.4.1 A QoS-managed stream binding

This example illustrates the management of a video stream binding between a camera and a video window object potentially on different network nodes. The

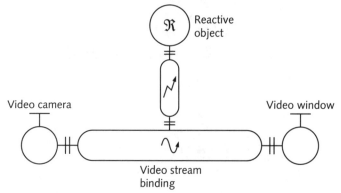

Figure 4.16 Overall design to achieve QoS management.

configuration of objects is shown in Figure 4.16. This diagram shows the following objects:

- a video camera object (videoCamera) offering a stream interface consisting of one outgoing flow together with an operational interface which can be used to control the camera,
- a video window object (videoWindow), also offering a stream interface with one incoming flow together with a signal interface indicating when a video frame has been presented,
- an explicit binding object (videoBinding) offering an input and output flow interface together with a signal interface supporting the QoS-management protocol,
- a reactive object implementing QoS management (qosManager) and offering two signal interfaces, the first interacting with videoBinding and the second offering an exception interface to an application object,
- an explicit binding object (qosBind) between the videoBinding interface and the reactive object, with an input and output signal interface corresponding to the transmission of signals in the binding together with a third signal interface for control.

In terms of quality of service, the videoBinding object should support the following QoS requirements:

- an average latency of 50 ms,
- a maximum delay jitter of ±10 ms, and
- a throughput of at least 25 frames per second.

We also assume that the producer and consumer stream interfaces can also support these requirements. Quality of service constraints should also be placed on the signal binding to the reactive object to place bounds on the latency of signals. For this example, we set this latency to a maximum of 5 ms for the binding. Such a tight constraint would normally *imply* that this binding is implemented locally (although the programming model does not explicitly define the distribution of objects).

The task of the qosManager reactive object is to monitor the quality of service offered by the video binding. Should the binding fail to deliver this desired quality of service, a signal should be sent to the application indicating a QoS violation. Furthermore, this violation should provide an indication of the type of violation (excessive delay or jitter or insufficient throughput).

4.4.2 Achieving lip synchronization

The second example illustrates how *lip synchronization* can be achieved between related audio and video connections. The high-level design to achieve lip synchronization is shown in Figure 4.17. This diagram shows an audio producer (a microphone), a video producer (a video camera), an audio consumer (a speaker) and a video consumer (a video window). The producers and consumers offer stream interfaces of the appropriate types and causalities. These are connected by an audio stream binding and a video stream binding. The consumer objects also support control interfaces which are used to implement lip synchronization. These are connected by signal bindings to a reactive object encapsulating the lip synchronization algorithm. This reactive object also requires input from an external clock operating at a granularity of 1 ms.

The QoS annotations for the various bindings mentioned above are as follows:

- the video stream binding offers a throughput of 25 frames per second and a delay of between 40 and 60 ms,

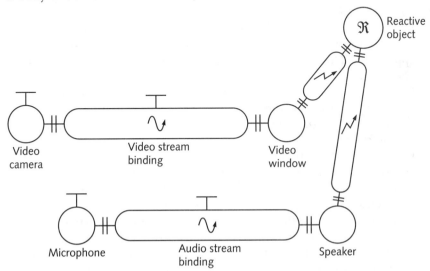

Figure 4.17 Overall design to achieve lip synchronization.

- the audio stream binding offers a throughput of 5 packets per second and a delay of between 40 and 60 ms,
- both the control bindings have a maximum delay of 10 ms, and
- the clock binding will deliver the time signal with a delay of precisely 1 millisecond with no jitter permitted.

(For simplicity, we ignore QoS annotations on the other object interfaces and merely note that they must be compatible with the established bindings.)

The protocol for lip synchronization is then as follows. The reactive object receives signals indicating when audio and video data items arrive at the respective presentation objects. The reactive object then informs the video consumer object when the data items should be displayed. The task of the reactive object is to issue this presentation signal at the appropriate times to ensure lip synchronization is preserved (for example by either speeding up or slowing down the video presentation).

4.4.3 A multimedia presentation

The final example is the real-time coordination of a multimedia presentation. This example illustrates how the programming model can support more complex applications that handle multiple, composite multimedia objects and that incorporate user interactions. More specifically, we consider the real-time coordination of the display of information relating to a museum collection. This application is designed to be placed in a museum foyer, where it can be interacted with by visitors through a special keyboard input device.

The presentation consists of three phases:

1. *The welcome phase*
   In this phase, the application presents a welcoming video sequence and associated audio commentary explaining how to start and use the application. This phase is terminated when the user presses a start key.
2. *The menu phase*
   In the menu phase, a menu is displayed and a short audio message is played repeatedly, inviting the user to select a presentation. This phase is terminated when the user selects a choice from a numerical keypad.
3. *The conference phase*
   In this phase, the application presents a sequence of N images accompanied by an associated audio commentary. An access map showing the exact location of the presented work in the museum building is also displayed in a second window. Image presentation is synchronized to the audio commentary which is therefore divided into N subunits in a one-to-one correspondence with the images. An image is displayed when the audio commentary of the previous image has finished. The new audio commentary starts two seconds after the display of the image. In addition, the access map is displayed simultaneously with the first picture of the conference.

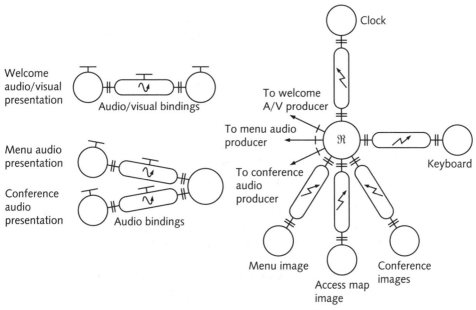

Figure 4.18 Overall design for the multimedia presentation.

When the presentation comes to an end, the application loops back to the menu phase. The user can temporarily suspend/resume the conference phase with a toggle key with values *suspend* and *resume*. The duration of suspension caused by a key press is, however, limited to a maximum of 30 seconds. The presentation is then automatically resumed, even if the user has not pressed *resume*. The user can also kill the menu and conference phases by pressing a *kill* key. The current phase (menu or conference) is then aborted and the application goes back to the welcome phase. A final feature is that the menu phase is guarded by a timeout: a selection has to be made within a delay of five minutes, otherwise the application assumes the user has left, and loops back to the welcome phase.

The overall object-oriented design for the application is then shown in Figure 4.18. This diagram shows a configuration of objects comprising:

- one audio/video producer (for the welcome phase), one corresponding audio/video consumer and associated stream binding with both an audio and a video flow,
- two audio producers (for the welcome phase and the conference phase), a single audio consumer and two audio stream bindings,
- a number of image sources (the menu image, the access map image and the conference images),
- a keyboard object,
- an external clock, and

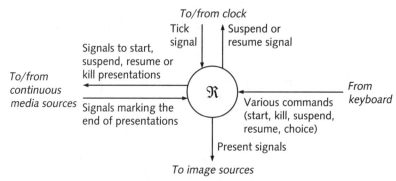

Figure 4.19 The reactive object.

- a reactive object (encapsulating the overall real-time coordination) with associated control (signal) bindings to the audio and video producers, the image sources, the keyboard and the external clock.

The quality of service annotations for the various bindings are given below (again ignoring the annotations for the other objects):

- video should be delivered at a rate of 25 frames per second with a delay of between 40 and 60 ms,
- audio should be delivered at a rate of 5 packets per second with a delay of between 40 and 60 ms,
- the various control bindings should have a maximum delay of 25 ms, and
- the clock should deliver the clock signal with a delay of precisely 1 ms with no permitted jitter.

The task of the reactive object is then to implement the required real-time coordination as defined above. The overall functionality of this object is summarized in Figure 4.19. As can be seen, the reactive object receives signals from the keyboard device (indicating a start, kill, suspend, resume or choice selection) and from the real-time clock. The reactive object also receives signals indicating the end of each of the phases. The reactive object must then respond by generating signals to initiate the presentations for the welcome and menu phases, to initiate the presentation of the i-th unit of audio and associated image for the conference phase, to present the access map, and, finally, to report exceptions to the appropriate objects.

4.5 Summary

This chapter has introduced an object-oriented programming model designed to support distributed multimedia computing. The main features of this object model are as follows:

- objects can offer multiple interfaces to the environment,
- support is provided for operational, stream or signal interfaces,
- all interfaces are described by an interface type,
- subtype relations are then defined between interface types,
- QoS annotations can be associated with each interface type as part of an environmental contract,
- explicit bindings can be created between compatible interfaces resulting in the creation of a binding object,
- static QoS management are encapsulated within explicit binding creation,
- dynamic QoS management are then supported by binding interface,
- access is provided to asynchronous events through the concept of signals, and
- reactive objects enable the programmer to provide arbitrary real-time synchronization or (dynamic) QoS management functionality.

This approach is closely related to the Computational Model defined in the RM-ODP. Our underlying object model is identical to RM-ODP. In addition, many of the extensions developed in this chapter are also now featured in the standard. In particular, the RM-ODP now includes the three styles of interface, QoS annotations and explicit binding. The one feature not supported is reactive objects. This is not a problem, however, as particular architectures based on RM-ODP can feature reactive objects as one particular object class. This then provides a specialized architecture providing direct support for real-time control. In our opinion, the added expressiveness of reactive objects is essential for multimedia programming.

Several examples were also given to illustrate the application of this programming model to typical multimedia problems. These examples will be revisited after specific notations to populate the programming model are introduced in the next chapter.

5 An approach based on the programming model

5.1 Introduction

As mentioned in the previous chapter, the role of the programming model is to provide a general framework for open distributed processing with specific features included to model multimedia computation. To provide a specific distributed system platform, it is necessary to populate this framework with specific notations. Firstly, notations are required to describe interface types and environmental contracts. These must conform to the abstract syntax defined in Chapter 4. Secondly, it is necessary to adopt a set of languages for the development of individual objects, including reactive objects. This relationship between the programming model and specific platforms is illustrated in Figure 5.1.

In this chapter, we consider one set of specific notations and languages to populate the architecture. In particular, we concentrate on languages for the following:

- interface type signatures (operational, stream and signal),
- QoS annotations,
- reactive objects.

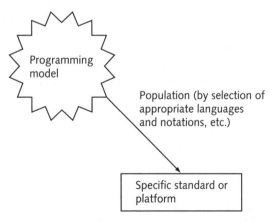

Figure 5.1 Populating the programming model.

The chapter is structured as follows. Section 5.2 introduces an extended CORBA IDL used to describe interface type signatures. The extensions enable the definition of signal and stream interfaces in CORBA. Section 5.3 then discusses a notation for quality of service annotations. In particular, this section introduces the real-time logic, QL. The programming language Esterel is then introduced in Section 5.4; this language is adopted for the programming of reactive objects. Finally Section 5.5 summarizes the chapter. Simple examples are used throughout this chapter to introduce the particular notations. More complex examples are presented in Chapter 6.

5.2 Expressing interface type signatures

5.2.1 Use of an extended CORBA IDL

In populating the programming model, the first requirement is for a notation to express interface type signatures (operational, stream and signal). The CORBA IDL has emerged as a *de facto* standard for the expression of operational interface type signatures. Rather than develop a new language, we take the approach of extending CORBA IDL to enable the expression of stream and signal interfaces. Our aim is that the extended IDL should be upwardly compatible with CORBA IDL; that is, everything expressible in CORBA IDL should be valid in the new IDL.

The key features of the extended IDL are described below.

5.2.2 Key features of the extended IDL

The extensions to CORBA IDL are the introduction of an interface role (operational, stream or signal), means of expressing stream and signal interfaces and the definition of subtyping rules for each interface style. These extensions are described below. Firstly, however, it is necessary to introduce some background on CORBA IDL (further discussion is given in Section 2.3.2).

Background on CORBA IDL
In this section, we provide a brief introduction to CORBA IDL. We do, however, assume some familiarity with IDL and hence do not present a full tutorial. Further details on CORBA IDL can be found in the CORBA specification (Object Management Group, 1995a).

Briefly, a CORBA specification consists of one or more interface definitions together with associated type, constant and exception definitions. A specification can also include modules which are themselves complete specifications providing an element of modularity in the construction of large specifications.

The grammar for an interface is then as follows (using an extended BNF notation):

```
<interface>              ::=<interface_header>
                            "{" <interface body> "}"

<interface_header>       ::="interface" <identifier> [<inheritance_spec>]

<interface_body>         ::=<export>*

<export>                 ::=<type_dcl> ";"
                         |    <const_dcl> ";"
                         |    <except_dcl> ";"
                         |    <attr_dcl> ";"
                         |    <op_dcl> ";"
```

In the above grammar, the optional <inheritance_spec> is used to list one or more specifications to be inherited by the new interface. In addition, the rules for <export> enable the specification of type and constant declarations required by the interface definition, a set of exceptions that can be raised by the interface and, finally, the attributes and operations defined on the interface (attributes are logically equivalent to state with associated access and set operations).

An operation is then defined as follows:

```
<op_dcl>      ::= [<op_attribute>] <op_type_spec> <identifier>
                  <parameter_dcls>
                  [<raises_expr>] [<context_expr>]
```

In this rule, the op_attribute can be used to denote 'oneway' operations (see Section 2.3.2), the <op_type_spec> describes the type returned by the operation, and the <parameter_dcls> describe one of more parameters qualified by 'in', 'out' or 'inout' attributes. In addition, the optional <raises_expr> and <context_expr> describe the exceptions that can be raised by the operation and elements describing the context of the invocation respectively.

Further expansion of this grammar is unnecessary for the discussion below.

Three styles of interface

CORBA IDL is extended to enable the expression of three styles of interface (operational, stream and signal). This is achieved by modifying the top level of the above grammar as follows:

```
<interface>   ::= <op_interface>
              |    <stream_interface>
              |    <signal_interface>
```

Note that this approach has the advantage of explicitly identifying the three different styles of interface in the syntax of the IDL. The disadvantage is that changes are required to CORBA IDL (although it is important to stress that the new IDL retains backward compatibility with CORBA IDL). Other (less explicit) approaches could also be taken, such as the use of pragmas to identify interaction styles.

We now look at each style of interface in turn below.

Expressing operational interfaces

The CORBA IDL described above already provides the necessary linguistic features for the expression of operational interfaces. The grammar for operational interfaces is therefore identical to CORBA but with the additional ability to identify the role of interfaces. This is however optional to allow existing CORBA specifications to be valid in the new IDL.

The revised grammar is shown below.

<op_interface>	::= <op_interface_header> "{" <op_interface_body> "}"
<op_interface_header>	::= "interface" [<op_role>] <identifier> [<inheritance_spec>]
<op_role>	::= "<operational>"
<op_interface_body>	::= <op_export>*

The grammar for op_export is then identical to <export> above.

If the role is not specified, it is assumed that the interface is operational. Hence, the following two specifications are identical:

```
interface <operational> name_service
interface name_service
```

We illustrate the definition of operational interfaces by example.

Example *Camera control interface*
The following IDL definition describes an example camera control interface:

```
interface <operational> cameraControl {
        start ();
        stop ();
        pan (in panDegrees integer);
        tilt (in tiltDegrees integer);
        zoom (in zoomFactor integer);
    };
```

(This interface will feature in Section 6.2.2.)

Note that in moving from the abstract syntax to the concrete syntax, a number of specific choices have been made. These choices are to a large extent determined by the choice of CORBA IDL as the basis for the interface definition language. For example, the use of CORBA enforces a particular choice of base types (boolean, short, object reference and so on). In addition, CORBA does not have a single syntactic representation of terminations. Rather, terminations can be results of operations, out parameters or exceptions. Similarly, there is no explicit identification of causality in CORBA. Therefore, the causality must be inferred from the overall context. Finally, CORBA provides a number of specific mechanisms to support the construction of large specifications (such as modules and interface inheritance). It is also necessary to adopt a particular approach to subtyping and ensure that the selected approach is compatible with the general rules introduced in Section 4.2.2. We defer a discussion of subtyping, however, until after the subsections on stream and signal interfaces.

Expressing stream interfaces
Stream interfaces are denoted by the role <stream> in the interface header. The interface body then describes the interface in terms of one or more flows, where each flow is given by:

- a direction (input or output flow),
- a name (a valid CORBA identifier unique to this interface), and
- a type (selected from an extended set of types for multimedia).

The corresponding grammar for stream interfaces is as follows:

<stream_interface>	::= <stream_interface_header> "{" <stream_interface body> "}"
<stream_interface_header>	::= "interface" [<stream_role>] <identifier> [<inheritance_spec>]
<stream_role>	::= "<stream>"
<stream_interface_body>	::= <stream_export>*
<stream_export>	::= <flow_dcl> ";"
<flow_dcl>	::= <flow_direction> <identifier> "(" <flow_type>")"
<flow_direction>	::= "flowOut" | "flowIn"
<flow_type>	::= "audio" | "video" | "animation"

Note that the expansion for <flow_type> is rather limited in the grammar above. In particular, it is only possible to define audio, video or animation flows. These can, of course, be further refined by appropriate QoS annotations (as discussed below). However, we do not see this as a complete solution and view this only as a placeholder for a richer type system. In particular, we see the solution to this problem as defining an *open* hierarchy of types and subtypes in a manner similar to the class hierarchy prescribed by MSS. The importance of having an open approach is that new formats can then readily be accommodated. This property is provided, however, as a consequence of the object-oriented approach by defining new subtypes.

Note that all types should provide at least two methods, `get_representation` and `set_representation`, to provide access to the underlying data structures representing the media type. This is important to enable applications to access and manipulate continuous media data.

We illustrate the use of the IDL by example.

Example *An audio/ video producer*
The following IDL definition describes a producer object generating a stream consisting of an audio and a video flow:

```
interface <stream> avProducer {
        flowOut audioOut (audio);
        flowOut videoOut (video);
    };
```

Again, the discussion of subtyping is deferred until the section below.

Expressing signal interfaces
Similarly, signal interfaces are denoted by the use of the role <signal> in the interface header. The body then describes each of the signals defined on that interface in terms of:

- a direction (input or output signal),
- a name (a valid CORBA identifier unique to this interface), and
- zero or more typed values associated with the signal (where the type is any valid CORBA type).

The corresponding grammar for signal interfaces is as follows:

<signal_interface>	::= <signal_interface_header> "{" <signal_interface body> "}"
<signal_interface_header>	::= "interface" [<signal_role>] <identifier> [<inheritance_spec>]
<signal_role>	::= "<signal>"
<signal_interface_body>	::= <signal_export>*

`<signal_export>`	::= `<type_dcl>` ";"
	| `<const_dcl>` ";"
	| `<signal_dcl>` ";"
`<signal_dcl>`	::= `<signal_direction>` `<identifier>`
	"(" [`<signal_values>`] ")"
`<signal_direction>`	::= "signalOut"
	| "signalIn"

where `<signal_values>` correspond to the values associated with the signals as described above. For input signals, these values are similar to 'in' parameters on operations and, for output signals, the values correspond to 'out' parameters. In both cases, the types should be CORBA data structures rather than continuous multimedia types to enable direct access to the data in the host language.

Again, we illustrate the description of signal interfaces by an example.

Example *A simple monitor*
The following IDL definition describes a monitor object which receives an input signal from a given device indicating the current temperature and pressure. The monitor can then issue a (pure) output signal if an exception is detected:

```
struct sensorData {
        unsigned long temperature;
        float pressure;
};


interface <signal> avProducer {
        signalIn report (audio);
        signalOut exception ();
};
```

The rules for subtyping are given below.

Subtyping in operational, stream and signal interfaces
To be compatible with the programming model, it is necessary to provide rules for subtyping for each interface style (operational, stream and signal interfaces). Furthermore, the rules must be compatible with the general rules presented in Chapter 4 as defined on the abstract syntax. Again, the selected approach is largely determined by the choice of CORBA IDL as the base notation. In particular, we adopt the rules from CORBA, where one interface I_1 is a subtype of another interface I_2 only if I_1 is directly derived from I_2 (that is, by interface inheritance). Furthermore, this rule applies equally to operational, stream and signal interfaces.

This is, however, a rather restricted view of subtyping. For example, it should be possible to have a subtype that is not a derived type. This restricted approach is adopted though to retain compatibility with CORBA. More advanced rules could be introduced at a later date.

Note that the proposed approach is compatible with the rules introduced in Chapter 4. In particular, a derived type will always be a subtype according to these rules.

5.2.3 Discussion

The IDL defined above provides a means of describing operational, stream and signal interfaces as required by the programming model. The precise mapping between the two concerns is considered in more detail below.

- *Operational interface signatures*
  The IDL enables the expression of both announcements and interrogations. An operation with the attribute 'oneway' is precisely equivalent to an announcement; other operations are then interrogations. The one limitation of the IDL is that interrogations can only return one result. The programming model requires the return of one or more results. The IDL can however also use out parameters and exceptions to provide additional results. In addition, the causality of interfaces is not explicitly stated (to retain compatibility with CORBA IDL). The causality is however implicit in the use of the IDL. For example, in a compilation chain the IDL would be used to generate either a client stub or a server stub. Finally, the concrete syntax can be seen to be compatible with the abstract syntax with particular choices in terms of the selection of base types, syntactic support for the construction of large specifications and so on.
- *Stream interface signatures*
  The IDL extensions enable the expression of stream interfaces consisting of one or more flows. In addition, the type and causality of flows is explicitly stated. In this case, it can be seen that the concrete syntax is trivially compatible with the abstract syntax.
- *Signal interfaces*
  The IDL extensions also enable the expression of signal interfaces consisting of one or more signals. Each signal can have associated values and also has an explicit causality. Again, the concrete syntax is trivially compatible with the abstract syntax.

In addition, subtyping is defined over the extended IDL (as required by the programming model). In particular, the subtyping rules defined for the abstract syntax have been reinterpreted for the concrete syntax.

The definition of templates will be reconsidered after the (concrete) language for QoS annotations is defined below.

Note that the notation for expressing stream interfaces and signal interfaces is rather similar. This should not be too surprising. As mentioned in Chapter 4, flows within streams can be interpreted as the production of valued signals from one interface followed by the consumption of that signal at another interface. The associated stream binding then encapsulates one particular style of interaction as required by continuous media. Therefore, signals can be seen as a more general, but more primitive, concept.

5.3 Expressing quality of service annotations

5.3.1 Choice of a real-time logic

We now consider the development of a language to express quality of service annotations (as part of the environmental contract). This is a much more difficult problem than providing a language for interface type signatures. We propose a particular approach based on a real-time logic QL. In order to understand this decision, it is first necessary to consider the requirements for a QoS annotation language.

Requirements for a QoS annotation language
In Chapter 4, it was decided to adopt a *contractual* approach to quality of service, enabling the specification of both provided and required clauses. (The provided clause describes the quality of service offered to the environment and the required clause describes dependencies on other objects.) In order to specify such clauses, it is necessary to define conditions over specific events. In terms of the programming model, the most natural approach is to specify conditions over the occurrence of *signals*. Signals are the most primitive events in the language, and, as discussed above, underpin both stream and operational interactions.

It is then necessary to define quality of service requirements in terms of signals. In particular, it is necessary to be able to specify relationships between arbitrary signals in a distributed configuration. This includes both local properties on an individual interface (such as the delay between a signal reception and a subsequent signal emission) and more general distributed properties (such as the delay between a signal emission and its reception at a remote object).

In terms of quality of service requirements, we would like to be able to express a *minimum* of:

- the timeliness properties of delay and delay jitter,
- the volume property of throughput, and
- reliability properties relating to transmission errors.

It would be an added advantage to have a *general approach* capable of expressing a wider range of properties. In each case, it is also necessary to be able to express *deterministic*, *probabilistic* or *stochastic* properties.

Finally, it is necessary to specify the *class of service* required in terms of, for example, whether the properties should be guaranteed or met on a best-effort basis.

Why a real-time logic?

As stated above, we propose the use of a real-time logic for the expression of QoS annotations. Our reasons for this decision are given below:

- *A declarative approach*
  Logics provide an abstract declarative specification of quality of service properties. In particular, they specify what is required rather than how it is to be achieved. This is important, as the Computational Viewpoint by definition should abstract away from engineering concerns.
- *Expressiveness of a logic*
  Logics have considerable expressive power, enabling the specification of a full range of quality of service properties. It is already recognized that logics can express a wide range of distributed systems properties. Real-time logics then enable the additional specification of real-time quality of service constraints.
- *Formal analysis*
  The mathematical foundation of a logic enables the use of a range of formal techniques. For example, logics often allow the automatic verification of requirements. In addition, it should be possible to check the consistency of a set of formulae. Finally, logics offer the interesting possibility of the automatic synthesis of controllers from logic constraints.

Note, however, that there is a trade-off between expressiveness and formal analysis. In particular, it is often necessary to constrain the expressiveness of a logic to retain tractability in the underlying mathematical model. Such trade-offs are crucial in the design of a logic. The particular design decisions in QL are described below.

5.3.2 Key features of the proposed logic

QL is a first-order real-time logic based closely on RTL (Jahanian and Mok, 1986). The language is also based on an event model inspired by the work of Caspi and Halbwachs (1986). We describe the key features of QL below under the headings of the underlying event model, the QL language and, finally, formal analysis and QL.

The underlying event model

We firstly introduce the general event model that is used for the interpretation (semantics) of QL.

Preliminaries

Consider a time domain $(T, \leqslant, +)$ where:

- T is an infinite set of instants with a minimal element $-\infty$ and a maximal element $+\infty$,
- $\leqslant$ is a total order relation on instants, and
- $+$ is a binary addition relation on T.

The time domain could be one of R, the set of reals, Z, the set of integers, or N, the set of positive numbers with the obvious interpretations in each case for $\leqslant$ and $+$.

Event types, events and histories

The three components in the underlying event model are *event types*, event occurrences (or simply *events*) and event histories (or simply *histories*). We look at each in turn below. Firstly, though, it is necessary to introduce some notation.

We use $\varepsilon, \varepsilon_1, \varepsilon_2$ to denote event types, e, e_1, e_2 to denote events, and h, h_1, h_2 to denote histories. We also use Π to denote the set of event types, E to denote the set of events and H to denote the set of histories. Finally, we write $e : \varepsilon$ to indicate that e is an occurrence of type ε.

We can now define the three basic components in the event model.

- *Event types*
  An event type, ε_i, then corresponds to a particular state transition in a system, for example, the arrival of a frame of video. The set Π thus corresponds to all the event types that can occur in a given system.
- *Events*
  An event, e_i, corresponds to a particular occurrence of an event type, for example, the arrival of a particular frame of video. The set E thus corresponds to all occurrences of this particular event type.
- *Histories*
  A history, h_i, is then a discrete sequence of events of the same event type, for example, a sequence of video frames arriving. The set H thus corresponds to the set of all histories in a system.

A history can be interpreted as a function from the set of positive integers to the set of events:

$$h : N \rightarrow E$$

This allows us to refer to the nth occurrence of a particular event type in a history, for example, the 40th frame of video arriving.

Dating and interpretation functions
Two key functions are defined over the event model. The first, a *dating function*, enables the assignment of a date (in time) to a particular event. The second, an *interpretation function*, enables access to a history for a given event type.

In more detail, a date is assigned to a particular event e using a function τ. Dates are selected from T and hence we have:

$$\tau : E \rightarrow T$$

As an illustration, the dating function would enable us to access the time at which a particular frame of video arrives. For example, if e_v is the arrival of a particular frame, then the time, t, of this event is given by:

$$t = \tau(e_v)$$

If we then have a particular history, h, we can also say that the nth element in the history occurs at a certain time. For example, if h_v is the history of video frames arriving, we can access the time of delivery of the 40th video frame:

$$t = \tau(h_v(40))$$

Often, it will be necessary to access a history by stating the event type of interest. The interpretation function, ϕ, provides this added level of expressiveness by defining a mapping from event types to histories:

$$\phi : \Pi \rightarrow H$$

Thus, if event e is the nth occurrence of the history associated with event type ε, the date t of the occurrence of e is expressed by:

$$t = \tau(\phi(e)\,(n))$$

The 40th occurrence of a video frame arriving can then be written as:

$$t = \tau(\phi(e_v)\,(40))$$

(compare this with the formula above when the history was directly accessible).
Note that when the context is known – when we are considering one particular interpretation ϕ – then we can shorten $\tau(\phi(\varepsilon)\,(n))$ to simply $\tau(\varepsilon, n)$.

Applying the event model
The above event model, when combined with standard first-order operators, is sufficient to express a range of quality of service properties. To illustrate this, we consider a representative selection of timeliness, volume and reliability properties below. In the examples, we use the following conventions:

- integer variables are denoted by $k, l, m, n, \ldots$
- integer constants are denoted by $\underline{k}, \underline{l}, \underline{m}, \underline{n} \ldots$
- delay constants are denoted by $\underline{\delta}, \underline{\delta_1}, \underline{\delta_2} \ldots$

Firstly, we consider the expression of three timeliness properties. The first two are concerned with the specification of latency and delay jitter between the sending and receiving of a video frame over a binding. The third property places a bound on the server execution time between the invocation reception and the subsequent termination emission. Note that all the examples are deterministic properties; the expression of probabilistic or stochastic properties is considered later.

- **Example** *Latency in video frame delivery*
  Let ε_s and ε_r be two event types corresponding to the sending and receiving of video frames. In addition, let $\underline{\delta}$ be an element in T. We can then express the fact that the same occurrence of ε_s and ε_r must not be exceeded by a delay exceeding $\underline{\delta}$ as follows:

  $$\forall n, |\tau(\varepsilon_r, n) - \tau(\varepsilon_s, n)| \leq \underline{\delta}$$

- **Example** *Delay jitter for video frame delivery*
  We can then trivially extend the above example to specify that the delay jitter is bounded by $\underline{\delta_1}$ and $\underline{\delta_2}$:

  $$\forall n, \underline{\delta_1} \leq |\tau(\varepsilon_r, n) - \tau(\varepsilon_s, n)| \leq \underline{\delta_2}$$

- **Example** *Bounded execution time*
  Let ε_r and ε_e be two event types corresponding to the invocation reception and termination emission respectively. In addition, let $\underline{\delta}$ be an element in T. The delay between reception and subsequent emission can be expressed as follows:

  $$\forall n, |\tau(\varepsilon_e, n) - \tau(\varepsilon_r, n)| \leq \underline{\delta}$$

Secondly, we consider the expression of the volume property, throughput. This implies we have to consider relationships between successive frames in a history.

- **Example** *Throughput of video frames*
  Let ε_r be an event type representing the arrival of video frames. In addition, let $\underline{\delta}$ be an element in T and $\underline{k}$ be an integer constant. We specify throughput by stating that every $\underline{\delta}$ units of time, we must receive at least $\underline{k}$ frames. More precisely, we state that the time between the nth occurrence and the $n + k$th occurrence must be no greater than $\underline{\delta}$. The formula for this is given below:

  $$\forall n, \tau(\varepsilon_r, n + k) - \tau(\varepsilon_r, n) \leq \underline{\delta}$$

Finally, we consider the expression of reliability properties. In particular, we would like to be able to express that m out of n frames are successfully delivered. This example requires the expression of a *fractional* property and is more complex, as will become apparent below.

Example *Bounded losses on video frame delivery*
Let ε_s and ε_r be two event types corresponding to the sending and receiving of video frames. In addition, let δ be an element in T. Let ε_v be an event type representing the arrival of video frames. In addition, let δ be an element in T and k and k' be integer constants. We can then express the fact that k messages are sent but only k' received by the following formula.

$$\forall n, \tau(\varepsilon_s, n + k) - \tau(\varepsilon_s, n) \leqslant \delta$$

$$\wedge \forall n, \tau(\varepsilon_r, n + k') - \tau(\varepsilon_r, n) \leqslant \delta$$

$$\wedge k' \leqslant k$$

This effectively states that k frames are sent but only k' frames received in each δ. The fact that messages are lost is however implicit in the above formulation. The loss of messages can be made more explicit by the addition of the following formula.

$$\forall m, \exists n, (\tau(\varepsilon_r, m) = t \wedge m \leqslant n)$$

$$\rightarrow (\tau(\varepsilon_s, n) = t' \wedge t' \leqslant t)$$

Also note that the formula for delay (and indeed delay jitter) would be invalidated by this consideration of errors. In particular, the formula for delay above assumes that a send is always followed by a receive. This problem can be avoided by combining the statement of delay with the formula immediately above, giving the following formula:

$$\forall m, \exists n, (\tau(\varepsilon_r, m) = t \wedge m \leqslant n)$$

$$\rightarrow (\tau(\varepsilon_s, n) = t' \wedge t' + \delta \leqslant t)$$

The event model therefore provides the basis for the expression of a range of (deterministic) quality of service properties. However, this approach, as it stands, is actually too expressive and cannot be formally analyzed. The design of QL therefore imposes a number of constraints on the event model. This design is described in more detail below.

The QL language
The QL language is presented in detail below. We first present the syntax and informal semantics, and then revisit the QoS constraints specified above in terms of the event model and show how they would be presented in QL.

Syntax and informal semantics
QL is interpreted over the event model introduced above, but with events corresponding directly to signals in the programming model. Event types are

then a particular type of signal emitted or received at an interface and event histories are the corresponding sequence of events of that type.

Event types in QL are expressed by concatenating an interface name, a signal name and a causality. The latter is denoted by SE for signal emission and SR for signal reception. For example, the following is a valid event type:

monitor.report.SR

It is also possible to access the signals underpinning operational and stream interfaces using the same syntax. In these cases, the signal name is the same as the operation or flow name. The interface name and causality are then used to provide a unique interpretation for the event type. For example, the following four event types denote the signals corresponding to an interrogation (the emission of an invocation by the client, the reception of this invocation at the server, the emission of the termination at the server and the reception of this termination back at the client):

client.op1.SE

server.op1.SR

server.op1.SE

client.op1.SR

Similarly, the following event types denote the emission and reception of signals corresponding to a video flow:

producer.frameOut.SE

consumer.frameIn.SR

The basic building blocks of a QL formula are then *constants* and *variables*. Constants can be either arbitrary integer constants, for example referring to events in a history, or delay constants selected from T. Following the convention above, we denote integer constant by $\underline{k}, \underline{l}, \underline{m}, \underline{n}$ and so on, and delay constants by $\underline{\delta}, \underline{\delta_1}, \underline{\delta_2}$ and so on. Variables can be over event types (denoted by $\varepsilon, \varepsilon_1, \varepsilon_2, \ldots$), integers (denoted by $k, l, m, n, \ldots$) or delay variables (denoted by $\delta, \delta_1, \delta_2, \ldots$).

Constants and variables can then be used in *functions* or *predicates*. Both are severely restricted, however, to enable formal analysis. Functions are restricted to the following:

- integer addition (+) and multiplication (×) by integer constants,
- delay addition (+),
- the dating function (τ), and
- uninterpreted functions with integer or delay ranges.

The latter are provided to enable the expressiveness of the logic to be extended. This facility should be used sparingly, however, to prevent problems with formal analysis.

Predicates can be involve the following:

- equality predicates (denoted by =) over event types, events, integers or delays, and
- inequality predicates (denoted by $\leqslant$ or $\geqslant$) over integers and delays.

Finally, formulae can be constructed with constants, variables, functions and predicates (as described above) together with universal and existential quantifiers ($\forall, \exists$), and boolean connectives ($\wedge, \vee, \neg, \rightarrow$).

QoS annotations are then constructed by providing a set of provided clauses and associated required clauses. A very simple example of a quality of service annotation could be:

Provided clause

$$\forall n, \tau(type1.S2.SE,n) \leqslant \tau(type1.S1.SR,n) + \underline{10}$$

Required clause

$$\forall n, \tau(type2.S4.SE,n) \leqslant \tau(type2.S3.SR,n) + \underline{5}$$

This says that the interface *type*1 can bound the delay between receiving a signal, S_1, and emitting a response to that signal to 10 units of time if a delay bound of 5 can be guaranteed for signals on a type *type2* (which presumably provides a service required by the object supporting interface *type*1).

Note that to enable formal analysis it is also necessary to impose a certain style of QL formulae. QL as given above is still undecidable (that is, no decision procedures exist for formal analysis). However, if the style defined below is followed then such a decision procedure does exist.

The style is as follows:

Rule 1
All basic formulae should have the form:

$$\tau(\varepsilon_1, n + j_1) + \underline{\delta} \leqslant \tau(\varepsilon_2, n + j_2)$$

Rule 2
An overall formula can then have the general form:

$$\exists i_1 \ldots \exists i_p \forall n \exists j_1 \ldots \exists j_m \forall n_1 \ldots \forall n_q \beta$$

where β is a boolean combination of the basic formulae defined by Rule 1.

The decision procedure is not presented in this book; the interested reader is referred to the literature for further details (Stefani, 1993).

Applying QL

In this section, we briefly revisit the examples presented above for the event model and show what they would be like in QL. To be consistent with the presentations above, we consider only provided clauses. Note that some of the formulae have to be reworked to be compatible with the QL syntax and the particular style outlined above.

The first three examples are the timeliness properties considered above.

Example *Delay in video frame delivery*
Let *camera.videoOut.SE* and *videoWindow.videoIn.SR* be two event types corresponding to the sending and receiving of video frames. In addition, let $\underline{\delta}$ be an element in T. Bounded delay is then expressed in QL as follows:

$$\forall n,\ \tau(videoWindow.videoIn.SR,n) \leqslant \tau(camera.videoOut.SE,n) + \underline{\delta}$$

Example *Delay jitter for video frame delivery*
To comply with the QL style, it is necessary to express delay jitter as the conjunction of two clauses as follows:

$$\forall n,\ \tau(videoWindow.videoIn.SR,n) \leqslant \tau(camera.videoOut.SE,n) + \underline{\delta_2}$$
$$\wedge \forall n,\ \tau(camera.videoOut.SE,n) + \underline{\delta_1} \leqslant \tau(videoWindow.videoIn.SR,n)$$

Example *Bounded execution time*
Let *server.invocation.SR* and *server.termination.SE* be two event types corresponding to the invocation reception and termination emission respectively. In addition, let $\underline{\delta}$ be an element in T. The delay between reception and subsequent emission can be expressed in QL as follows:

$$\forall n,\ \tau(server.termination.SE,n) \leqslant \tau(server.invocation.SR) + \underline{\delta}$$

We now consider the expression of throughput in QL.

Example *Throughput of video frames*
Again, let *videoWindow.videoIn.SR* be an event type representing the arrival of video frames. In addition, let $\underline{\delta}$ be an element in T and $\underline{k}$ be an integer constant. The equivalent QL formula is given by:

$$\forall n,\ \tau(videoWindow.videoIn.SR,n + \underline{k}) \leqslant \tau(videoWindow.videoIn.SR,n) + \underline{\delta}$$

Finally, we consider the expression of bounded frame loss in QL.

Example *Bounded losses on video frame delivery*
Let *camera.videoOut.SE* and *videoWindow.videoIn.SR* be two event types corresponding to the sending and receiving of video frames. In addition, let $\underline{\delta}$ be an element in T and $\underline{k}$ and $\underline{k}'$ be integer constants. We can then

express the fact that k messages are sent but only k' received by the following set of formulae.

$$\forall n, \tau(camera.videoOut.SE,n + \underline{k}) \leqslant \tau(camera.videoOut.SE,n) + \underline{\delta}$$

$$\forall n, \tau(videoWindow.videoIn.SE,n + \underline{k'}) \leqslant \tau(videoWindow.videoIn.SE,n) + \underline{\delta}$$

$$\wedge \underline{k'} \leqslant \underline{k}$$

As with the previous example, the loss of messages can be made more explicit by the addition of the following formula. Note that this has been reworked considerably to be compatible with the desired QL style.

$$\forall n, \exists j, (\tau(videoWindow.videoIn.SR,n) = t)$$

$$\rightarrow (\tau(camera.videoOut.SE,n + j) = t' \wedge t' \leqslant t) \wedge j \leqslant k$$

In addition, the following formula deals correctly with delay when frames can be lost:

$$\forall n, \exists j, (\tau(videoWindow.videoIn.SR,n) = t)$$

$$\rightarrow (\tau(camera.videoOut.SE,n + j) = t' \wedge t' \leqslant t + \underline{\delta}) \wedge j \leqslant k$$

It can therefore be seen that QL can express all the formulae written previously in terms of the event model.

Formal analysis and QL

Considerable benefits can be gained from adhering to the particular style of QL described above. In particular, as mentioned above, this style of QL is decidable and hence can be formally analyzed. In this section, we consider the particular uses of formal analysis for quality of service management.

Firstly, it is possible to define *weaker* and *stronger* relations over QoS annotations. These relations can then be used with subtyping rules to determine substitutability; that is, one type can be substituted for another if it is a subtype *and* the QoS clause is weaker.

Formally, a QL clause Q_1 is weaker than a QL clause Q_2 if and only if:

$$Q_2 \rightarrow Q_1$$

Conversely, Q_2 is said to be stronger than Q_1.

For example, consider the following two QL formulae:

$$Q_1 = \forall n. \tau(server.termination.SE, n) \leqslant \tau(server.invocation.SR, n) + 10$$

$$Q_2 = \forall n. \tau(server.termination.SE, n) \leqslant \tau(server.invocation.SR, n) + 5$$

In this case, it is clear that $Q_2 \rightarrow Q_1$ and hence Q_2 is stronger than Q_1.

Secondly, it is possible to check *consistency* of the QoS annotations associated with a particular interface type. Assume an interface type contains the following QoS declarations:

$$\{(Qp_1,Qr_1),\ldots(Qp_n,Qr_n)\}$$

This can be represented by the following QL formula:

$$((Qp_1 \wedge Qr_1) \vee \ldots \vee (Qp_n \wedge Qr_n))$$

This states that there is a choice between several QoS alternatives (pairs of provided and required clauses). For a given choice, both the provided and required clauses must hold.

Checking the consistency of this formula means checking if the formula is logically *satisfiable*. This process is normally carried out by checking its negation for logical validity (if the negation is logically valid, then the formula is not satisfiable and hence the interface type definition is inconsistent).

As an example, the following is an inconsistent QoS annotation and would be found to be logically unsatisfiable:

$$Q_p = \forall n.\, \tau(compressor.videoIn.SR,n+1) \leqslant \tau(compressor.videoIn.SR,n) + 10$$

$$Q_r = \forall n.\, \tau(compressor.videoOut.SE,n) \leqslant \tau(compressor.videoIn.SR,n) + 1$$

$$\vee\, \forall n.\, \tau(compressor.videoIn.SR,n) \leqslant \tau(compressor.videoOut.SE,n) + 0$$

$$\vee\, \forall n.\, \tau(compressor.videoOut.SE,n+1) \leqslant \tau(compressor.videoOut.SE,n) + 2$$

A more comprehensive test can also be carried out to check the consistency of the constraints associated with one interface (q_0) against all other constraints in the environment ($q_1,\ldots,q_n$). This is achieved simply by testing the logical satisfiability of the following formula:

$$q_0 \wedge \ldots \wedge q_n$$

Note that a satisfiability check proves that a particular formula can be met. This does not mean the level of QoS *will* be met. The latter requires considerable support in terms of QoS management.

The formality of QL can also be exploited in supporting QoS management functions. For example, logics enable controllers to be synthesized directly from the logic. Such monitors can be used both for QoS monitoring and QoS policing functions. Interestingly, a mapping exists from QL to the language Esterel, as used to program reactive objects (see below). This enables the direct translation of QL formulae to QoS monitors implemented as reactive objects in the architecture. The concepts of weaker and stronger defied above also provide support for the QoS negotiation function.

Direct support for other QoS management functions is more difficult. For example, admission control and resource reservation require the translation from QL formulae to underlying scheduling and real-time constraints. In general, this is an intractable problem. However, heuristics can be employed to provide a partial solution to this translation process. The most promising approach is to identify particular patterns of QL formulae, for example relating to delay or throughput, and extract parameters directly from such patterns.

5.3.3 Discussion

From our analysis, we believe that QL meets the majority of our requirements for the specification of QoS annotations. In particular, we have been able to specify the timeliness properties of delay and delay jitter, the volume property of throughput and the reliability property of lost frames. In addition, the formality of QL provides a means to analyze QL formulae in terms of consistency and to derive weaker and stronger relations. It is also possible to support QoS management by the synthesis of QoS monitors and policing objects.

There are a number of limitations with QL however. Most importantly, the logic does not support the specification of probabilistic or stochastic properties; the expression of such properties would require significant extensions to the logic. This has implications for the expressiveness of the logic. For example, QL cannot express more general reliability requirements such as Mean Time Between Failure (MTBF) and Mean Time To Repair (MTTR). In addition, QL does not directly support the specification of the class of commitment for QoS contracts. It is assumed that this is expressed elsewhere in the environmental contract.

Note that there are a number of other notations that could be used in place of QL. Lamport's Temporal Logic of Actions (TLA) is receiving considerable interest in the distributed systems community and could be used for the expression of QoS (Lamport, 1994). A real-time temporal logic such as MTL, TPTL, XCTL could also be employed (Alur and Henzinger, 1990). In addition, real-time temporal logics are now being developed specifically for the expression of quality of service properties (Blair, 1995). Finally, a number of probabilistic and/or stochastic logics have been developed, including TPCTL (Hansson, 1991) and SQTL (Lakas *et al.*, 1996) (again, the latter being designed particularly for the expression of QoS properties). In all cases, care would be required to ensure that the logic can be formally analyzed.

Finally, it would be possible to define higher level, more user-friendly notations for QoS annotation and then translate this representation into the underlying logic.

5.4 Programming reactive objects

5.4.1 Use of Esterel

Finally, we consider the language to be used in the programming of reactive objects. Our overriding requirement is that the choice of language must enable the synchrony hypothesis to be met. As mentioned in Chapter 4, a number of such languages, known as synchronous languages, have been developed. Examples of synchronous languages include Esterel, Lustre, Signal and Statecharts.

In our work, we have adopted the synchronous language Esterel (Berry, 1988) to develop reactive objects. The particular reasons for selecting Esterel are given below:

- Esterel is an imperative programming language, making it relatively easy to understand by the majority of programmers. The other synchronous languages mentioned above are not imperative (Lustre and Signal are declarative data flow languages and Statecharts is based on the hierarchical composition of automata).
- Esterel provides high-level constructs (including parallel constructs) allowing a concise description of the complex relationships between events governing the behaviour of a reactive system (see the examples in Chapter 6).
- The language has clearly defined semantics with respect to temporal execution and allows the behaviour of reactive systems to be specified *and* verified formally.
- Programs in Esterel are deterministic. They can be translated into a deterministic finite automaton that can be used for an efficient implementation. The automaton may be also used to formally analyze behavioural properties and derive execution bounds.

The key features of Esterel are described below. Note that we do not present a full tutorial on Esterel. Rather, we limit the presentation to the level necessary to understand the examples later in the book. Further information on Esterel can be found in the literature (Berry, 1988).

5.4.2 Key features of Esterel

Overview of an Esterel program

An Esterel program consists of a set of parallel processes that execute synchronously and communicate with each other and with the environment by sending and receiving *signals*. The signals present at each instant are broadcast instantaneously to all processes. Signals may carry a value, in which case they are called *valued signals*, or be used just for synchronization, in which case they are called *pure signals*.

Local signals correspond to internal communication between processes and input/output signals to communication with the environment. There is no absolute time in Esterel; time only appears as input signals generated by an external clock.

An overall Esterel program is denoted by a module with the following syntax:

```
module <name> :
   declaration part
          data declarations
          interface declarations
body.
```

As denoted above, the declaration part consists of data declarations and interface declarations. Data declarations supported directly by Esterel are rather limited. In particular, variables and constants can be declared of simple types such as integer, boolean, string and float. No complex types are supported. The programmer can however provide abstract types which are not interpreted in Esterel. The programmer must then provide external functions or procedures, written in a host language, to manipulate these abstract types.

Abstract types are declared as follows:

```
type VideoFrame, AudioFrame;
```

The interface declarations describe the interface of an Esterel program to the outside environment and are written in terms of input and output signals. Individual signal declarations can have associated values. An example interface declaration is given below:

```
input
        VideoReady (integer),
        AudioReady (integer),
        Restart,
        Millisecond;
output
        VideoPresent (),
        timerStart (integer);
```

(As will be seen in Chapter 6, this is the interface to a reactive object implementing lip synchronization).

In addition, it is possible to declare explicit relations between different input signals. In particular, two styles of relation are defined. The first enables the programmer to state that two (or more) signals are incompatible in a given instant:

```
relation S₁#S₂# ... Sn
```

The second form enables the programmer to state that the occurrence of one signal implies that a second signal should also be present. This is written:

```
relation S₁=>S₂
```

It is also possible in Esterel to have a signal declaration local to a block. This is achieved by the syntax:

```
signal SIG in stat end
```

Such signals are then only visible in `stat` (where `stat` can be an arbitrary compound statement).

Finally, combination functions are required in Esterel when several emitters emit the same signal but with a different value. Esterel solves this problem by allowing the programmer to specify an arbitrary function, such as `comb`, the resulting value of the signal being (for n signals):

```
comb (v₁, comb (v₂, ... comb (vₙ₋₁, vₙ) ...))
```

Combine functions can be associated with output signals or local signals as follows:

```
output S (combine type with comb)
signal S (combine type with comb) in stat end
```

Details of the body of an Esterel program are given below. We look firstly at standard imperative statements and then consider temporal statements concerned with signal broadcasting and reception. To conclude, a simple example is presented.

Imperative statements in Esterel

Esterel provides a range of standard imperative statements as summarized in Table 5.1.

In addition, Esterel provides a powerful exception handling mechanism:

```
trap T in stat end
```

which is then combined with

```
exit T
```

The `trap` declares an exception while an `exit` raises an exception. The body of the `trap` construct is executed normally until an `exit T` is encountered. The body is then immediately terminated.

The programmer also has the option of attaching a handler using the syntax:

```
handle T in stat end
```

Table 5.1 Imperative statements in Esterel

Statement	Syntax	Informal semantics
Assignment	`variable:=expression`	assigns expression to variable
Iteration	`loop stat end`	infinite loop
Selection	`if exp then stat1 else stat2 end`	executes `stat1` or `stat2` depending on the value of `exp`
Sequence	`stat1; stat2`	`stat2` starts as soon as `stat1` is finished
Parallel	`stat1 || stat2`	stat1 and stat2 start instantaneously; statement terminates when both are completed
Null statement	`nothing`	no action
Halt statement	`halt`	sends automata into halt state
External procedure call	`call proc (vars) (exprs)`	calls an external procedure (potentially manipulating an abstract type); `vars` are passed by reference and `exprs` by value
Compound statement	`[ stats ]`	combines simple statements into one compound statement

If present, the `handle` clause will be executed before terminating the `trap` block.

Finally, Esterel possesses a `copymodule` statement which provides for in-place expansion, together with constant and signal renaming facilities. It has the syntax:

```
copymodule module_ident [substitution-list]
```

where a substitution can be either a signal substitution or a constant substitution. For example, the following is a valid substitution list:

```
[constant 10/delay; 5/jitter; signal video_arrived/frame_in;
QoS_violation/ QoS_error]
```

The module is then textually copied with the indicated substitutions.

This facility offers a simple but powerful mechanism to build a composite object from child objects. This facility can be used in multimedia to reuse modules which capture basic and general media functionalities.

Temporal statements in Esterel

The temporal statements in Esterel realize broadcast communication of signals. The main temporal statements are given in Table 5.2.

Table 5.2 Temporal statements in Esterel

Statement	Syntax	Informal semantics
Signal emission	`emit sig (exp)`	broadcast a signal with or without a value
Signal presence	`present S then stat1 else stat2 end`	if S is present execute `stat1` else execute `stat2`
Watchdog	`do stat watching S`	execute `stat` normally unless S occurs; if S occurs terminate `stat`
Await signal	`await S`	blocks until S is present
Watchdog with timeout	`do stat1 watching S timeout stat2 end`	extends the watchdog by enabling a `timeout` clause to be executed if S occurs before `stat1` finishes
Every statement	`every S do stat end`	execute `stat` for every occurrence of S

Further details on each of these statements is given below.

A signal is broadcast through the instruction *emit*. Signals carry two types of information:

- an (optional) *value* which is persistent and may be accessed as any other variable or constant, and
- control information which indicates whether or not a signal is present during an execution instant.

The current value of a signal is accessed through the ? operator. In addition, the presence of signals can be determined by the signal presence statement.

Reaction to signals relies on a unique basic primitive:

```
do stat watching [exp] SIG
```

Stat starts immediately. If `stat` finishes before the next occurrence of the signal S, so does the `do watching` statement. Otherwise, the `do watching` statement is terminated as soon as the next occurrence of S occurs. In this case `stat` is immediately killed. This statement can also be extended by having `[exp] SIG` which then watches for the `exp`th occurrence of `SIG` rather than the next.

Esterel also offers an `await` statement:

```
await [exp] SIG
```

This blocks a process until the next (the expth) occurrence of SIG occurs. Strictly speaking, this is a higher level statement in Esterel constructed out of the do watching statement. In particular, await is precisely equivalent to:

```
do
halt
watching [exp] SIG
```

A further higher level statement is provided which extends do watching with a timeout clause:

```
do stat1 watching [exp] S timeout stat2 end
```

In this construct, stat1 starts immediately. If stat1 finishes before the next (the expth) occurrence of the signal S, so does the statement. Otherwise stat1 is immediately killed and stat2 started. This is precisely equivalent to:

```
trap T in
   do
            stat1;
            exit T
   watching S;
   stat2
end
```

A final higher level statement is the *every* statement which has the form:

```
every SIG do stat end
```

This statement executes stat on every occurrence of the signal SIG. More specifically, the statement has the following expansion:

```
await SIG;
loop
  do
     stat;
     halt
  watching SIG
end
```

In other words, the block waits for the first occurrence of SIG and then loops, executing stat and then halting. This is interrupted by the next occurrence of SIG and a further iteration of the loop is carried out.

A simple example

We illustrate the use of Esterel by a simple example. Further examples are given in Chapter 6.

Example *A simple QoS monitor in Esterel*

This example considers a simple QoS monitor, monitoring the delay in consuming video frames at a video window object. We assume the video window offers two input signals to the Esterel program: `data_available` and `data_consumed`. `Data_available` is used to indicate the delivery of a data sample at the video window. `Data_consumed` indicates that the window object has consumed the data sample. We also assume the availability of a clock generating `tick` signals. The Esterel module `DeviceMonitor`, shown below, performs the necessary monitoring. In particular, the module checks that `data_consumed` occurs `DELAY` units of time (ticks) after `data_available`. The constant `TOLERANCE` specifies acceptable variations on the occurrence of the `data_consumed` event from its ideal occurrence time: `data_available + DELAY`. If the `data_consumed` signal does not occur within the required delay, taking into account the specified acceptable tolerance, the signal `QoS_violation` is emitted. The value of this signal is used to indicate a particular kind of quality of service violation, a missed deadline in this case.

```
module DeviceMonitor:
type            QoS_violation_type;
constant        DELAY, TOLERANCE : integer,
                QOS_MISSED_DEADLINE : QoS_violation_type;
input           data_available, data_consumed, tick, stop;
output          QoS_violation(QoS_violation_type);

trap terminate in
  loop
    await data_available;
    do
      await data_consumed
    watching DELAY + TOLERANCE tick
    timeout
      emit QoS_violation(QOS_MISSED_DEADLINE)
    end %do
  end %loop
  ||
  await stop; exit terminate;
end % trap
  .
```

A more sophisticated QoS manager will be developed in Chapter 6.

5.4.3 Discussion

As stated earlier, reactive objects can be programmed in any language as long as they adhere to the synchrony hypothesis. Indeed, in an open environment, different reactive objects can be implemented in different languages.

However, we believe that Esterel is a strong candidate for programming reactive objects for the real-time control and QoS management of multimedia applications. Firstly, it is an imperative language and hence is simple to understand for the majority of programmers. Secondly, the language supports the elegant expression of a range of multimedia behaviours (this point will be revisited after the multimedia examples are presented in the next chapter). Thirdly, the language has a formal semantics and supports automatic verification of Esterel programs. Finally, the language is deterministic and supports the generation of small and efficient automata. The size of an automaton and its execution time can be derived formally from an Esterel script.

Esterel does, however, suffer from some significant problems. For example, it is often difficult to understand the rules for causality in the language and this can lead to problems of introducing causality paradoxes in specifications. The rules of causality also make it difficult to implement separate compilation. These problems are currently being addressed in the language SL (Boussinot and de Simone, 1996). In particular, SL removes problems of causality by introducing a weaker form of pre-emption in the language. This also has the effect of making separate compilation trivial to implement.

5.5 Summary

This chapter has developed specific notations to populate the programming model introduced in Chapter 4. The three notations introduced are:

- an extended CORBA IDL with facilities to support the specification of both stream and signal interfaces,
- the QL logic designed to specify QoS annotations on interfaces, and
- the Esterel language, which is used to program reactive objects.

The first two notations are particularly important as together they have the central role of describing interfaces in the open distributed environment. Their selection effectively characterizes one approach to open distributed processing. The choice of other languages would lead to a different standard (albeit one that also conforms to the programming model framework). The choice of Esterel, while important, is less crucial, as different languages for reactive objects can coexist in a given distributed environment.

Small examples were presented throughout the chapter providing an initial illustration of the proposed approach. A more comprehensive illustration of the new approach can be found in the next chapter when three complete multimedia examples are presented.

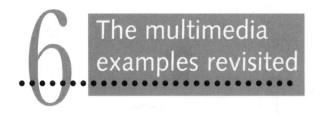

6 The multimedia examples revisited

6.1 Introduction

In this chapter, we present three case studies illustrating the use of the particular approach described in Chapter 5. More specifically, we revisit the examples presented in Chapter 4, namely:

- a QoS-managed stream binding,
- achieving lip synchronization between audio and video streams, and
- a more general multimedia presentation.

In Chapter 4, the presentation was restricted to a high-level object-oriented design. In this chapter, we refine the design by presenting the full *interface type signatures* and *QoS annotations* for each interface (written in the extended IDL and QL respectively). In addition, we present code for each of the *reactive objects* involved in each example (written in Esterel).

The chapter is structured as follows. The QoS-managed stream binding and the lip synchronization example are presented in Sections 6.2 and 6.3 respectively. The multimedia presentation is then described in Section 6.4. Finally, Section 6.5 concludes the chapter and presents an overall evaluation of the examples.

6.2 A QoS-managed stream binding

6.2.1 The design revisited

The first example is the QoS management of a video stream. More specifically, we monitor a video stream binding between a video camera and a video window to ensure the desired delay, jitter and throughput rates are maintained (for the purposes of the example, we ignore the possibility of lost frames). This example was first presented in Section 4.4.1, where the following high-level design was given (see Figure 6.1).

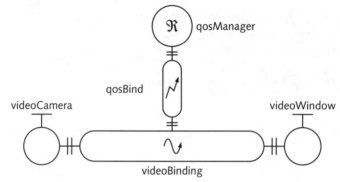

Figure 6.1 Overall design to achieve QoS management.

Briefly, this diagram shows five objects:

- a video camera object (videoCamera) offering a stream interface consisting of one outgoing flow together with an operational interface which can be used to control the camera,
- a video window object (videoWindow), also offering a stream interface with one incoming flow together with a signal interface indicating when a video frame has been presented,
- an explicit binding object (videoBinding) offering an input and output stream interface together with a signal interface supporting the QoS-management protocol,
- a reactive object implementing QoS management (qosManager) and offering two signal interfaces, the first interacting with videoBinding and the second offering an exception interface to an application object,
- an explicit binding object (qosBind) between the videoBinding interface and the reactive object, with an input and output signal interface corresponding to the transmission of signals in the binding together with a third signal interface for control.

The task of the qosManager is to monitor the video stream binding to ensure that the following QoS requirements are met:

- an average latency of 50 ms,
- a maximum delay jitter of ±10 ms, and
- a throughput of at least 25 frames per second.

Should the binding fail to deliver this desired quality of service, a signal should be sent to the application indicating a QoS violation. Furthermore, this violation should provide an indication of the type of violation (excessive delay or jitter or insufficient throughput).

The following subsections refine this informal and high-level specification by providing interface type signatures and QoS annotations for the above interfaces together with the Esterel script implementing the desired QoS-management behaviour.

6.2.2 The interface types and QoS annotations

We consider each of the objects in turn below and consider the interfaces and associated QoS annotations. In all examples, time is measured in milliseconds.

The video camera object

The video camera object offers a stream interface representing the production of video frames and an operational interface to control the camera. The signature for these two interfaces is as follows:

```
interface <stream> videoCameraOut {
    flowOut videoOut (video);
}

interface <operational> cameraControl {
    start ();
    stop ();
    pan (in panDegrees integer);
    tilt (in tiltDegrees integer);
    zoom (in zoomFactor integer);
}
```

The associated QoS annotation for this object is:

Provided clause

$\forall n, \tau(videoCameroOut.videoOut.SR, n + 24)$

$\leqslant \tau(videoCameraOut.videoOut.SR, n) + 1000$

$\wedge$

$\tau(videoCameraOut.videoOut.SE, 1)$

$\leqslant \tau(cameraControl.start.SR, 1) + 10$

Required clause

None.

The provided clause indicates that this camera will provide at least 25 frames in a given second. In addition, there will be a maximum delay of 10 ms between the start operation and the production of the first frame. The null required clause indicates that this provided quality of service is unconditional.

The video window object

The video window object offers an input stream interface with a single video flow together with a signal interface indicating when a frame has been presented:

```
interface <stream> videoWindowIn {
    flowIn videoIn (video);
}

interface <signal> videoWindowStatus {
    signalOut videoPresented ();
}
```

The associated QoS annotation is then as follows:

Provided clause

$\forall n, \tau(videoWindowStatus.videoPresented.SE,n + 24)$

$\leqslant \tau(videoWindowStatus.videoPresented.SE,n) + 1000$

$\wedge$

$\forall n, \tau(videoWindowStatus.videoPresented.SE,n)$

$\leqslant \tau(videoWindowIn.videoIn.SR,n) + 10$

Required clause

$\forall n, \tau(videoWindowIn.videoIn.SR,n + 24)$

$\leqslant \tau(videoWindowIn.videoIn.SR,n) + 1000$

This states that the video window will present frames at a rate of at least 25 frames per second providing that the object receives frames at the same rate (from the binding). In addition, there will be a maximum delay of 10 ms between the arrival of a frame and its subsequent presentation.

The video binding object

The video binding object has both an input and an output stream interface together with a signal interface providing access to events for QoS management. The signatures for the three interfaces are as follows:

```
type timestamp integer;

interface <stream> videoBindingIn {
    flowIn videoIn (video);
}

interface <stream> videoBindingOut {
    flowOut videoOut (video);
}

interface <signal> qosControl {
    signalOut videoSent (timestamp);
    signalIn videoDelivered (timestamp);
}
```

The qosControl interface provides a minimal interface enabling the monitoring of the QoS provided by the binding. Note that we assume the existence of a global clock for the timestamps associated with the signals *videoSent* and *videoDelivered*.

The QoS annotation for this object is then as follows:

Provided clause

$\forall n, \tau(videoBindingOut.videoOut.SE, n + 24)$

$\leqslant \tau(videoBindingOut.videoOut.SE, n) + 1000$

$\wedge$

$\forall n, \tau(videoBindingOut.videoOut.SE, n)$

$\leqslant \tau(videoBindingIn.videoIn.SR, n) + 60$

$\wedge$

$\forall n, \tau(videoBindingIn.videoIn.SR, n) + 40$

$\leqslant \tau(videoBindingOut.videoOut.SE, n)$

$\wedge$

$\forall n, \tau(qosControl.videoSent.SE, n) = \tau(videoBindingIn.videoIn.SR, n)$

$\wedge$

$\forall n, \tau(qosControl.videoDelivered.SE, n) = \tau(videoBindingOut.videoOut.SE, n)$

Required clause

$\forall n, \tau(videoBindingIn.videoIn.SR, n + 24)$

$\leqslant \tau(videoBindingIn.videoIn.SR, n) + 1000$

This states that the binding will provide a throughput of 25 frames per second and a delay of between 40 and 60 ms if the binding receives video frames at a rate of 25 frames per second from a producer. Additionally, the binding guarantees that the monitoring signals will be emitted through the *qosControl* interface at the time of occurrence of the monitored signals.

It can be seen by inspection that the interfaces provided by this object are compatible with the interfaces offered by the video camera and the video window. In particular, the stream interface of the video camera offers a single outgoing flow of type video. This matches the signature of the input interface to the binding. Similarly, the video window has a stream interface with a single input flow of type video. Again, this matches the output interface of the binding. Finally, the QoS annotations are compatible. The binding requires 25 frames per second from the producer and this can be supported by the camera. In addition, the video window requires 25 frames per second from the binding, and this is precisely what the binding will deliver.

The reactive object

The reactive object provides two signal interfaces as follows:

```
type timestamp integer;
type violationType integer;

interface <signal> reactIn {
    signalIn videoSent (timestamp);
    signalIn videoDelivered (timestamp);
}

interface <signal> reactOut {
    signalOut qosViolation (violationType);
}
```

The first interface corresponds to signals into the reactive object and the second to signals emitted by the object.

Note that reactive objects do not have associated QoS annotations; such annotations are only required to constrain asynchronous behaviour and hence do not apply to synchronous objects. In one sense, reactive objects have an implicit quality of service that their execution should be instantaneous.

The QoS management binding

Finally, the QoS management binding has two signal interfaces corresponding to the delivery of the signals between the video binding and the reactive object. This object also has a control interface which could be used for further QoS management (this is not used in this example). The three interfaces are as follows:

```
type timestamp integer;

interface <signal> qosBindingIn {
    signalIn videoSentIn (timestamp);
    signalIn videoDeliveredIn (timestamp);
}

interface <signal> qosBindingOut {
    signalOut videoSentOut (timestamp);
    signalOut videoDeliveredOut (timestamp);
}

interface <signal> qosControl {
    signalIn qosPoll ();
    signalOut qosAverageDelay (integer);
}
```

The control interface, in this case, reports on the average delay in delivering signals. This information is provided in response to a qosPoll signal.

The associated QoS annotations for this binding object are then:

Provided clause

$\forall n, \tau(qosBindingOut.videoSentOut.SE,n)$

$\leqslant \tau(qosBindingIn.videoSentIn.SR,n) + 5$

$\wedge$

$\forall n, \tau(qosBindingOut.videoDeliveredOut.SE,n)$

$\leqslant \tau(qosBindingIn.videoDeliveredIn.SR,n) + 5$

Required clause

None.

This states that the binding will guarantee a maximum delay of 5 ms for the transmission of signals across the binding. There is no required clause in this case, indicating that this QoS provision is unconditional.

Again, it can be seen that the type and QoS annotations for this binding object are compatible with the appropriate interfaces on the video binding object and the reactive object and hence the binding would succeed (providing resources are available from the engineering infrastructure).

6.2.3 The reactive object

The script for the reactive object is given below.

```
module qosManager:

% Declaration part follows....

% We declare the interface in terms of signals
% msec stands for millisecond

input
        videoSent (integer),
        videoDelivered (integer),
        msec;
output
        qosViolation;

% The body of the module follows....

[ every videoDelivered
    do await 24 videoDelivered
    watching 1000 msec
    timeout emit qosViolation
    end
```

```
||
every videoSent
   do await videoDelivered
   watching 60 msec
   timeout emit qosViolation
   end
||
every videoSent
   do await 40 msec
   watching videoDelivered
   timeout emit qosViolation
   end
]
.
```

This script shows how the different QoS provisions can be monitored. Each clause in the provisions of the video binding object is monitored by a branch of the parallel construct in the `qosManager` body. The behaviour of the `qosManager` is fairly elementary since it only emits a `qosViolation` every time a provision is violated.

Note that this Esterel program is developed directly from the QoS annotations for the video binding object as given above. In this case, the translation process was manual; however, it is possible to automate the translation from QL to Esterel (as discussed in Section 5.3.2).

6.2.4 Analysis

This example illustrates how the specific approach developed in Chapter 5 can be used to design a QoS-managed stream binding. The example also provides evidence of how QoS monitoring of timeliness and volume properties can be implemented using reactive objects and how the implementation of such reactive objects can be synthesized directly from QoS annotations. The resultant Esterel script provides a concise and elegant implementation of the required QoS monitoring functionality.

We argue that the use of reactive objects generalizes to other (dynamic) QoS management functions. For example, the same technique can be used for the following:

- to provide more sophisticated QoS monitors for a range of other properties, including reliability properties,
- to develop reactive objects which support both QoS monitoring and renegotiation functions,
- to implement QoS policing functions, and
- to realize control loops for QoS maintenance within the engineering infrastructure.

This approach has the important advantage that it is not necessary to consider the time taken for management functions (it can be assumed that this takes zero time). Thus it is not necessary to manage the management functions, hence breaking the potential recursion in QoS management.

6.3 Achieving lip synchronization

6.3.1 The design revisited

The second example is concerned with achieving lip synchronization between audio and video connections. The overall design as presented in Section 4.4.2 is shown in Figure 6.2. This diagram shows an audio producer (a microphone), a video producer (a video camera), an audio consumer (a speaker) and a video consumer (a video window). The producers and consumers offer stream interfaces of the appropriate types and causalities. These are connected by an audio stream binding and a video stream binding. The consumer objects also support control interfaces which are used to implement lip synchronization. These are connected by signal bindings to a reactive object encapsulating the lip synchronization algorithm. This reactive object also requires interaction with an external timer (as discussed below).

Note that this example has been implemented on the platform described in Chapter 10. As will become apparent, the implementation strategy was actually affected by practical considerations emerging from the prototype development; this issue will be revisited in Section 6.3.4. The details given below match the implementation (apart from some minor changes to simplify the presentation).

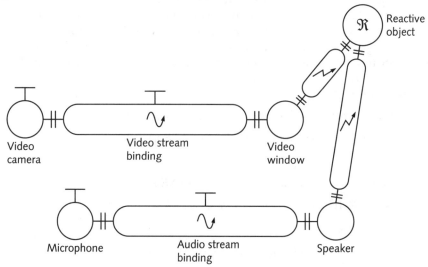

Figure 6.2 Object configuration to achieve lip synchronization.

6.3.2 The interface types and QoS annotations

We consider each of the objects in turn below and consider the interfaces and associated QoS annotations. We consider the video subsystem, the audio subsystem and then the control subsystem. Again, time is measured in milliseconds.

The video subsystem

The video subsystem consists of a video camera object, a video window object and a video binding. The video camera and video binding objects provide exactly the same interface as for the example above (see Section 6.2.2). The video window object also supports the same `videoWindowIn` interface as above. However, the `videoWindowStatus` interface is replaced by the following more sophisticated control interface:

```
type timestamp integer;

interface <signal> videoWindowControl {
    signalOut videoReady (timestamp);
    signalIn videoPresent ();
    signalOut videoPresented ();
}
```

The `videoReady` signal is emitted by the interface when a frame is delivered. The associated timestamp indicates the time when this frame was captured at the source. The input signal is then used to control the precise time at which the frame should be presented based on this information, the lip synchronization requirements and the permissible delays. This can be delayed or generated early to synchronize the video frame to the associated audio track. Finally, `videoPresented` is emitted when the presentation is completed.

The QoS annotations for the video camera and video binding are also assumed to be identical to the first example (again, refer to Section 6.2.2 for full details). The QoS annotations for the video camera are however slightly modified:

Provided clause

$$\forall n, \tau(videoWindowControl.videoPresented.SE,n + 24)$$
$$\leqslant \tau(videoWindowControl.videoPresented.SE,n) + 1000$$

$$\wedge$$

$$\forall n, \tau(videoWindowControl.videoPresented.SE,n)$$
$$\leqslant \tau(videoWindowControl.videoPresented.SR,n) + 10$$

Required clause

$$\forall n, \tau(videoWindowIn.videoIn.SR,n + 24)$$
$$\leqslant \tau(videoWndowIn.videoIn.SR,n) + 1000$$

As before, the video window will provide a throughput of 25 frames per second if it receives frames at this rate from the binding. The above provided clause also states that the time delay between the *videoPresent* signal and the *videoPresented* signal will be at most 10 ms.

The audio subsystem
The audio subsystem consists of a microphone, a speaker and an audio binding. Full details of each of the objects is given below.

The microphone object
The microphone object offers a stream interface representing the production of audio packets and an operational interface to control the microphone. The signatures for these two interfaces are as follows:

```
interface <stream> microphoneOut {
    flowOut audioOut (audio);
}

interface <operational> microphoneControl {
    start ();
    stop ();
    setVolume (in volume integer);
}
```

The associated QoS annotation for this object is:

Provided clause

$\forall n, \tau(microphoneOut.audioOut.SR,n + 4)$

$\leqslant \tau(microphoneOut.audioOut.SR,n) + 1000$

$\wedge$

$\tau(microphoneOut.audioOut.SE,1)$

$\leqslant \tau(microphoneControl.start.SR,1) + 10$

Required clause

None.

The provided clause indicates that the microphone will provide at least five audio packets in a given second. In addition, there will be a maximum delay of 10 ms between the `start` operation and the production of the first packet. The null required clause indicates that this provided quality of service is unconditional.

The speaker object

The speaker object offers an input stream interface consisting of a single audio flow together with a control interface as follows:

```
type timestamp integer;

interface <stream> speakerIn {
    flowIn audioIn (audio);
}

interface <signal> speakerControl {
    signalOut audioReady (timestamp);
    signalOut audioPresented ();
}
```

In this case, the control interface emits an `audioReady` signal when a packet is delivered. As with the video window object, the associated timestamp indicates the time at which this information was captured at the source. Unlike the video window object, however, the interface does not support a present signal. Rather, the audio packet is processed for presentation immediately. The `audioPresented` signal is then emitted when the presentation is completed.

The associated QoS annotation is then as follows:

Provided clause

$\forall n, \tau(speakerControl.audioPresented.SE,n + 4)$

$\leqslant \tau(speakerControl.audioPresented.SE,n) + 1000$

$\wedge$

$\forall n, \tau(speakerControl.audioPresented.SE,n)$

$\leqslant \tau(speakerIn.audioIn.SR,n) + 200$

Required clause

$\forall n, \tau(speakerIn.audioIn.SR,n + 4)$

$\leqslant \tau(speakerIn.audioIn.SR,n) + 1000$

This states that the speaker will present packets at a rate of at least five packets per second providing that the object receives packets at the same rate (from the binding). In addition, there will be a maximum delay of 200 ms between the arrival of a packet and its subsequent presentation.

The audio binding object

The audio binding object has both an input and an output stream interface together with a signal interface providing access to events for QoS management.

The signatures for the three interfaces are as follows:

```
type timestamp integer;

interface <stream> audioBindingIn {
    flowIn audioIn (audio);
}

interface <stream> audioBindingOut {
    flowOut audioOut (audio);
}

interface <signal> qosControl {
    signalOut audioSent (timestamp);
    signalIn audioDelivered (timestamp);
}
```

The QoS annotation for this object is then as follows:

Provided clause

$\forall n, \tau(audioBindingOut.audioOut.SE,n+4)$

$\leqslant \tau(audioBindingOut.audioOut.SE,n) + 1000$

$\wedge$

$\forall n, \tau(audioBindingOut.audioOut.SE,n)$

$\leqslant \tau(audioBindingIn.audioIn.SR,n) + 60$

$\wedge$

$\forall n, \tau(audioBindingIn.audioIn.SE,n) + 40$

$\leqslant \tau(audioBindingOut.audioOut.SR,n)$

Required clause

$\forall n, \tau(audioBindingIn.audioIn.SR,n+4)$

$\leqslant \tau(audioBindingIn.audioIn.SR,n) + 1000$

This states that the binding will provide a throughput of 5 packets per second and a delay of between 40 and 60 ms if the binding receives audio packets at a rate of 5 frames per second from a producer.

The control subsystem

The control subsystem consists of a reactive object, an external timer and three signal bindings from the reactive object to the control interfaces of the video window and the speaker and to the timer. Full details of these objects are given below. For the sake of simplicity we ignore the control interfaces of the binding objects.

The reactive object
The reactive object provides four signal interfaces, as follows:

```
type timestamp integer;
type violationType integer;
type delay integer;

interface <signal> videoControlIn {
    signalIn videoReady (timestamp);
    signalOut videoPresent ();
}

interface <signal> audioControlIn {
    signalIn audioReady (timestamp);
}

interface <signal> timerInOut {
    signalOut timerStart (delay);
    signalIn timerEnd ();
}

interface <signal> applicationControl {
    signalIn restart ();
}
```

The first two interfaces are connected to the corresponding control interfaces of the video window and speaker objects respectively. The third interface is connected to the timer object. Finally, the fourth interface can be used by an application to restart the reactive object. As above, the reactive object does not require QoS annotations.

The timer
The timer object offers a single signal interface as follows:

```
interface <signal> timer {
    signalIn timerStart (delay);
    signalOut timerEnd ();
}
```

The timer must then emit the timerEnd signal in the number of milliseconds designated by delay after the reception of timerStart. We also allow a tolerance of 1 ms for the operation of the timer. The required QoS annotation to capture this requirement is as follows:

Provided clause

$\forall n, \tau(timer.timerEnd.SE,n)$

$\leqslant \tau(timer.timerStart.SR,n) + (delay + 1)$

$\wedge$

$\forall n, \tau(timer.timerEnd.SE,n) + (delay - 1)$

$\leqslant \tau(clock.timerStart.SR,n)$

Required clause

None.

This simply states that the *timerEnd* signal is emitted *delay* $\pm$ 1 milliseconds after the reception of *timerStart*.

The video control binding
The video control binding has two signal interfaces corresponding to the incoming and outgoing signals respectively:

```
type timestamp integer;

interface <signal> videoControlBindingIn {
    signalIn videoReadyIn (timestamp);
    signalIn videoPresentedIn ()
}

interface <signal> videoControlBindingOut {
    signalOut videoReadyOut (timestamp);
    signalOut videoPresentedOut ()
}
```

The associated QoS annotations for this binding object are then:

Provided clause

$\forall n, \tau(videoControlBindingOut.videoReadyOut.SE,n)$

$\leqslant \tau(videoControlBindingIn.videoReadyIn.SR,n) + 10$

$\wedge$

$\forall n, \tau(videoControlBindingOut.videoPresentedOut.SE,n)$

$\leqslant \tau(videoControlBindingIn.videoPresentedIn.SR,n) + 10$

Required clause

None.

This states that the binding will guarantee a maximum delay of 10 ms for the transmission of signals across the binding. There is no required clause in this case indicating that this QoS provision is unconditional.

The audio control binding
The audio control binding is very similar to the video control binding. Again, the binding offers two interfaces:

```
type timestamp integer;

interface <signal> audioControlBindingIn {
    signalIn audioReadyIn (timestamp);
}

interface <signal> audioControlBindingOut {
    signalOut audioReadyOut (timestamp);
}
```

The associated QoS annotations for this binding object are then:

Provided clause

$\forall n, \tau (audioControlBindingOut.audioReadyOut.SE, n)$

$\leqslant \tau (audioControlBindingIn.audioReadyIn.SR, n) + 10$

Required clause

None.

This again indicates that there is a maximum delay of 10 ms in delivering the signals.

The timer binding
Finally, the timer binding has two interfaces corresponding to the two ends of the binding (the reactive object end and the timer end respectively):

```
interface <signal> timerBinding1 {

    signalIn timerStartIn (delay);
    signalOut timerEndOut ();
}

interface <signal> timerBinding2 {
    signalOut timerStartOut (delay);
    signalIn timerEndIn ();
}
```

In this case, it is important that delay is kept to a minimum. This condition is indicated by the following QoS annotation:

Provided clause

$\forall n, \tau(timerBinding2.timerStartOut.SE, n)$

$\leqslant \tau(timerBinding1.timerStartIn.SR, n) + 1$

$\wedge$

$\forall n, \tau(timerBinding1.timerEndOut.SE, n)$

$\leqslant \tau(timerBinding2.timerEndIn.SR, n) + 1$

Required clause

None.

This states that the binding will deliver the signal *timerStart* from interface 1 to interface 2 and *timerEnd* from interface 2 to interface 1 in less than or equal to one millisecond.

6.3.3 The reactive object

The Esterel module to implement lip synchronization is given below. As the specification is rather large, we first present the declaration part and then the body of the module.

The declaration part

The declaration part describes the data declarations and signal interface for the lip synchronization module. The full specification for the declaration part is given below:

```
module LIPSYNC:

% Declaration part follows....

% Firstly, we define the data declarations

constant
        VideoTheoRate : integer,
        VideoSlowRate : integer,
        VideoFastRate : integer,
        DisplayVideoDelay : integer,

        AudioTheoRate : integer,
        DisplayAudioDelay : integer,

        VideoGoodDelay : integer,
        MaximumSyncDiff : integer;

function
        systemTime (): integer;
```

```
% Secondly, we declare the interface in terms of signals

input
        videoReady (integer),
        audioReady (integer),
        restart,
        timerEnd;
output
        videoPresent,
        timerStart (integer);

% The body of this module is as presented below
...

.
```

The constants represent the characteristics of the audio and video flows and the requirements in terms of lip synchronization.

For the video stream, `VideoTheoRate` represents the theoretical rate of video frame presentation measured in terms of the delay between successive frames. For a throughput of 25 frames per second, the correct value for this constant is 40 ms. `VideoSlowRate` and `VideoFastRate` then define the maximum and minimum gaps between successive video frames. These are set to 45 ms and 35 ms respectively. Finally, `DisplayVideoDelay` corresponds to the delay between the output of the `videoPresent` signal and the actual presentation on the screen. From the QoS annotations above, this can be seen to be 10 ms.

For the audio stream, `AudioTheoRate` defines the theoretical delay between successive audio frames. For a throughput of 5 packets per second, this is set to 200 ms. `DisplayAudioDelay` then defines the delay between the generation of the `audioReady` signal and the actual presentation. Again, the QoS annotations above gave this figure as 200 ms.

The final two constants relate to the lip synchronization between audio and video. `MaximumSyncDiff` defines the maximum acceptable difference between the respective delays for audio and video. We set this to 5 ms. `VideoGoodDelay` is concerned with the case when audio packets are missing. In this case, the strategy is to speed up video if the delay is above this threshold (see below).

The above discussion is summarized in Table 6.1.

The function `systemTime` provides access to an underlying system clock. Finally, the signal interface corresponds exactly to the signal interface defined for the reactive object. Note that both *videoReady* and *audioReady* are valued signals; the value corresponds to the timestamp placed on associated packet at time of capture at the source.

The body of the Esterel program

The lip synchronization program makes use of the Esterel copymodule facility to achieve a level of modularity. In particular, a top-level Esterel module relies

Table 6.1 Constants defined in the lip synchronization program

Constant	Interpretation	Value (ms)
VideoTheoRate	Ideal inter-frame gap for video	40
VideoSlowRate	Maximum inter-frame gap for video	45
VideoFastRate	Minimum inter-frame gap for video	35
DisplayVideoDelay	Delay between videoPresent and actual presentation	10
AudioTheoRate	Ideal inter-packet gap for audio	200
DisplayAudioDelay	Delay between audioReady and actual presentation	200
MaxSyncDiff	Maximum acceptable difference between audio and video delays	5
VideoGoodDelay	Threshold for speeding up video when audio is missing	5

on an AudioModule and a VideoModule to deal with the incoming audio and video respectively.

We look at the top-level module and then the two sub-modules below.

The top-level module
The top-level module is presented below.

```
module LIPSYNC:

% The declaration part is as given above

...

% Body follows...

every Restart do

   signal audioDelay (integer), timeNow (integer) in [

   % Initialise the value of the signal audioDelay to 0

      emit audioDelay (0);

      % Now execute the audio and video modules and a clock
      % process in parallel
      [
        [ % audioReady signal processing

            copymodule AudioModule [
                           constant AudioTheoRate/AudTheoRate,
                           VideoTheoRate/VidTheoRate,

                           signal audioReady/audReady,
                           audioDelay/audDelay,
```

```
                                    videoReady/vidReady,
                                    timeNow/now;
                                    ]

        ] % End audioReady signal processing

    ||

        [ % videoReady signal processing

            copymodule VideoModule [

                                constant VideoTheoRate/VidTheoRate;
                                VideoSlowRate/VidSlowRate,
                                VideoFastRate/VidFastRate,
                                DisplayVideoDelay/DispVidDelay,
                                AudioTheoRate/AudTheoRate,
                                DisplayAudioDelay/DispAudDelay,
                                MaximumSyncDiff/MaxSyncDiff,
                                VideoGoodDelay/VidGoodDelay;

                                signal videoReady/vidReady,
                                timeNow/now,
                                audioDelay/audDelay,
                                videoPresent/vidPresent
                                timerStart/timStart
                                timerEnd/timEnd;
                                ]
        ]% End videoReady signal processing

    ||

            every tick do emit timeNow (systemTime() ) end

        ] % parallel blocks

    ] end % signal

    end % every


        .
```

This script declares some additional signals which are not visible to the environment. These signals are as follows:

- audioDelay is the current delay (positive or negative) for the audio presentation, and
- timeNow is the current real-time measured in milliseconds.

The main body then reacts to every restart signal by first emitting an initial value of zero for the local signal audioDelay and then executing three processes in parallel, namely the AudioModule, the VideoModule and a process generating the current time. This latter process updates the value of the signal timeNow on every tick signal by using an external function (systemTime). The tick signal is a special signal generated by Esterel on every execution. Hence, this process has the effect of generating an up-to-date value of the current time.

Further details of the actions of AudioModule and VideoModule are given below.

The audio module

The complete specification of AudioModule is as follows.

```
module AudioModule:

constant    AudTheoRate: integer,
            VidTheoRate: integer;

input       audReady (integer), vidReady (integer), now (integer);
output      audDelay (integer);

var AudThisDelay, MaxWait : integer in [
  AudThisDelay := 0;
  MaxWait := (AudTheoRate / VidTheoRate) + 2;
  every audReady do
    AudThisDelay := ?now - ?audReady;
    emit audDelay (AudThisDelay);
    await (MaxWait) vidReady; % usually interrupted by the "every"
    emit audDelay (0);
  end % every
] end % var
.
```

This module is relatively straightforward. The program reacts to every audReady signal by firstly calculating the delay for the corresponding audio packet (given by the time now minus the timestamp on the audio packet) and then emitting this delay to the environment. As will be seen, this information is used by the video module to achieve lip synchronization. Following this, the program blocks awaiting MaxWait occurrences of the vidReady signal. MaxWait was earlier calculated as:

```
AudTheoRate/VidTheoRate + 2
```

AudTheoRate/VidTheoRate gives the number of video packets expected per audio packet. Adding two on to this provides an acceptable maximum wait for the next audio packet. For the values given above, MaxWait will hence be:

```
200/40+2
= 7 video packets
```

Normally, the await statement will be interrupted by another audReady signal and then the behaviour described above will be repeated. If this statement terminates, implying seven video packets have been received before the next audio packet, the program assumes that the next audio packet is missing and emits a delay of zero to indicate this fact. This should be unambiguous, as AudThisDelay should never be zero as time should pass between the capturing of the audio packet and its reception at the destination.

The video module

The specification of VideoModule is as follows:

```
module VideoModule:

constant    VidTheoRate: integer,
            VidSlowRate : integer,
            VidFastRate : integer,
            DispVidDelay : integer,

            AudTheoRate: integer,
            DispAudDelay: integer,

            MaxSyncDiff : integer,
            VidGoodDelay : integer;
;

input       vidReady (integer), now (integer),
            audDelay (integer), timEnd;
output      vidPresent, timStart (integer);

var VidThisDelay := 0, VidThisTime := 0, VidLastTime := 0,
ComparedDelay := 0, VidAdjust := 0, VidWait := 0 : integer in [

    % await first video frame...

    await VidReady;

    % initialise value for VidThisTime

    VidThisTime := ?vidReady - VidTheoRate;

    loop

        % calculate VidLastTime, VidThisTime, VidThisDelay for
        % current packet

        VidLastTime := VidThisTime;
        VidThisTime := ?vidReady;
        VidThisDelay := ?now - VidThisTime+ DispVidDelay;

        % calculate adjustment factor based on above variables and
        % ComparedDelay

        ComparedDelay := ?audDelay + DispAudDelay;
```

```
        if (?audDelay = 0)
          then % Audio not being presented
            if (VidThisDelay > (VidGoodDelay + DispVidDelay))
              then VidAdjust := -1
              else VidAdjust := 0
            end
          else
            if (VidThisDelay > (comparedDelay + MaxSyncDiff))
              then
                VidAdjust := VidFastRate - VidTheoRate;
              else
                if (VidThisDelay < (ComparedDelay - MaxSyncDiff))
                  then VidAdjust := VidSlowRate - VidTheoRate;
                  else VidAdjust := 0;
                end
            end
        end;

        % emit signal to present current video frame

        emit VidPresent;

        % calculate how long to wait with respect to this reaction

        VidWait := VidThisTime - VidLastTime;
        if (VidWait > VidSlowRate) then VidWait := VidSlowRate end;
        VidWait := VidWait + VidAdjust;

        % await next video packet and wait time (whichever takes
        % longest

        [
          await vidReady
        ||
          if (VidWait > 0)
            then
              emit timStart (Vidwait);
              await timEnd;
          end
        ];

      end % loop
    ] end % var
    .
```

This is considerably more complicated than AudioModule and requires some careful explanation. The program declares a number of local variables as follows:

• VidThisDelay, representing the delay associated with the current video frame,

- VidThisTime, representing the actual capture time of the current video packet,
- VidLastTime, representing the actual capture time of the previous video packet,
- ComparedDelay, representing the corresponding delay for the current audio packet,
- VidAdjust, representing the adjustment factor required by the current video frame, and
- VidWait, representing the actual delay to be incurred by the automata in dealing with this video frame,

The program starts by awaiting the first video frame and then sets an initial value for VidThisTime as the timestamp for the first frame minus the ideal gap. This value represents the timestamp for an ideal previous frame (given that none exists). Following this, the program loops indefinitely processing this and further video packets. The main body of the loop follows the following steps:

1. *Calculate* VidLastTime, VidThisTime *and* VidThisDelay
   The loop starts by calculating values for the above three values.
   VidLastTime is set to the previous value of VidThisTime (given by the ideal value mentioned above for the first iteration). VidThisTime is then taken from the timestamp on the current video packet. Finally, VidThisDelay is calculated by first subtracting VidThisTime from the current time (represented by the signal, now). It is then necessary to add in the value of DispVidDelay allowing for the fact that the frame will not be presented immediately after vidPresent is emitted. The final value provides an indication of whether the current frame is on time, early or late.
2. *Calculate adjustment factor*
   The next step effectively implements the strategy for lip synchronization by deciding whether to speed up or slow down the inter-frame gap. Firstly, ComparedDelay is calculated giving the corresponding delay for audio. This takes the value for audDelay as emitted by the audio module and then adds on DispAudDelay allowing for the delay to the actual presentation. This then provides a reference point for the further calculations. The strategy is then summarized by Table 6.2.
3. *Display video frame*
   The step consists simply of the emitting of the signal vidPresent. This signal will result in the presentation of the associated video frame. Note that, because of the semantics of the reactive object, this happens instantaneously with respect to this reaction. The required delay is then imposed between this frame and the next frame (see below).
4. *Calculate required waiting time*
   The next step is to calculate how long to wait before processing the next frame. This calculation is based on the inter-frame gap of the previous two frames. With this strategy, synchronization errors are corrected in the

Table 6.2 Strategy for achieving lip synchronization

Condition	Indicator	Action
Audio missing	`?audDelay = 0`	Speed up by 1 ms if delay above threshold (`VidGoodDelay`)
Video late	`VidThisDelay >` `(ComparedDelay +` `MaxSyncDiff)`	Adjustment of `VidFastRate -` `VidTheoRate`
Video early	`VidThisDelay <` `(ComparedDelay -` `MaxSyncDiff)`	Adjustment of `VidSlowRate -` `VidTheoRate`
Otherwise	None of above	No adjustment

future. The required wait time, `VidWait`, is initially set to the time between the generation of the current frame and the previous frame. If this is greater than the maximum inter-frame gap (given by `VidSlowRate`) then this is set to `VidSlowRate`. This is necessary to deal with the case where, for some reason, there is a problem with the camera and a frame has not been generated for a relatively long period of time (resulting in a large value of `VidWait`). This exceptional value should not adversely affect the presentation of the future frame and hence a maximum bound is placed on the wait time (given by `VidSlowRate`). The accumulated value is then modified by the required adjustment factor (as calculated in step 2).

5. *Impose inter-frame gap*
   The final step is to wait in parallel for both the next frame and the required wait time (using the external timer). This will terminate when the slower component terminates. The effect is to impose the required delay before dealing with the next video frame.

Note that the above cycle (together with the audio module) can be interrupted at any point by a `restart` signal. This signal will result in an effective reinitialization of the object's behaviour.

6.3.4 Analysis

This example illustrates that inter-media real-time synchronization can be realized using our approach. The example also provides further evidence of the expressiveness and elegance of Esterel for programming real-time control strategies. We also believe that Esterel, as a general real-time programming language, can be used to program a full range of intra- and inter-media synchronization strategies.

As with the previous example, it is also possible to develop the solution to this problem at a computational level without concern about the execution time for this object (it can be assumed that this takes zero time). All real-time assumptions are then explicitly stated as QoS annotations on the audio and video producer and consumer objects, on the associated bindings, on the bindings to the reactive object and even to the value offered by the real-time clock.

The above Esterel program also results in a highly efficient automaton. In particular, the Esterel script compiles to an automaton with approximately 10 states. The total execution time for the automaton is around 1 ms, although about 90% of this time is spent in the supporting execution machine (see Chapter 11); the actual execution of the automaton takes less than 100 microseconds.

It is worth re-emphasizing that this is a real Esterel script from a working prototype. This is reflected directly in the approach to achieving lip synchronization. In particular, the script would be considerably simplified with the introduction of a millisecond signal. For example, it would no longer be necessary to use the external timer or await a certain amount of video frames in the audio module. However, the introduction of a millisecond signal would mean that the execution machine must react at least every millisecond. Given that the total execution time for the reactive object is 1 ms, this is clearly impractical. In contrast, the above script operates at a much coarser granularity but still achieves the desired effect.

6.4 A multimedia presentation

6.4.1 The design revisited

The final example is the real-time coordination of a multimedia presentation. This example was first presented in Section 4.4.2 and involves a three phase interactive presentation of a museum (welcome phase, menu phase and conference phase). The reader should refer back to Chapter 4 for the full definition of the problem. Chapter 4 presented the high-level design shown in Figure 6.3 as a solution to the problem. This diagram shows a sizeable configuration of objects comprising:

- one audio/video producer (for the welcome phase), one corresponding audio/video consumer and associated stream binding with both an audio and a video flow,
- two audio producers (for the welcome phase and the conference phase), a single audio consumer and two audio stream bindings,
- a number of image sources (the menu image, the access map image and the conference images),
- a keyboard object,
- an external clock, and
- a reactive object (encapsulating the overall real-time coordination) with associated control (signal) bindings to the audio and video producers, the image sources, the keyboard and the external clock.

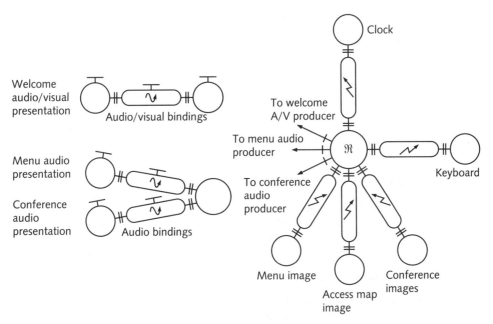

Figure 6.3 Coordinating a multimedia presentation.

The interface type signatures, QoS annotation and the implementation of the reactive object are now presented below.

6.4.2 The interface types and QoS annotations

Because of the larger number of objects in this example, we do not provide full detail for all objects. For example, we only present QoS annotations for binding objects and assume that the participants in the binding offer compliant levels of QoS. Other simplifications are described in the text below.

The audio-visual subsystem

The audio-visual subsystem features a number of continuous media producers corresponding to sources of stored media. In particular, there is one joint audio/video producer for the welcome phase and two separate audio producers for the menu and conference phases. The audio/video producer is connected to a corresponding audio/video consumer by an appropriate binding (featuring two flows). The other audio producers are connected to a single audio consumer by two separate bindings. Note also that the audio track for the conference phase is broken into a number of distinct sequences; the correct sequence is selected by providing a sequence number. The full interfaces are given below.

The audio/video producer (welcome phase)

```
interface <stream> welcomeAvOut {
        flowOut audioOut (audio);
        flowOut videoOut (video);
}

interface <signal> welcomeAvControl {
        signalIn welcomeAvStart ();
        signalOut welcomeAvEnd ();
}
```

The audio/video consumer (welcome phase)

```
interface <stream> welcomeAvIn {
        flowIn audioIn (audio);
        flowIn videoIn (video);
}
```

The audio producer (menu phase)

```
interface <stream> menuAudioOut {
        flowOut audioOut (audio);
}

interface <signal> menuAudioControl {
        signalIn menuAudioStart ();
        signalOut menuAudioEnd ();
        signalIn killMenu ();
}
```

The audio producer (conference phase)

```
type SequenceNumber integer;

interface <stream> menuAudioOut {
        flowOut audioOut (audio);
}

interface <signal> confAudioControl {
        signalIn confAudioStart (sequenceNumber);
        signalOut confAudioEnd ();
        signalIn killConf ();
        signalIn suspendConf ();
        signalIn resumeConf ();
}
```

The audio consumer (menu and conference phases)

```
interface <stream> audioConsumerIn {
        flowIn audioIn (audio);
}
```

One audio/video binding and two audio bindings are then required to complete this subsystem. To shorten the presentation, we only present details for the audio/video binding. The other bindings (and QoS annotations) can be assumed to be similar to the audio bindings presented in Section 6.3.2.

Type signature

```
interface <stream> avBindingIn {
      flowIn audioIn (audio);
      flowIn videoIn (video);
}

interface <stream> avBindingOut {
      flowOut audioOut (audio);
      flowOut videoOut (video)
}
```

Provided clause

$\forall n, \tau(avBindingOut.videoOut.SE,n + 24)$

$\leqslant \tau(avBindingOut.videoOut.SE,n) + 1000$

$\wedge$

$\forall n, \tau(avBindingOut.videoOut.SE,n)$

$\leqslant \tau(avBindingIn.videoIn.SR,n) + 60$

$\wedge$

$\forall n, \tau(avBindingIn.videoIn.SE,n) + 40$

$\leqslant \tau(avBindingOut.videoOut.SR,n)$

$\wedge$

$\forall n, \tau(avBindingOut.audioOut.SE,n + 4)$

$\leqslant \tau(avBindingOut.audioOut.SE,n) + 1000$

$\wedge$

$\forall n, \tau(avBindingOut.audioOut.SE,n)$

$\leqslant \tau(avBindingIn.audioIn.SR,n) + 60$

$\wedge$

$\forall n, \tau(avBindingIn.audioIn.SE,n) + 40$

$\leqslant \tau(avBindingOut.audioOut.SR,n)$

Required clause

$$\forall n, \tau(avBindingIn.videoIn.SR,n + 24)$$

$$\leqslant \tau(avBindingIn.videoIn.SR,n) + 1000$$

$$\wedge$$

$$\forall n, \tau(avBindingIn.audioIn.SR,n + 4)$$

$$\leqslant \tau(avBindingIn.audioIn.SR,n) + 1000$$

This states that the binding will provide a throughput of 25 frames per second and 5 packets per second. For both, the delay will be between 40 and 60 ms per frame/packet. There is an assumption, however, that the binding receives video frames and audio packets at a rate of 25 frames per second and 5 packets per second respectively from the producer.

The image sources

There are three image sources in the configuration, corresponding to the menu phase, the access map for the conference phase and the set of images required for the conference phase. The latter requires a sequence number to select the appropriate image. The full interfaces are given below:

The menu image

```
interface <signal> menuImageControl {
      signalIn menuImagePresent ();
}
```

The access map image

```
interface <signal> accessMapImageControl {
      signalIn accessMapImagePresent ();
}
```

The conference images

```
type sequenceNumber integer;

interface <signal> conferenceImageControl {
      signalIn conferenceImagePresent (sequenceNumber);
}
```

We do not provide QoS annotations for these discrete media objects, but rather assume that the images will be presented immediately the signal is received (without any perceivable delay).

The keyboard and clock objects

The configuration also features two objects representing basic devices, a keyboard and a clock. The keyboard is a restricted keyboard featuring the following keys:

kill, suspend, resume, start and a numerical keypad to select from the menu. The keyboard then offers outgoing signals corresponding to each of these keys (the numerical keypad maps to a valued signal indicating the user's choice):

The keyboard object

```
interface <signal> keyboardOut {
        signalOut killOut ();
        signalOut suspendOut ();
        signalOut resumeOut ();
        signalOut startOut ();
        signalOut choiceOut (integer);
}
```

Again, we do not present QoS annotations for this object.

The external clock simply provides a second signal as follows:

The clock object

```
interface <signal> clockOut {
        signalOut secondOut;
}
```

The QoS annotation for this object is similar to the clock presented in Section 6.3.2 above (but with a granularity of one second):

Provided clause

$\forall n, \tau(clock.secondOut.SE,n)$

$\leqslant \tau(clock.secondOut.SE,n+1) + 1050$

$\wedge$

$\forall n, \tau(clock.secondOut.SE,n) + 950$

$\leqslant \tau(clock.secondOut.SE,n+1)$

Required clause

None.

This simply states that the second signal is emitted precisely every 1000 milliseconds with a permitted jitter of ±50 ms.

The control subsystem

The reactive object is at the heart of the control subsystem. This object is then connected to the objects under its control (the welcome audio/ video producer, the menu and conference audio producers and the three image sources). The object also receives input from the keyboard and clock objects.

To support this configuration, the reactive object supports a number of distinct interfaces corresponding to each of the connected objects given above. The full set of interfaces is given below:

```
interface <signal> welcomeAvInterface {
      signalOut welcomeAvStart ();
      signalIn welcomeAvEnd ();
}

interface <signal> menuAudioInterface {
      signalOut menuAudioStart ();
      signalIn menuAudioEnd ();
      signalOut killMenu ();
}

interface <signal> confAudioInterface {
      signalOut confAudioStart (sequenceNumber);
      signalIn confAudioEnd ();
      signalOut killConf ();
      signalOut suspendConf ();
      signalOut resumeConf ();
}

interface <signal> menuImageInterface {
      signalOut menuImagePresent ();
}

interface <signal> accessMapImageInterface {
      signalOut accessMapImagePresent ();
}

type sequenceNumber integer;

interface <signal> conferenceImageInterface {
      signalOut conferenceImagePresent (sequenceNumber);
}

interface <signal> keyboardInterface {
      signalIn killIn ();
      signalIn suspendIn ();
      signalIn resumeIn ();
      signalIn startIn ();
      signalIn choiceIn (integer);
}

interface <signal> clockInterface {
      signalIn secondIn ();
}
```

(As will be seen below, this set of interfaces provides a template for the Esterel implementation for the reactive object.)

The subsystem then features eight signal bindings connecting the various reactive object interfaces to the corresponding control interface. Apart from the clock binding, these are all fairly similar. We therefore restrict the presentation to the welcome control binding. This binding has the following type signature and QoS annotations:

The welcome control binding

```
interface <signal> welcomeControlBindingA {
        signalOut welcomeAvStartOut ();
        signalIn welcomeAvEndIn ();
}

interface <signal> welcomeControlBindingB {
        signalIn welcomeAvStartIn ();
        signalOut welcomeAvEndOut ();
}
```

Provided clause

$\forall n, \tau(welcomeControlBindingA.welcomeAvStartOut.SE,n)$

$\leqslant \tau(welcomeControlBindingB.welcomeAvStartIn.SR,n) + 25$

$\wedge$

$\forall n, \tau(welcomeControlBindingB.welcomeAvEndOut.SE,n)$

$\leqslant \tau(welcomeControlBindingA.welcomeAvEndIn.SR,n) + 25$

Required clause

None.

This states that the binding delivers *welcomeAvStart* signals from interface A to interface B and *welcomeAvEnd* signals from interface B to interface A. Interface A corresponds to the reactive object and interface B to the corresponding control interface. The QoS annotation states that the maximum delay for each signal is 25 ms.

The clock binding has stronger QoS constraints to preserve the integrity of the second signal. The definition for this binding is as follows:

The clock binding

```
interface <signal> clockBindingIn {
        signalIn secondIn ();
}

interface <signal> clockBindingOut {
        signalOut secondOut ();
}
```

Provided clause

$\forall n, \tau(clockBindingOut.secondOut.SE,n)$

$\leqslant \tau(clockBindingIn.secondIn.SR,n) + 1$

$\wedge$

$\forall n, \tau(clockBindingIn.secondIn.SR,n) + 1$

$\leqslant \tau(clockBindingOut.secondOut.SE,n)$

Required clause

None.

The QoS annotation states that the binding will deliver the signal in precisely 1 ms with no permitted jitter.

6.4.3 The reactive object

Overall structure

The reactive object, museum, is a composite object exploiting the copymodule facility (as used above). In particular, museum consists of a top-level object, three child objects representing each of the presentation phases, and a clock object (which embodies general time services and also realizes the suspend/ resume feature). This structure is illustrated in Figure 6.4.

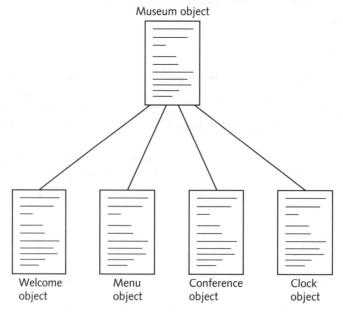

Museum object

Welcome object   Menu object   Conference object   Clock object

Figure 6.4 The hierarchy of Esterel modules.

Each of the modules is presented in detail below (note that a slightly different form of this Esterel program was previously presented in Horn (1993) and, in a shorter form, in Blair *et al.* (1996)).

The museum object
The Esterel script for the top-level museum object is as follows:

```
module museum:

constant MENU, CONFERENCE: integer;

input      killIn, suspendIn, resumeIn, startIn, choiceIn(integer)
           secondIn, welcomeAvEnd,
           menuAudioEnd, confAudioEnd;

output     killMenu, killConf, suspendConf, resumeConf,
           welcomeAvStart, menuAudioStart, menuImagePresent,
           confAudioStart(integer), confImagePresent(integer),
           accessMapPresent;

signal appliSecond, phase(integer) in
  loop
    trap restart in
        copymodule welcome [signal welcomeAvStart/avStart,
                                   welcomeAvEnd/avEnd,
                                   startIn/terminate];
      do
       loop
        emit phase(MENU);
          do
             copymodule menu [signal menuImagePresent/imagePresent,
                 menuAudioStart/audStart,
                 menuAudioEnd/audEnd,
                 choiceIn/choice]
           watching 5*60 second timeout exit restart end;
           emit phase(CONFERENCE);
           copymodule conference [constant 2/AUDIO_DELAY;
               signal accessMapPresent/mapPresent,
               confImagePresent/imagePresent,
               confAudioStart/audioStart,
               confAudioEnd/audioEnd,
               choiceIn/choice,
               appliSecond/sec]

          ||
          copymodule clock [signal appliSecond/appliTick,
              secondIn/tick,
              suspendIn/suspIn,resumeIn/resIn
```

```
                        suspendConf/suspConf,
                        resumeConf/resConf]
            end % loop
        watching killIn timeout
            if (?phase=MENU) emit killMenu else emit killConf end
        end
      end % trap
    end % main loop
  end.
```

The interface to this object consists of a number of input and output signals. These signals correspond precisely to the external interface as presented above. The module then defines two local signals:

- appliSecond is emitted by the clock module and is used by the other modules to provide a reference point for real-time (the reason why this is used and not the external clock signal, second, will be explained below).
- phase is used to record the current phase and is accessible from all modules.

The main body of the module is then relatively straightforward. The program consists of two loops. The outer loop never terminates and encapsulates the three phases of the presentation. The inner loop cycles through the menu phase and conference phase and can be terminated by the user hitting the kill key (resulting in the KillIn signal). This effect is achieved by using the do ... watching ... timeout construct. Similarly, a timeout is placed around the menu using the do watching 5 MINUTE construct. In this case, the exception GOTO_WELCOME is used to return control to the start of the outer loop.

The welcome object
The welcome object is shown below.

```
module welcome:

input       avEnd, terminate;
output      avStart;

do
  loop
    emit avStart;
    await avEnd
  end
watching terminate.
```

This script loops repeatedly until the terminate signal is detected. Inside the loop, the script presents the welcoming video and audio using the signal avStart. The script then synchronizes awaiting the corresponding end signal (avEnd). Note that the three signals used by the module correspond to the signals welcomeAvStart, welcomeAvEnd and startIn through the use of the copymodule renaming facility.

The menu object

The menu object is given below.

```
module menu:

input      avEnd, choice;
output     imagePresent, audStart;

do
  emit imagePresent:
  loop
    emit audStart;
    await audEnd;
  end
watching choice.
```

With this module, a single image is displayed (using the imagePresent signal). The script then loops playing the audio commentary repeatedly. The presentation is then terminated by the reception of a choice signal (indicating that the user has made a selection from the menu).

The conference object

The conference module is shown below.

```
module conference:

constant AUDIO_DELAY: integer;

input      audioEnd, choice (integer), sec;
output     mapPresent, imagePresent(integer),
           audioStart(integer);

function GetNoUnits (integer): integer;
function AudioAddress (integer, integer): integer;
function ImageAddress (integer, integer): integer;

emit mapPresent;
var index:=0, N, addressA, addressI : integer in [
  N := GetNoUnits (?choice);
  repeat N times;
    index := index+1;
    addressI := ImageAddress (?choice, N);
    emit imagePresent(addressI);
    await AUDIO_DELAY sec;
```

```
        addressA := AudioAddress (?choice, N);
        emit audioStart(addressA);
        await audioEnd
    end ]
end.
```

This module outputs signals to present the map and to present the appropriate image and the associated audio. The latter signals are valued signals carrying the logical address for the image and audio respectively. We assume the existence of two functions, `ImageAddress` and `AudioAddress`, which compute the desired addresses from the user's choice and the position in the presentation. We also assume a function, `GetNoUnits`, which indicates the number of units for a particular choice. The user's choice is indicated by the valued input signal, `choice`. The module also receives two other input signals. The `audioEnd` indicates that the previous audio unit has been presented. The signal, `second`, presents a real-time clock. Note again that this is the signal emitted by the internal clock rather than the external clock (see explanation below).

The body of the module then simply emits the signal to present the map and then loops N times, presenting the ith image and starting the corresponding audio presentation; this then synchronizes on the end of the audio segment. The script also provides a delay between the presentation of the image and the start of the associated audio sequence.

The clock
The clock has a central role to play in implementing the suspend/resume functionality. The Esterel is presented below.

```
appliTick, tick, suspIn, resumeIn, suspConf, resumeConf
module clock:

constant SUSPENDED, RUNNING, MAX_SUSPENDED_DELAY: integer;

input tick, suspIn, resIn;

output appliTick, suspOut, resOut;

relation resIn#suspIn
function clash(integer, integer): integer;

signal state (combine integer with clash) in
    emit state(RUNNING);
    every suspIn do
        trap resume in
            emit state(SUSPENDED); emit suspOut;
            [await MAX_SUSPEND_DELAY; exit RESUME]
            ||
            [await resIn; exit RESUME]
```

```
        end
    handle RESUME do emit state(RUNNING); emit resOut
    end
    every tick if (?state=RUNNING) then emit appliTick end end
end.
```

This script takes as input a `tick` (corresponding to the `second` signal from the external clock) and also the `suspIn` and `resIn` signals (corresponding to `suspendIn` and `resumeIn` from the keyboard). The script then produces a filtered clock signal called `appliTick` (corresponding to `appliSecond`). The script also produces `suspConf` and `resConf` corresponding to `suspendConf` and `resumeConf` respectively. Note that a relation declaration is included to state that `suspIn` and `resIn` are incompatible in a given instant.

The body of the module has the task of filtering the clock tick and producing a modified clock `appliTick` as output. The filter state toggles from `SUSPENDED` to `RUNNING` based on the input signals `suspIn` and `resIn`. The module then only produces an `appliTick` when in the `RUNNING` state. In more detail, the initial state is set to `RUNNING`. A subsequent `suspIn` sets the state to `SUSPENDED` until either a corresponding `resIn` is received or `MAX_SUSPEND_DELAY` elapses. In both cases, the state is set back to `RUNNING`. When a state change occurs the appropriate signal (`suspOut` or `resOut`) is emitted, enabling the corresponding objects to react.

Note that it is also necessary to deal with the case when `emit state(RUNNING)` and `emit state(SUSPENDED)` occur in the same instant. We assume the existence of an external function `clash` which should combine the two values. The correct action for `clash` is to set the state to `SUSPENDED` in precedence over `RUNNING`.

6.4.4 Analysis

This example illustrates how it is possible to synchronize a multimedia presentation using the approach developed in the previous two chapters. As with the previous examples, all real-time requirements are explicitly stated as QoS annotations on objects (including binding objects). These annotations provide constraints for the underlying engineering infrastructure. The remainder of the design is developed in an engineering-independent manner. In particular, the reactive object provides a declarative, engineering-independent statement of the casual ordering between events.

The Esterel modules for the reactive object again illustrate the expressiveness and elegance of the language for expressing real-time synchronization. The script can also be compiled to a highly efficient automaton consisting of (again) approximately 10 states.

The use of `copymodule` has particular benefits in this example in reflecting the hierarchical structure of the corresponding multimedia document. The approach can also be compared to alternative notations for document presentation including MHEG (Meyer-Boudnik and Effelsberg, 1995), HyTime (ISO/IEC, 1992) and PREMO (ISO/IEC, 1996). Such notations provide a limited number of constructs for specifying presentation scripts (such as sequential and parallel operators, conditional action sets and restricted blocking). In contrast, Esterel provides a general purpose and comprehensive language which can model the above constructs and also a range of other synchronization options. Our approach is therefore to provide reactive objects and Esterel as the most general means of achieving real-time synchronization of multimedia documents and other structures, and then provide mappings to Esterel from appropriate standard notations.

A final observation from this example is that reuse can be supported with this approach by developing libraries of common modules. For example, the clock module in the example above is clearly reusable in other Esterel scripts. Alternative clocks could also be provided, for example supporting fast forward or slow down functionality, offering the programmer a number of options to select from.

6.5 Summary

This chapter has presented three case studies illustrating the use of the approach developed in Chapters 4 and 5. The first example illustrated how the approach can be used to implement a QoS management function: QoS monitoring. It was also argued that the approach could be generalized to other dynamic QoS management functions, including renegotiation, policing and maintenance. The second example then illustrated how the approach can be used to achieve inter-media synchronization between an audio and a video stream. Again, we believe that the approach can be used for the full range of inter- and intra-media synchronization requirements. Finally, the third example shows how the approach can be used to coordinate the presentation of multimedia documents. It was again argued that the approach was more general than presentation standards such as MHEG and HyTime and that appropriate mappings can be defined between such standard notations and Esterel.

Overall, the examples provide further illustration of the benefits of the approach. Firstly, the examples demonstrate the style of programming imposed by the approach where all real-time requirements are explicitly specified as QoS annotations on objects. As argued previously, this contributes significantly to our requirement for portability of real-time applications in an open environment. This also enables analysis of overall real-time performance of configurations. Secondly, reactive objects can be developed for QoS management and real-time synchronization in a declarative, engineering-independent manner. Again, this contributes to portability of applications. Thirdly, the synchrony hypothesis enables real-time analysis. Finally, Esterel scripts compile to highly efficient automata. This was illustrated by the sizes of the automata for the latter two examples (approximately 10 states in both cases).

7 Concurrent object-oriented programming within the new approach

7.1 Introduction

The aim of this chapter is to develop an approach to concurrent object-oriented programming based on the programming model of Chapter 4. There has been considerable research on concurrency and object-oriented programming, but this is one of the first attempts to combine this work with support for real-time and multimedia (that is, via the programming model). The foundations for this work can be found in the literature (Papathomas *et al.*, 1995a, b). The most recent developments with respect to reuse have been carried out by Papathomas at IMAG and can be found in Papathomas (1996).

Note that it is important to clarify the relationship between the concurrent model developed in this chapter and the programming model defined earlier in the book. The extended object model of Chapter 4 provides the conceptual framework for the concurrent model. The concurrent model is then a particular specialization based on this framework (there could of course be many others). The particular role of the model developed in this chapter is to enable the exploitation of concurrent object-oriented concepts in the development of multimedia applications. For example, the model enables the development of object-oriented applications featuring both intra- and inter-object concurrency. More significantly, the concurrent model adds value to the programming model in two key areas:

- by enabling the use of (multiple) inheritance in distributed multimedia applications, and
- by providing sophisticated techniques for inter-object synchronization and coordination (including real-time aspects).

This makes the model comparable with MSS as discussed in Chapter 2 (which features a *particular* inheritance hierarchy for multimedia together with an event notification mechanism based on the COSS Event Service). However, we believe that by adopting the programming model developed in this book, the resultant concurrent model is more open and complete in its treatment of distributed multimedia programming.

The remainder of this chapter is structured as follows. Section 7.2 identifies two key problems in achieving inheritance and coordination in concurrent object-oriented languages. Section 7.3. then describes the concurrent object model intended to overcome these problems. A prototype implementation is then introduced in Section 7.4. Following this, Section 7.5 provides some simple examples illustrating the key features of the approach and Section 7.6 describes a more complete multimedia example. Finally, Section 7.7 presents some concluding remarks.

7.2 Analysis of the problem

7.2.1 The importance of reuse

As stated above, there has recently been considerable research on the design of concurrent object-oriented programming languages (Papathomas, 1995). To achieve this goal, it is necessary to achieve an integration between concurrent programming and object-oriented paradigms. It is generally recognized that such a step can considerably enhance the expressiveness of object-oriented languages. One goal of object-oriented programming is to model the real world directly in software. Concurrency adds to the *expressiveness* by making it easier to model the inherently concurrent aspects of the real world. The integration of the two paradigms also encourages the *reuse* of generic concurrent behaviour. Other advantages include *improved execution speeds* and the potential *sharing* of distributed, persistent objects (Papathomas, 1995).

In terms of this chapter, we are interested in the potential for reuse, especially the reuse of inter-object synchronization and coordination patterns. Such a facility is important in multimedia programming, for example to encourage the reuse of generic real-time synchronization patterns, such as lip synchronization.

However, combining the two paradigms has proved to be rather difficult. The main problem is that the features found in concurrent and object-oriented languages are not orthogonal and consequently cannot be combined in an arbitrary way. More specifically, it is now recognized that, unless great care is taken, introducing concurrency into object-oriented languages can lead to significant problems with reuse:

- there are a number of potential problems between inheritance and (local) synchronization constraints,
- existing approaches make it difficult to reuse (global) coordination patterns.

We consider each issue in more detail below.

Reuse and local synchronization
Local synchronization is concerned with the synchronization of methods and, more generally, threads within a given object. The main problem with

inheritance is to interpret synchronization constraints in subclasses correctly. In particular, there can be problems associated with achieving the correct execution of inherited, overridden and newly defined methods without breaking the encapsulation between classes.

The potential problems are highlighted by Matsuoka *et al.* (1993) who highlight a number of *inheritance anomalies* in concurrent object-oriented languages. More specifically, this paper identifies problems whereby, in many languages, 'synchronization code cannot be effectively inherited without non-trivial class re-definitions'. They also highlight several areas where inheritance anomalies can arise. For example, consider the definition of a bounded buffer class where synchronization is based on a statement of acceptable states: states in which particular methods can be executed (Kafura and Lee, 1989). A definition of such a bounded buffer is shown below (taken from Matsuoka *et al.* (1993)):

```
Class b-buf: ACTOR {
    int in, out, buf[SIZE];
behaviour:
    empty = {put}; partial = {put, get}; full = {get}
public:
void Buffer ()
{
    in = out = 0:
}
void put (int item)
{
    in++; // store an item
    if (in == out + size) become full
    else become partial;
}
void get ()
{
    out++; // remove an item
    if (in == out) become empty
    else become partial;
}
```

The acceptable states are specified in the behaviour clause. This clause states that the put () method can be executed if the buffer is in the states empty or partial, and the get() method can execute in states partial or full. Consider now the definition of a specialized bounded buffer class x-buf2 which supports an additional method get2(). This method removes the two oldest items from the buffer. This cannot be specified, however, without redefining put() and get(). The problem is that get2() can only be executed if at least two items are in the buffer. To achieve this, it is necessary to

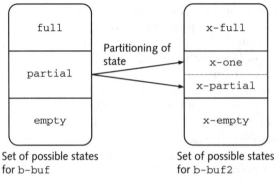

Figure 7.1 The state partitioning anomaly.

partition the state partial into two states: x-one, indicating that one item remains and x-partial, indicating that the buffer is partially full but with more than one item. This, however, requires modification to the methods put() and get(). The paper refers to this problem as partitioning of acceptable states. This problem is illustrated in Figure 7.1.

As a further illustration, it is often useful to be able to inherit (and hence reuse) generic local synchronization patterns in the construction of concurrent objects. This would be achieved by inheriting from predefined classes specifying the required (local) synchronization patterns. Such classes are often referred to as *mix-in* classes, as the behaviour is mixed into the new class. It is important, however, that this can be achieved in such a way that the old behaviour of the object need not be modified. In other words, the specification of the mix-in class should be independent of the behaviour of the object. Similarly, the specification of the mix-in classes must be independent of any instance variables defined in the underlying object.

Consider, for example, a lock mix-in for the bounded buffer class. This class accepts two methods: lock() and unlock(). The effect of the lock() method is to suspend the acceptance of all other methods until an unlock() method is received. Again, however, this cannot be achieved without modifying the behaviour of the bounded buffer class. In particular, the synchronization conditions for put() and get() must be modified to take into account, whether the object is locked or unlocked. This problem is referred to by Matsuoka *et al.* as the state modification anomaly (see Figure 7.2).

This analysis also applies to real-time patterns. For example, it would be desirable to specify a mix-in which defines a real-time synchronization pattern to provide rate-based flow control on the production of continuous media data items. Again, however, this can be difficult to achieve in many existing concurrent object-oriented languages.

Reuse and global coordination
Global coordination is concerned with the mutual synchronization of a set of objects in achieving a given task. The most common approach to achieve such

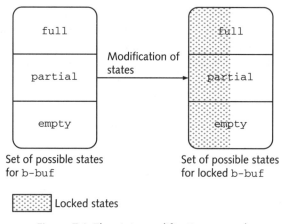

Figure 7.2 The state modification anomaly.

coordination is to embed synchronization actions in the methods of individual objects. For example, objects may include actions to notify other objects if a particular event occurs. This, however, makes it difficult to identify general coordination patterns and hence reuse such patterns in different applications. This stems from the fact that such algorithms are distributed across multiple objects and also intermixed with local functional computations. However, as with local patterns, it is often desirable to be able to reuse such patterns. For example, it would be advantageous to be able to identify and reuse a coordination algorithm to solve the dining philosophers problem. It would also be useful to reuse real-time synchronization patterns such as lip synchronization of an audio and a video channel or the mixing of two audio channels.

Careful design and programming can overcome the problem identified above. However, there is no well-defined and widely accepted method to achieve the desired effect. We therefore believe that languages should be designed to support the reuse of such global coordination patterns.

As a final point, the language used to express object behaviour may not be the most appropriate language to express coordination patterns. This is particularly true when real-time coordination patterns are considered. By achieving a separation between these different concerns we hope to allow the most appropriate language to be used in each part of the coordination. In particular, reactive objects written in Esterel can be exploited for real-time coordination (see Section 7.3.3).

7.2.2 Summary of requirements

The discussion above has highlighted a number of problems in achieving reuse in concurrent object-oriented languages. In considering these problems, we have identified the following key requirements for the design of a concurrent object-oriented language:

- there is a need to be able to identify and reuse local synchronization constraints in the execution of an object's methods and threads,
- there is a need to be able to identify and reuse local synchronization patterns (including real-time patterns) in the form of mix-in classes, and
- there is a need to be able to identify and reuse global coordination patterns (again, including real-time patterns).

We return to each of these requirements in the examples of Sections 7.5 and 7.6.

7.3 The object model

7.3.1 The overall approach

The object model, referred to as ATOM (for AcTive Object Model) (Papathomas, 1996), is based on the concept of *active objects*. Active objects encapsulate arbitrary processing (including the real-time processing of multimedia). They provide support for concurrent execution within objects through lightweight threads. A new thread will be created to support the execution of an incoming method request. Active objects can also have additional threads created at object instantiation time. Synchronization within an object is supported by two novel features: *abstract states and state predicates*. Synchronization between objects is then achieved by *state notifications*, which inform other objects of changes in the abstract state of an object. These features are described in more detail below. The key to the approach, however, is to define *synchronization* (both local and remote) in terms of abstract states rather than concrete states. This crucial separation enables interaction between components to be designed, in principle, independently of the behavioural components in the system.

The relationship with the programming model is as follows. As with the programming model, objects are either asynchronous or reactive. Reactive objects are included to support the expression of real-time coordination patterns, as required in multimedia applications. They can be written in specialized languages more suited to the expression of real-time synchronization concerns (for the purposes of this chapter, we assume the use of Esterel for the development of reactive objects). Reactive objects are simply defined as subclasses of active objects, albeit with a special mode of implementation to ensure that the synchrony hypothesis is met (see Section 7.3.3). This enables the benefits of active objects to be used throughout an application. Signals are then represented as state notifications; abstract states and state predicates effectively provide a linguistic notation for specifying and managing the occurrence of such signals. ATOM also provides a mechanism to map such (asynchronous) signals to synchronous events in reactive objects (again see Section 7.3.3).

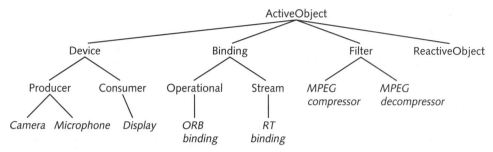

Figure 7.3 A typical class hierarchy.

Crucially, bindings are also represented as a subclass of active objects. Further subclasses are then defined for operational, stream and signal bindings. This tree can then be extended arbitrarily depending on the binding classes provided in a given environment. In addition, each subclass can define its own parameters including quality of service parameters on the binding. Similarly, virtual devices are also subclasses of active objects. As with MSS, it is then possible to generate a range of subclasses of virtual device representing different styles of multimedia device in the system. Unlike MSS, however, we do not prescribe a particular active object hierarchy but leave this open for a particular class library to define. A typical class hierarchy is shown in Figure 7.3.

7.3.2 Supporting active objects

Intra-object synchronization
As mentioned above, intra-object synchronization is supported by the novel concepts of abstract states and state predicates together with conditions expressed over abstract states. These are considered in turn below.

An *abstract state* represents some aspect of the real state of execution of an object at a level of abstraction that hides implementation details. For example, a bounded buffer could have abstract states, full and empty. These abstract states hide whether the bounded buffer is defined using a linked list or a linear array.

State predicates then provide an interpretation of abstract states over the state of execution. Note that we interpret state of execution in the broadest sense. This could be interpreted over the values of the actual instance variables, the incoming messages for the object or the state of the object's threads. The role of state predicates is to define whether the property associated with an abstract state holds at a given instant. Note that the mapping between abstract states and state of execution (as defined by state predicates) can vary from class to class, thus introducing a level of polymorphism for abstract states.

More formally, a state predicate can be defined as a function P from $CS \times AS_p$ to {*true*, *false*}, where CS is the set of concrete object states and AS_p is a subset of the object's abstract states AS. State predicates also have the following properties:

- a set of abstract states may be true at one (concrete) object state,
- an object may be associated with a set of state predicates and each predicate is associated to a subset of the object's abstract states, and
- the subsets of abstract states associated with different state predicates of an object are disjoint.

From a practical point of view, state predicates are objects that encapsulate the information necessary to determine whether or not the property described by the abstract state is true at a certain instant in the execution of the program. They are defined by the programmer and can contain arbitrary behaviour.

Finally, the execution of an object can be controlled by *activation conditions* and *thread suspension conditions*. These are both described in terms of abstract states. Activation conditions define constraints over the execution of threads, including threads created to execute incoming methods. As an example, an activation condition can specify that an `insert` into a bounded buffer can only execute when the buffer is not `full`. Conversely, a thread associated with a `remove` can only execute when the abstract state of the buffer is not `empty`. In general, activation conditions can be arbitrary boolean expressions defined over a number of abstract states. Executing threads can also explicitly suspend themselves until a particular condition is reached. Again, the condition can be expressed in terms of an arbitrary boolean expression over abstract states. The thread will remain suspended until the condition is true and until the activation condition for the method being executed is also true.

The execution of threads is managed by an *object manager*. In particular, the object manager creates new threads and suspends and resumes existing threads in accordance with the activation conditions. The object manager is entered at various points during execution, including the arrival of an operational, stream or signal method, the completion of a method execution, the requested suspension of an executing thread, or the notification of an external event (see below).

Note that abstract states, state predicates and activation conditions can be inherited by subclasses and redefined or extended without compromising encapsulation. This property of ATOM is considered in more depth in Section 7.5.

Inter-object synchronization
Inter-object notification allows active objects to synchronize with state changes in other objects, expressed in terms of abstract states. State notification is supported by a protocol inherited by every active object. This protocol is executed by the object manager and supports both asynchronous and synchronous state notifications. In the asynchronous case, the object manager checks all notification requests and despatches notification events for those which evaluate to true. The object manager then proceeds with the normal execution of the object's threads: there is no blocking. In the synchronous case, however, the notifier and the object requesting notification must rendezvous

on the occurrence of the event: the notifier will block until the other object has dealt with the notification. This variant guarantees that the notified object will get the chance to invoke methods on the notifying object while it is still in the requested state.

Note that state notification is a general concept and can be instantiated with different interfaces and implementations. For example, it would be possible to introduce a specialized state notification protocol which defined the quality of service on the notification event (for example in terms of maximum latency).

7.3.3 Supporting reactive objects

Reactive objects are used to describe potentially reusable real-time coordination patterns in a distributed application. As mentioned earlier, they can be written in a more specialist notation such as Esterel. Steps must therefore be taken to integrate reactive objects with active objects. This is achieved by introducing reactive object *proxies* into the language. Crucially, the proxies are defined as active objects. When a new reactive object is instantiated, the external reactive object is created with its own support environment (to realize the synchrony hypothesis). In addition, a reactive object proxy is created as an instance of an active object. All communication with the reactive object is then through this proxy object. In implementation, however, the proxy will communicate directly to the external object using a private protocol. This mechanism is illustrated in Figure 7.4.

The proxy object has methods to attach to a particular input signal and output signal of the associated automaton. The methods are called `getInputSignal()` and `getOutputSignal()` which return an object of class `InputSignal` and `OutputSignal` respectively. The `InputSignal` and `OutputSignal` classes are active objects with abstract states `On`, `Off`, `Connected` and `Disconnected`. `InputSignal` classes have one method, called `Set()`, which sets the signal for the associated Esterel automaton. This also moves the abstract state to `On`. The object will remain in this abstract state

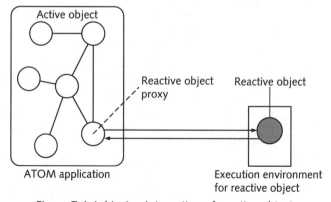

Figure 7.4 Achieving integration of reactive objects.

until the automaton consumes the signal; at this point the abstract state will revert to Off. OutputSignals have a method called IsItSet() which can be used to determine whether a particular output signal has been emitted. This is also indicated by the abstract state of the output signal being set to On. Thus, an interested party can either interrogate the OutputSignal object using IsItSet() or can use the state notification mechanism to be informed when the abstract state moves to On. The abstract states Connected and Disconnected are required to indicate whether particular signals are connected via a proxy object. A signal will remain Disconnected until a call of getInputSignal() or getOutputSignal() respectively. Note that the method Set() can only be called when the corresponding signal is Connected. This is specified as an activation condition associated with the method.

7.4 A prototype implementation

7.4.1 Use of Python

The model described above is sufficiently general to be incorporated into a variety of languages. For example, prototypes have been developed using both Smalltalk (Papathomas *et al.*, 1995a) and C++ (Papathomas *et al.*, 1995b). A more recent and complete version has been developed by Papathomas using the Python language (Papathomas, 1996). The following descriptions are based on the Python-based implementation.

Python is an interpreted and interactive object-oriented language (Watters *et al.*, 1996). It is often referred to as a scripting language and hence can be compared to languages such as Tcl, Perl, Scheme and Java. A complete description of Python is beyond the scope of this chapter. We therefore restrict the discussion to the features necessary to follow the examples in the next two sections.

Python supports a range of traditional imperative control structures including if/elif/else, while/else and for/else. The else clause on while and for statements allows the programmer to specify actions to be executed at the end of the loop if the loop terminates normally (that is, it is not terminated by a break or continue construct). More interestingly, Python supports the concepts of objects, classes and inheritance. Objects are created as instances of classes where classes are defined in terms of a set of methods defined on that class plus associated instance variables. One particular method, called __init__() acts as a constructor for the class; that is, this method is always called when a new instance is created of that class. Classes can inherit from one or more other classes: multiple inheritance is supported.

Note that Python supports two useful and pervasive data types, known as *tuples* and *dictionaries*. Tuples are variable length ordered lists of elements, where individual elements can be of different types. For example, the following are all valid tuples in Python:

```
('blair', 'gordon', 10)
()
('stefani',)
```

Note that a tuple with one element must have a comma in the Python syntax.

Dictionaries are mappings from Python objects to an arbitrary list of values. The Python objects are referred to as the keys of the dictionary. As an example, the following Python dictionary defines a mapping between people and email addresses:

```
contacts = {'blair' : 'gordon@comp.lancs.ac.uk',
            'stefani' : 'stefani@issy.cnet.fr' }
```

Dictionaries are implemented using hashing techniques, which leads to highly efficient implementation.

Further details of Python can be found in Watters *et al*. (1996).

7.4.2 Supporting active objects in Python

Defining and creating an active object

In order to create an active object, it is first necessary to define a class that inherits from the class ActiveObjectSupport. The ActiveObjectSupport class provides the functionality to support abstract states, state predicates, and activation and thread suspension conditions. Following this, it is necessary to call the function ActiveObject() with the newly defined class as parameter. This then creates an active object class that can be used to create the required instances. For example, consider the following outline of a buffer class (the body is not shown for simplicity):

```
class Buffer(ActiveObjectSupport)
# definition of the buffer class inserted here
```

Given this definition, an active object class can be created with the following step:

```
BoundedBufferClass = ActiveObject(Buffer)
```

Subsequently, a bounded buffer can be created of size 10 as follows:

```
aBoundedBuffer = BoundedBufferClass(10)
```

Alternatively, the previous two steps can be replaced by a single instruction (thus avoiding the additional variable):

```
aBoundedBuffer = ActiveObject(Buffer)(10)
```

Note that the definition of the Buffer class should define a number of variables representing the required behaviour of the active object. These variables are methods, states, state_predicates, conditions, pre_actions, post_actions, receipt_actions and activities. The first variable, methods, provides a list of the methods to be exported by the active object class. The roles of the remaining variables are described in more detail below.

Abstract states and state predicates

In the ATOM prototype in Python, abstract states are represented as tuples, where each tuple must contain at least one element; that is, a string representing the name of the abstract state. Further elements, if specified, can be of arbitrary type and are used to qualify a particular abstract state. They are interpreted by the state predicate for the abstract state.

Abstract states are defined by assigning a list of abstract state definitions to the variable states. For example, the following definition introduces abstract states empty and full for a bounded buffer:

```
states = ['empty', 'full']
```

In a similar manner, a state_predicates variable is used to specify the association between abstract states and state predicates (remember that a state predicate is required to evaluate each abstract state). In general, an object can have a set of state predicates where each state predicate is associated with a disjoint subset of the set of abstract states defined on that object. This is specified in the Python implementation by associating a Python dictionary with the state predicate variable. This dictionary should have one or more entries where each entry has a state predicate class as key and a list of associated abstract states as values. The object manager selects the appropriate class by examining the associated set of states.

A state predicate class must provide a method called evalState() that takes three arguments: an indication of self, the object to be tested and a tuple representing the abstract state. The method should then return true if the object is at the required abstract state. Users define their own state predicate classes by adhering to this protocol.

As an example, the following statement introduces two state predicate classes, is_empty and is_full, to determine whether a bounded buffer object is in abstract states empty or full respectively:

```
state_predicates = {is_empty : ['empty'], is_full : ['full']}
```

The corresponding state predicate classes would then be defined as follows:

```
class is_empty:
def evalState (self, object, state)
   return self.inbuffer == 0
```

```
class is_full:
def evalState (self, object, state)
   return self.inbuffer == self.lim
```

If no state predicate is specified explicitly for an abstract state, the object should have a method with the same name as the abstract state. This method should return true if the object is in this abstract state. Therefore, in the above example it would be possible to omit the `state_predicate` assignment and simply include the following methods:

```
def empty(self, state):
   return self.inbuffer == 0
def full(self, state):
   return self.inbuffer == self.lim
```

This is often the most convenient mechanism for introducing state predicates. However, the explicit notation can be useful either to rename functions in subclasses or to associate an arbitrary object with the state predicate functionality.

Activation conditions

As mentioned previously, activation conditions constrain the execution of methods or, more generally, object threads. To achieve this, they associate a condition with a particular method, expressed in terms of abstract states. This condition must be true in order to execute the associated method.

The variable `conditions` is used to introduce activation conditions. In particular, this variable should be set to a Python dictionary where the keys of this dictionary are a set of methods and the values are boolean functions which specify the required condition. Keys are normally defined as a single string or a list of strings. In the first case, the condition applies to the method with the name given by the string. In the second case, the condition applies to all the methods given in the list. The language also allows a function to be used as a key. In this case, the function must return a list of strings. This is useful to determine dynamically the list of methods to be associated with a given condition. These functions can be specified by the programmer. In addition, a number of predefined functions are provided, including `allMethods()`, which returns the list of all methods defined on an object. The boolean functions can be arbitrary functions defined over abstract states. They can use the predefined function `atState()` that takes as argument an abstract state and returns true or false depending on whether the object is at this abstract state. Note that boolean functions are written in lambda notation of the following form:

```
lambda o: <arbitrary expression over o>
```

The variable o is bound to the object under consideration in the activation condition.

We return to the bounded buffer example to illustrate the use of activation conditions. The activation conditions associated with the methods put() and get() are as follows:

```
conditions = {
    'put': (lambda o: not o.atState(('full',))),
    'get': (lambda o: not o.atState(('empty',)))
}
```

The first condition states that the method put() can only occur if the object is not at abstract state full (as determined by the atState() method). Similarly, the second condition states that get() can only occur if the object is not at abstract state empty.

Note that, for activation conditions to take effect, it is necessary to invoke methods indirectly via a special Python interface on the object. For example, the following is the correct way for a bounded buffer object to invoke its get() method (ensuring that the above activation condition is met):

```
self.interface.get()
```

It is also possible to invoke the method directly but this would bypass the ATOM mechanisms.

Thread suspension conditions

The ATOM prototype also enables the specification of thread suspension conditions. This facility enables threads to be suspended until a particular abstract state condition is reached. This is achieved using the suspendUntilState() method as defined in ActiveObjectSupport. This method takes as parameter an expression defined over abstract states and suspends the calling thread until this expression is true (other threads in the object can execute, however).

In its most simple form, suspendUntilState() can be used to suspend a thread until a particular abstract state is reached. For example, the following statement suspends the calling thread until the object reaches the abstract state initialized:

```
self.suspendUntilState (('initialised',))
```

Alternatively, it is possible to construct an arbitrary lambda expression as follows:

```
self.suspendUntilState      (lambda o: o.atState (('initialised',))
                             and not o.atState (('terminated',)))
```

This statement suspends the calling thread until the object is initialized and has not yet entered the terminated state.

The above statements are all based on the abstract state of the current object. It is also possible to suspend a thread based on the abstract states of other objects. To achieve this, it is necessary, however, to use the state notification mechanisms (described below).

State notification

As discussed above, there are two forms of state notification in the language, namely asynchronous and synchronous state notification. We consider each in turn below.

Asynchronous state notification

With asynchronous state notification, an object issues a request to be notified when a particular abstract state condition is reached in another object. This is achieved using the `notifyRequest()` method. This method takes as parameter an abstract state expression. This can take the same form as abstract state expressions as defined above: either an abstract state or an arbitrary lambda expression. The method also returns an object representing the potential notification event. This object can then be used to synchronize with the external event.

For example, consider the following statement:

```
reachedFrame = videoPlayer.notifyRequest (('endSequence1',))
```

This statement issues a request to the video player object to notify the calling object when the video player reaches the abstract state indicating that it is at the end of sequence 1. The calling object can then synchronize with this notification event by calling the `suspendUntil()` method. This method takes a notification event as parameter and blocks the calling thread until this event has been received. For example, the following call will block the calling thread until the appropriate frame has been reached in the video player:

```
self.suspendUntil (reachedFrame)
```

Note that, by default, the request is persistent in that notifications continue indefinitely every time the required condition is reached. This notification can, however, be stopped using the `quit()` method on the notification event as follows:

```
reachedFrame.quit()
```

It is also sometimes useful to suspend not just the calling thread but also all other concurrent activity in the object. This can be achieved using the `waitUntil()` method. For example, the following statement will block all activity in the calling object until the driver object has been initialized (indicated by a variable `is_initialised`):

```
self.waitUntil (is_initialised)
```

The calling object will then resume by executing the statement following the `waitUntil`.

Finally, the language enables an object to block awaiting a combination of events. This is achieved using either `suspendUntilComplexEvent()` or `waitUntilComplexEvent()`. As above, the former blocks the calling thread whereas the latter blocks the entire object. Both methods take two parameters. The first parameter defines the complex event in terms of a Python dictionary. This dictionary creates a mapping between a string key and an associated event notification variable. For example, the following would be a valid complex event:

```
boundaries = {'highWaterMark': reachedHigh, 'lowWaterMark':
reachedLow}
```

The second parameter then is one of the strings `Any` or `All`. In the former case, the event is reached when one of the associated events in the dictionary is notified. The string associated with the event is then returned as a result of the method call. In the latter case, notifications are required for all events.

As an example, the complex event defined above could be used as follows:

```
ev = self.suspendUntilComplexEvent (boundaries, 'Any')
```

This method will suspend the calling thread until notification is received indicating that either the high water mark or the low water mark has been reached. The precise event will be indicated by returning (in variable `ev`) either `highWaterMark` or `lowWaterMark`.

Synchronous state notification
The language also provides support for synchronous state notification where a form of rendezvous is created between the notifying and the notified objects. This can be required, for example, when the notified object would like to respond to an event and also be confident that the notifying object is still in the same abstract state For example, in a safety critical application, it could be important to issue a close down method to a device if it has reached a dangerous state; in this case, it is important that no further activity is carried out. This is not possible with asynchronous notification, as the notifying object will continue executing concurrently once the notification has been sent.

Synchronous notification is achieved using the `syncBlock()` method. This method takes as parameter a Python dictionary describing the required synchronization. More specifically, the dictionary contains one entry with key `'with'` which specifies a list of objects and associated state notification conditions (this list is itself a dictionary), and a second key `'do'` which specifies the required actions to be carried out during the rendezvous. The method will then achieve synchronization when all the conditions on all the objects are true. At this point, the actions are carried out on the objects as specified in the 'do' part of the dictionary. All objects are blocked until these actions complete.

We illustrate this further by an example:

```
syncBlock (
    {'with' : {'private' : (valve, ('overheating') ) },
     'do'    : "private.shutdown ()"
    }
)
```

This statement achieves synchronization between the calling object and the object represented by valve when the abstract state overheating is reached on valve. At this point a shutdown() method is invoked on valve using a private interface active only during the synchronization. All other activity is blocked on valve. In this way, the programmer can ensure that a shutdown() method is executed as soon as the overheating condition is detected.

7.4.3 Additional features

The ATOM prototype also includes a number of additional features as enhancements to the basic model defined above. These features are described in turn below.

Specifying the level of concurrency
The language enables the programmer to specify the level of concurrency within an object. A new thread is always created to service an incoming invocation. In addition to this, however, it is possible to specify that a number of threads should be created at object instantiation time. This is achieved by assigning a list of methods to a variable called activities. The effect of this statement is to create a running thread for each method in the list (by default an object is created without any running threads).

As an example, the following statement will create one new thread at object instantiation time, executing the method called qosMonitor():

```
activities = ['qosMonitor']
```

Further threads will then be created as method invocations are received. All the threads are subject to the thread suspension conditions as described above.

Additional styles of method invocation
By default, method invocation is carried out using the normal Python method call syntax. As an example, the following Python statement invokes a method reset() on an object called camera:

```
camera.reset ()
```

The effect of this call is, however, to block the entire object until the method has been executed (compare a blocking remote procedure call). This is too restrictive for many applications. The ATOM prototype therefore introduces two additional methods called aSend() and sendAndSuspend().

The aSend() method takes as parameter a dictionary representing the message to be sent. The fields of this dictionary are summarized in Table 7.1.

The effect of the aSend() method is to send the message representing the invocation to the object specified in the target field. This object will then execute the desired method and (optionally) return the result to the object specified in the replyTo field. This field can be set to any object representing a reply destination. If this field is null, a reply is not sent. The programmer can also explicitly create an object of class reply to represent the incoming reply message. This name of this object would be specified in the replyTo field of the message. To receive a reply objects can call the getResult method defined on this class. This method can, however, only be accepted if the reply object is in abstract state ready (indicating that a reply has been received), otherwise the calling thread will be suspended. This blocking can be avoided, however, by using state notification to indicate when the reply object moves to abstract state ready. This facility is similar to future messages or Cboxes, although more flexible, as reply objects are first-class objects which can be passed in messages.

The sendAndSuspend() method also sends a message of the same form as specified in Table 7.1. This method, however, blocks the calling thread until a reply is received. Other threads in the object can continue execution (this is in contrast to remote procedure calls which block the entire object). The method returns when the following conditions are met: (1) a reply has been received, (2) there is no other concurrent thread execution within the object, and (3) the normal activation conditions are met.

Synchronization actions

The programmer can specify a number of actions to be executed when certain events occur. For example, the programmer can specify pre-actions and post-actions to be executed before and after method execution respectively. In addition, actions can be associated with the events of thread suspension, thread

Table 7.1 Fields of the message dictionary

Field	Status	Interpretation
'target'	compulsory	The object to which the message is sent
'key'	compulsory	The name of the method to be called
'args'	compulsory	Arguments for the method
'replyTo'	optional	The destination for any reply messages
'condition'	optional	Associates an activation condition with the message

Table 7.2 Synchronization actions

Action	Interpretation
pre_actions	Actions carried out before a particular method is executed
post_actions	Actions carried out after a particular method is executed
suspend_actions	Actions carried out when a thread is suspended
resume_actions	Actions carried out when a thread is resumed
receipt_actions	Actions carried out on the receipt of messages

resumption and message reception. The complete list of such actions are summarized in Table 7.2.

Synchronization actions are specified in ATOM prototype by introducing dictionaries with the names `pre_actions`, `post_actions`, `suspend_actions`, `resume_actions` and `receipt_actions` respectively. The keys in these dictionaries are lists of method names (or functions that evaluate to such lists); the values are then the actions associated with the execution of these methods. For example, the following statement associates appropriate post-actions with the execution of `getChopsticks` and `release Chopsticks()` methods as part of a solution to the dining philosophers problem:

```
post_actions = {
'getChopsticks' : "eating = 1",
'releaseChopsticks' : "eating = 0"
}
```

Note that synchronization actions could also be embedded directly in the code of methods. However, this approach has the advantage of introducing a separation of concerns, thus avoiding unnecessary complexity in an object's methods.

Dynamic creation of abstract states and activation conditions

Finally, the ATOM prototype allows the dynamic creation of abstract states (together with associated state predicates) and also additional activation conditions (perhaps defined in terms of the new abstract states).

New abstract states can be established by invoking the `newPred()` method on an active object. This method has the following parameters:

- a state predicate class, and
- a list of associated abstract states.

As before, the task of the state predicate class is to determine whether the object is in a particular abstract state. The ATOM prototype also offers a `newPredObject()` method which is identical to `newPred()` except that the first parameter is an object rather than a class.

These facilities can be very useful to introduce state predicates that are required for a particular context (which may not be anticipated when the object is created). For example, Papathomas (1996) provides an example whereby a new abstract state called ('contains', n) is created on a buffer object. This abstract state is then used to implement rate control on the production of buffer items.

Similarly, new activation conditions are introduced by calling the addCondition() method. This method takes as parameter a dictionary specifying the new activation condition and returns an object representing the condition. This object can later be used with the method removeCondition() to dynamically delete the condition. In general, the addCondition() facility can be used to dynamically add new constraints to objects.

7.5 Some simple examples

This section provides some simple examples illustrating the capabilities of the ATOM prototype based on Python. More specifically, the examples illustrate how the object model can support local synchronization and global coordination (as discussed in Section 7.2). The following section also provides a larger multimedia example illustrating the real-time features of the model. A more comprehensive set of examples can be found in Papathomas (1996).

7.5.1 Supporting local synchronization

The bounded buffer example revisited
We firstly consider how the ATOM prototype can support the inheritance of local synchronization constraints and patterns. To illustrate this, we revisit the two examples presented in Section 7.2.1, namely the provision of a get2() method on a bounded buffer and the definition of a lock mix-in class for a bounded buffer. In both cases, we assume the definition of a bounded buffer class as given below:

```
class Buffer (ActiveObjectSupport):
states = ['empty', 'full']
methods = ['put', 'get']
conditions = {
    'put':      (lambda o: not o.atState(('full',)),),
    'get':      (lambda o: not o.atState(('empty',)),)
}

# state predicate functions

def empty(self,state):
    return self.inbuffer == 0
```

```
def full(self,state):
    return self.inbuffer == self.lim

# methods

def __init__(self,size):
    inbuffer = 0
    self.lim = size
    self.store = []

def put(self,data):
    self.store.append(data)
    self.inbuffer = self.inbuffer + 1

def get(self):
    self.inbuffer = self.inbuffer - 1
    d = self.store[0]; del self.store[0]
    return d
```

This shows the definition of a bounded buffer class, `Buffer`, inheriting from `ActiveObjectSupport`. This inherited class provides all the facilities defined on active objects as defined in Section 7.4.2. The abstract states, state predicates and activation conditions are identical to those introduced in Section 7.4.2 and hence do not require further commentary.

We now reconsider the two examples in turn and show how the ATOM prototype can overcome the inheritance anomalies described in Section 7.2.

Overcoming the state partitioning anomaly
A solution to the first problem is given below:

```
class g2Buffer(Buffer):
states = ['twoLeft']
methods = ['get2']
conditions = {'get2' : (lambda o: o.atState(('twoLeft',)),) }

# state predicate functions

def twoLeft(self, state):
return self.inbuffer >= 2

# methods

def get2(self):
return (self.get(), self.get())
```

This program creates a new class, `g2Buffer`, as a specialization of `Buffer`. This new class features a new abstract state, `twoLeft`, and an associated state predicate function. The class also defines a new method, `get2()`, which returns the two oldest items in the bounded buffer. An additional activation condition also ensures that this method can only be executed when the object is at state twoLeft. All other abstract states, state predicates and methods are inherited from the Buffer class.

Crucially, in this solution, it is not necessary to modify the definition of the Buffer class to accommodate the new behaviour. There are two reasons for this. Firstly, there is a separation of concerns between abstract states (together with their associated state predicates) and the behaviour of objects. This enables synchronization constraints to be specified independently of the object's behaviour. Secondly, and crucially, new abstract states can coexist and, indeed, overlap with the previous abstract states. This allows the composition of new constraints with existing, predefined constraints. The net effect is that the new behaviour can be achieved by simply providing the additional behaviour and constraints in terms of the new method, abstract state/state predicate and activation condition. Thus, the ATOM prototype can overcome the state partitioning anomaly. (Note that in ATOM it is possible to have conflicts between new activation conditions and inherited activation conditions. This problem is, however, less severe than the inheritance anomalies because conflicts are in terms of published interfaces (as opposed to embedded code). Conflicts at this level can thus be interpreted as a design problem rather than an implementation problem.)

Overcoming the state modification anomaly
We now consider the definition of a Lock mix-in class in the ATOM prototype. A definition of this class is given below:

```
class Lock:
states = ['locked']
methods = ['lock', 'unlock']
conditions = {
    lambda o: o.allMethodsExcept(['unlock']):
            (lambda o: not o.atState(('locked',)),)
    }

# instance variables
isLocked = 0

# state predicate functions

def locked(self,state):
    return self.isLocked

# methods

def lock(self):
    self.isLocked = 1

def unlock(self):
    self.isLocked = 0
```

This class defines an abstract state `locked`. This is implemented in terms of a variable called `islocked` which is set to true (1) and false (0) by the `lock()` and `unlock()` methods respectively. The activation condition then specifies that no methods except `unlock()` can be accepted if the object is in abstract state `locked`. This relies on the predefined function `allMethodsExcept()` to return the set of all methods except `unlock()`.

The `Lock` mix-in can now be used to create a new bounded buffer class with the additional capabilities to lock the buffer object. This would be created as follows:

```
class LockedBuffer(Lock, Buffer):
def __init__(self, size):
    Buffer.__init__(self, size)
```

Again, it is not necessary in this solution to change the behaviour of the original bounded buffer class. This can also be explained in terms of the separation offered by abstract states and also the ability for new abstract states to supplement existing states. More specifically, the new activation condition provides added constraints over those already defined in the class `Buffer`. Thus, the ATOM prototype can also overcome the state modification anomaly.

7.5.2 Supporting global coordination

This section now considers how the ATOM prototype can support global coordination. More specifically, we illustrate that the language supports the separate specification of global coordination patterns, hence encouraging reuse. The example we consider is the classical dining philosophers problem. In this problem, a number of philosophers sit around a circular table (see Figure 7.5). The philosophers alternate between eating and thinking. To eat, they must possess two chopsticks (those on the left and right of the philosopher). They are therefore competing with other philosophers for these chopsticks. The solution must ensure fair access to chopsticks and also avoid deadlock.

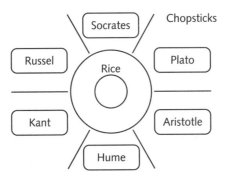

Figure 7.5 The dining philosophers problem.

The behaviour of each philosopher is described by the `Philosopher` class as given below:

```
class Philosopher(ActiveObjectSupport):
states = ['alive','eating','thinking','hungry','hasChopsticks']
methods = ['die', 'getHungry', 'eat','getChopsticks',
           'releaseChopsticks']

activities = ['cycle']

post_actions = {
   'getChopsticks':
         ["self.isEating = 1", "self.obtainedChopsticks = 1" ],
   'releaseChopsticks':
           ["self.isEating = 0","self.obtainedChopsticks = 0"]
}

# instance variables

isAlive = 1
isEating = 0
isHungry = 0
obtainedChopsticks = 0

# state predicate functions

def alive(self,state):              return self.isAlive
def eating(self,state):             return self.isEating
def thinking(self,state):           return self.isAlive and not
                                    self.isEating
def hungry(self,state):             return self.isHungry
def hasChopsticks(self,state):      return self.obtainedChopsticks

# methods

def __init__(self,str):
   self.name = str

def die(self):
   self.isAlive = 0

def getHungry(self,n):
   self.isHungry = n

def eat(self):
   self.isHungry = self.isHungry - 1

def getChopsticks(self):
   time.sleep(3)
   print "philo: %s: get first chopstick" % self.name,
   time.sleep(3)
```

```
      print "philo: %s: get second chopstick" % self.name,

  def releaseChopsticks(self):
    print "philo: %s: released chopsticks\n" % self.name,

  def cycle(self):
    while self.atState(('alive',)):
        self.suspendUntilState(lambda o: o.atState(('hungry',)))
        self.sendAndSuspend(('target': self.interface,
                             'key': 'getChopsticks', 'args': ))
        while self.atState(('hungry',)):
            self.sendAndSuspend(('target': self.interface,
                                 'key': 'eat', 'args': ))
        self.sendAndSuspend(('target': self.interface,
                             'key': 'releaseChopsticks',
                             'args':))
```

This class has five abstract states, namely `alive`, `eating`, `thinking`, `hungry` and `hasChopsticks`, supported by a set of associated state predicate functions. These state predicate functions simply return the values of the corresponding instance variables as shown. These instance variables are set at appropriate points in the code. For example, the `isAlive` variable is set to true at initialization and remains true until the `die()` method is called. More interestingly, `isEating` and `obtainedChopsticks` are both set to the correct values in `post_actions` for the `getChopsticks()` and `releaseChopsticks()` methods. As stated earlier, the use of such post actions creates a separation of concerns between the synchronization code and the main body of methods.

The main behaviour of the object is given in the `cycle()` method. This method name is assigned to the activities variable. Hence, as stated in Section 7.4.3, this method will be assigned a new thread and set running on instantiation of the object. The method loops while the philosopher is in abstract state `alive`; that is, until the `die()` method is called, executing the following behaviour:

1. wait until the philosopher is in abstract state `hungry`,
2. obtain the two chopsticks,
3. eat until the philosopher is no longer in abstract state `hungry`,
4. release the two chopsticks.

Crucially, the `Philosopher` class does not contain any code pertaining to the global synchronization of philosophers. Rather, this is encapsulated within a `PhiloCoordinator` object as given below (for simplicity, this object is defined for two philosophers, but the code can clearly generalize to other numbers):

```
class PhiloCoordinator(ActiveObjectSupport):
activities = ['coordinate']
def __init__(self,p1,p2):
    self.ph1 = p1
    self.ph2 = p2

def coordinate(self):
    self.p1.newPredObject(self, ['myTurn'])
    self.p1.addCondition(
            {['getChopsticks'], lambda o: o.atState(('myTurn',))}
    )

    self.p2.newPredObject(self.interface, ['myTurn'])
    self.p2.addCondition(
            {['getChopsticks'], lambda o: o.atState(('myTurn',))}
    )

def evalState(self,object,state):
    self.reply(1)
    eats = object.interface.notifyRequest (('eating',))
    self.waitUntil(eats)
```

This coordinator object introduces a new abstract state, myTurn, on each
philosopher. This is achieved by calling the newPredObject() method on
the corresponding objects. The coordinator object also introduces a new
activation condition on each philosopher based on myTurn (in this case by
calling addCondition()). This new activation condition ensures that
getChopsticks() can only be executed when the object is at abstract state
myTurn. To check this, the object manager must call the associated state
predicate for myTurn. In this case, the state predicate is given by the
coordinator's evalState() method. This method uses a predefined
method, called reply(), which returns a result to the caller immediately but
allows the method to continue execution. In this case, the method returns true
(1), indicating that the object is in abstract state myTurn. This allows
getChopsticks() to proceed. The method, however, then uses
waitUntil() to ensure that the object will not accept any more methods
until the philosopher is at state eating. This ensures that the actions of
acquiring chopsticks are executed atomically with respect to other
philosophers.

This example illustrates how the ATOM prototype can support the
separate specification of global coordination patterns. By isolating
coordination, it is possible to modify or replace the global coordination
algorithm without affecting the behaviour of individual philosophers. For
example, by modifying the evalState function, it would be possible to
introduce a more sophisticated scheduling policy for controlling access to
chopsticks.

7.6 A larger multimedia example

7.6.1 The problem

We now consider a larger multimedia example based on the decompression and presentation of a continuous media stream. This example illustrates the ability to separate out, and hence potentially reuse, *real-time* local and global coordination patterns. The example consists of a producer and consumer of video data connected by a continuous media stream. The producer transmits compressed data (for example in MPEG format). The role of the consumer is then to decompress the data and present the decompressed images on an appropriate display. The problem is illustrated in Figure 7.6.

The crucial factor in this example is to maintain a particular frame rate as specified by the required throughput and jitter parameters. To achieve this, we adopt an algorithm whereby the next frame is presented if it is received by an appropriate deadline (as derived from the QoS parameters), otherwise the previous frame is displayed. For the purposes of this example, we assume a required frame rate of one frame every 100 ms with an acceptable jitter of 10 ms.

For the sake of simplicity, we focus on the behaviour of the consumer end and assume that the continuous media stream upcalls the consumer when a full buffer has been received.

Note that an earlier version of this problem appeared in Papathomas *et al.* (1995b).

7.6.2 A generic class framework

Before presenting the solution to this problem, we first introduce some generic classes to represent multimedia objects. These classes can be compared to the class framework presented by Gibbs and Tzichritzis (1994) for multimedia programming. The generic classes are referred to as activities and real-time activities respectively and are intended to be reusable across a range of multimedia problems. We consider each in turn below.

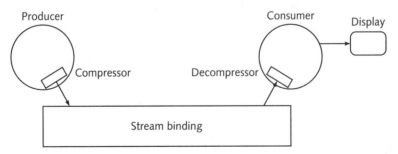

Figure 7.6 The multimedia example.

Activities

Activities are abstract classes (mix-ins) which can be inherited to obtain an interface to control the behaviour of multimedia objects. By inheriting an activity class, the program also reuses the local synchronization patterns contained in the class. Activities provide a public interface consisting of the methods start(), stop(), pause(), resume() and stepAction(). In addition, they support the following abstract states: idle, running, paused and stopped. They also have a set of activation conditions controlling the acceptance of methods in particular abstract states (see below). The behaviour of instances of this class is summarized in Figure 7.7.

When created, objects are in state idle and can only accept the start() method. They then move to the abstract state running. In this state, they can accept the methods stepAction(), pause() or stop(), either remaining in the running state or moving to the states paused and stopped respectively. The stepAction() method is used to represent a single step of an ongoing activity (assuming activities can be represented as a series of discrete steps). This is primarily used to represent continuous media where, for example, a step may represent the arrival of a video frame or audio packet. This method should be redefined in subclasses to provide the required behaviour associated with the processing of an item of continuous media data. From the paused state, the object can accept a resume() method, returning the object to the running state, or can accept a stop() method, moving the object to the stopped state. In the stopped state, the object cannot accept any more methods. Moving to this state triggers some internal actions to release resources associated with the multimedia object.

The full definition for the activity class is given below:

```
class Activity(ActiveObjectSupport):
states = ['idle','running','paused','stopped']
methods = ['start','stop','pause','resume','stepAction']
activities = ['cycle']
conditions = {
    'start':         (lambda o: o.atState(('idle',)),),
    'stepAction':    (lambda o: o.atState(('running',)),)
}

# instance variables

step =            0
hasStarted =      0
hasPaused =       0
hasStopped =      0

# state predicate functions

def idle(self,state):     return not self.hasStarted
def running(self,state):  return self.hasStarted
```

```
                              and not self.hasPaused
                              and not self.hasStopped
def paused(self,state):       return self.hasPaused
def stopped(self,state):      return self.hasStopped

# methods

def start(self):
   self.hasStarted = 1

def stop():
   self.hasStopped = 1

def pause(self):
   self.hasPaused = 1

def resume(self):
   self.hasPaused = 0

def stepAction(self):
   pass          # actual behaviour to be specified in subclasses

def cycle(self):
   while 1:
         self.suspendUntilState (
               lambda o: o.atState(('running',)) or
               o.atState(('stopped',))
         )
         if self.atState(('stopped',)):
               break
         else:
               self.sendAndSuspend(
                     {'target': self.interface,
                      'key':    'stepAction',
                      'args':   ()
                     }
               )
```

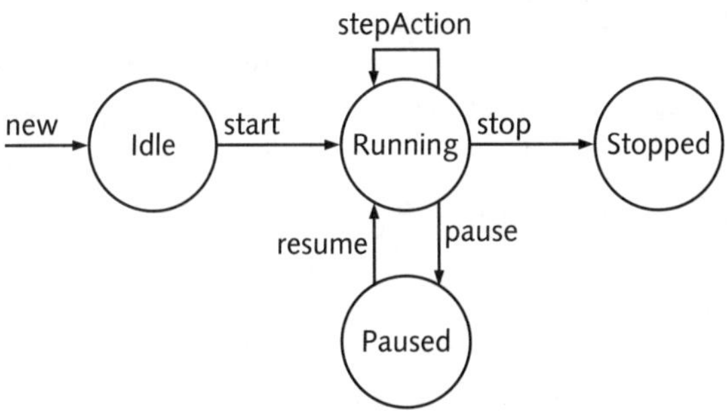

Figure 7.7 State diagram representing the activity abstract class.

Note that the object starts by executing the `cycle()` method (as specified in the `activities` variable). This method loops, blocking until the object is at state `stopped` or `running`. If the object is at state `stopped`, the method returns immediately, otherwise the object uses `sendAndSuspend()` to call the `stepAction()` method. It is assumed that the actual behaviour of this method is provided in subclasses. The remainder of the code is straightforward and does not require any further explanation.

Real-time activities

Real-time activities provide support for the real-time execution of activities. The real-time requirements are specified in terms of the instance variables `period`, `jitter` and `tolerance`, representing the period of time between each step action, the acceptable jitter over this period and also a small tolerance to compensate for the delay between calling `start()` or `resume()` and the actual time that `stepAction()` is called.

The definition of the real-time activity class, `RTactivity`, is given below:

```
class RTactivity(Activity):
methods = ['setPeriod','getPeriod','errorHandler']
activities = ['cycle']

# instance variables

period = 40           # ms
jitter = 5            # ms
delta = 0.5           # ms
# Note that these can be considered as default values and can be
# re-defined in subclasses (e.g. see Timer below)

# methods

def setPeriod(self,np):
    self.period = np

def getPeriod(self):
    return self.period
# Note that the class should also provide methods to set/ get the
# jitter and delta parameters; these are not shown for simplicity

def errorHandler(self,step):
    self.nextime = time.time() + 2*self.period
    return 0

def start(self):
    self.step = 0
    Activity.start(self)
    self.nextime = time.time() + self.delta
```

```
def resume(self):
   Activity.resume(self)
   self.nextime = time.time() + self.delta

def cycle(self):
   while not self.atState(('stopped',)):
           self.step = self.step + 1
           self.suspendUntilState(lambda o: o.atState(('running',)))
           now = time.time()
           then = self.nextime
           self.nextime = self.nextime + self.period
           self.step = self.step +1
           if now > then + self.jitter:
                   action = self.errorHandler(self.step)
                   if action == 0:
                           # skip
                           pass
                   else:
                           self.stepAction()
           else:
                   t = then - now
                   if t > 0:
                           self.sleep(t)
                   self.stepAction()
```

The RTactivity class is defined as a subclass of Activity and hence inherits all the methods, abstract states, state predicates and activation conditions from that class. The RTactivity class, however, introduces the new methods setPeriod() and getPeriod() to establish and retrieve the value for the period of the real-time activity respectively. The new class also introduces a method, called errorHandler(), which is called if the real-time requirements are violated; that is, if a step is not executed by the previous execution time plus the period plus the acceptable jitter. This method should return 1 if the action is to continue, otherwise 0 to abort the action. The definition above provides a default error handler which effectively skips the current period; this can be overridden by the programmer in a subclass. The RTactivity class also redefines the methods start(), resume() and activity(). The rationale for these changes is to ensure that the stepAction() method should be called periodically according to the real-time requirements. As stated above, a null stepAction() method is defined in the Activity class. It is expected that subclasses of RTactivity will redefine this method, thus providing their own step action.

The start() and resume() methods call the corresponding methods defined in the Activity class but also make a small modification to the nextime variable to compensate for the delay in reacting to these method calls (see above). In addition, the cycle() method ensures that the `stepAction()` method is called with the required period. The method loops continuously until the object reaches abstract state `stopped`. Within the loop, the method waits until the object is `running` using `suspendUntilState()` then carries out the following steps:

- establish the current time (`now`) and the start of the next period (`then`), and also calculate the start of the next period (`nextime`),
- decide whether a real-time violation has occurred (signified by the current time being greater than the required start of the period),
- if a violation has occurred, decide whether to continue execution or abort by calling `errorHandler()`,
- if there is no violation, calculate the time to wait and, if this is still positive, sleep for the required time and then call `stepAction()`.

Note that this class assumes that the `time()` and `sleep()` operations provided by the underlying operating system function with the required accuracy.

7.6.3 Applying this framework

We now consider the solution to the decompression problem in the ATOM prototype. This solution exploits the `RTactivity` classes as defined above.

The overall design
The overall object configuration for the consumer is shown in Figure 7.8. The decompressor object, `dc`, receives a buffer item from the continuous media stream, decompresses this buffer and then makes this available for consumption by the display object, `display`. More specifically, we assume that the stream upcalls the consumer when a frame arrives. The handler associated with this upcall then presents the buffer to the decompressor object and starts the decompression process. The display object then displays the decompressed buffer on the appropriate video display. The `synchDisplay` object, together with the reactive object, `qosMonitor`, maintains the required

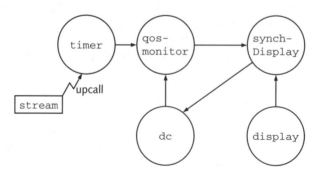

Figure 7.8 Overview of the solution.

synchronization between the decompressor and the display. The timer provides a reference time signal indicating when frames should be presented (derived from a set of QoS parameters).

We consider each object in more detail below.

The decompressor object

The decompressor object is an active object of class `Decompressor`. The object provides three methods, namely `setBuffer()`, `start()` and `getBuffer()`. In addition, the object supports the abstract states `idle`, `ready`, `active` and `finished`. The overall behaviour of the object is depicted in Figure 7.9.

The object is initially in state `idle`. At this state, the decompressor can accept a `setBuffer()` method call providing a new compressed data item for processing. The object then moves to the `ready` state. At this point, the `start()` method can be called to initiate the decompression process. The object now enters the `active` state and will remain in this state until decompression is completed. The object will then spontaneously enter the `finished` state (as indicated by the τ symbol). At this point, the object can accept a call to `getBuffer()` to provide access to the decompressed buffer. The decompressor object then returns to the `idle` state to restart the cycle.

The definition of the `Decompressor` object is given below:

```
class Decompressor(ActiveObjectSupport)
states = ['idle', 'ready', 'active', 'finished']
methods = ['setBuffer','start','getBuffer']
pre_actions = {'setBuffer':["self.isIdle=0", "self.isReady=1"],
              'start': ["self.isReady=0", "self.isActive=1"],
              'setBuffer':["self.isFinished=0", "self.isIdle=1"]}
conditions = {
   'start' :          (lambda o: o.atState(('ready',))),
   'getBuffer' :      (lambda o: o.atState(('finished',))),
   'setBuffer' :      (lambda o: o.atState(('idle',)))
}
```

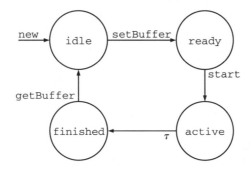

Figure 7.9 Overall behaviour of the decompressor class.

```
# instance variables (as required by the state predicates)

isIdle = 1              # true
isActive = 0            # false
isReady = 0             # false
isFinished = 0          # false

# state predicate functions

def idle(self,state):      return self.isIdle
def active(self,state):    return self.isActive
def ready(self,state):     return self.isReady
def finished(self,state):  return self.isFinished

# methods

def setBuffer(self):
    # main body not given

def start(self):
    # main body not given

def getBuffer(self):
    # main body not given
```

`Pre_actions` are used in this class definition to manipulate abstract states. This has the advantage of simplifying the corresponding methods. Note also that we omit the implementation details of the three methods for simplicity. In addition, further instance variables will be required to represent the local state of the object. We also assume that the end of the decompression process changes the variable `self.isActive` to false and `self.isFinished` to true.

The display object
The display object is more straightforward. The object provides one method, called `display()`, to display a given frame on the appropriate video device. The object also supports the abstract states `active` and `idle` to serialize calls to display. More specifically, the object is in the `active` state when it is in the process of displaying a video frame, otherwise it is in the `idle` state. The object can only accept the `display()` method when the object is in the `idle` state.

The definition of the `Display` object is given below:

```
class Display(ActiveObjectSupport)
states = ['active', 'idle']
methods = ['display']
pre_actions = {'display': ["self.isIdle=0", "self.isActive=1"]}
post_actions = {'display': ["self.isActive=0", "self.isIdle=1"]}
```

```
conditions = {
   'display' :          (lambda o: o.atState(('idle',)),)
}

# instance variables (as required by the state predicates)

isActive = 0          # false
isIdle = 1            # true

# state predicate functions

def active(self,state):    return self.isActive
def idle(self,state):      return self.isIdle

# methods

def display(self):
   # main body not given
```

This class uses pre_actions and post_actions to manipulate the instance variables representing abstract states. In addition, again for simplicity, we omit the implementation details of the display() method.

The timer object

The role of the timer object is to generate the signal deadline, indicating the real-time deadline for the next frame of video to be presented. This object is implemented as a subclass of RTactivity as defined above. The pre_actions and post_actions defined on the stepAction() method ensure that the abstract state alarm is on for a short period. This is then detected by the main program which then generates the deadline signal (see below).

The definition of the timer object is given below:

```
class Timer(RTactivity)
states = ['alarm']
pre_actions = {'stepAction': "self.alarmON=1"}
post_actions = {'stepAction': "self.alarmON=0"}

# instance variables (as required by the state predicate)

alarmON = 0           # false

# state predicate functions

def alarm(self,state):     return self.alarmON

# methods

def __init__ (self, qos1, qos2, qos3):
   # establish required QoS parameters
   self.period = qos1
```

```
        self.jitter = qos2
        self.delta = qos3

    def errorHandler(self):
        # exception handler code not given

    def stepAction(self):
        # delay for a few milliseconds
```

In this case, we omit the body of the exception handler for simplicity. The constructor method, __init__(), is used in this case to initialize the real-time activity object.

The reactive object

The reactive object has the generic task of monitoring a periodic event and reporting if it happens by the desired time. An arrival of the signal target indicates the occurrence of an event. Similarly, an arrival of the signal deadline marks the desired timing for this event. The reactive object will then generate a signal qos_ok if the operation is completed by the arrival of deadline, otherwise it will generate a qos_violation signal.

The code for the reactive object is given below (in Esterel):

```
module QoSMonitor
input       deadline, target;
output      qos_ok, qos_indication;

var ok: integer in
    loop
            ok := 0;
            do
                    await target; ok := 1;
            upto deadline;

            present target then
                    ok := 1;
            end;

            if ok = 1 then
                    emit qos_ok
            else
                    emit qos_violation
            end
    end
end
```

This reactive object loops awaiting the arrival of the next target signal. This can be interrupted by the arrival of the deadline signal using the do-upto clause (see Chapter 5). The reactive object checks to ensure the target signal is actually present and then emits either qos_ok or qos_violation accordingly.

In the context of this problem, the reactive object is used to monitor the performance of the stream and decompression process and to indicate the late availability of frames. The target signal is generated when a frame is ready for display and the deadline signal is provided by the timer object (see below). The qos_ok and qos_violation information is then used by the synchDisplay object (again, see below).

The synchDisplay *object*

The synchDisplay object has the crucial role of synchronizing the decompressor and the display object and implementing the strategy to deal with the late availability of frames.

The code for the corresponding SynchDisplay class is given below:

```
class SynchDisplay(ActiveObjectSupport)
methods = ['setSignals','start']

# methods

def __init__ (self, disp, decomp)
    self.display = disp
    self.dc = decomp
    self.myFrame = NONE

def setSignals (self, sigOk, sigViolation):
    self.isOk = sigOk.notifyRequest(('ON',))
    self.isViolation = sigViolation.notifyRequest(('ON',))

def start(self):
    while self.atState(('active',)):
        res = self.waitUntilComplexEvent (({'ok': self.isOk,
                                    'violation: self.isViolation,}
                                    ), "Any")
        if res = 'ok':
            dc.getBuffer(self.myFrame)
        display.display(self.myFrame)
```

The __init__() method establishes the correct (initial) values at object creation time for the variables display, dc and myFrame. The setSignals() method must also be called before use to initialize the values for the active objects representing the qosOk and qosViolation signals respectively. The main behaviour of the object is then contained in the start() method. This method loops while the object is active, awaiting an event notification and taking the appropriate action. More specifically, the method uses waitUntilComplexEvent() to block until one of two notifications is received (isOk or isViolation), indicating whether the next frame has been decompressed in time or not. If the decompression has been successful (isOk), the object will get the buffer from the decompressor and present this buffer to the display object. Otherwise, the object will display the previous value of myFrame.

The main program

The main program has the task of creating the appropriate objects, establishing the appropriate interconnections and then initializing the different activities. Before considering this program, we first introduce a class, called signalEachState. This class is extensively used by the main program to provide a link between abstract states and the generation of signals. The code for this class is given below:

```
class SignalEachState(ActiveObjectSupport)
activities = ['monitor']

# methods

def __init__ (self, obj, state, sig)
   self.targetObject = obj
   self.targetState = state
   self.signal = sig

def monitor(self):
   event = self.targetObject.notifyRequest(self.targetState)
   while 1:
         self.suspendUntil(self.event)
         self.signal.set()
```

As can be seen, this class suspends itself until a designated object is at a designated abstract state. The class then emits the corresponding signal.

The main program is then as follows:

```
# first, create the required set of objects ...

dc =              ActiveObject(Decompressor)()
display =         ActiveObject(Display)()
synchDisplay =    ActiveObject(SynchDisplay)(display, dc)
timer =           ActiveObject(Timer)(100,10,1) # qos parameters
qosMonitor =      ActiveObject(QoSMonitor)

# and then create links to the reactive object (proxy)

target = qosMonitor.getInputSignal('target')
deadline = qosMonitor.getInputSignal('deadline')

qosOk = qosMonitor.getOutputSignal('opOk')
qosViolation = qosMonitor.getOutputSignal('opViolation')
```

```
# create two objects to monitor the required abstract states

SignalEachState(dc, ('finished',), target)
SignalEachState(timer, ('alarm',), deadline)

# finally, initialise the various objects

synchDisplay.setSignals(qosOk, qosViolation)
synchDisplay.start()
qosMonitor.start()
streamControl.start()
timer.start()
```

The first task of this program is to create the required objects: the decompressor, the display, the synchDisplay object, the timer and the reactive object. Note that the class QoSMonitor is of class ReactiveObject (a subclass of ActiveObject). This class is automatically constructed from the Esterel program of the same name. The program then uses getInputSignal() and getOutputSignal() to establish active objects representing the set of signals associated with the reactive object (see Section 7.3.3). We assume that the strings 'target', 'deadline', 'opOk', 'opViolation' are used to denote the various signals uniquely. Following this, the program creates two instances of signalEachState corresponding to the signals target and deadline respectively. The first instance generates the signal target each time the decompressor object reaches abstract state finished; that is, when the decompression process is completed and a frame is available for display. The second instance generates the signal deadline each time the timer object reaches abstract state alarm: it marks the end of each period.

Finally, the main program initializes the various objects. Firstly, the setSignals() method is called on the synchDisplay object to inform the object of the correct signals to monitor. This synchDisplay() object and the active object are then set running by invoking their respective start() methods. Following this, the stream object is started (we assume the control interface on the stream active object is called streamControl). This will then result in periodic upcalls of the methods setBuffer() and start() on the decompressor object as compressed frames are delivered by the stream. The precise timings of the method executions will, of course, be governed by the associated abstract states and state predicates (see above). Finally, the start() method is called on the timer object. This will then result in a call of the start() method defined on its superclass, RTactivity, leading to the periodic invocation of the stepAction() method.

7.6.4 Analysis

This final example illustrates the use of the ATOM prototype for the programming of multimedia applications. More specifically, the example illustrates how the language can be used to specify the required real-time behaviour of such examples. Crucially, the language supports the creation of separate and hence reusable classes representing local and global real-time coordination patterns. For example, the RTactivity class encapsulates the necessary local coordination pattern for the timer object. This class (and the associated Activity class) are clearly reusable across a wide range of multimedia applications. In addition, the SynchDisplay class encapsulates the particular strategy for real-time global coordination of the decompressor and display devices. By separating out this behaviour, the particular strategy for coordination can easily be changed. In addition, the strategy can be reused for other devices. The reactive object class provides a further example of a re-usable global coordination pattern. The QoSMonitor can clearly be used in a variety of situations where a given operation should be completed by a given deadline. This class also illustrates the use of Esterel to specify particular real-time behaviours and demonstrates how the language can be used to develop hybrid applications consisting of both asynchronous and synchronous objects (as required by the programming model of Chapter 4).

7.7 Summary

This chapter has introduced an approach to concurrent object-oriented programming based on the concepts in the programming model of Chapter 4. The resultant concurrent object model, ATOM, is based on the general concepts of active objects, abstract states, state predicates, state notifications, and activation and thread suspension conditions. Reactive objects are incorporated into the language as a particular subclass of active objects. The chapter has also introduced a prototype implementation of ATOM as an extension to Python.

ATOM can be viewed as one particular specialization based on the general framework offered by the programming model. ATOM adds value to the programming model by providing linguistic support for multiple inheritance and also offering particular features for both local and global synchronization (including real-time synchronization). Crucially, the use of abstract states enables the reuse of such coordination patterns across a range of applications (overcoming, for example, the inheritance anomalies identified by Matsuoka *et al* (1993)). The capabilities of ATOM have been demonstrated through a number of examples, including a multimedia example featuring local and global real-time synchronization patterns.

PART 3
Building distributed multimedia systems

8 Engineering support for multimedia

8.1 Introduction

Part 3 of the book examines support for multimedia in open distributed processing from an engineering and technology viewpoint. This first chapter considers an engineering model for multimedia based on the RM-ODP Engineering Model. This model is technology independent in that the engineering concepts can be realized using a number of different technology components (operating systems, protocols and so on). The latter chapters in this part then consider a specific technology approach based on microkernel operating system technology.

Again, our engineering model should be viewed as a framework for engineering support (see corresponding discussion on the programming model in Section 4.1). To develop a standard platform, it is necessary to populate this framework with specific interfaces and notations for the concepts defined in the engineering model.

The chapter is structured as follows. Section 8.2 describes in detail the RM-ODP Engineering Model. The mapping from the Computational Model to the Engineering Model is also highlighted. Section 8.3 then introduces a number of extensions to the RM-ODP Engineering Model to accommodate multimedia. These refinements are presented under the headings of support for explicit binding, support for QoS management and support for reactive objects. Following this, Section 8.4 discusses a number of available technologies to populate this engineering model and Section 8.5 presents a summary of the chapter.

8.2 The existing RM-ODP Engineering Model

8.2.1 General approach

As with the Computational Model, the RM-ODP Engineering Model adopts an object-oriented approach. However, there is a crucial difference between the two models: the Computational Model describes an idealized model of objects and interaction and does not consider distribution; in contrast, the

Engineering Model explicitly addresses how objects are configured in a distributed environment and how interaction is to be achieved. More specifically, the Computational Model recognizes that objects are potentially distributed (in that bindings are asynchronous) while the Engineering Model identifies the precise allocation of objects to nodes and address spaces. The Engineering Model also identifies the resources required to support the configuration.

Note that the Computational Model does identify *constraints* on the distribution in terms of the environmental contract. Such constraints are, however, declarative. The Engineering Model must identify how such declarative constraints are to be met. For example, the Computational Model might identify a QoS requirement for operational bindings such that invocations have a maximum latency of 1 ms. The Engineering Model would then denote that this requires a configuration where the objects share the same address space.

We now describe the main features of the Engineering Model as defined in RM-ODP. This description expands on the short introduction to the Engineering Model included in Section 2.2.2. We firstly describe the resource model used to describe the configuration of objects in terms of system resources and then describe the communication model supporting interaction between objects. As will be seen, both models are defined in terms of an abstract framework and hence retain independence of underlying technology. Finally, we describe the mapping between the Computational Model and the Engineering Model in more detail. Note that, to distinguish objects in the Engineering Model from objects in the Computational Model, we will refer to the former as *engineering objects* throughout this section.

8.2.2 The resource model

To enable object configurations to be described, the Engineering Model must provide an abstract means of specifying system resources. The model achieves this goal by defining a nested set of abstractions, namely nodes, capsules and clusters. We look at each in turn below.

- *Nodes*
  A node is a representation of a complete computing resource featuring processing and storage capabilities together with a number of devices (including communication devices). A distributed system can then be thought of as a collection of nodes interconnected by a (potentially complex) communications infrastructure; each node represents a location in space within the distributed system. Nodes can vary in their precise configuration. For example, a node could be a single-processor workstation or a tightly coupled multiprocessor. The defining feature of a node is that all its resources are managed together in an integrated manner. This management is provided in RM-ODP by the *nucleus*, which offers an abstraction over the underlying operating system. Each node will

therefore have precisely one nucleus. The nucleus provides an *open* interface to the underlying operating system resources. This includes access to communication facilities and processing/storage resources. The interface also supports the creation of (unique) *interface references* for new interfaces and also enables access to low-level resources such as clocks.

- *Capsules*
  Each node can contain a number of capsules where each capsule provides an encapsulation of the resources necessary to perform a computation. In particular, a capsule owns a share of the node's processing and storage capabilities. Capsules can be likened to the traditional operating system concept of a process or execution environment. They therefore provide the unit of protection in the system and also the smallest unit of independent failure. In the Engineering Model, capsules can either have a single flow of control (as in a Unix process) or can be multi-threaded. This level of detail is determined by a particular implementation of an RM-ODP conformant platform.

- *Clusters*
  A particular capsule can contain one or more objects. Normally, a capsule would contain multiple objects as the overhead of having a capsule per object would usually be too great (both in terms of the resources required and the cost of crossing capsule boundaries for all object interactions). Objects within a capsule must be grouped into clusters. Therefore a particular capsule will contain one or more clusters, with each cluster containing one or more objects. Clusters provide the smallest unit of management for objects in terms of checkpointing, recovery, reactivation or migration. Again, to provide this for every object would be prohibitively expensive, especially if objects have fine granularity.

The relationship between nodes, capsules and clusters is shown in Figure 8.1. This diagram also shows the nucleus managing the resources associated with a node.

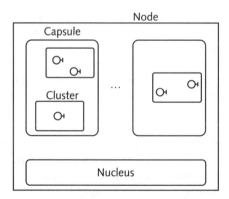

Figure 8.1 The relationship between nodes, capsules and clusters.

Nodes, capsules, clusters and objects are all subject to management. This management is provided by the various management functions introduced in Section 2.2.2. Each aspect of management is considered in turn below:

- *Node management*

  Node management is encapsulated in the nucleus and is accessed through a node management interface on the nucleus. This interface supports the creation of capsules within that node from an appropriate capsule template. The interface also supports the creation of channels: communication paths between objects (as discussed below). Finally, the node management function allows the creation of threads within capsules and also provides access to low-level devices such as clocks.

- *Capsule management*

  Capsule management is encapsulated within *capsule managers* with one capsule manager existing for each capsule. These managers support the creation of clusters within their capsule and also enable checkpointing or deactivation of complete capsules. The latter two activities involve checkpointing or deactivating all clusters within the capsule. Hence it is necessary for the capsule manager to communicate with all cluster managers under its control (see below). The capsule manager also enables the deletion of the capsule; again, this will mean the deletion of all clusters within the capsule.

- *Cluster management*

  Cluster management is encapsulated within *cluster managers*, with one cluster manager per cluster. These managers support the checkpointing, recovery, migration, deactivation and reactivation of complete clusters. These, in turn, will involve actions on the individual objects within a cluster. This involves accessing object management interfaces directly (see below). The cluster manager operations might fail if individual objects do not support the appropriate action. Finally, the cluster manager supports the deletion of clusters which will delete all objects within that cluster.

- *Object management*

  The object management function is assumed to be encapsulated within individual objects, with such objects offering an object management interface. This interface is accessed directly by cluster managers, as discussed above. For cluster management to be carried out, the object management interface must support a minimum of checkpointing and deletion. This is sufficient to support the various cluster management functions described above.

This overall management structure is depicted in Figure 8.2.

The various management functions are also potentially under the control of higher level managers implementing coordination functions (again, see Section 2.2.2). For example, migration managers can coordinate the migration of a cluster between capsules on potentially different nodes. This manager will

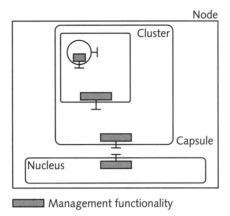

Management functionality

Figure 8.2 Management structure for system resources.

encapsulate the policy for when the cluster should migrate and where it should be relocated. It will then rely on the underlying capsule and cluster managers to offer the appropriate functionality to achieve the migration.

8.2.3 The communications model

The Engineering Model also provides an abstract means of representing the communications infrastructure. This centres on the concept of a *channel* as an abstraction over the communications infrastructure necessary to support object interaction. The concept of a channel is illustrated in Figure 8.3.

Channels are actually composite objects which rely on a number of more specific engineering objects to provide their overall functionality. The detailed structure of a channel is shown in Figure 8.4.

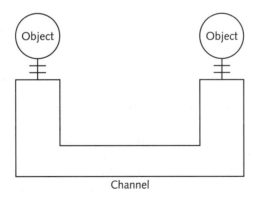

Channel

Figure 8.3 The concept of a channel.

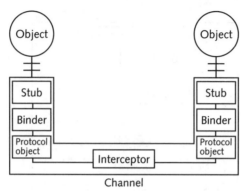

Channel

Figure 8.4 The detailed structure of a channel.

The various components of a channel are discussed in some detail below:

- *Stubs*
  Stubs are engineering objects which provide an interface between the host
  object and the underlying communications infrastructure. As such, they
  are a generalization of the concept of stubs as found in remote procedure
  call protocols. In the engineering model, stubs are the only parts of a
  channel which are aware of the nature of the interaction with the host
  object (in terms of the type of information conveyed). Based on this
  knowledge, they are responsible for marshalling and unmarshalling the
  required information into appropriate buffers and interfacing with the
  other objects in the channel to achieve physical communication.
- *Binders*
  Binders are responsible for creating and subsequently maintaining the
  integrity of a channel. To perform this task, they must be aware of the status
  of both the channel and all objects connected to a channel. In particular,
  they must detect failures in the underlying infrastructure and also failure or
  relocation of objects. They will also take actions to overcome these problems.
  They are therefore responsible for many of the distribution transparencies
  offered by an RM-ODP platform. Note that, to implement transparencies,
  they may interact with specific engineering objects implementing
  transparency functions. For example, binders will often interact with the
  relocator object (see Section 2.2.2) to rediscover the location of an object
  after a reconfiguration (using the interface reference as the key).
- *Protocol objects*
  Protocol objects encapsulate the underlying communications protocols
  required to perform the given task. They therefore provide an abstraction
  over protocol services such as sockets or remote procedure calls. Protocol
  objects also may rely on other services to perform address translation as
  required by the protocol stack. Protocol objects will interact with the
  corresponding protocol objects in other objects in the channel to effect
  communication. They may exploit information about the particular object

configuration to optimize the costs of communication. For example, objects within the same cluster can communicate directly in the knowledge that they will remain colocated with each other. Similarly, objects in the same capsule can exploit shared memory to improve the latency and reliability of communication. Similar optimizations can also be made between objects on the same node (depending on the underlying operating system facilities).

- *Interceptors*
  Interceptors are engineering objects which enable objects in different management domains to interact. As such, they are a generalization of gateways or bridges. Objects within a particular management domain will share the same protocol families and will have the same policies, for example for security. They can therefore communicate directly. Objects in different management domains cannot, however, rely on this level of homogeneity. It is therefore necessary to use interceptors in this case to effect a communication path. Interceptors perform two distinct roles. Firstly, they perform checks to enforce policies on permitted interactions between domains. Secondly, they perform the necessary transformation to ensure that communication can take place across domains (for example by translating between different protocol formats).

There is considerable flexibility within the overall structure defined above. Firstly, by exploiting the object-oriented framework, it is possible to provide a range of different implementations of each of the components described above. For example, different stubs can be provided for operational, stream or signal interfaces and for different language bindings; different binders can offer varying levels of distribution transparency; different protocol objects can offer different styles of communication (perhaps reflecting signal, stream or operational interaction) or different qualities of service; finally, different interceptors can implement different protocol translations. A particular channel can then be constructed by selecting an appropriate configuration of objects and then contacting the correct stub, binder, protocol object and interceptor factories to create the components in the configuration.

Secondly, the individual objects can be private to a particular channel or shared across channels. The latter would imply that the various channels are *multiplexed* through the one object.

Thirdly, a range of different binding services can be supported. For example, services can be offered for signal, stream and operational interactions. Similarly, both *point-to-point* and *multiparty* communications can be constructed.

An example of a multiparty channel is shown in Figure 8.5.

The one invariant that must be maintained in a channel structure is that a particular path from object to object must consist of either

- stub – binder – protocol object – interceptor – protocol object – binder – stub, or
- stub – binder – protocol object – protocol object – binder – stub.

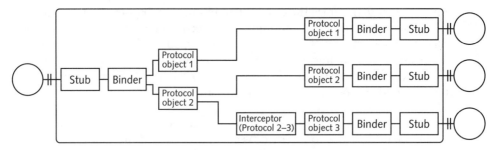

Figure 8.5 A multiparty channel.

(As will be seen later, we weaken the above constraint in our extensions for multimedia.)

Finally, note that there is some provision for management of channels in the Engineering Model. In particular, all the above engineering objects can offer management interfaces providing access to management information or enabling the control of the particular functionality. RM-ODP does not, however, specify particular management functions to exploit this capability. This feature will be revisited in Section 8.3.2 when we consider quality of service management.

8.2.4 Mapping from the Computational Model

There is a strong correspondence between a description of a system in the Computational Model and the corresponding description in the Engineering Model in RM-ODP. Firstly, computational objects are represented by basic engineering objects in the Engineering Model. Normally, there will be a one-to-one correspondence between a computational object and a basic engineering object. However, it is possible for one computational object to map on to a set of basic engineering objects. Secondly, bindings are represented by appropriate channels. The one key difference (as discussed above) is that the Engineering Model makes distribution explicit and shows the configuration of objects and the required communications channels. The Engineering Model may also feature additional engineering objects to implement a transparency or a particular management function.

Example *A client–server interaction*
To illustrate this mapping, consider a simple (computational)
configuration of a client object interacting with a server object through an
operational binding. The computational configuration is shown in
Figure 8.6(a). The corresponding engineering configuration is shown in
Figure 8.6(b).

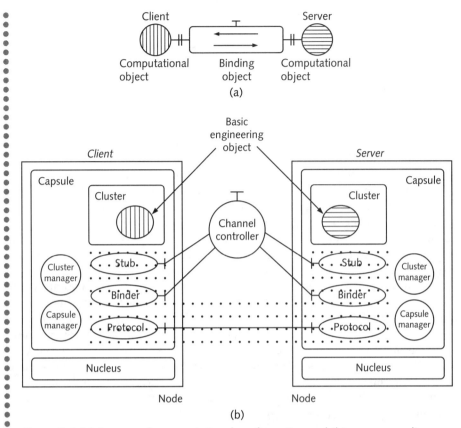

Figure 8.6 (a) An example computational configuration and (b) a corresponding engineering configuration.

8.3 Extensions for multimedia

This section now describes an engineering model, based on the RM-ODP Engineering Model, but with extensions to support multimedia. As will become apparent, there is a close mapping between the extensions required for the engineering model and the extensions already proposed for our programming model. In particular, it is necessary to provide direct support for explicit binding, for QoS management of objects (including bindings) and for reactive objects. We consider each of these areas in turn below. Firstly, however, it is necessary to revisit the concept of an object in the RM-ODP Engineering Model.

8.3.1 What is an engineering object?

The Engineering Model as defined in the RM-ODP standard is rather vague in its description of the underlying object model. The standard merely identifies a set of objects, such as basic engineering objects, capsules and channels, but does not discuss the meaning of an engineering object or specify the means of interaction between such objects. In our extended engineering model, we are more specific and state that *engineering objects are simply objects* and share precisely the same programming model as described in Chapter 4 in terms of objects, interfaces, types, factories and the various styles of interaction (signal, stream and operational). An engineering specification can thus be seen as a refinement of a computational specification but sharing the same object model.

The distinction between the two specifications is then one of perspective. The computational specification considers a system from the application perspective and describes a set of interacting application-level objects. In contrast, the engineering specification describes the system in terms of engineering components which are grounded in actual computer and communications resources. The engineering specification then defines a virtual machine and the computational specification is refined towards this virtual machine. The one crucial difference, however, is that the engineering specification must identify the placement of objects in terms of nodes, capsules and clusters.

It is important to realize that the boundary between the two viewpoints is fluid, depending on the level of the virtual machine offered by the system's infrastructure. Some systems will provide a rich and abstract set of engineering objects whereas others will provide a more minimal set of objects leaving more responsibility to the applications developer. For example, some systems will provide implementations of bindings that directly support the establishment of $m : n$ conference calls; other systems will only provide $1 : n$ multicast services and hence the application will need to take responsibility for building $m : n$ communications from the $1 : n$ service.

Example *An analogy with object-oriented programming*
A comparison can be drawn with programming in an object-oriented language such as Smalltalk. The programmer starts with a high-level object-oriented design and refines this towards realizable components. At one point in the refinement, the objects in the design can be supported directly by the object classes supported by the class library. This corresponds to an underlying virtual machine and hence marks the boundary between the Computational and Engineering Viewpoints. In languages such as Smalltalk, the programmer can also extend the class library with higher level classes. This corresponds to raising the level of the virtual machine and hence moves the boundary between the two viewpoints.

To summarize, our programming model defines an object-oriented model for the design of distributed applications, whereas the engineering model defines a virtual machine to support such applications. Designs proceed through a series of refinements until they can be implemented in terms of the virtual machine. As with object-oriented programming languages, refinement and eventual implementation is seamless, sharing the same object model.

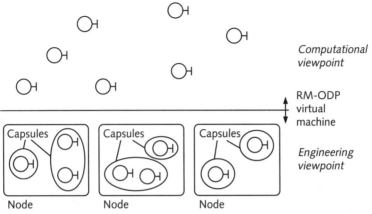

Figure 8.7 The Computational and Engineering Viewpoints.

This overall approach is illustrated in Figure 8.7. This diagram shows the same object model being used in the Computational and Engineering Viewpoints. The one distinction is that the Engineering Viewpoint considers the mapping of objects to nodes and capsules (for simplicity, clusters are not shown). The diagram also emphasizes the fluidity of the boundary between the virtual machine and the application.

8.3.2 Support for explicit binding

We now describe our extended engineering model to support explicit binding. Before examining the details of the proposed approach, it is helpful to consider the requirements in terms of engineering support for bindings. (These requirements will then be revisited at the end of the section to demonstrate the completeness of the approach.)

Requirements

The most general requirement for our refined engineering model is to support the concept of explicit binding as defined in the extended programming model (see Section 4.3.3). The programming model defines a flexible approach to explicit binding where bindings are simply another class of object and binding creation is the same as object instantiation. Binding objects can then encapsulate arbitrary behaviour so long as they perform the required task of communicating information from one or more senders to one or more receivers.

A set of more specific requirements are identified below:

- to retain the inherent flexibility and generality of bindings as defined in the programming model,
- to support client-initiated bindings, server-initiated bindings or the more general case of third-party bindings, and
- to enable implicit bindings to be established.

The proposed approach to meeting these requirements is given below.

The proposed approach

We firstly describe a generalized model of bindings and then consider an abstract protocol to support this model.

The generalized binding model

The proposed approach relies on a more general model of communication than the one proposed in the RM-ODP Engineering Model. Recall that RM-ODP defines channels as an abstraction over communications resources. Furthermore, channels are constructed using stubs, binders, protocol objects and optional interceptors. Bindings at the computational level are then realized in terms of channels in the Engineering Model. In contrast, our approach is based on a *recursive model* of binding objects. In this approach, binding objects can be constructed using arbitrary object configurations which might contain further binding objects. The internal binding objects might themselves contain further binding objects, with this recursion ending with primitive binding objects offered by the engineering infrastructure.

The one constraint on binding objects is that they must contain stubs (as defined in RM-ODP). The role of a stub is to support an interface which is connected to the binding; to do so, it may have to provide some functionality, such as marshalling/unmarshalling or more general encoding/decoding. Stubs must be provided for all interfaces connected to the binding, although one stub can be shared across multiple interfaces. We relax the constraint in RM-ODP that bindings must contain binder objects. Some bindings will support binder objects, for example implementing transparencies. However, other classes of binding will not. Furthermore, other objects can be included within a binding. For example, filter objects can be inserted into a flow of continuous media data. Finally, there is no need for protocol objects in the revised engineering model as the concept of bindings applies in both the programming and engineering models; this removes the need for a separate concept at the engineering level. Protocol objects can thus be reinterpreted as primitive binding objects supported by the infrastructure. Overall, this view is in sympathy with the overall object model defined in Section 8.2.2 in supporting a more seamless refinement from computational to engineering specifications.

This view of a recursive binding is illustrated in Figure 8.8. This figure shows a producer object and a consumer object linked together with a stream binding object. A producer stub and a consumer stub perform the necessary mappings between the binding and the producer and consumer interfaces. In this case, this will be a lightweight function supporting minimal marshalling and unmarshalling. The stream binding itself is a binding object which contains compression and decompression objects. Again, stubs are required to support the bound interfaces. Finally, the compression and decompression objects are bound together by a further nested binding. In this example, this binding is

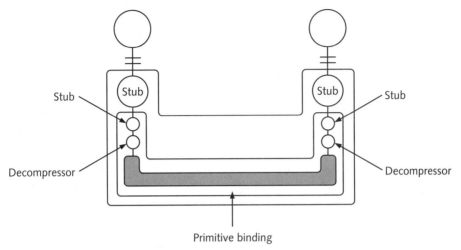

Primitive binding

Figure 8.8 A recursive model of bindings.

primitive and is supported directly by the infrastructure. For example, this binding could be a rate-based transport protocol (see Section 8.4.1).

The abstract binding protocol
In order to support the creation of explicit bindings, we further propose an *abstract binding protocol*. This protocol relies on the existence of one or more *binding factories* which create particular classes of binding object. These are similar to other factories apart from the fact that they generate distributed objects (objects that span multiple nodes); in contrast, most other objects are created on a single site. To support this process, it is likely (but not required) that binding factories will themselves be distributed objects with representatives on each node. The protocol also assumes the existence of a localBind operation to bind a participating interface to the binding. Without this operation, it would be necessary to create a binding to link the participating object to the binding; this process would then become recursive, requiring an infinite number of bindings. The concept of a localBind is illustrated in Figure 8.9.

The localBind operation must be offered by all interfaces through a special *link interface*. The operation must also be supported by the nucleus (as defined

Local binding between adjacent interfaces

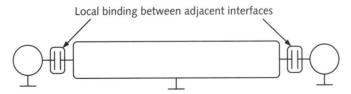

Figure 8.9 The localBind operation.

above) and hence by the underlying operating system. The precise semantics of localBind are as follows:

- information (signals, flow items or operations) delivered to the binding should be instantaneously visible to all participants in the (local) bindings, and
- information cannot be lost or corrupted by a local binding.

This corresponds closely to the semantics of shared memory. Although the engineering model does not prescribe a particular implementation, this would normally imply that local bindings are contained within the same cluster.

In order to describe the abstract protocol, we introduce the following notations:

- C is the object that requests the creation of the binding,
- A_j are objects whose interfaces AI_j are to participate in the binding,
- B is the binding object of the appropriate type created to support the binding,
- BF is the binding factory responsible for instantiating B, and
- BI_j is the interface in B adjacent to AI_j (that is to be locally bound to AI_j).

The binding protocol is then as follows:

Step 1: Requesting a binding object
C selects an appropriate binding factory, BF, and then asks BF to create a binding object (see Figure 8.10(a)). This is achieved by invoking a new operation on BF. The parameters to this operation will include the set of interfaces to be bound, AI_j. The parameters may also include a statement of QoS annotations or other management related items (the precise details will vary from factory to factory).

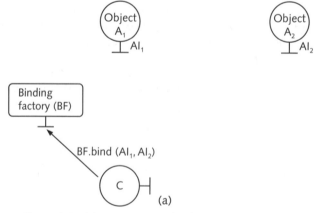

Figure 8.10 (a) Requesting a binding object – *continues.*

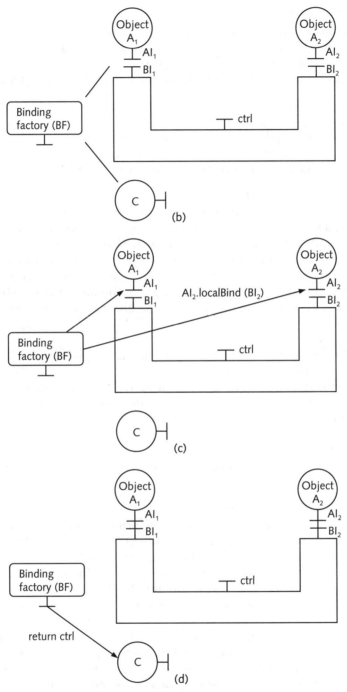

Figure 8.10 – continued (b) creating the binding object; (c) creating the local bindings; (d) returning the result.

Step 2: Creating the binding object
BF instantiates a binding object *B* with the right (i.e. type conformant) binding interfaces BI_j in the right nodes (see Figure 8.10(b)). This step may fail for a number of reasons, including the factory not being able to produce interfaces of the correct type or a failure to achieve the required quality of service.

Step 3: Linking adjacent interfaces
If the previous step has been successful, the binding factory, *B*, links each pair of adjacent interfaces (AI_j, BI_j) by upcalling `localBind()` on each interface AI_j quoting BI_j as parameter (see Figure 8.10(c)).

Step 4: Returning the result
If all the previous steps have been successful, the binding factory, *BF*, returns an interface reference corresponding to the control interface of *B* (see Figure 8.10(d)); otherwise, it returns an exception. (Note that the engineering model does not prescribe the nature of this control interface. It is likely, however, that this interface will provide a local view of the binding. With this approach, other objects joining the binding would also obtain their own local interfaces, thus offering a degree of autonomy and local control.)

Step 2 is by far the most complex step in the above process and the precise details will vary from factory to factory.

In the simplest case, a binding will be primitive and will hence be supported directly by the engineering infrastructure. In this case, the following protocol is carried out for Step 2:

Step 2.1: Locating the interfaces
It is firstly necessary to resolve the precise location of the set of interfaces AI_j.

Step 2.2: Creating the binding
The second step then involves creating the primitive binding. More specifically, this involves creating a stub object of the appropriate type for each interface associated with the binding, and then the associated communications resources. Note that there are no objects associated with the communications resources for primitive bindings (by definition) and hence the implementation details are closed.

Alternatively, a binding may be composite and hence contain further objects and nested bindings. In this case, it is be necessary to invoke factories to create the full set of encapsulated objects (including the nested binding objects). It is then necessary to link the various objects together into the required configuration. This could involve the creation of further bindings or, depending on the configuration, local bindings may be employed.

The requirements revisited

The generic binding protocol presented above is carefully designed to meet the set of requirements identified at the start of this section. The main benefit of the binding protocol in addressing the requirements is the clear separation between (1) the generic binding protocol and (2) the specific and arbitrary functionality encapsulated in various binding factories. This provides a highly flexible and general architecture. For example, factories can offer signal, stream or operational services and such services can either be point-to-point or multiparty. Similarly, they can encapsulate arbitrary behaviour, for example in terms of compression and decompression, filtering, real-time synchronization or QoS management. In addition, the generic binding protocol can be reused across the full range of binding services. In order to develop specific personalities, it is then simply a matter of constructing a particular set of factories able to create a particular set of binding services. For example, a CORBA personality could be provided by constructing binding factories encapsulating the CORBA interoperability protocols (see Section 2.3.3).

The approach is more general than the approach described in RM-ODP. In particular, the binding architecture can model channels as defined in the RM-ODP Engineering Model, but can also represent other structures. In particular, it is possible to construct arbitrary configurations of objects (including binding objects) where any of the objects can be composite. This provides the level of generality required of multimedia communications.

The same approach can also be used at both the computational and engineering levels. This means that the applications designer has the freedom to develop arbitrary bindings featuring arbitrary configurations of objects. Alternatively, the applications designer can rely on (potentially complex) bindings provided by the underlying virtual machine.

The protocol defined above is also designed to support third-party binding. In particular, the initiating object (C in the protocol above) can be any object in the distributed environment. Client-initiated or server-initiated bindings are then special cases where C is associated with the client or server object respectively.

Finally, implicit binding can be supported by the model. This is achieved by offering default binding factories which are invoked by the infrastructure either when an interface is imported or, more dynamically, on the first invocation of this interface. Note that the use of an implicit binding mechanism would be required for the CORBA personality in the example above.

8.3.3 Support for QoS management

The second extension is to support QoS management of objects. Again, it is helpful to identify the precise requirements before introducing the proposed extensions to the engineering model.

Requirements

In terms of QoS management, the main role of the engineering model is to support the creation of an abstract machine with explicit support for both static and dynamic QoS management functions. In terms of static QoS management, this corresponds to the use of appropriate QoS management functions (negotiation, admission control and resource reservation) in order to meet a given QoS contract. Note that this QoS contract may be given by the computational specification. Alternatively, the QoS contract may be generated in the engineering viewpoint itself. For example, consider the creation of a stream binding with a given QoS. This might, in turn, involve the creation of an underlying primitive binding object (such as representing an ATM connection) with a related QoS contract.

In terms of dynamic QoS management, the engineering model must support the creation of interfaces for QoS monitoring, policing, maintenance and renegotiation. Note, however, that these functions can also feature within other viewpoints. For example, application developers can provide their own strategy for QoS monitoring and renegotiation as part of the computational specification. Similarly, primitive bindings can encapsulate a particular strategy for policing or maintenance (corresponding to the technology viewpoint). The role of the engineering model, however, is, as stated above, the creation of a virtual machine with appropriate QoS management capabilities to then support the development of applications.

It is also important to stress that QoS management for bindings must be considered to be *end-to-end*. Hence, it is not sufficient only to consider communications resources. It is also important to consider end systems resources as encapsulated in the engineering concepts of nodes, capsules and clusters. In particular, QoS constraints can apply equally to devices, threads and (virtual) memory.

Finally, QoS management can apply to *all* objects. Most significantly, QoS management will be carried out on binding objects. It is also important to remember that QoS management will be required for other classes of object as well, for example on a multimedia storage server.

To summarize, we identify the following requirements for QoS management within the engineering model:

- support for static QoS management functions in interpreting (computational or engineering) QoS specifications,
- support for dynamic QoS management functions on engineering objects,
- support for end-to-end QoS management, and
- the above should apply to all objects (bindings and others).

The precise details of the proposed approach are now considered below.

The proposed approach

In presenting the proposed approach, we first consider the issue of resource allocation and multiplexing before then considering the provision of static and dynamic QoS management functions. We conclude the section with an example.

Resource allocation and multiplexing
In order to support QoS management, it is first necessary to be able to allocate end system resources with a given quality of service. In order to support this, we assume that each capsule has an interface supporting the allocation of threads and virtual memory with appropriate QoS parameters. The precise details of the interfaces are not, however, prescribed, to allow flexibility in developing conformant platforms. For example, thread creation based on deadlines or fixed priorities should both be valid implementations. Whatever approach is adopted, each capsule then has access to its own set of virtual resources which it can allocate based on local policies (such as using split level resource management as discussed in Chapter 10).

It is then necessary to extend the node management function to deal with multiplexing these virtual resources associated with capsules on to the physical resources associated with a particular machine. Again, the precise details of this function are not prescribed; for example, a rate monotonic scheduler or an earliest deadline first scheduler would be an appropriate management policy for real-time threads. This overall approach is summarized in Figure 8.11.

All other aspects of QoS management can then be constructed on top of this basic infrastructure. In particular, it is interesting to note that the equivalent resource management strategies for communications resources are encapsulated within bindings. The end system need only provide the localBind functionality with the required semantics in terms of atomicity and failure (see above). We now look at the other aspects of QoS structure in terms of both static and dynamic QoS management.

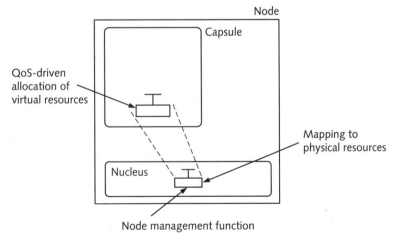

Figure 8.11 QoS-driven resource management.

Static QoS management

Static QoS management is assumed to be encapsulated within factories, with the level of QoS management varying from factory to factory. Some factories will offer no QoS management while others will offer comprehensive QoS management offering absolute guarantees. The precise support in terms of static QoS management is advertised as part of the interface for each factory (for example, as properties associated with the service offer). More specifically, factories can contain one or more of the following static QoS management functions:

- the QoS negotiation function,
- the QoS admission control function, and
- the QoS resource reservation function.

The QoS negotiation function assumes that the engineering infrastructure has already determined the engineering objects required to support the corresponding computational activity. This could be in terms of basic engineering objects or a configuration of engineering objects and channels. The negotiation function also assumes the existence of a QoS specification which is created by translating the computational specification into a corresponding specification in terms of engineering requirements. This specification is then negotiated between all participants in the engineering infrastructure to determine the precise resources required by each participant in the configuration. For example, for end-to-end binding, this might involve a producer thread, a channel implementing a stream interaction and a consumer thread. Note that, in order to support such end-to-end activity, it is assumed that the nucleus supports the creation of end system resources with real-time guarantees (such as real-time threads). This negotiation step will succeed if a suitable partitioning can be accepted by all participants.

The negotiation function can be supplemented by admission control tests or by resource reservation strategies depending on the requirements in terms of QoS guarantees. Admission control determines whether an overall resource allocation should proceed by examining the resource requirements of the request against the current state of the system. Resource reservation ensures that resources are dedicated to an activity to enable QoS constraints to be met. Different resources require different combinations of negotiation, admission control and resource reservation to ensure a given QoS requirement. This issue is revisited in Chapters 10 and 11 when different implementations of the static QoS manager are considered. As an added feature, some static QoS managers could also offer transactional allocation or reservation of resources: the negotiation will succeed if all resources all available, otherwise the allocation will abort and the resources will be returned to the system.

Dynamic QoS management

In contrast, *dynamic QoS management* at the engineering level is achieved by introducing *managed objects* in the engineering configuration (a similar

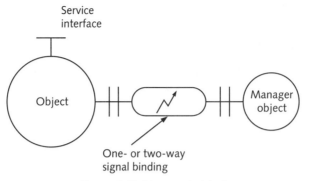

Figure 8.12 Managed objects.

approach can also be adopted at the computational level). The precise configuration can be generated automatically by factory objects depending on the stated QoS management requirements in the environmental contract. A managed object is simply an object whose activities are monitored and potentially controlled by an associated manager object. Such manager objects rely on an appropriate management interface supporting a management protocol between the object and the manager. The precise details of this interface and associated protocol will vary from object class to object class. The concept of a managed object is illustrated in Figure 8.12. Managed objects can implement one or more of the following QoS management functions:

- the QoS monitoring function,
- the QoS policing function,
- the QoS maintenance function, and
- the QoS renegotiation function.

The simplest style of manager will simply offer a monitoring capability. In particular, the manager will observe the occurrence of events in the object being managed and determine whether the object is maintaining the desired level of quality of service. If violations are detected, the manager will simply raise an exception. More sophisticated managers can carry out renegotiation on QoS violations. This effectively completes the control loop illustrated in Figure 8.12. There is an assumption, however, that the underlying management interface supports renegotiation operations (for example to reduce the frame rate).

QoS policing is similar to monitoring. The distinction is that whereas monitoring observes the behaviour of the underlying object, policing observes the behaviour of the user of the object. This is necessary to ensure that the user does not break its part of the contract by, for example, swamping the object with too many signals. QoS policing can be achieved using managed objects simply by having access to signals generated by the management interface indicating the frequency and style of service requests.

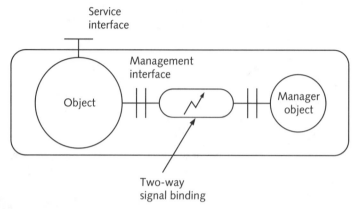

Figure 8.13 The use of managed objects for dynamic QoS maintenance.

Finally, QoS maintenance can be viewed as monitoring and renegotiation at a finer level of granularity. The use of managed objects to achieve QoS maintenance is illustrated in Figure 8.13. This is similar to Figure 8.12 but, in this case, management is encapsulated within the outermost object. The user perceives a single object, with this object taking actions internally to maintain the desired level of QoS.

As with factories, manager objects are simply arbitrary objects, normally provided at the engineering level (that is, provided as part of the underlying virtual machine). A number of distinct classes of such object can coexist, supporting a level of flexibility in the QoS management process.

To illustrate the above approach we consider a simple example.

Example *A multiparty video binding*
Consider the problem of multicasting the output from a video device to a number of interested participants. In particular, we consider the specific case of the video being sent to three participants, two of which are connected by a high-performance multi-service network and the third connected by a low-bandwidth mobile network. Figure 8.14(a) shows a configuration of computational objects able to support this scenario. In this figure, we assume the existence of a binding factory which can create video bindings supporting heterogeneous levels of QoS.

We now focus on the creation of the binding object as an example of the multimedia support in the extended engineering model. The first task of the binding factory is to check (at the computational level) whether the binding is type-safe. This function is performed within the binding factory as each factory has the local knowledge of the types of interface it can support. In this case, the binding can support the producer interface with the given level of QoS and the multiple consumer interfaces with their different QoS requirements. The factory will therefore proceed to create the appropriate engineering infrastructure. The factory creates the

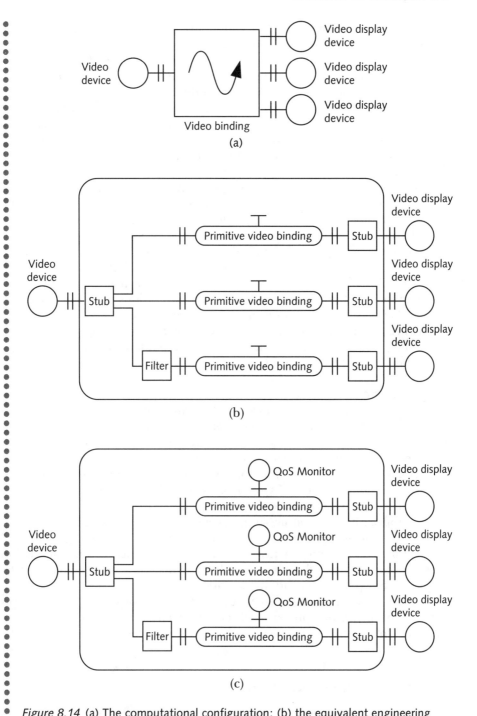

Figure 8.14 (a) The computational configuration; (b) the equivalent engineering configuration; (c) the final engineering configuration.

engineering configuration shown in Figure 8.14(b) using the generic
binding protocol discussed above.

In this case, the video is compressed at the producer end and
decompressed at the consumer end using the MPEG standard. This
process of encoding and decoding is, in this example, encapsulated within
the stubs for the binding. The multiparty binding is then engineered out
of a number of point-to-point bindings (in this case, a direct multiparty
service is not available). Furthermore, to support the mobile recipient,
filtering is carried out on the MPEG video flow at the source end of that
particular binding to reduce the bandwidth requirements. This recipient
will therefore see a much reduced quality of service. We assume for
simplicity that the bindings shown in this configuration are primitive and
hence are not decomposed further in terms of engineering objects.

This particular factory also supports both static and dynamic QoS
management. In particular, negotiation and resource reservation is carried
out on the above configuration. This will involve deciding on the required
resource allocation for each of the components shown above (MPEG
compression, decompression, filtering and the various primitive bindings)
and then ensuring that appropriate resources are reserved to guarantee
this activity. The factory also introduces dynamic QoS management of the
binding by generating QoS monitors on each binding. The final
configuration is illustrated in Figure 8.14(c).

The requirements revisited

The above approach clearly addresses the requirements identified above. In
particular, factories and managed objects directly implement static and
dynamic aspects of QoS management. In addition, this functionality is
provided by ordinary engineering objects, and hence different classes of object
can coexist. This provides considerable flexibility in the management process,
both in terms of the range of QoS management functions supported and the
precise mechanisms and policies for each function.

The approach also naturally supports end-to-end QoS management. Firstly,
static QoS management functions can be carried out on configurations of
engineering objects and not just individual objects. Such configurations can
represent an end-to-end path. Secondly, dynamic QoS management can be
inserted at any point in an end-to-end path.

Finally, the above management is not specific to binding objects. The concepts
defined above can be applied to all objects. Hence, it is equally possible to
provide QoS management for end system resources such as multimedia
storage servers.

8.3.4 Support for reactive objects

The third extension is to provide engineering support for reactive objects. As
mentioned in Section 4.3.4, reactive objects are synchronous objects whose

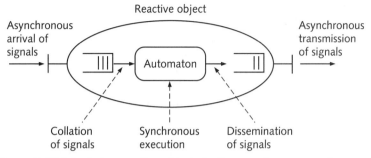

Figure 8.15 Interfacing reactive objects to the asynchronous environment.

execution must conform to the synchrony hypothesis. In order to support such objects, two distinct problems must be addressed:

- it is necessary to provide an interface between the synchronous interaction of reactive objects and the asynchronous interaction of distributed systems, and
- it is necessary to preserve the synchrony hypothesis for the reaction of reactive objects.

These problems are discussed in turn below.

Synchronous objects interface to the asynchronous environment through incoming and outgoing signal bindings. Incoming bindings deliver RM-ODP signals asynchronously to the reactive object for execution. The stub in the binding then performs the necessary language translations to map the incoming signals to signals in the language implementing the reactive object, such as Esterel. Outgoing bindings then deliver the results of the reaction to the intended recipients. Again, the stub will perform the necessary language mapping (this time in the opposite direction).

This is, however, not sufficient to interface to the asynchronous environment. It is also necessary to provide a mapping from the asynchronous RM-ODP signals and signals for synchronous execution. On the input side, this means collecting asynchronous signals into input signal occurrences. In order to achieve this goal, it is necessary to define when two (asynchronous) signals are instantaneous and when they are distinct in time. This will inevitably involve heuristics. It is also necessary at this stage to take into account any constraints on signal occurrence, such as using the relation statement in Esterel. The final input signal occurrences will then be presented for execution. At the output site, it is also necessary to collect output signal occurrences for transmission to the associated outgoing binding. This overall process is summarized in Figure 8.15.

The second problem is to preserve the synchrony hypothesis during reactions. As discussed earlier, this implies that the reaction time of the machine must be sufficiently fast to deal atomically with all incoming signals; that is, it must never be possible for two sequential signals of the same type to be waiting when the machine is ready for execution. The expected arrival pattern of signals is given by the quality of service declarations on interfaces. In particular, the throughput and jitter quality of service parameters of the input interfaces provide a bound on the permissible run-time of the execution machine: the run-time must be no more than the minimum inter-packet gap for each incoming event stream. This information can be used to derive QoS constraints for the basic engineering object realizing the reactive object. This in turn will result in suitable resource allocations in terms of, for example, real-time threads. Again, this process must involve an element of heuristics.

A specific implementation of reactive objects conforming to the above approach will be presented in Chapter 11.

To summarize, engineering support for reactive objects can be provided in terms of:

1. stubs performing the necessary language translation between the incoming and outgoing bindings and the language used for the reactive object,
2. strategies encapsulated within the reactive object to collate input signal occurrences and output signal occurrences, and
3. suitable QoS management strategies to ensure the synchrony hypothesis is met.

(1) and (3) are already supported by the engineering model; (2) can also be provided by an encapsulated execution environment for reactive objects (for example available as a library). Therefore, we conclude that no extra support facilities are required in the engineering model to meet the requirements of reactive objects.

8.4 A note on technology support

The goal of the engineering model is to remain technology-independent; it is the task of the technology viewpoint to consider specific technologies that can support the engineering framework. It is important, however, that concrete technologies do exist and that the engineering model provides suitable abstractions over such technologies. This section examines these issues. Firstly, we examine communications support for the engineering model and then consider the more general issue of end system support.

8.4.1 Appropriate communications technologies

Over the last few years, there have been a number of significant developments in communications services which can underpin distributed systems platforms. We look at the most significant areas below.

Transport services

In terms of transport services, the most important technologies are the TCP/IP protocol suite and the OSI Transport Service Class 4. The former is deployed in the Internet and offers a reliable connection-oriented service (TCP) and an unreliable datagram service (UDP) on top of the internetworking protocol IP. The latter is an international standard and offers a reliable connection-oriented service similar to TCP.

While such services provide support for traditional distributed applications, it is now recognized that they have major limitations in terms of multimedia. Most significantly, services such as TCP/IP and TP4 are not well suited to high-speed networks. This is largely due to window-based flow control strategies which (1) generate a large amount of acknowledgement traffic requiring relatively long latencies in a high-speed network, and (2) link the functions of error control and flow control. In addition, such services do not offer configurability in terms of quality of service parameters (to the extent demanded by multimedia applications).

Consequently, there has recently been considerable research and development activity directed towards the development of communication architectures for multimedia systems. Early work addressed the provision of new transport services designed to operate over high-speed networks; for example, XTP (Chesson, 1988), VMTP (Cheriton, 1986) and NetBlt (Clark *et al.*, 1987). Such protocols are often referred to as *rate-based* because of their reliance on clock-driven rather than window-based flow control. This has the significant advantage that acknowledgements are not required for flow control. In addition, such protocols maintain a separation between flow control and error control.

More recently, a number of protocols have emerged which are designed specifically to meet the needs of continuous media; for example, TPX (Danthine, 1994) and HeiTS (Hehmann *et al.*, 1991). In addition, a new version of XTP (XTPX) has recently been developed by the Technical University of Berlin (Miloucheva *et al.*, 1993). These protocols are generally configurable in terms of quality of service specification for use by a range of different media types.

Other significant work on QoS provision at the transport layer has come from the Tenet Group at the University of California at Berkeley (Wolfinger and Moran, 1991; Ferrari *et al.*, 1994). This group have developed a family of protocols including the Real Time Internet Protocol (RTIP), the Continuous Media Transport Protocol (CMTP) and the Real Time Channel Administration Protocol (RCAP). The latter provides generic connection establishment, resource reservation, and signalling functions for the rest of the protocol family. CMTP is explicitly designed for continuous media support. It is a lightweight protocol which runs on top of RTIP and provides sequenced and periodic delivery of continuous media samples with QoS control over throughput, delays and error bounds. Notification of all undelivered and/or corrupted data can optionally be provided to the client. The client interface to CMTP includes facilities to specify traffic characteristics in terms of burstiness (useful for variable bit rate encoding techniques) and workahead (which allows the protocol to deliver faster than the nominal rate if data is available). CMTP also permits dynamic QoS renegotiation.

Standards organizations are now responding to these new developments. For example, ISO have recently set up a new work item on Enhanced Communication Functions and Facilities (ECFF) which will address, among other things, multimedia services over high-speed networks. The outcome of this work is likely to be a new generation of protocols to coexist with TP4 and other related services. The Internet also now offers the real-time transport protocol, RTP. This protocol resides on top of TCP or UDP and enables timestamp and other related information to be associated with real-time data. It should be noted however that RTP relies on the underlying transport service for the delivery of the data.

Multiparty services

A number of services are also available to support multiparty communications. Early work centred on the Multicast Backbone (or *MBONE*) experiment in the Internet. MBONE supports the multicasting of audio and video streams and is now in regular use by a large number of users of the Internet (Eriksson, 1994). MBONE provides a multicasting service to subscribers including both audio and video channels. A number of applications have also been developed, including *ivs* (inria video conferencing system) and *nv* (network video). MBONE uses existing Internet protocols, in particular UDP and multicast IP although a number of the applications rely on RTP for real-time data such as continuous media (as discussed above).

While MBONE was a considerable success, the experiment highlighted a number of deficiencies, particularly with respect to the lack of resource reservation. The *RSVP* protocol (Zhang *et al.*, 1993) was introduced to overcome this problem. RSVP enables the construction of multicast groups and ensures that the necessary resources are reserved. The protocol is layered on top of the Internet IP protocol and hence assumes a connectionless environment. Consequently, RSVP maintains a clean separation between resource reservation (using RSVP) and data transfer (relying on the underlying IP). This separation is beneficial in terms of re-routing packets on failure but can cause problems in maintaining the mapping between reserved resources and the underlying IP-based forwarding algorithms. RSVP allows the construction of multiple-sender to multiple-receiver communications with resource reservation being receiver-initiated as new receivers join the group.

Similar facilities are offered by the connection-oriented *ST-II* protocol (Delgrossi *et al.*, 1994a). However, there are significant differences between RSVP and ST-II. Firstly, ST-II integrates the functions of resource reservation and routing. To support this, the protocol is connection-oriented with resources reserved and the route established at connection setup time. This approach therefore carries a more significant overhead on network failures as the connection must be renegotiated. However, ST-II does not suffer from the problems of relating reserved resources to routing decisions (this is fixed). ST-II supports single-sender to multiple-receiver connections but also allows multiple connections to be grouped together. The resulting trees are sender-initiated. A good comparison of RSVP and ST-II can be found in Delgrossi *et al*. (1994c).

Finally, the Tenet group at Berkeley are also working on an extended protocol suite offering multiparty communications with statistical guarantees on the quality of service (Gupta *et al*., 1995).

Some networks also support multicasting directly. Researchers are also developing techniques to extend ATM to enable multicasting of messages using the inherent flexibility of ATM switches (ATM Forum, 1996). It is crucial that the programming model can be mapped on to such developments.

Upper layer services

A number of services have also been defined on top of these transport services. In general terms, however, these developments focus on operational interactions and do not offer support for stream interactions.

The most significant development in this area has been in *remote procedure call* protocols (RPC) with a number of technologies now widely available, such as DCE RPC (as discussed in Chapter 2) and SUN RPC (as used by the SUN Network File System). In addition, there has also been a considerable amount of research in optimizing RPC for different environments. Most significantly, Bershad's lightweight RPC optimizes local calls by removing the need for context switching and data copying (Bershad *et al*., 1990). In terms of the engineering model, such developments enable optimizations to be made in inter-cluster, inter-capsule and inter-node communications.

Upper layer services have also been defined for multiparty communication Again, however, such developments focus on operational interaction. The most important developments in this area include the ISIS (Birman, 1993), Horus (van Renesse *et al*., 1996) and Psync (Peterson *et al*., 1989) protocols. ISIS is based on the concept of a process group. Process groups can have many members and processes can join or leave at any time. Messages sent to the group are then sent to all members of the group. The delivery semantics is based on the concept of virtual synchrony whereby all sites in a broadcast see the same events (message deliveries or failure notifications) in precisely the same order. ISIS is implemented in user space on top of the underlying operating system. In contrast, Horus is a group communication service which can be implemented within the kernel for maximum efficiency. Horus also extends the group communications model of ISIS, offering unreliable or reliable FIFO delivery, causal or total group multicasts. Finally, Psync is developed in the framework offered by the x-kernel and provides causal ordering of messages to group participants. Psync is also used as the basis for a range of higher level protocols referred to collectively as Consul (Mishra *et al*., 1993).

Such developments provide strong technology support for multiparty operational interactions. There has been much less work in providing higher level services for multiparty stream interactions. Such services should provide lightweight access to the underlying resource reservation and multicast transport services, but should also enable the construction of $m : n$ conference calls. Higher level services are also required which support multiparty communications where different participants have different quality of service requirements. This latter issue is discussed in more detail below when filtering technologies are highlighted.

Compression and filters

A wide range of technologies are now available for the compression and decompression of continuous media. The area of compression was discussed in Section 1.3.1 and therefore will not be considered in great depth here. It is sufficient to mention that software and hardware implementations of the major compression standards are now readily available (including JPEG, MPEG and H.261).

There have recently been interesting developments in the area of filters. Filters are essentially processing elements which carry out some manipulation on one or more continuous media flows. They are most often used in multiparty communications where different participants require different qualities of service. For example, one group of users requires full motion colour video, whereas another prefers grey-scale video (for reasons of cost or because of limited communications or end system resources). Filters can also provide a level of flexibility in dynamic QoS management by providing functions which can alter the quality of service of the data at run-time.

A range of filter mechanisms can be identified including (Yeadon *et al.*, 1996):

- *Transcoding filters*
  Transcoding filters perform transformations between different compression standards. For example, transcoding filters can be provided to convert motion JPEG to MPEG.
- *Frame dropping filters*
  Frame dropping filters reduce bandwidth requirements by selectively losing frames. Such services can have knowledge of the frame types and can drop frames according to their importance. For example, with MPEG a filter could drop B-frames, P-frames and then I-frames until the bandwidth requirements are met.
- *Frequency filters*
  Frequency filters again reduce bandwidth requirements by operating on the frequency domain. A range of frequency filters can be provided, including low-pass filters which remove the higher frequency elements of an image and colour reduction filters which manipulate the chrominance information to reduce or remove colour information.
- *Mixing filters*
  Mixing filters combine separate continuous media flows either by overlaying or multiplexing the information. For example, one video image can be overlaid on top of another. Similarly, two audio channels can be multiplexed into a single encoding.

- *Hierarchical filters*
  Hierarchical filters can parse an incoming hierarchically encoded continuous media stream and separate the stream into its various components. This can then enable the different components to be transmitted using different qualities of services.

Most of the research on filtering is still experimental. For example, research on filtering of MPEG and motion JPEG streams is being carried out at Lancaster University (Yeadon *et al.*, 1996). In addition, researchers at the University of California at San Diego are developing strategies for the placement of filters in multicast dissemination trees (Pasquale *et al.*, 1994).

8.4.2 Appropriate end systems technologies

There has similarly been a wide range of developments in end systems technology. In particular, a range of operating systems exist which provide support for the engineering abstractions of nodes, capsules, clusters and the nucleus. Examples of such operating systems include Unix, VMS, Windows, and Windows 95. More specific end systems technologies have also emerged, including the IEEE POSIX standard for lightweight threads (*pthreads*) as used in DCE. It is notable, however, that such technologies do not yet provide the real-time guarantees required by continuous media applications.

A number of real-time operating systems have been developed, including Alpha (Jensen and Northcutt, 1990), ARTS (Tokuda and Mercer, 1989), Mars (Kopetz *et al.*, 1989), Spring (Stankovic and Ramamrithan, 1991) and Delta-4 (Powell, 1991). Such systems, however, have generally been used for hard real-time systems and do not meet the soft real-time requirements of multimedia applications. They also do not allow real-time applications to coexist with other, non-real-time, activities.

Operating system support for multimedia applications therefore remains a matter for research; important projects in this area include RT-Mach (Tokuda *et al.*, 1990), Yartos (Jeffay *et al.*, 1991), μ-Choices (Campbell and Tan, 1995), Scout (Montz *et al.*, 1994) and Pegasus (Leslie *et al.*, 1993). This issue is also revisited in Chapters 9, 10 and 11 of this book, when an approach is developed based on emerging microkernel technology.

8.4.3 Discussion

From the discussion above, it should be apparent that a wide range of communications technologies are available to support the engineering concept of a channel. The most important technologies are:

- new transport services, such as XTP, HeiTS and CMTP, which incorporate rate-based flow control and which enable the specification of QoS requirements,

- emerging protocols such as RSVP, which enable the construction of dissemination trees for multiparty multimedia and which also ensure that appropriate resources are reserved to support the multiparty interaction, and
- compression techniques, such as MPEG and JPEG, which reduce the bandwidth requirements of continuous media data.

In addition, new techniques such as filtering are emerging which introduce more variety in the styles of channel that can be supported, for example where different participants in a multiparty interaction can receive different levels of quality of service.

In contrast, end systems support for the engineering model is more limited. Existing operating systems such as Unix provide direct support for the engineering model in terms of nodes, capsules and clusters. They do not, however, provide (soft) real-time guarantees as required by multimedia applications. This area therefore remains a matter for further research.

8.5 Summary

This chapter has described an engineering model designed to support distributed multimedia computing. This model is based closely on the RM-ODP Engineering Model which features, firstly, a model of end system resources consisting of nodes, capsules, clusters and the nucleus together with appropriate resource management functions and, secondly, a model of communications based on arbitrary point-to-point or multiparty channels which can encapsulate stubs, binders, protocol objects and interceptors.

The RM-ODP Engineering Model was then extended with support for the concepts of explicit binding, QoS management and reactive objects. The main extensions required to support these concepts are:

- a more precise view of an engineering specification as a refinement of a computational specification and sharing the same object-oriented approach,
- a recursive model of bindings supported by a generic binding protocol, replacing the channel structure described in RM-ODP,
- QoS-driven resource allocation for end system resources accessed through a capsule interface and supported by an extended node management function,
- the incorporation of the static QoS management functions of QoS negotiation, resource reservation and admission control within factory objects, and
- the use of the concept of managed objects to provide dynamic QoS management functionality such as QoS monitoring, policing, maintenance and renegotiation.

The factory has a particularly important role in supporting the above extensions. Factories in RM-ODP are arbitrary objects which have the particular role of introducing new objects into the environment. We retain the flexibility inherent in this approach, but introduce an optional (and potentially reusable) functionality that particular classes of factory can support, including the generic binding protocol, static QoS management functions and the automatic generation of managed objects supporting dynamic QoS management functions.

The chapter concluded by considering the range of technology available to support the (technology-independent) engineering model. This discussion highlighted a wide range of communications technologies to support channels. In contrast, end system support for multimedia remains a matter for research. The next three chapters present a new technology approach to operating system support for multimedia, based on emerging microkernel technology.

9 A technology approach based on microkernels

9.1 Introduction

The previous chapter presented an engineering model designed to support distributed multimedia computing. This engineering model allows systems to be described independently of the underlying technology. In developing a system, however, it is also necessary to identify particular technologies that can be used to realize the system defined in the engineering model. This identification of technology corresponds to the technology viewpoint in RM-ODP (see Section 2.2).

The previous chapter also considered the range of technologies that are emerging to support the multimedia aspects of the engineering model. This discussion highlighted the wide range of communications technologies that are either available or are at an advanced stage of development. In contrast, there is a lack of end systems technologies which address the particular requirements of multimedia. This chapter addresses this deficiency in the state of the art by examining the issue of operating system support for multimedia. The chapter introduces a new approach based on the use of microkernel technology.

The chapter is structured as follows. Section 9.2 presents the motivation for adopting the microkernel approach to meet the needs of multimedia applications. More specifically, this section examines the challenges of multimedia for operating systems and highlights deficiencies in the state of the art in meeting these challenges. The section then considers alternative strategies to respond to these deficiencies and concludes that the microkernel approach has a number of distinct advantages. Section 9.3 then examines the selected microkernel technology, Chorus, in detail. This section examines the overall architecture of Chorus and then examines in depth the various components with particular reference to the scheduling, communications and memory management facilities. Section 9.4 then introduces an architecture based on the Chorus microkernel, but with specific support for multimedia. Finally, Section 9.5 summarizes the contributions of the chapter.

9.2 Motivation

9.2.1 The challenge of multimedia for operating systems

In order to support our approach to multimedia, as captured in the programming and engineering models, the most crucial requirement is the ability to support end-to-end communication paths (bindings) governed by an overall QoS requirement. Such paths may involve an arbitrary amount of processing in the producer, transmission through an arbitrary communications infrastructure, and finally arbitrary processing at the consumer end. With such end-to-end activities, it is crucial that QoS management applies not just to the network but also to end systems resources. There is little point in the network delivering data with the required quality of service only for the operating system to be busy processing other activity, leading to QoS violations.

> **Example** *An analogy of a hi-fi system*
> When purchasing a hi-fi system, it is crucial to consider every component involved in the production of sound. The overall quality of service is determined by the interaction between all components. Indeed, the quality will largely be determined by the weakest link in the chain. For example, there is little point having a high-quality CD player and amplifier if the speakers are of poor quality.

As mentioned above, a number of important advances have been made in communications support for multimedia. In order to meet end-to-end requirements, it is crucial that such advances are matched by similar advances in operating systems technologies. The particular challenges of multimedia for operating systems are examined in more depth below.

The first set of challenges stem from the overall *real-time performance* required by continuous media data:

Requirement 1: Predictable real-time behaviour
The first challenge imposed by multimedia is for operating systems to offer predictable real-time behaviour to applications. This in turn implies having *quality of service guarantees* on each of the components of the operating system: thread scheduling, communications, device management and virtual memory management. Furthermore, an *integrated* approach must be adopted to ensure that the end-to-end quality of service can be achieved.

Requirement 2: Efficiency
A number of multimedia applications are required to process continuous media data, for example to carry out image processing on an incoming video sequence. This can place considerable demands on the underlying hardware resources (particularly with respect to video data). It is hence important that the operating system provides efficient mechanisms to

support this processing. Hence the operating system must not impose unnecessary overheads in accessing continuous media data.

A second set of requirements arise because of the *variety* of applications that a future workstation will be required to support.

Requirement 3: Diversity in terms of quality of service requests
Future workstations will support a *range* of applications, including multimedia applications featuring audio and video streams, interactive applications and more processor-intensive applications. Furthermore, such applications must be able to *coexist* and share the available resources. This implies that the underlying operating system must be able to manage a wide *variety* of resource requests with quite distinct quality of service requirements. For example, continuous media applications require predictable throughput and minimal jitter. This should not, however, be at the expense of interactive or processor-intensive applications, which require short latencies and high throughput respectively.

Requirement 4: Diversity in terms of guarantees
There is further diversity in the level of *guarantees* demanded by different applications. Some applications will tolerate a best effort service and will tolerate occasional degradation in the quality of service delivered. In contrast, other applications will require absolute guarantees on the level of quality of service offered by the operating system. For example, safety-critical applications such as medical applications may require guarantees on the quality of incoming video data.

Finally, it should be recognized that the operating system will occasionally be asked to operate near or over maximum capacity (*overload*). This adds a final requirement:

Requirement 5: Dealing with overload
Given that the operating system may enter periods of overload, it is essential to ensure that mechanisms are in place to deal with overload. In particular it is crucial that temporary periods of overload do not bring the system to a halt.

The operating system has a crucial role in ensuring that the above challenges can be met (Steinmetz and Nahrstedt, 1995). Note that some researchers take the position that, with advances in hardware, the quality and efficiency of the operating system is no longer so crucial. In particular, they argue that with advances in processor speeds, memory access times and disk technology, a modern workstation has plentiful resources and hence efficiency and optimal management is no longer so important. We disagree with this position and believe that for the foreseeable future operating system support will remain

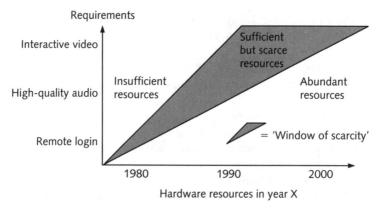

Figure 9.1 The window of scarcity.

crucial for the support of multimedia applications. In particular, we believe that the increasing demands of applications are more than keeping pace with the increasing capabilities of modern workstations.

This position is captured nicely by Figure 9.1 by Anderson *et al.* (1990). This diagram shows that there are sufficient resources for emerging multimedia applications but only if they are managed correctly.

9.2.2 Problems with existing operating systems

It is now clear that existing (commercially available) operating systems do not meet the requirements identified above. We look in more detail at the reasons for this below.

Real-time performance

Firstly, existing operating systems do not provide the level of predictable performance required by multimedia applications (*Requirement 1*). In contrast, they tend to be very unpredictable in the real-time characteristics of the services they provide. This stems from a lack of quality of service management in operating systems. For most services, it is simply not possible to specify the quality required of the service. This is certainly true of areas such as memory and device management. In addition, most operating systems fail to provide interfaces which can exploit emerging quality of service parametrization in communications protocols (for example, refer to the sockets interface in Berkeley Unix or the messages and streams based interface in System V). Some systems do allow control over thread scheduling, for example in terms of specifying priority bands. This support, however, is not sufficiently refined for a multimedia workstation. Many schedulers also suffer from the problem that they will spend relatively long periods of time in interrupt service routines rather than servicing user requests. This introduces a significant element of unpredictability in the quality of service obtained by application threads.

More significantly, there is currently little integration between the different areas of resource management in operating systems. For example, when packets arrive from the network, the operating system has no information on the urgency or importance of the data. If this information exists, it is encapsulated in higher layer protocols. Hence it is not possible for the scheduler to correctly schedule the processing of this packet. This can lead to less important activity being scheduled in preference to activity with tight quality of service requirements (a problem known as *priority inversion*). Similarly, there is a lack of integration between the scheduler and memory management. For example, there is no guarantee that when threads are scheduled the data required by the thread will be in main memory. Both of these effects can lead to significant delays in processing data and hence unpredictable real-time performance.

Secondly, existing operating systems are often very inefficient in terms of supporting manipulation of continuous media data (*Requirement 2*). There are three major reasons for this potential inefficiency:

- *System call/domain crossing overheads*
  Multimedia applications will typically require a significant number of domain crossings between system space and user space. At a minimum, there will be one system call per frame of data sent or received. In addition, there may be more calls associated with synchronization of activity, file access and so on. In existing operating systems, such domain crossings tend to be a relatively expensive operation and hence the number of system calls can jeopardize the performance of continuous media manipulations.
- *Context switches*
  Similarly, many (distributed) multimedia applications will be structured as a set of cooperating processes in order to achieve concurrent activity. This can lead to a large number of context switches. Furthermore, system calls can themselves result in additional context switches, for example involving costly virtual memory context changes. Again, context switches are relatively expensive operations in existing operating systems. Even lightweight processes sharing virtual memory carry a significant overhead in terms of performance.
- *Copy operations*
  Finally, existing implementations of communications protocols typically include a number of copy operations as data is manipulated by a layered stack (for example, the protocol stack in Berkeley Unix performs an initial copy from the network card and up to two additional copies as data is passed through the protocol layers). Further copying is then required as data crosses between user and system space. Copying is also an expensive operation involving processing time and two accesses to virtual memory. Again, this poses a threat to the performance of multimedia applications.

Overall, the overheads in each of the above areas must be minimized for multimedia applications either by minimizing the number of domain crossings, context switches and copy operations or by reducing the cost of each operation.

Dealing with variety

Further problems arise when dealing with a variety of application styles (*Requirement 3*). It is noticeable that modern operating systems are biased towards interactive applications. For example, schedulers will be optimized to offer a level of fairness and minimum delays. This is reflected in the popularity of policies such as round robin schedulers. There is also considerable experience in the operating system world in optimizing such approaches to deal with a mixture of interactive and computer-intensive applications. It is becoming clear, however, that existing schedulers fail to deal with the addition of multimedia applications to this mix. This problem was demonstrated by a series of experiments carried out by Nieh on the scheduler in Berkeley Unix (Nieh *et al.*, 1994). These experiments involved running a mixture of continuous media, interactive and computer-intensive applications on a relatively powerful workstation. The results showed that even on a relatively lightly loaded workstation pathological cases were detected when one of the classes of application would be completely starved of resources. Furthermore, Nieh discovered specific solutions to a number of the problems, but failed to identify general solutions which would deal with arbitrary applications using the existing approach to scheduling. His conclusions were as follows:

> *Through trial and error, it may be possible to find a particular combination of priorities and scheduling class assignments to make the SVR4 scheduling pathologies go away. However, such a solution would be extremely fragile and would require discovering a new setting for any change in the mix of applications.*

One of the problems with respect to real-time scheduling (Kopetz, 1994; Stankovic *et al.*, 1995) is that applications can have two very distinct metrics for their criticality. In particular, metrics can be expressed in terms of one of the following:

- the *urgency* of the activity, or
- the *importance* of the activity.

Most existing schedulers are biased in terms of one or the other. This is also true for the styles of scheduler considered for multimedia. In particular, most of the research is either considering fixed priority schedulers (based on a measure of importance) or earliest deadline first schedulers (based on a measure of urgency). In either case, requirements which are most naturally expressed in terms of one metric must be re-expressed in terms of the other metric. For example, if a fixed priority scheme is chosen, activity with a given deadline must be re-expressed in terms of a priority which can then deliver this deadline. Conversely, if an earliest deadline first scheduler is implemented, priorities of activities must be expressed in terms of deadlines. This is a major dilemma for operating system developers. Some researchers are looking at schedulers which contain elements of both styles of metric. For example, Nieh has proposed a scheme where scheduling is carried out on the basis of both urgency and importance (Nieh and Lam, 1995). Similarly, researchers have proposed an extension to earliest deadline first scheduling, called D^{over}, which employs an importance metric in overload situations (see also discussion on overload below) (Koren and Shasha, 1992). This work has not yet propagated into commercial operating systems.

As a further criticism, existing operating systems completely fail to allow different levels of guarantee to be specified, for example best effort or guaranteed quality of service (*Requirement 4*).

Dealing with overload

Finally, there is currently little support in operating systems to handle overload conditions. Indeed, operating systems tend to suffer from problems such as thrashing as the load increases. A number of researchers are examining this problem, however, in the context of multimedia systems. Two different approaches have been proposed.

In the first approach, overload situations are avoided by the use of appropriate static QoS management strategies. In particular, a combination of admission control tests and resource reservation can guarantee that an application has all the required resources to complete the task. If all applications perform these functions, then overload cannot occur. The problem with this approach is that it can be rather conservative and inflexible. It also requires all applications to perform the appropriate QoS management functions.

The second approach allows overload to occur but then takes actions to ensure *graceful degradation*. This can partly be achieved by the adoption of particular scheduling algorithms. For example, it is recognized that fixed priority schemes, such as rate monotonic scheduling, perform better than earliest deadline first policies in overload situations. (Earliest deadline first algorithms tend to select tasks whose deadline is in the past, leading to a cascade of missed deadlines (Locke, 1986)). Alternatively, earliest deadline first policies can be used with the extensions defined in the D^{over} algorithm (mentioned above). Graceful degradation can also be supported by appropriate dynamic QoS management strategies. In particular, a combination of QoS monitoring and renegotiation can be used to adapt the behaviour of applications to the available resources. With many applications, the scope for adaptability is rather limited. However, with media types such as video and (to a lesser extent) audio, there is the potential to adapt the incoming data stream to reduce the loading on the system, for example by dropping frames or reducing the colour element.

In practice, a combination of the two approaches outlined above can also be employed. In particular, one class of application would have guaranteed performance by employing resource reservation and admission control,

Table 9.1 Summary of problems with existing operating systems

Requirement	Analysis of existing systems
Predictable real-time behaviour	Unpredictable real-time responses; lack of integration between different components; problems of priority inversion
Efficiency	Expensive and excessive domain crossings and context switches; unnecessary data copies
Diversity in terms of QoS	Bias towards interactive applications; lack of mechanisms to specify alternative styles of traffic
Diversity in terms of guarantees	Best effort only
Dealing with overload	Lack of admission control tests or resource reservations; do not offer graceful degradation

whereas another class of application would compete for the remaining resources employing dynamic strategies to ensure graceful degradation. Such a scheme requires the partitioning of resources between the two classes; this partition can either be static or can alter at run-time.

In conclusion, there are a number of approaches to dealing with overload in operating systems (in terms of improved scheduling algorithms and static and dynamic QoS management functions). However, such schemes are not yet employed in commercial operating systems.

Summary

It should be clear from the discussion above that existing operating systems completely fail to address the requirements of multimedia. The overall analysis is summarized in Table 9.1. Hence significant changes are required before operating systems are able to address the requirements of multimedia and hence enable the quality of service on end-to-end bindings to be achieved.

9.2.3 Responding to these challenges

There are essentially two main approaches to respond to the challenges outlined above. The first is to *modify* existing operating systems to address the various requirements of multimedia. The second approach is to consider *alternative* implementation strategies better suited to meeting these demands. The first is essentially an evolutionary approach, whereas the second is by nature more revolutionary. We look at each approach in more detail below.

Modifying existing systems

The first approach involves modifying existing operating systems to meet the demands of multimedia in terms of real-time performance, dealing with a variety of application requirements and dealing with overload. This involves two separate activities as discussed below.

Firstly, it is necessary to alter the implementation of the various system components to better address the needs of multimedia. For example, the existing scheduler can be altered from, say, a round robin scheduler to earliest deadline first or a fixed priority-based scheduler. Similarly, the communications architecture could be extended with, for example, a rate-based transport protocol.

Secondly, it is necessary to introduce overall resource management strategies to meet end-to-end requirements. Such an approach was adopted by Sun in their modification of the Unix operating system. Their position is that workstations have ample processing power but their weaknesses lie in inappropriate resource management. Their proposal is for *time-driven resource management* (Hanko *et al.*, 1991), which allows applications to signal their likely forthcoming resource requirements in terms of parameters such as quantity, deadline and priority. The system will not attempt to guarantee performance, but will instead bias available resources in the requested directions and concentrate on graceful degradation of service, optionally accompanied by notification of degradation to the affected process. It is argued that this is an appropriate strategy in general purpose multi-programmed workstations.

Alternative implementation strategies

The second approach is to re-engineer operating systems based on an architecture which is better suited to the demands of multimedia. A number of researchers are investigating this route. In particular, research is investigating the role of microkernels in the support of multimedia applications. Microkernels are essentially minimal kernels providing generic functionality to enable the construction of more open operating system services. The general approach is to provide a set of primitives to enable the construction of concurrent activities which can then communicate via message passing. This approach is well suited to distributed systems, as message passing can extend to a networked environment. The lightweight nature of a microkernel also encourages the development of systems with improved real-time behaviour. Operating system functionality is then constructed on top of a microkernel by the development of an operating system personality. For example, a Unix personality can be developed on top of a microkernel. One interesting feature of microkernels is that multiple personalities can coexist, enhancing the level of flexibility in the system architecture. Microkernel technology is now widely available and used in industry and commerce. Examples of mature microkernel technology include Chorus (Bricker *et al.*, 1991), Mach (Rashid *et al.*, 1989) and Amoeba (Tanenbaum *et al.*, 1990).

The attraction of microkernels for multimedia is twofold. Firstly, microkernels can potentially offer the real-time performance required by multimedia applications by providing lightweight and direct access to low-level facilities. Secondly, microkernels provide the level of necessary flexibility to enable specialized support for multimedia to be developed. Furthermore, this support can coexist with traditional operating system functionality through the use of personalities: a real-time personality can coexist with a Unix personality.

With these benefits, a number of researchers are developing refinements or extensions to microkernels to support multimedia and real-time activity. For example, work has been carried out in a Mach environment to provide processor scheduling more appropriate to continuous media (Govindan and Anderson, 1991). In addition, work has been undertaken at CWI, Amsterdam to support continuous media in an Amoeba-based Unix environment. The approach is to use coprocessor-based intelligent device controllers and to give applications controlled direct access to physical devices (Bulterman and van Liere, 1991).

Note that recent research has investigated the development of extensible and adaptable operating systems. For example, the operating system Spin enables the user to insert selected modules (called Spindles) dynamically into the kernel in a type-safe manner (Bershad *et al.*, 1995). Other examples of extensible operating systems include the Exokernel (Engler *et al.*, 1995) and Spring (Mitchell *et al.*, 1994). Such systems provide another interesting approach to offering the flexibility required by multimedia applications.

Discussion

In this book, we adopt the microkernel approach as discussed above. We believe that the advantages of microkernels in terms of flexibility and real-time performance make them more suitable in the longer term for the support of multimedia applications. More specifically, we adopt the Chorus microkernel as developed by Chorus Systèmes in France. This particular microkernel has a number of advantages in terms of its flexible and open architecture. The system is developed using object-oriented programming techniques (in particular, using C++). In addition, the various subcomponents of the operating system (virtual memory, communications and scheduling) are all designed to enable different classes of policy to coexist. These features make it a strong candidate for the support of multimedia. In particular, the required extensions in terms of real-time functionality and QoS management can readily be incorporated into the system framework. It should be noted, though, that the principles developed in the remainder of Part 3 can equally be applied to other microkernel technologies.

The next section provides a detailed introduction of the Chorus microkernel and also contains a more in-depth analysis of the potential support for multimedia.

9.3 The Chorus microkernel

9.3.1 Overall approach

The Chorus operating system (Bricker *et al.*, 1991) is a microkernel-based operating system originally developed at INRIA in France and now produced by a commercial company, Chorus Systèmes. The design goals of Chorus are

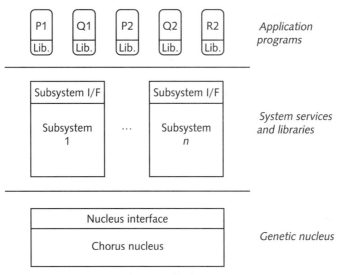

Figure 9.2 The overall Chorus architecture.

to enable the development of more modular and flexible operating systems through the use of a microkernel approach. They contrast this with more traditional monolithic operating systems where all operating system services reside in a large *monolithic* kernel; such kernels have severe problems in terms of maintenance, the complexity of introducing new services and real-time performance.

The overall Chorus architecture is shown in Figure 9.2. This diagram shows a lightweight Chorus nucleus (the microkernel) at the bottom of the architecture. This nucleus provides a minimal set of generic operating system services to support a range of operating systems. In particular, the nucleus provides a basic environment in terms of support for address spaces, multi-threaded execution and communication primitives (both in terms of inter- and intra-address spaces). The particular services provide basic mechanisms and are intended to be policy free. This allows particular policies to be developed at a higher level. (Note that it is important to avoid confusion over the different uses of the term *nucleus* in this book. The RM-ODP uses the term nucleus to represent an abstraction over the underlying operating system. In contrast, Chorus Systèmes use the term more specifically to denote the microkernel at the heart of their operating system.)

The nucleus can then support one or more *subsystems*. The most common use of a subsystem is to provide a particular operating system personality. For example, Chorus provides a subsystem which offers a Unix personality (strictly speaking a System V personality). Unlike monolithic implementations of Unix, however, the operating system is structured as a set of cooperating services using the features offered by the nucleus. Subsystems can also implement other personalities, such as a support environment for a particular programming language or a distributed systems platform. For example, Chorus currently also offer the COOL subsystem, which is a generic object-oriented platform offering a CORBA interface.

Finally, a range of application programs can be constructed on top of the various subsystems. Application programs can access the services offered by a particular subsystem or can access the nucleus directly. In accessing a subsystem, they need not know that the interface is implemented using a microkernel. For example, standard Unix applications will run on Chorus/MiX without the need for recompilation (binary compatibility).

The designers of Chorus argue that this architecture has a number of significant benefits over monolithic kernels:

- the architecture is inherently *portable* as the machine-dependent aspects of an operating system are isolated in the nucleus,
- the architecture is highly *flexible*, both in terms of allowing different subsystems to coexist and also in terms of the configuration of subsystem services in the distributed environment,
- the architecture can provide *real-time performance* by enabling direct access to low-level resources and also by enabling real-time management policies to be offered in an appropriate subsystem, and
- the architecture enables the development of more *open* operating systems which naturally support *evolution* in terms of the introduction of new services or the modification of existing services.

We also believe that the above benefits make the Chorus microkernel a suitable basis for the development of open distributed processing platforms with multimedia capabilities. More specifically, the microkernel can offer multiple personalities including a standard operating system personality and a real-time personality. For example, the architecture can offer a traditional Unix personality supporting a range of existing applications together with a real-time personality supporting multimedia applications. The nucleus, together with the subsystems, then has the crucial task of multiplexing the available resources between the different personalities (effectively implementing the required node management function as described in Section 8.2.2). The real-time personality can have more direct and lightweight access to underlying hardware resources to maximize performance. In addition, the real-time personality can contain appropriate resource management strategies to ensure that real-time guarantees are met. Finally, access to services can be provided through an open distributed processing platform. Because of the open nature of the operating system, access can extend to services within each subsystem.

This general architecture will provide the basis for the remainder of the discussion in Part 3 of the book. Before proceeding, however, we will examine the details of the Chorus nucleus in more detail, starting with the abstractions and then looking at details of the implementation.

9.3.2 The nucleus abstractions

We now present a detailed description of the services offered by the Chorus nucleus. We first present a brief overview of the programming model offered by the nucleus and then look at the various aspects of the service interface in some detail. The discussion is based on version 3, release 5 (v3 r5) of the nucleus.

Overview of the programming model
The programming model offered by the Chorus nucleus is illustrated in Figure 9.3. A Chorus system consists of one or more *sites* connected by a communication medium. Each site can contain a number of *actors* which encapsulate a set of resources necessary to carry out the execution of a program. In particular, actors encapsulate virtual memory in terms of *regions* and *segments*. Actors are *multi-threaded* and can also support one or more *ports*. Actors then communicate by passing *messages* between ports. The nucleus also provides *semaphores* and *mutual exclusion variables* to support concurrency control within an actor. Finally, all entities supported by the nucleus are identified by a unique identifier which is generated by the nucleus.

Each of these aspects is discussed in more detail below under the headings of processing entities, communication entities, virtual memory management, and naming and addressing.

Processing entities
The Chorus abstractions for processing are sites, actors and threads. *Sites* represent tightly coupled computing resources featuring one or more processors, some memory and a set of devices. Sites are then connected by a communications medium, which can either be a network or a bus. By definition, there should be precisely one copy of the nucleus per site.

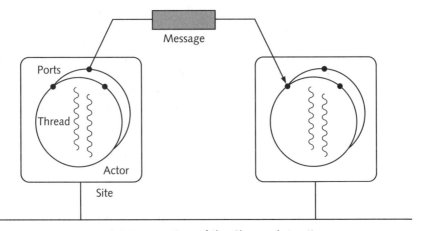

Figure 9.3 An overview of the Chorus abstractions.

The concept of sites can therefore map on to a variety of architectures. For example, in a typical distributed architecture sites would represent workstations; in a loosely coupled multiprocessor, sites would represent processors; in a more tightly coupled multiprocessor, the whole machine would be one site; finally, it is possible to have sites consisting of clusters of processors which are then connected by an appropriate communication medium in a distributed configuration.

An actor in Chorus is then a collection of resources necessary to support processing. More precisely, an actor defines a protected address space supporting the execution of threads (see below). A given site can support a number of actors with actors remaining at that site; it is not possible for actors to migrate to another site.

Three styles of actor are defined in Chorus, namely *user actors*, *system actors* and *supervisor actors*. User actors are normal actors with ordinary access to the nucleus interface. System actors are then like user actors, but are trusted by the kernel. They have access to a number of sensitive nucleus operations such as allocating a unique identifier to a Chorus entity (such as a port). They are often used to implement security functions. Finally, supervisor actors have the same privileges as system actors, but also have access to primitives, for example to an interrupt or trap, or to send a mini-message (a highly optimized form of IPC used within the nucleus). In the current release of the nucleus, supervisor actors actually execute in the same address space as the nucleus for reasons of efficiency. The role of supervisor actors is normally to implement device management and critical subsystem functionality.

Finally, a thread is the unit of execution in Chorus and provides a sequential flow of control through an address space (an actor). A given actor can support one or more threads, offering a level of concurrency within actors. These threads then remain tied to that actor and cannot migrate to another address space. Each thread is defined by a thread context which defines among other things the current state of registers and the program counter, a pointer to the stack, and the privilege level of the thread (user or supervisor).

Threads in Chorus are supported directly by the nucleus and hence are correctly termed *system threads* (as opposed to *user threads* as discussed in Chapter 11). They offer a lightweight model of concurrency with a thread context switch being approximately 10 times more efficient than an actor context switch (Marsh *et al.*, 1991). The nucleus also supports scheduling at the granularity of individual threads. This aspect of threads support is discussed in more detail in Section 9.3.3.

The kernel interface defines a number of different primitives for actors and threads (there are no calls for sites). A selection of the most important calls are given in Table 9.2.

Communication entities

The Chorus nucleus supports communication between threads in terms of a set of shared memory primitives (for within an actor) and message passing

Table 9.2 A selection of nucleus primitives for actors and threads

Primitive	Description
actorCreate()	Create an actor
actorDelete()	Destroy an actor
actorPriority()	Set the priority of the actor
threadCreate()	Create a thread
threadDelete()	Destroy a thread
threadPriority()	Set the priority of the thread
threadSuspend()	Suspend a thread
threadResume()	Resume a thread

primitives (for communication either within or between actors). We look at each in turn below.

The shared memory primitives are required to support concurrency control between threads within an actor. The nucleus provides both semaphores and mutexes for this purpose. Semaphores are non-negative integers which can only be accessed by the operations semInit(), semV() and semP(). semInit() sets the initial value of the semaphore to a chosen positive value. semV() then has the effect of increasing the value of the semaphore by 1. Finally, semP() then decrements the value of the semaphore by 1; if, however, this would result in a negative result, the calling thread is blocked on this semaphore until a semV() operation increases the value. All three operations are performed atomically. It is well recognized that this technique can implement a variety of concurrency control strategies.

Mutexes are simply a restricted form of semaphore where the value can be either 1 or 0. They are used as gates to allow or prevent access to a critical section of code (enforcing mutual exclusion). Note that mutexes offer one additional operation over semaphores, mutexTry(), which enables the thread to poll the status of the mutex variable.

The key primitives for shared memory concurrency control are summarized in Table 9.3. (Note that the nucleus also supports a lightweight style of mutex variable called a *spin lock*, which is specifically designed for short critical sections and for implementations on multiprocessors; the use of spin locks is, however, restricted to supervisor threads.)

The nucleus provides more general primitives for communication between threads in the form of message passing. This service can be used for threads to communicate whether they are in the same address space or in a separate address space. The precise location is transparent to the programmer. Messages in Chorus consist of a message body and an optional message annexe. The message body is an untyped byte string of variable size (but with an upper limit on the size); the message annexe is also an untyped byte string but of fixed size (currently 80 bytes). This fixed size allows the nucleus to optimize the sending of the annexe. Note that the annexe is always copied to the receiver's address space. The sending of the message body can, however,

Table 9.3 A selection of nucleus primitives for shared memory concurrency control

Primitive	Description
semInit()	Initialize a semaphore
semP()	Wait on a semaphore
semV()	Signal a semaphore
mutexInit()	Initialize a mutex
mutexGet()	Acquire a mutex
mutexRelease()	Release a mutex
mutexTry()	Try to acquire a mutex

exploit the virtual memory management architecture to avoid unnecessary copies (see below).

Messages are sent to ports rather than to actors or threads. A port is a fixed size queue of incoming messages. For an actor to be able to access a port, the port must be attached to the actor. A port can only be attached to a single actor at a given time, with the initial attachment carried out when the port is created. Ports can, however, migrate between actors over time. Consequently, ports provide the basis for reconfiguration in a Chorus system.

Ports can also be collected into *port groups* (see Figure 9.4). The precise membership of a port group can then change dynamically as new ports are added or removed. Port groups provide the basis for a multicast service. More specifically, the following services are offered:

- multicast the message to all ports currently in the group,
- send the message to any member of the group, and
- send the message to any member of the group matching certain constraints.

A number of different styles of message passing are offered by the nucleus. In the *asynchronous mode*, the sender sends a message using ipcSend() and then continues processing: the sender thread is not blocked. This message can then be received using ipcReceive() by the destination actor. The primitive

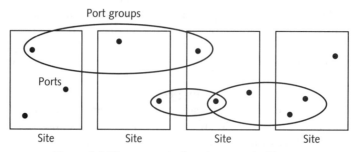

Figure 9.4 The concept of port groups in Chorus.

Table 9.4 A selection of nucleus primitives for message passing

Primitive	Description
portCreate()	Create a port
portDelete()	Destroy a port
portMigrate()	Migrate a port
grpAllocate()	Create a new group address
grpPortInsert()	Add a port to a group
grpPortRemove()	Remove a port from a group
ipcSend()	Send a message asynchronously
ipcReceive()	Receive a message
ipcCall()	Send an RPC message
ipcReply()	Reply to an RPC message

ipcReceive() will block the calling thread until the message has been received.

In the remote procedure call (RPC) mode, the sender sends a message using ipcCall(). The sending thread then blocks awaiting a reply. The receiver can receive the message using ipcReceive() and then reply to the original sender by using ipcReply(). This latter message will then unblock the sender on its arrival. The underlying RPC protocol implements *at-most-once* semantics (see Section 2.3.2).

Finally, the Chorus nucleus supports a style of interaction where message handlers can be attached to ports. A thread will then be generated to execute this handler on the receipt of the message. This service is, however, restricted to supervisor actors.

A selection of the most important primitives supporting message passing is given in Table 9.4.

Virtual memory management

Each actor has its own virtual address space, referred to as a *context*, which is then divided into a number of different *regions*. For example, an actor might consist of separate, non-overlapping, regions for text, data and the stack. Each region has an associated set of access rights for that actor. Regions can also be created and destroyed dynamically within an actor. Supervisor actors also have the capability to create a region in a different actor.

Regions are generally mapped on to secondary storage objects called *segments*. A region can map directly on to an entire segment. More generally, however, a region will map on to a portion of a segment. Furthermore, different regions can access potentially overlapping portions of a segment and hence segments can be shared. This relationship between regions and segments is illustrated in Figure 9.5.

A segment can be thought of as a unit of representation for a portion of the address space. Most segments are persistent and consequently are represented in terms of files or swapping areas. Other segments can, however, be transient

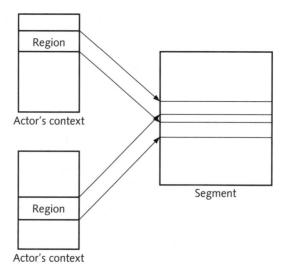

Figure 9.5 Regions and segments in Chorus.

Table 9.5 A selection of nucleus primitives for virtual memory management

Primitive	Description
rgnAllocate()	Allocates a new region in an actor
rgnFree()	Deallocates a region
rgnSetProtect()	Change protection on a region
sgRead()	Reads data from a segment to an address space
sgWrite()	Writes data to a segment from an address space
sgFlush()	Flush a local cache to a segment

and hence be defined in terms of main memory. Larger persistent segments are subject to paging, with the nucleus providing a cache of recently accessed pages.

A selection of the most important primitives supporting virtual memory management is given in Table 9.5.

Naming and addressing

The Chorus entities of actors, ports, port groups and segments are all named using a global unique identifier (UI); that is, this unique identifier is guaranteed to be unique in a global distributed environment. A unique identifier is a 64-bit structure which includes a number indicating the site of creation (used as a hint by the location service), a type and a unique stamp. The type field defines the type of entity represented by the UI (port, port group or site). The stamp is the part of the data structure which must be globally unique.

Unique identifiers are normally generated by the nucleus, which will guarantee the uniqueness in both space and time. It is also possible for

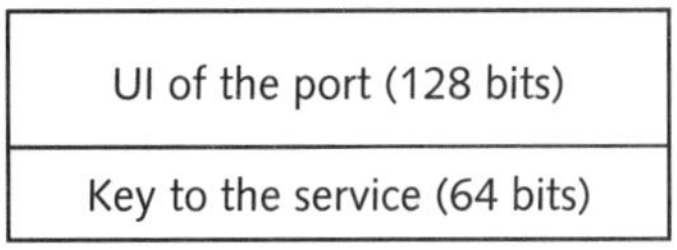

UI of the port (128 bits)
Key to the service (64 bits)

Figure 9.6 The structure of a capability in Chorus.

Table 9.6 A selection of nucleus primitives for virtual memory management

Primitive	Description
uiBuild()	Builds a user defined unique identifier
uiClear()	Clears a user defined unique identifier
uiIsLocal()	Determines if the corresponding entity is local

applications or services to construct their own UIs. In this case, it is their responsibility to ensure the resultant UIs are unique. The nucleus also supports a localization service which will determine the locality of a Chorus entity based on the UI.

It is also possible in Chorus to introduce an additional level of protection in accessing services through the use of *capabilities*. Capabilities are data structures consisting of the 64-bit unique identifier for the port corresponding to the service together with a 64-bit key defining access rights to the service (see Figure 9.6). The Chorus nucleus does not define any particular structure for keys. Key structure must therefore be defined and managed by services outside the nucleus.

A selection of the most important primitives supporting unique identifiers is given in Table 9.6. Note that unique identifiers are also generated by the nucleus as a result of primitives such as portCreate() and grpAllocate().

9.3.3 Chorus implementation

Overall structure of the nucleus

The Chorus nucleus is divided into a number of distinct parts, as shown in Figure 9.7. The *supervisor* is the lowest level of the nucleus and contains a significant portion of the machine-dependent parts of the nucleus. In particular, the supervisor deals with hardware event handling (in terms of traps, exceptions and interrupts) and also provides low-level support for threads. The thread support consists of mapping threads to physical processors and implementing thread context switches.

The *real-time executive* then implements the abstractions of actors and threads and provides underlying support in terms of thread scheduling and thread synchronization. The real-time executive also implements the nucleus interface, calling the appropriate internal nucleus operations to realize each primitive.

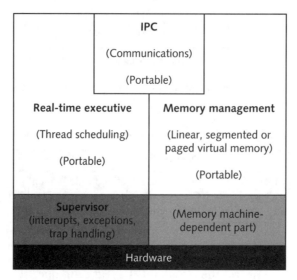

Figure 9.7 The structure of the Chorus nucleus.

The *IPC subsystem* implements the concepts of ports and port groups together with the two styles of message passing defined in Chorus (asynchronous message passing and RPC). The subsystem encapsulates the protocol stack supporting these message-passing services.

Finally, the *memory management subsystem* supports the abstractions of regions and segments and provides the necessary underlying mechanisms to support these concepts. The subsystem is divided into two components. The top-level component, called the virtual memory manager, contains all the machine-independent parts of the subsystem and hence is portable. The lower level component, referred to as the memory management unit, contains the machine-dependent aspects of memory management.

The next subsections examine the various components in more detail. The discussion focuses on the real-time executive (focusing on the thread scheduler), the IPC subsystem and the memory management subsystem. These are the components which are most affected by multimedia. The supervisor is not addressed further in this book. As will become apparent, the implementation of scheduling, IPC and memory management are all flexible in that they support the coexistence of different mechanisms and policies and also readily allow the introduction of new approaches.

The real-time executive

As mentioned above, the real-time executive supports the abstractions of actors and threads. The heart of the executive is the thread scheduler, which determines which thread in a given site should run next. The approach in Chorus is to provide a minimal, efficient scheduler at the lowest level and then provide an extensible set of scheduling classes above this scheduler. This

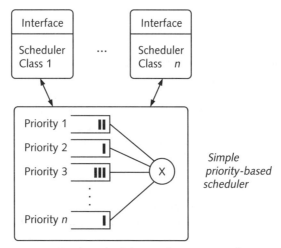

Figure 9.8 The scheduling architecture in Chorus.

architecture is illustrated in Figure 9.8. The underlying scheduler is a simple priority-based scheduler. This scheduler operates on the basis of a kernel priority associated with each thread, with 256 different priority levels supported. To support this, the kernel maintains a set of lists, one per priority level. The scheduler will then maintain one of the following invariants:

- on a single-processor system, the running thread is always the ready thread with the highest absolute kernel priority, or
- on a tightly coupled multiprocessor (managed by one nucleus) featuring N processors, the N ready threads with the N highest absolute priorities are running.

It is also important to note that, in order to support these invariants, the scheduler is preemptive: the arrival of a higher priority thread will preempt the current thread. This also has the crucial effect of minimizing latency for real-time threads.

The kernel priorities are actually hidden from the user. Instead, the user is presented with the abstraction of *scheduling classes*. A given scheduling class implements a particular policy for managing a set of threads. Threads can also be assigned to scheduling classes on an individual basis.

The task of each scheduling class is to determine the kernel priority for a given thread based on its own scheduling policy, together with a set of scheduling attributes. The interpretation of the scheduling attributes varies from class to class. For example, a scheduling class for real-time periodic threads would have attributes representing the period and (optionally) the deadline of the thread.

Chorus also defines a default class. This class implements a simple priority-based scheme with the absolute kernel priority determined from a relative thread priority specified by the user, together with the priority of the associated actor.

The IPC subsystem

The IPC subsystem in Chorus has recently been substantially revised to introduce more flexibility into the architecture. These revisions took place between v3 r4 and v3 r5. We describe the new version of the architecture in this book.

The revised architecture has the following key requirements:

- to obtain outstanding performance on a range of network architectures with particular attention to addressing the requirements of tightly coupled multi-computers and telecommunications networks,
- to provide a framework which enables the introduction of new protocols such as multicast protocols,
- to enable the introduction of more sophisticated (for example quality of service-driven) resource management, and
- to provide extensibility with respect to real-time and multimedia applications.

In order to address these new requirements, significant changes have been made to the communications architecture. Perhaps the most radical innovation is the introduction of a reliable data link layer which provides guaranteed delivery of packets and monitors the availability of the data link. In addition, a number of changes have been made to enable the coexistence of different protocols at various layers. The overall architecture is shown in Figure 9.9.

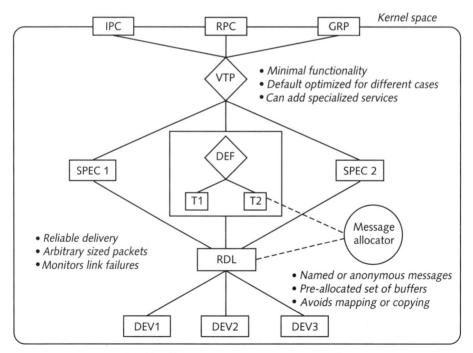

Figure 9.9 The Chorus v3 r5 communications architecture.

The kernel implements the standard Chorus interprocess communication primitives for IPC and RPC and will also in the future provided an additional, reliable group service. These protocols rely on the service of a virtual transport protocol (VTP) which selects the most appropriate transport service for the interaction. To support this, each protocol must offer a generic interface as defined by the Transport Protocol Object. The selected service can either be the default protocol or one of a number of specialist protocols, such as for real-time communications. The default protocol offered by the nucleus is also highly flexible in that it can select from a number of transport strategies depending on the size and destination of the messages. For example, optimizations are provided for local traffic, for fixed size messages or for large messages. Each transport service effectively implements a suitable flow control policy for the style of traffic. For example, the fixed size message protocol operates a credit-based scheme designed to optimize latencies on messages. In addition, the large message protocol in the default stack is optimized for high throughput.

The transport service can also (optionally) make use of a *router*. This functionality is not offered in the v3 r5 release of the software and hence is not shown in the figure above. Future releases will, however, offer this service between the transport and RDL layers to enable protocols to span multiple subnets. This service can also be bypassed to improve performance if interaction is contained within a subnet.

The transport services rely on the RDL service mentioned above to provide a reliable data link. Note that this link supports arbitrary sized messages: fragmentation and reassembly are included in the RDL. The architecture allows for this layer to be null, for example if the underlying network is highly reliable. The rationale for changes at this level is to enable lightweight and highly efficient transport protocols over essentially reliable networks. The transport protocol can therefore implement flow control strategies for the appropriate application requirements and network needs and can assume that this lower level will successfully transmit the underlying messages. The RDL can also select (dynamically) from a range of underlying network devices, such as ATM or Ethernet. The various devices are encapsulated in a Network Device Manager (NDM).

The final component in the new architecture is the message allocator. This is shared between the transport service and the RDL and is responsible for allocating resources to a connection (primarily buffer resources). Connections are provided with a resource object which maps on to a set of physical buffers. It is also proposed to allow the direct mapping of incoming data into user space (although this is not yet implemented). In addition, data can be sent directly to named buffers which correspond to actual physical locations in memory.

The memory management subsystem

The memory management subsystem implements the abstractions of contexts, segments and regions as discussed above. The particular goals of the implementation are as follows (Abrossimov *et al.*, 1989):

- to enable the creation of separate and protected address spaces for actors (contexts), defined in terms of regions mapping on to segments,
- to provide efficient and versatile mechanisms for data transfer between secondary storage and contexts and also between contexts,
- to be adaptable to a wide range of hardware architectures.

The overall architecture offers a Generic Memory Interface (GMI) to other subsystems. Several implementations of this GMI are provided matching different hardware architectures, the most important one being a demand-paged virtual memory implementation (referred to as PVM). We focus on this paged architecture in the remainder of this section. As with all implementations of the GMI, PVM is divided into a machine-independent virtual memory manager and a (smaller) machine-dependent memory management unit. The overall architecture is illustrated in Figure 9.10. (Note that the implementation of segments is done above the Generic Memory Interface; this aspect is discussed in more detail below).

The virtual memory manager implements the abstractions of contexts and regions. To support this, the virtual memory manager maintains a number of data structures: *a list of all contexts* on a given site, a *context descriptor* per context containing a doubly linked list of regions, and a *region descriptor* per region defining the region start address, size and access rights together with a pointer to the local cache for the associated segment (again, see below), together with an offset within the segment for the start of the region.

Segments are represented in the virtual memory manager by *local caches*. There is one local cache per segment on a site. Therefore, if this segment is shared between regions, the local cache will also be shared. Care must therefore be taken to ensure cache consistency. The local cache maintains a doubly linked list of page descriptors for currently cached pages. On access to a

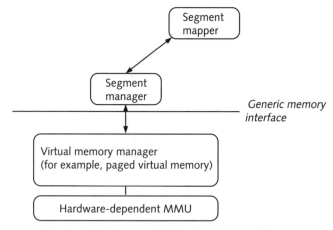

Figure 9.10 The paged virtual memory architecture.

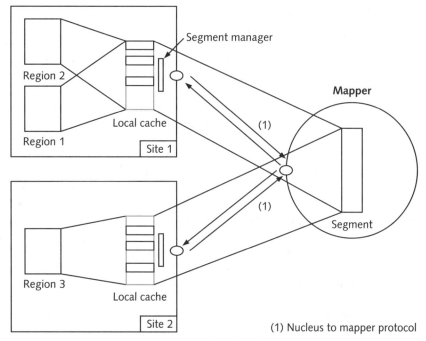

Figure 9.11 The role of the local cache.

page, this local cache is searched. If the appropriate page is found, the request can be serviced immediately. If the page is absent, the local cache must access the segment to obtain the appropriate page.

Segments in Chorus are implemented by *segment managers* in the nucleus together with *segment mappers* in user space. The segment manager deals with requests from the local cache to pull in or to push out a particular page. To satisfy this request, the segment manager must interact with the appropriate segment mapper (see Figure 9.11). This mapper actually implements the segment, defining the representation of the segment on secondary storage. The mapper also encapsulates the policy for cache management (for example in terms of locking pages in physical memory or flushing the contents of the cache to the segment). Thus, the architecture maintains a clean separation between mechanism and policy. Segment mappers are implemented as normal user-level actors and are accessed by using interprocess communication on a port address for the actor. This increases the flexibility of the memory management architecture in that different implementations of segment mappers can coexist. Chorus provides a default mapper with the microkernel, but users are free to define their own. This flexibility has been exploited by researchers in defining mappers to implement *distributed virtual memory* (Coulouris *et al.*, 1994). In this case, a number of mappers interact to implement distributed virtual memory and to ensure the coherency of a set of local caches.

The memory management architecture features a number of optimizations designed to improve the efficiency of Chorus subsystems. The most notable optimization is the *deferred copy technique* designed to improve the performance of copy operations. Using this technique, pages are not automatically copied when a portion of a segment is copied. Rather, pages are shared until the page is actually written; at this point, a new page must be allocated and data copied.

This technique is implemented by a refinement of the concept of local caches as introduced above. When a segment is copied, a history object is created as a descendant of the local cache for the source segment. This history object is used to access the new segment (this is effectively the local cache for the new segment). In particular, the history object is searched for a page and, if it is not found, the local cache for the source is then searched. Initially, the history object is empty and hence all searches will be resolved by the source object (in other words, all pages are shared at this stage). An action must, however, be taken when a page is written in either the source or the copy. This action is necessary to preserve the correct view of both copies of the data. Write attempts are detected by setting all pages in the source to read-only. On a write violation, the following algorithm is then executed:

> If the write attempt was on the segment represented by the history object, then a new page is allocated and the contents copied from the corresponding page in the source. The write action can then proceed. If, however, the write attempt was on the source object then it is first necessary to check whether the history object already has a copy of this page. If a copy exists, it is only necessary to make the source page writable. If a copy does not exist, it is necessary to allocate a new page and update the contents from the source page. The source page is then made writable and the write action is carried out.

Because of the above semantics, the technique is also referred to as copy-on-write.

We further illustrate the operation of history objects by example (taken from Abrossimov *et al.* (1989)). Figure 9.12 illustrates a segment, cpy, as a partial copy of a source segment, src. In particular, cpy is a copy of the first three pages of src. In the diagram, page 1 is unmodified. Hence, a search from cpy will be passed on to src. Page 2 however has been updated in src and page 3 in cpy. Hence new pages have been allocated in each case (shown in the figure as 2' and 3' respectively). Note that the algorithm generalizes for further copying of the source or history objects. The net result is a tree of objects with the original source at the head; a new leaf is added for each copy operation. The full algorithm is reported in Abrossimov *et al.* (1989).

This technique is useful in Chorus to optimize the copying of large amounts of data. For example, deferred copying is used to improve the efficiency of fork operations in the Unix subsystem. The same technique can also be used to improve the efficiency of message passing between actors in the same site by

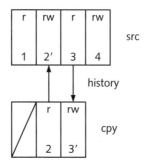

Figure 9.12 Illustration of history objects.

only copying the data when it is written. Note that a different technique is used in Chorus when small amounts of data are being copied. The alternative technique operates at the granularity of individual pages and is hence referred to as the per-virtual-page technique. Again, further details can be found in Abrossimov *et al.* (1989).

Finally, the memory management unit for the paged implementation contains the machine-dependent aspects mapping paging on to the underlying hardware. In particular, the memory management unit provides a range of services including:

- the allocation and deallocation of physical pages,
- the mapping of pages into a context,
- the invalidation of physical pages,
- the implementation of protection on physical pages, and
- the maintenance of state on each page (whether the dirty bit is set).

The memory management unit is relatively small and is easy to port on to alternative architectures.

9.3.4 Discussion

From the descriptions above, it is now possible to appreciate more fully the benefits of Chorus in terms of real-time performance and flexibility. In terms of real-time performance, Chorus provides a lightweight and highly efficient platform for distributed processing. In addition, the Chorus nucleus offers features such as preemptive scheduling and page locking, which assist the attainment of real-time guarantees. More importantly, the system is highly flexible. The overall architecture is flexible in that it allows specialized subsystems to be developed. Furthermore, different subsystems can coexist on the same site. Each of the components in the nucleus offers a similar level of flexibility:

- the real-time executive enables users to develop their own scheduling classes,

- the IPC subsystem supports the insertion of specialized transport protocols through the virtual transport protocol, and
- the memory management subsystem supports the creation of specialized implementations of segments through the mapper concept.

Again, the different services can coexist on the one site.

The Chorus microkernel therefore provides a promising approach to the support of our engineering model (and in particular, the multimedia aspects of the model) through both the development of a specialized subsystem and the specialization of each of the nucleus services to support this subsystem. It should be stressed, however, that the specializations are necessary. The Chorus microkernel does not yet provide the level of service or guarantees of performance for multimedia applications. For example, the communications architecture is tailored towards the reliable delivery of messages and does not consider signal or stream interactions, the scheduling subsystem has a rather simple view of scheduling tailored towards the support of Unix subsystems, and the memory management subsystem provides no guarantees on the latency of page accesses. Furthermore, there is a lack of integration between these various components. Chorus also does not currently support QoS management of resources. It is therefore necessary to consider refinements and extensions to the Chorus approach to meet our full set of requirements.

9.4 Extensions for multimedia

9.4.1 General approach

Overall architecture

In this section, we describe an overall approach to the development of a microkernel-based, RM-ODP-compliant platform offering explicit support for distributed multimedia applications. Our overall architecture is shown in Figure 9.13.

The overall approach is based closely on a microkernel-based architecture as discussed in Section 9.3.1. In particular, the architecture features a low-level operating system nucleus which can support a number of subsystems. The figure then shows an ODP subsystem coexisting with other subsystems (for example, a Unix subsystem). The role of this subsystem is to provide an RM-ODP-compliant virtual machine. More specifically, this virtual machine conforms to our engineering model and provides access to a range of underlying services to support the creation of open applications (including real-time services supporting multimedia application). Note that the figure shows the ODP subsystem spanning over the other subsystems; this simply indicates that the ODP subsystem can provide open access to other services, for example those offered by the Unix subsystem. The top layer is then a set of

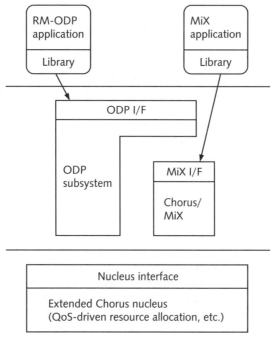

Figure 9.13 The overall architecture.

RM-ODP-compliant applications and services. This layer corresponds to the programming model as defined in Chapter 4. It should be stressed, however, that the precise boundary between the virtual machine and the applications and services is fluid (see the discussion in Section 8.3.1). Indeed, as discussed above, both layers share precisely the same object model.

We discuss the nucleus and ODP subsystem in more detail below, with particular emphasis on the facilities required to support multimedia.

The nucleus

The nucleus is at the bottom level of this architecture. This layer provides the nucleus services as defined in the engineering model. In particular, the layer supports the creation of virtual resources in capsules and also the multiplexing of these virtual resources on to the underlying physical resources (corresponding to the node management function in RM-ODP). The layer should also provide access to primitive bindings as required by the recursive binding model.

In terms of multimedia, we require a nucleus with particular properties:

- it should be possible to create resources (threads, communications and memory resources) with a particular quality of service,
- there should be a level of integration between the various aspects of the nucleus to enable end-to-end quality of service to be attained,

- the node management function should allow different resource management strategies to coexist and should honour quality of service requirements where provided,
- the nucleus should adopt a strategy to deal with overload (this could be null if appropriate static QoS management strategies are employed),
- the implementation of multimedia services in the nucleus should be optimized for efficiency (for example by minimizing domain crossings, context switches and physical data copies), and
- the nucleus should support a set of primitive QoS-driven bindings (at a minimum, signal bindings).

The services offered by the nucleus are then used by the ODP subsystem as discussed below.

The ODP subsystem

The implementation of the virtual machine is based on the engineering model as defined in Section 8.3. In particular, the virtual machine offers a set of services to support the creation of engineering objects and bindings. In terms of multimedia, the most important aspect of the ODP subsystem is the provision of a set of binding factories enabling the creation of bindings with quality of service guarantees. The bindings factories can also offer varying levels of quality of service management.

More specifically, the following requirements can be identified for multimedia bindings:

- the subsystem should implement the recursive binding model as proposed in Section 8.3.2,
- as part of this model, the subsystem should exploit the abstract binding protocol defined in Section 8.3.2,
- the subsystem should provide a range of binding factories enabling the creation of signal, stream and operational bindings with QoS guarantees,
- the above binding factories should encapsulate static QoS management (negotiation, admission control and resource reservation) functions as required by the class of binding,
- the above binding factories should generate managed objects for dynamic QoS management functions (monitoring, policing, maintenance and re-negotiation) as required by the class of binding.

The subsystem should also support the creation of other multimedia objects with QoS guarantees, such as producer or consumer objects.

9.4.2 Two implementations

Two implementations have been developed based on the architecture described above and using the Chorus microkernel. The main features of the two implementations are described below (full details can be found in Chapters 10 and 11).

- *The Sumo-CORE*

  The goal of this platform is to provide specialized real-time support for multimedia applications in a microkernel-based environment. The emphasis of the work is therefore to develop specialized resource management strategies (communications, scheduling and memory management) to meet the demands of multimedia. Particular attention is given to achieving integration between the various aspects of resource management to enable end-to-end bindings to be achieved. Considerable attention is also given to underlying support for QoS management. In particular, a set of QoS management functions are developed which are intended to provide the required level of guarantees in heterogeneous environments. The Sumo-CORE platform was developed at Lancaster University.

- *The Sumo-ORB*

  The goal of this platform is to provide an open distributed processing environment for telecommunications services and applications. The platform adopts CORBA as a basic technology but extends CORBA with support for real-time and multimedia applications, following the programming and engineering models developed earlier in this book. The platform can thus be viewed as a telecommunications ORB with appropriate real-time support for that domain. The current implementation of Sumo-ORB operates over an FDDI network which offers deterministic guarantees on the underlying quality of service. This implementation therefore features more specialized QoS management services designed for the FDDI environment. The Sumo-ORB platform was developed at CNET.

The two platforms are therefore complementary. The first focuses on the nucleus in terms of the above architecture and hence provides real-time (integrated) resource management, but with less attention on the structure and facilities offered by the ODP subsystem. In contrast, the latter focuses on the ODP subsystem in terms of the above architecture but with less attention to the underlying operating system support. In addition, the first implementation provides QoS management functions for general non-deterministic networks, whereas the latter concentrates on providing deterministic guarantees for FDDI networks.

It is important, however, to stress the commonalities between the two implementations. Both implementations adhere to the systems architecture described in Section 9.4.1 and also adopt the programming and engineering models developed in Chapters 4, 5 and 8. Similarly, both implementations make the same technology choice: to adopt the Chorus microkernel as the basis for the implementation. The two platforms should therefore be viewed as exploring different and complementary aspects of the overall approach to open distributed processing and multimedia as developed in this book.

9.5 Summary

This chapter has considered the issue of operating system support for multimedia and has presented the case for a microkernel approach to meeting the particular demands of multimedia applications. The chapter started by considering the demands of multimedia on operating systems in terms of predictable real-time performance, efficiency, support for diversity and the need for graceful degradation on overload. The chapter then argued that existing operating system structures are not able to meet these demands but highlighted the potential contribution of microkernels in this area. In particular, the chapter highlighted the following potential benefits of microkernels:

- the lightweight nature of microkernels provides a more supportive environment for attaining real-time performance,
- the inherent flexibility of microkernels encourages specialization of various operating system components for a particular application domain, such as multimedia.

The chapter then described in detail the Chorus microkernel. This description focused on the overall architecture, the service offered by the Chorus nucleus (the microkernel) and finally the implementation of this nucleus. The subsequent discussion then highlighted the particular features of Chorus which support specialization.

Finally, the chapter concluded by presenting an implementation architecture for an open distributed processing platform based on microkernels. The chapter also outlined two experimental implementations based on this overall architecture: the Sumo-CORE platform developed at Lancaster University and the Sumo-ORB platform developed at CNET. The next two chapters will describe these two platforms in considerable detail.

10 Sumo-CORE: a specialized microkernel-based operating system for multimedia

10.1 Introduction

This chapter describes the design and implementation of Sumo-CORE, an operating system designed to support multimedia (Coulson *et al.*, 1994a, b, 1995). More specifically, the operating system is designed to provide explicit support for the engineering model as described in Chapter 8. In particular, the operating system fulfils the role of the RM-ODP nucleus and hence supports the creation of virtual resources (with optional quality of service) and the multiplexing of these virtual resources on to the underlying physical resources. The operating system also provides primitive bindings to support the recursive binding architecture.

The most important research goals of the platform are as follows:

- to investigate efficient quality of service-driven resource management strategies (particularly for communications and scheduling),
- to achieve integration between the various aspects of resource management to support the construction of end-to-end bindings,
- to enable coexistence with alternative resource management strategies in other subsystems (such as in a Unix subsystem),
- to investigate quality of service management strategies for end-to-end bindings in heterogeneous environments, and
- to achieve integration between the various aspects of quality of service management for end-to-end bindings.

The chapter is structured as follows. Section 10.2 describes the overall approach to the design of Sumo-CORE. This section highlights two key principles behind the design: active bindings and split level resource management. Section 10.3 then describes the extended programming interface offered by Sumo-CORE. This interface is based on the Chorus programming interface, but with additional operations for real-time and multimedia applications. The implementation of the platform is then described in Section 10.4. This section describes scheduling and communications in some depth and also outlines the solution for the management of communications buffers. The section also highlights how the implementation supports the engineering model (in terms of explicit binding, QoS management and reactive objects). Following this, Section 10.5 describes the quality of service management features in Sumo-CORE, discussing the approach to both static and dynamic QoS management. Section 10.6 presents some performance figures for Sumo-CORE and Section 10.7 summarizes the major contributions of the chapter.

10.2 Overall approach

10.2.1 Refinements to Chorus

The Sumo-CORE platform retains the overall programming model of Chorus but refines this programming model to provide explicit support for multimedia. This is achieved to retain backward compatibility with the Chorus nucleus, so that all Chorus applications will operate correctly on a Sumo-CORE platform.

The major refinements are summarized below:

- *QoS-driven resource allocation*
  The Chorus nucleus provides a number of primitives for the allocation of resources: `portCreate()` and `threadCreate()`, corresponding to the creation of ports and threads respectively. However, such primitives do not generally include QoS directives. The Sumo-CORE platform therefore supports an additional set of primitives for quality of service-driven resource allocation: `rt_portCreate()` and `rt_threadCreate()`, corresponding to the creation of the new abstractions of `rt_ports` and `rt_threads` respectively (the allocation of buffers is encapsulated within `rt_ports`). In addition, all primitives defined on ports and threads are also supported on `rt_ports` and `rt_threads` (for example `ipcSend()`, `ipcReceive()` on `rt_ports` and `threadSuspend()`, `threadResume()` on `rt_threads`).
- *Explicit QoS-managed bindings*
  Sumo-CORE supports explicit binding between `rt_ports` through an `rt_portBind()` primitive. This binding takes a set of quality of service requirements as a parameter and returns a control port supporting the subsequent management of the binding. The creation of a binding therefore encapsulates static resource management functions, including negotiation, admission control and resource reservation. The control port then supports dynamic QoS management functions, including monitoring and renegotiation. Crucially, bindings in Sumo-CORE are *active* rather than the more traditional passive model of interaction. This important aspect of the design is discussed in more depth in Section 10.2.2.
- *Specialized resource management*
  Sumo-CORE also features specialized resource management strategies for scheduling, communications and buffer management (with particular

emphasis on the first two areas). The approach to scheduling is based on an earliest deadline first policy, which ensures that deadlines for both periodic and aperiodic tasks can be met. Similarly, the communications architecture features specialized strategies for multimedia, including rate-based flow control and minimal error control. In each case, these policies can coexist with other policies, for example as required by the Unix subsystem (MiX). Crucially, the implementation of each of the components features a split level approach. This aspect of the design is central to Sumo-CORE and is discussed more fully in Section 10.2.3.

We now look at the rationale for active bindings and split level resource management in some detail.

10.2.2 Active bindings

What is an active binding?

Bindings provide an explicit representation of the means of communicating data between rt_ports. In most systems, this process would be passive, with applications taking the active role; that is, applications will actively send and receive data by invoking appropriate system calls. The application will also provide buffers for the data being received or sent. In contrast, bindings between rt_ports in Sumo-CORE are *active* (see discussion in Section 4.3.3). In other words, the implementation of the binding takes responsibility for collecting the data and delivering the data. The binding also takes responsibility for providing buffers for this data.

More specifically, the binding upcalls the application when either data is required or data is to be delivered. At this stage, a thread is created to deal with the event. The role of the application is to provide handlers for different categories of event (referred to as rt_handlers in Sumo-CORE). Producer rt_handlers are expected to fill buffers with data to be sent, and consumer rt_handlers to use the data as provided. The distinction between passive and active styles of binding is illustrated in Figure 10.1 (repeated from Section 4.3.3).

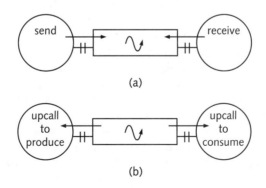

(a)

(b)

Figure 10.1 (a) Passive and (b) active stream binding.

Advantages of active bindings

We believe that there are a number of advantages to active bindings for multimedia. The most important advantages relate to quality of service management. In particular, the binding can take full responsibility for the provision of the desired level of quality of service. This involves the following steps:

1. the establishment of an appropriate communications protocol with the desired QoS characteristics,
2. upcalling the producer or consumer at the appropriate times as determined by the quality of service requirements,
3. the assignment of deadlines to threads for the execution of upcalls (again determined from the overall QoS requirements), and
4. the allocation of sufficient buffers to support the desired level of quality of service.

Thus, active bindings achieve a level of *integration* in the *quality of service management* of threads, communications and buffers. Furthermore, the application need not be concerned with any of these issues. As a side effect of this approach, it is also not necessary to provide QoS policing (ensuring that the application does not attempt to inject data at a higher rate than that contracted at binding establishment time).

We also contend that active bindings provide a *natural and effective model* for real-time programming. Real-time programming is considerably simplified when programmers can structure applications to react to events and delegate to the system the responsibility for initiating communication events. The programmer is still ultimately in control of event occurrence, but this control is expressed declaratively through the provision of QoS parameters at binding establishment time, and need not be explicitly programmed in a procedural style.

The implementation of active bindings also exhibits a *separation of control transfer and data transfer*. In traditional systems, the transfer of control and the transfer of data are usually tightly coupled. For example, the execution of a Unix *write* system call passes data to the kernel and simultaneously transfers control to the kernel. Similarly, the return of a call such as *read* transfers control back to the application and simultaneously transfers the received data to the application. In Sumo-CORE, these aspects are kept quite separate. On the consumer side, this implies maintaining a separation between the notification of data arrival and the actual receipt of this data by the application. Similarly, on the producer side, there is a clear separation between the notification that data should be sent and the actual sending of the data. This separation is particularly useful when dealing with data that should be delivered directly to a device. For example, consider the case of video frames being delivered directly to a frame buffer for display. In this case, the application can be notified of the arrival of video frames but need not physically receive the data; the data can be delivered directly to the frame buffer. This separation of control and data is an important optimization in Sumo-CORE, as many multimedia applications are only interested in the control aspects of an interaction (either for purposes of synchronization or monitoring).

10.2.3 Split level resource management

What is split level resource management?

Resource management in Sumo-CORE has a split level structure in that management is split between the nucleus and user space. More specifically, management is carried out between a kernel-level manager in the nucleus and a user-level manager in a user actor. This general principle applies to both scheduling and communications and is the key to achieving integration between the two aspects of resource management (see below). In general, the minimum of functionality is placed in the kernel-level manager, leaving the majority of resource management functionality in user space. More specifically, the high-level policy for resource management is largely determined by the user-level managers. The two levels of management then function cooperatively by sharing management information in an area of shared memory (a *bulletin board*). The user-level functionality is contained in a Sumo-CORE library that can be linked into applications.

In terms of RM-ODP, split level resource management can be interpreted as the nucleus supporting the creation of virtual resources and then multiplexing the virtual resources on to physical resources; the user-level manager then creates higher level abstractions and multiplexes these on to the virtual resources offered by the kernel.

The concept of split level resource management applies to specific resources as follows:

- *Split level scheduling*
  In split level scheduling, management is split between a kernel-level scheduler and a user-level scheduler. The kernel-level scheduler creates the abstraction of virtual processors and schedules the virtual processors on to the available physical processor. The user-level scheduler then creates the abstraction of user-level *lightweight threads* and determines which lightweight thread should be scheduled next (on the available virtual processor). Information on the urgency of virtual processors is then conveyed to the kernel through an area of shared memory.
- *Split level communications*
  In the split level communications architecture, the protocol stack is split between kernel and user space. More specifically, the kernel deals with the data link and network layers with the transport protocol being implemented in user space. The task of the kernel is to multiplex and demultiplex network packets to application address spaces, but to let

application address spaces perform transport level processing. As will become apparent in Section 10.4.2, communication between the two components again relies on an area of shared memory.

The split level approach relies on efficient and lightweight communications between user and kernel space. This is achieved by having an area of shared memory between the two areas. It is also necessary to pass events between the two areas, such as the arrival of a packet or a request to send a packet. This is achieved by the use of asynchronous *upcalls* and *downcalls* (corresponding to signals in RM-ODP). Note that the implementation of upcalls and downcalls also relies on the use of the bulletin board; further details are, however, deferred to Section 10.4.

Advantages of split level resource management

One major advantage of this approach is that the majority of functionality is in user space and hence can exploit inexpensive user-level concurrency. Lightweight threads are an order of magnitude cheaper than kernel-supported threads (which are in turn an order of magnitude cheaper than Unix-like processes, as discussed in Chapter 2). This improvement in efficiency stems from the fact that context switches between lightweight threads are essentially a coroutine switch. We also believe that, in general, multimedia applications will feature a high level of internal concurrency and hence will be able to exploit the benefits of lightweight threads. For example, many multimedia applications will be structured as pipelines, where continuous media data is passed through a number of concurrent processing stages.

The split level approach also achieves a level of *integration* between communications and scheduling in that the execution of the transport protocol and the subsequent application processing are both carried out in user space and hence can be carried out by a single lightweight thread (or set of interacting threads) with a clearly identifiable deadline. (This deadline can be derived from the quality of service requirements for the associated binding.) In conventional systems, the transport processing would be carried out in the kernel and there would be no knowledge of the importance or urgency of the encapsulated information until the protocol processing had been carried out. Similarly, the kernel must deal with multiple transport connections with competing requirements. According to Tennenhouse (1990), it is much more difficult to meet quality of service requirements of particular connections in such *multiplexed* implementations.

A level of integration is also achieved with buffer management in that, for example, the number of buffers devoted to a connection can be determined from the expected execution time of protocol and application processing. Thus a combination of active bindings and split level resource management achieves integration of both QoS management and resource management for the full set of resources (hence achieving two of our key objectives listed in the introduction).

Similarly, by having transport processing and application processing in the same address space, we do not incur any context switches or domain crossings in their interaction. There will be some overhead associated with interaction between the user-level and kernel-level resource managers, but this can be minimized by the use of upcalls and downcalls, as discussed above.

Finally, the split level approach is inherently *flexible* in that user space management can be specialized to meet the needs of the particular application. For example, one actor can have a reliable connection-oriented transport protocol, such as TCP, while another may have an unreliable rate-based protocol for continuous media interactions. Similar arguments apply for scheduling and buffer management. It is also relatively easy for application programmers to develop their own user-level services for scheduling, communications and buffer management.

10.3 Programming interface and abstractions

We now describe the additional primitives offered by Sumo-CORE to support real-time and multimedia programming. We first describe the primitives offered by the platform and then provide two examples illustrating their use in typical multimedia scenarios. Note that some details of the interface are omitted to simplify the presentation in the book.

10.3.1 Additional primitives in Sumo-CORE

The additional primitives offered by Sumo-CORE are as follows:

- `rt_ports` – communication end-points for real-time communications,
- `rt_handlers` – user defined procedures which manipulate real-time data coming from or going to an `rt_port`,
- QoS-managed bindings – communication channels with a specific QoS, and
- `rt_threads` – real-time lightweight threads.

These primitives are described in turn below.

Rt_ports
`Rt_ports` are an extension of standard Chorus ports and serve as end-points for both continuous media communications and real-time messages with bounded latency. They are offered by Chorus actors requiring real-time communication with other actors (such as producer or consumer devices, filters or arbitrary multimedia services). Like Chorus ports, `rt_ports` are named globally and can be accessed in a location independent fashion from anywhere in the distributed system.

There are, however, the following differences between Chorus ports and `rt_ports`:

- `rt_ports` can support explicit binding with a specified level of QoS,
- the internal buffers of `rt_ports` can be directly accessed by the application programmer without the overhead of a system call,
- `rt_ports` may not migrate because the QoS commitments offered by the `rt_port` must be sustained.

Rt_ports are created with the following call:

```
logicalID rt_portCreate(KnCap *host; rt_Port *p);
```

The parameters to this call are as follows. The first parameter, `host`, is a capability for a Chorus actor specifying the required location for the new `rt_port`. With the semantics of `rt_ports`, this must be an actor on the local site. The second parameter, `p`, returns a pointer to the created `rt_port`. The call returns a logical identifier used to uniquely identify the new port; if an error occurs, this identifier will have the value -1. Note that no resources are created at this stage. Resources are allocated to `rt_ports` as a result of an `rt_portBind()` call (see below), taking into account the desired level of quality of service for the binding.

Rt_handlers

Rt_handlers are user-supplied C functions which are attached to `rt_ports` to realize active bindings. As described in Section 10.2.2, `rt_handlers` are upcalled from their associated `rt_port` whenever data is required at a producer `rt_port` or has been delivered, by a binding, to a consumer `rt_port`. The upcall indicates the occurrence of an event. This event may be related to the required production or consumption of data, in which case the `rt_handler` can directly access the buffer associated with the `rt_port`. Alternatively, the event could be related to QoS management and indicate, for example, a QoS violation. More generally, the event can be any asynchronous notification as defined in the particular implementation and can have associated data of arbitrary size.

The call to attach an `rt_handler` to an `rt_port` is as follows:

```
typedef struct {
  int eventType;
  VmAddr buffer;
  VmSize size;
  VmFlags flags;
} rt_portEvent;

typedef int(Rthandler)(rtportEvent event);

status rt_portAttachRt_handler(rtport *p; rt_handler f;
                    Time *cputime);
```

Table 10.1 Fields of `rt_portEvent` structure

Parameter	Interpretation
eventType	The type of the event
buffer	Virtual memory address for the associated buffer
size	Size of the associated buffer
flags	Flags concerning virtual memory management, for example if the data is remapped

The first two parameters to the `rt_portAttachRt_handler()` call specify the `rt_port` to which the `rt_handler` is to be attached and the address of the `rt_handler` function. The third parameter, `cputime`, is a programmer-supplied estimate of the execution time of the handler. This is used for scheduling purposes and is added to the *a priori* known time for protocol processing to help derive the deadline of the handler thread. Note that the `rt_portAttachRt_handler()` call will fail if the specified `rt_port` does not reside in the current address space.

It is assumed that `rt_handlers` offer a common interface as specified by the `typedef` above. In particular, an `rt_handler` is assumed to receive one parameter, which is a structure defining the incoming event. The interpretation of the various fields is given in Table 10.1.

An event can also explicitly be delivered to an `rt_port` (as opposed to being raised by the active binding), resulting in the execution of the associated `rt_handler`. This is achieved by the following call:

```
status rt_portRaiseEvent (rtport *p, rt_portEvent event);
```

Events are normally dealt with by invoking appropriate `rt_handlers`. However, it is also possible to suspend a thread awaiting an event as follows:

```
status rt_portAwaitEvent (rtport *p, rt_portEvent *event);
```

This call blocks until an event has been raised on the specified `rt_port` and then returns the event in the specified `rt_portEvent` structure.

QoS-managed bindings
QoS-managed bindings are explicit bindings between `rt_ports` which are governed by an overall statement of the desired quality of service. As discussed above, such bindings in Sumo-CORE are active in that they upcall the application when they require data for transmission and also when data is to be delivered. Bindings encapsulate the static QoS management functions of negotiation, resource reservation and admission control. In addition, they support dynamic QoS management through a management port attached to the binding.

At present, only point-to-point bindings are supported in Sumo-CORE. The call to establish such a binding is as follows:

```
typedef enum {
   RT_MESSAGE, RT_STREAM
} bindingType;

typedef enum {RT_BESTEFFORT, RT_GUARANTEED} com;
typedef enum {RT_ISOCHRONOUS, RT_WORKAHEAD} del;

                                 typedef struct {
typedef struct {                     com commitment;
   com commitment;                   int buffsize;
   int buffsize;                     int priority
   int priority;                     int latency;
   int latency;                      int error;
   int error;                    } MessageQoS;
   int errorInterval;
   int buffrate;                 typedef union {
   int jitter;                       MessageQoS mq;
   del delivery;                     StreamQoS sq;
} StreamQoS;                      } QoSVector;

status rt_portBind(rtport *producer, *consumer;
                   bindingType service;
                   QoSVector *qos; rt_port *ctl);
```

The rt_portBind() call takes two rt_ports, a producer and a consumer, as its primary parameters. Note that because of the global naming of rt_ports, it is possible to call rt_portBind() from a third-party site. This is a useful facility, as distributed multimedia applications are often structured as a centralized master process supervising and controlling a number of physically distributed producer and consumer objects (see the discussion in Section 8.3.2).

The third parameter specifies the type of service for the binding. This can be either RT_MESSAGE or RT_STREAM. The fourth parameter, qos, then indicates the quality of service required by the binding. QoS parameters are specified to the system by means of a data structure called a QoSVector. Different definitions of this data structure are used depending on the service type required (RT_MESSAGE or RT_STREAM). The interpretation for each of these parameters in QoSVector is given in Table 10.2.

The delivery parameter requires some additional explanation. If delivery is isochronous, the stream service delivers precisely at the rate specified by buffrate; otherwise, it attempts to workahead (ignoring the jitter parameter) at rates temporarily faster than buffrate. One use of the workahead delivery mode is to support applications such as real-time file transfer. Its primary use, however, is for pipelines of processing stages (see below).

Table 10.2 QoS parameters for streams and messages

Parameter	Interpretation for streams	Interpretation for messages
commitment	Whether QoS is best effort or guaranteed	As for streams
buffsize	Size of internal buffer	As for streams
priority	Measure of relative priority	As for streams
latency	Maximum end-to-end delay (including application processing)	As for streams
error	Maximum number of buffer losses in a given interval	Probability of message loss
errorInterval	Interval for error measurements	Not used
buffrate	Required delivery rate for buffers	Rate for transmission of fragments for large messages
jitter	Tolerable variance in delivery times	Not used
delivery	Whether rate should be isochronous or workahead	Not used

The final argument to rt_portBind() is a result parameter which returns a new rt_port used to dynamically control the behaviour of the binding. The operations available on the control rt_port are as follows:

- *renegotiate* – this allows the user to dynamically change the QoS of the binding by supplying a new QoSVector argument,
- *disconnect* – to destroy a binding,
- *start, stop* – to respectively activate and deactivate the binding, and
- *prime* – ready the end-to-end binding by filling the receive buffers so that a subsequent start will take immediate effect.

The last three operations are only applicable on stream bindings.

Rt_threads

Normally, lightweight threads are implicitly created as a result of establishing a binding. However, we also allow applications to explicitly create lightweight threads. For example, an rt_handler can spawn one or more threads to deal with the incoming event. A real-time lightweight thread is created by using an rt_threadCreate() primitive as specified below:

```
typedef enum {
    RT_BAND1, RT_BAND2, RT_BAND3;
} priorityBand;

typedef struct {
```

```
        timeValue schedTime;
        timeValue relDeadline;
        priorityBand band;
        timeValue period;
        timeValue worstCaseExecution;
        int criticality;
        int flags;
    } schedParams;

    status rt_threadCreate (int status; schedParams *sp;
                            VmAddr entryPoint);
```

The first parameter, status, is used to determine whether the thread should be created in a suspended state or a running state. The second parameter then defines the scheduling parameters for this particular thread. We examine the interpretation of this structure in more detail below. Finally, the third parameter defines the virtual memory address of the entry point for the thread: the thread will start executing at this address.

The scheduling parameters allow a number of different types of user-level rt_thread to be created. The particular type is determined by the value of the flags field in the above structure. The permissible types are depicted in Figure 10.2. From this figure, it can be seen that rt_threads can either be scheduled according to a given deadline or on the basis of priority. We consider each general category in turn below:

- *Deadline-based threads*
  Deadline-based threads are scheduled on the basis of the relative deadline as specified in the relDeadline field. The schedTime specifies the earliest (relative) time at which the thread can be scheduled. As a refinement, they are also scheduled according to priority bands (as specified in the band field). Three priority bands are supported: $band_1$, $band_2$ and $band_3$. The interpretation of this field is described in Section 10.5.2. Deadline-based threads can also be either periodic or aperiodic: they can either execute repeatedly or can execute once with the given deadline. For periodic threads, the period is determined from the period field. The next execution is then determined by the absolute deadline for the previous thread execution plus the period. Finally, periodic threads can be either workahead or isochronous. This is used to determine the reaction to an incoming event from a binding. Suppose an event is delivered early by the binding. In this case, workahead threads would execute eagerly. However, isochronous threads would be executed according to the required deadline and would therefore wait until the normal scheduling time. For all deadline-based threads, it is also necessary to have a worst-case execution time for the thread give by the worstCaseExecution field. This is used by the underlying infrastructure to determine the expected latency of this component of a binding.

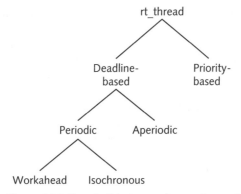

Figure 10.2 Permissible types of rt_thread.

- *Priority-based threads*
  For priority-based threads, the only other applicable field is the criticality field which determines the priority for this thread. Note that deadline-based threads execute with a priority greater than the highest priority allowed for priority-based threads. Hence, priority-based threads are used for non real-time behaviour.

The interpretations of the various fields in the schedParams structure are summarized in Table 10.3.

Sumo-CORE supports a set of primitives operating on rt_threads, corresponding to the primitives defined on kernel threads (see Section 9.3.2). These include rt_threadDelete(), rt_threadSuspend(), and rt_threadResume(). In addition, the operating system provides a number of primitives for thread synchronization. These are based on the Chorus primitives for semaphores and mutexes as discussed in Section 9.3.2. The system also supports one additional primitive, rt_threadRestart(), which resets the thread to its original state ready for the next periodic execution (without this call, a thread would normally terminate on completing its task).

Table 10.3 Fields of schedParams structure

Parameter	Interpretation
schedTime	The permissible scheduling time for deadline-based threads
relDeadline	The relative deadline for deadline-based threads
band	The priority band for a deadline-based thread
period	The period for periodic deadline-based threads
worstCaseExecution	The worst-case execution time for deadline-based threads
criticality	The priority for priority-based threads
flags	Flags determining the type of thread

Note that there is a strong requirement in dealing with concurrent real-time threads to consider deadline inheritance. With deadline inheritance, a deadline can be associated with an entire logical computation rather than with an individual thread. The overall deadline is then passed on from thread to thread as the computation progresses. This can occur either when a thread spawns a new thread or when one thread wakes up another thread using semaphores or mutexes. In both cases, the second thread should inherit the deadline of the first. Deadline inheritance is included in the design of Sumo-CORE, but is not yet provided in the current implementation.

10.3.2 Examples of use

A simple example

The first example illustrates the creation of a stream binding between an audio device on one site and a speaker device on another site. For this example, we assume that both devices are managed in user space. An application actor on a third-party site is responsible for creating the binding between the two devices and starting the interaction. This actor uses a trader service (also located on the third site) to locate the devices. This service provides a means of locating objects in the distributed environment (as discussed in Section 2.2.2). The overall configuration is shown in Figure 10.3.

The audio device and speaker device both create `rt_ports` and then make these `rt_ports` available by exporting their unique identifiers to the trader service. The audio device provides an `rt_handler` which has the task of producing audio data on demand. Similarly, the speaker device provides an `rt_handler` which consumes audio data on demand. Both actors also provide QoS handlers to react to QoS violations detected by the infrastructure.

Code for this example is shown in Figure 10.4 (written in pseudo-C++). In this example, we assume access to the unique identifier for the local actor (K_MYACTOR) and also the port defined on the trader service (`traderPort`). We also assume access to a function, `QoSViolation`, which examines the event type to determine if it is a violation indication.

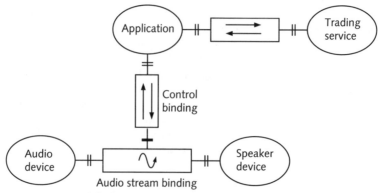

Figure 10.3 Configuration for the simple example.

Producer

```
main ()
{
  rt_port srcPort;

  rt_portCreate (K-MYACTOR, &srcPort);
  rt_portAttachRt_handler  (&srcPort,
                  srcHandler,10);
  traderExport (&traderPort, &srcPort,
                  "producer");
  // delay the thread indefinitely
  // or do some other work
}


sourceHandler (rt_portEvent event)
{
  if (QoSViolation (event))
    // see what type of violation &
    // take appropriate action
  else
    // process the buffer for sending,
    // according to application reqs
    rt_threadRestart ();
}
```

Consumer

```
main ()
{
  rt_port sinkPort;

  rt_portCreate (K-MYACTOR, &sinkPort);
  rt_portAttachRt_handler  (&sinkPort,
                  sinkHandler,10);
  traderExport (&traderPort, &sinkPort,
                  "consumer");
  // delay the thread indefinitely
  // or do some other work
}


sinkHandler (rt_portEvent event)
{
  if (QoSViolation (event))
    // see what type of violation &
    // take appropriate action
  else
    // process the buffer received,
    // according to application reqs
    rt_threadRestart ();
}
```

Application

```
main()
{
  QoSVector actualQos;
  rt_port producer, consumer, control;

  //set Qos parameters  . . .
  myQos.commitment = RT_GUARANTEED;
  //      . . .etc . . . .

  traderInput (&traderPort, &producer,
                "producer");
  traderInput (&traderPort. &consumer,
                "consumer");
  rt_portBind (&producer, &consumer,
                RT_STREAM, &actualQos,
                &control);
}
```

Figure 10.4 Outline code for the simple example.

A more complex example

The second example is a simple distributed MPEG player. The configuration consists of a stored MPEG video sequence implemented in user space, which is then connected with a video binding to a filter object on the same site (again implemented in user space). The filter object reduces the bandwidth

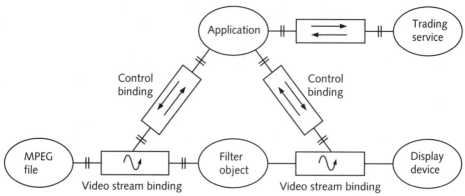

Figure 10.5 Configuration for the more complex example.

requirements of the film by, firstly, dropping B-frames and P-frames and, secondly, applying colour reduction techniques on the remaining frames (see Section 8.4.1 for a discussion of MPEG filtering). The output of the filter object is then connected by a video binding to a kernel-managed display device on another site. This display device decodes the incoming MPEG stream and displays it in an appropriate user window. Again, the configuration is created and managed by an application actor running on a remote site. This actor also has access to a trader running on the same site. The configuration is shown in Figure 10.5.

We now consider the implementation of each actor in turn (in each case, we omit the QoS handlers to simplify the presentation):

- *The storage server*
  This object creates an rt_port and makes this rt_port available through the trader service. The actor also provides an rt_handler to produce the video data. This handler reads the required data from the stored object and then fills the buffer provided by the rt_port on the upcall.
- *The filter object*
  The filter object creates two external rt_ports, one for the incoming MPEG stream and one for the outgoing MPEG stream and makes them available through the trading service. The object also provides two rt_handlers to deal with incoming and outgoing data. These two rt_handlers then consume and produce data respectively. As will become apparent, they also carry out the necessary filtering on the MPEG stream. An internal rt_port is also used to convey data between the two handlers. Consider the arrival of an MPEG frame at the incoming rt_port. This will cause the execution of the first rt_handler. This handler determines whether the frame is a B-frame, P-frame or I-frame. If it is an I-frame, the rt_handler raises an event directly on the intermediary rt_port using rt_portRaiseEvent(). This event will

contain a pointer to the appropriate I-frame. If it is not an I-frame, the rt_handler takes no action and immediately returns (B-frames and P-frames are discarded). The second rt_handler executes at the rate determined by the outgoing binding. On each execution, the rt_handler will block, awaiting an event on the intermediary rt_port, and will then process this event. More specifically, the rt_handler will take the associated I-frame and perform the necessary colour reduction. It will then make the fully processed MPEG frame available for transmission across the binding. Note that further data might arrive at the incoming rt_port before the above process is completed. This next data item will be processed after a period determined by the quality of service on the incoming binding. This can result in a level of concurrency within the object. The overall structure for the filter object is summarized in Figure 10.6.

- *The display device*
  The object representing the display device creates an rt_port for communication and makes this available, for example through a trader service. Note, however, that the display device is different from the other objects considered above as it is implemented in kernel space. The device is also optimized by delivering incoming data directly to internal buffers for display. The device offers an rt_port for communication with the outside world. Hence, the display device object can only monitor events associated with the incoming data and cannot access the data directly. The rt_handler associated with the rt_port thus simply monitors the rate of the arriving MPEG packets.

- *The application object*
  The application object firstly imports the unique identifiers for the various rt_ports using the trader service and then creates the required configuration by establishing a binding between the MPEG source and the filter object and also between the filter object and the MPEG device. The first binding is declared as a workahead binding: it can deliver data faster than the required rate. Finally, the application object initiates the flow of data by starting both bindings.

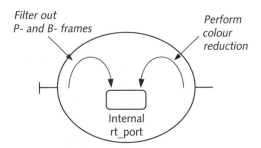

Figure 10.6 The filter object in more detail.

Main Program

```
main()
{
  rt_port mpegIN, mpegOUT, intermediary;

  rt_portCreate (K_MYACTOR,&mpegIN);
  rt_portAttachRt_handler (&mpegIN),
                   handler1,30);
  traderExport (&traderPort, &mpegIN.
                   "mpegIN");

  rt_portCreate (K_MYACTOR,&mpegOUT);
  rt_portAttachRt_handler (&mpegOUT,
                   handler2,100);
  traderExport (&traderPort, &mpegOUT,
                   "mpegOUT");

  rt_portCreate (K_MYACTOR,&intermediary);

  // delay the thread indefinitely
  // or do some other work
  }
```

First Filter

```
handler1 (rt_portEvent event)
{
  rt_portEvent continuation;

  if (isI-frame (event.buffer)) {
    continuation.eventType= I-frame;
    continuation.buffer=event.size;
    continuation.size=event.size;
    rt_portRaiseEvent (&intermediary, continuation)
}
rt_threadRestart ();
}
```

Second Filter

```
handler2 (rt_portEvent event)
{
  rt_portEvent next;

  rt_portAwaitEvent (&intermediary, next);
  colourReduction (next.buffer, next.size);

  // finally, set the event buffer to point
  // to next.buffer

  rt_threadRestart ();
}
```

Figure 10.7 Outline code for the filter object.

We present pseudo-code for the filter object in Figure 10.7 (the others are fairly straightforward and similar to the example presented above). Note that we again assume access to the unique identifier for the local actor (K_MYACTOR) and also the port defined on the trader service (traderPort). We also assume access to a function, isI-frame(), which examines the incoming buffer attached to the event to determine if it is an I-frame, and a function, `colourReduction()`, which performs the necessary colour reduction on an I-frame.

10.4 Implementation

10.4.1 Scheduling

Preliminaries
Sumo-CORE supports the concept of lightweight (user-level) threads which are created and managed in a single user-level actor. As mentioned above, this approach has significant benefits in terms of minimizing the overhead in terms of system calls and context switches. Lightweight threads also have additional benefits in terms of the low cost of thread creation and the ability to scale to large numbers of threads providing potentially high levels of concurrency. Before proceeding with the description of the implementation, it is important, however, to clarify some terminology. The following text will refer to three different styles of thread:

- *system threads* are kernel supported threads which run in supervisor mode,
- *kernel threads* are kernel supported threads which run in user mode, and
- *lightweight threads* are implemented in user space and are multiplexed on top of kernel threads.

A decision was taken to adopt an *earliest deadline first* (Liu and Layland, 1973) policy for real-time threads in Sumo-CORE. As mentioned in Section 9.2.2, there has been considerable debate in the multimedia community over scheduling policies for real-time threads. Most of the discussion has centred on the relative merits of earliest deadline first and fixed priority schemes. The results of this discussion have, however, been inconclusive. Earliest deadline first schedulers have some advantages in terms of utilization of the processor. They also retain deadline information at run-time which can be useful for system monitoring. In addition, earliest deadline first schedulers have the property that they will guarantee to find a valid schedule (one that honours the deadline of all its threads) if such a schedule exists. However, it is recognized that such schemes do suffer from problems on overload. In contrast, fixed priority schemes have a number of advantages in terms of coexistence with existing (priority-based) operating systems and support for mathematical analysis. We selected earliest deadline first as the policy for Sumo-CORE, but also recognize the contributions of fixed priority schemes. Indeed, the second implementation described in the next chapter adopts the latter approach to enable a fuller comparison to be carried out. We also recognize the benefits of schemes that can capture a mixture of urgency and importance information (again see the discussion in Section 9.2.2). At the time of writing, however, this remains a matter for further research.

More accurately, we adopt an earliest deadline first policy with three distinct priority bands: $band_1$, $band_2$ and $band_3$ (as described above). A $band_1$ thread will always run in preference to a $band_2$ thread, and a $band_2$ thread in preference to a $band_3$ thread. Within a band, threads are scheduled according to earliest deadline first. The different priority bands are required to support the resource classes introduced for QoS management (see Section 10.5).

Finally, all non real-time threads are scheduled according to standard Chorus policies and share whatever processor time is left after real-time threads have taken their requirements.

Split level scheduling

We now describe the split level approach to scheduling. We first describe the overall approach and then discuss the supporting mechanism of asynchronous upcalls and downcalls.

The overall approach

The implementation architecture for real-time thread scheduling consists of a single kernel scheduler (KLS) and cooperating user-level thread schedulers (ULS) with one ULS per actor (Govindan and Anderson, 1991). This approach has the advantages of user-level thread schemes as discussed above, but also enables the kernel to make optimal decisions in order to achieve real-time guarantees. With a split level scheme, each actor multiplexes lightweight user-level threads on a small number of kernel threads dedicated to the actor. In the current implementation, there is one kernel thread per ULS. This could, however, be extended, for example, for a multiprocessor environment. Kernel threads supporting lightweight threads are referred to as *virtual processors* in the discussion below. This overall architecture is shown in Figure 10.8.

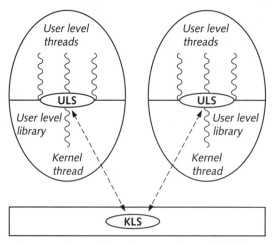

Figure 10.8 A split level approach to scheduling.

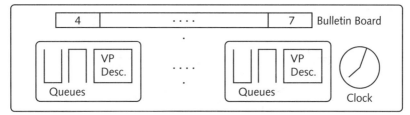

Figure 10.9 Structure of the shared memory.

The scheme maintains the following invariants with respect to the two types of scheduler:

- each user scheduler runs the lightweight thread in its actor from the highest non-empty priority band and then with the earliest deadline within this band, and
- the kernel scheduler runs a kernel thread which is executing in the actor with the *globally* highest non-empty priority band and then with the *globally* earliest deadline within this band.

The necessary information exchange between the kernel scheduler and the user-level schedulers is accomplished via a combination of shared data structures and asynchronous events. Both of these are implemented using an area of shared memory which is visible to the kernel and to each user-level scheduler. The overall structure of this area of shared memory is depicted in Figure 10.9. This figure shows the following components:

- a *bulletin board* containing global deadline information,
- a number of pairs of *FIFO queues* supporting asynchronous upcalls and downcalls,
- a set of *virtual processor descriptors*, one per virtual processor,
- the value of the *current time*.

We now consider how the bulletin board supports the split level scheduling invariants described above. Other aspects of the shared memory area are covered below.

The bulletin board contains one entry per ULS. On each scheduling operation, the ULS updates this entry to reflect the highest band/earliest deadline from its set of lightweight threads. Note that the deadlines are all specified as absolute deadlines. These are calculated simply by adding the relative deadlines of the threads to the site clock value, also stored in the area of shared memory. The KLS can then use this information to make an informed scheduling decision. In particular, the KLS will run the kernel thread corresponding to the ULS with the globally highest band/shortest deadline. The ULS can then schedule the corresponding lightweight thread. For example, consider the scenario depicted in Figure 10.10. In this case, the KLS will run the kernel thread

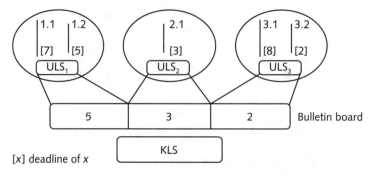

Figure 10.10 A simple scheduling scenario.

corresponding to ULS$_3$. The scheduler can then schedule lightweight thread 3.2, thus maintaining the invariants described above.

Note that we also support priority-based rt_threads as well as deadline-based rt_threads in our design (see Section 10.3.1). To achieve this, we transform the priority field threads to an equivalent absolute deadline metric using the following formula:

```
absDeadline = maxEDF + (maxPriority - priority)
```

The constant maxEDF indicates the maximum possible deadline for deadline-based threads. The above formula therefore ensures that priority-based threads will all have lower urgency than deadline-based threads by giving them deadlines after the last possible deadline-based thread. They are then ranked according to the priority field (with maximum value given by maxPriority).

Asynchronous upcalls and downcalls

The area of shared memory also features a number of pairs of FIFOs, one supporting upcalls from the kernel and the other supporting downcalls from user space. There is one pair of FIFOs per actor. The FIFOs are used for two distinct purposes:

- to communicate events between the kernel space and user space, and
- to implement asynchronous system calls.

We look at each of these aspects in more detail below.

The first use of the FIFO queues is to convey *communications events* from the kernel to a particular rt_port; that is, the arrival of a particular message on an rt_port. To support this, a data structure of type rt_portEvent is placed on the appropriate FIFO for the actor containing the rt_port. The corresponding ULS must respond to this event by delivering it to the correct rt_port, which should in turn execute the appropriate rt_handler.

This mechanism is used to achieve integration between communications and scheduling. At bind time, an `rt_thread` is created and assigned to each `rt_port` in the binding The scheduling parameters of the various `rt_threads` are determined from the required QoS of the binding (see Section 10.5). For example, consider the case of a continuous media stream. In this case, the deadline and period will be calculated from the required throughput of the incoming or outgoing continuous media data. The entry point of the created thread is also set to `rt_handler` for the corresponding `rt_port`. The task of the ULS in delivering an event to an `rt_port` is therefore to resume the corresponding `rt_thread` to execute an instance of the `rt_handler` (which will execute with the desired real-time characteristics).

The second use of FIFO queues is to support *asynchronous system calls*. The problem with normal system calls is that they block awaiting the result of the operation. Consider, for example, a lightweight thread performing an `ipcReceive()` operation. This would block the lightweight thread and the underlying kernel thread until the system call has been processed. This would mean that no other threads in that actor would be able to execute until the system call returns. This can lead to a problem of *priority inversion*, whereby the highest priority (in our case, earliest deadline) lightweight thread might not be able to run because another thread in that address space has executed a blocking system call.

Asynchronous system calls are introduced to overcome this problem. The execution of system calls proceeds as follows. Firstly, an event is placed in the downcall FIFO for execution by the kernel. The corresponding lightweight thread is then suspended, but the kernel thread is free to run other lightweight threads in that actor. The kernel will then perform the system call and post an event in the upcall FIFO. This will then result in a resume of the appropriate lightweight thread.

Further implementation details

We now consider in more detail the implementation of the user-level and kernel-level schedulers.

The user-level scheduler

The ULS maintains two main data structures: a set of linked lists of runnable lightweight threads awaiting execution (one per band) and a linked list of suspended lightweight threads. Threads can be suspended awaiting an incoming event or because the start time for their execution has not arrived. Note that periodic lightweight threads which have completed their previous execution are placed on this suspended list.

The ULS executes at each scheduling point; that is, on the invocation of an Sumo-CORE primitive or at the end of the execution of a lightweight thread. On each execution, the ULS carries out the following steps:

- *Step 1*

  The ULS first examines the current absolute time in the shared memory area and then resumes all suspended threads whose start time is now in the past (the threads are moved from the suspended list to the appropriate runnable list).

- *Step 2*
  The ULS then examines the associated upcall FIFO for any incoming events. If the FIFO contains some events, the ULS identifies the rt_ports for each of the events and then optionally resumes the corresponding rt_thread. In particular, if the rt_thread is workahead, the rt_thread is resumed immediately, otherwise the rt_thread is only resumed if the scheduling time has been reached.
- *Step 3*
  Finally, the ULS selects its most urgent lightweight thread (according to the band and deadline information) and updates the entry in the bulletin board. The ULS then searches the bulletin board to determine if this local thread is the globally most urgent (again considering band and deadline information). If the local thread is the most urgent, the ULS executes the local thread until completion and then suspends itself; otherwise the ULS yields the CPU, resulting in the immediate suspension of the underlying kernel thread.

Note that it is crucial for this algorithm that the KLS schedules the underlying kernel thread with the desired frequency in order to support the real-time requirements of the lightweight threads. To achieve this, the ULS places a *wakeup time* in the corresponding virtual processor descriptor before each suspend operation. This wakeup time is determined from the start times of the current set of rt_threads. The KLS will then respond to the wakeup times as discussed below.

The kernel-level scheduler
The kernel-level scheduler is a modified version of the Chorus scheduler described in Section 9.3.3. As with the Chorus scheduler, the KLS maintains a set of lists, one per priority level. All kernel threads supporting rt_threads are mapped to a single high-priority band. All other Chorus kernel threads are spread across the lower priority bands. This allocation is summarized in Figure 10.11.

The modified scheduler, however, has access to the shared memory area (as discussed above). Crucially, the scheduler can access the set of virtual processor

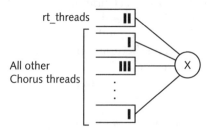

Figure 10.11 Allocation of kernel threads to priority bands.

descriptors in this area. Each virtual processor descriptor contains information pertaining to the virtual processor, including the unique identifier of the kernel thread supporting the virtual processor and the wakeup time for this thread (as set by the ULS).

The KLS executes on every clock tick from the underlying system clock and carries out the following steps:

- *Step 1*
  The KLS first updates the current time in the shared memory area and then examines the wakeup times in the set of virtual processor descriptors. The KLS then resumes all suspended kernel threads whose wakeup time has arrived. These threads are inserted in the priority-based linked list for subsequent execution.
- *Step 2*
  The KLS then examines downcall FIFOs for each of the virtual processors. On detecting events, the KLS despatches the events to the appropriate parts of the system, for example an appropriate part of the Sumo-CORE library. To minimize the overhead in the KLS, this is achieved by the deferred interrupt technique supported in the Chorus nucleus. Deferred interrupts are a lightweight means of achieving interprocess communication within the single address space of the microkernel. They operate by sending lightweight mini-messages to mini-ports. This approach has the benefit of minimizing the time spent in the interrupt routine.
- *Step 3*
  Finally, the KLS performs a schedule operation on the set of kernel threads. Scheduling is performed using the standard Chorus preemptive, priority-based scheduler.

Some further discussion on the design of the KLS and ULS is included below.

Discussion

An alternative solution would be for the KLS to select the highest band/earliest deadline from the bulletin board and then manipulate the priority of the corresponding kernel thread to ensure that this is the next virtual processor to execute. This would also be the most natural solution given the scheduling class framework provided by Chorus (see Section 9.3.3). In our solution, however, the kernel threads corresponding to virtual processors remain fixed at the same high priority band. The desired effect is then achieved by the user-level scheduler choosing either to execute a lightweight thread or yield the processor on the basis of information from the bulletin board.

The main reason for this decision was to avoid the overhead of manipulating the priority lists in every schedule operation. The experience of other researchers suggests that the overhead of such manipulations can be prohibitively high (Gaultier and Metais, 1994). The one drawback of the implemented scheme is that virtual processors may be scheduled only to yield the processor to other activities. Nevertheless, this overhead is compensated by the fact that the data structures are updated during this operation, providing more global information for the scheduling of other threads.

10.4.2 Communications

A split level communications architecture

Protocol processing in Sumo-CORE is split between user and kernel space. In particular, a user-level protocol (ULP) executes in user space and communicates with a kernel-level protocol (KLP) in the microkernel. This communication is achieved using asynchronous upcalls and downcalls via an `rt_port` as discussed above. The KLP deals with the data link and network layers of the protocol stack whereas the ULP provides the transport service. (The network layer could alternatively be implemented in user space; this remains a matter for ongoing research in the Sumo Project.) Therefore, the task of the kernel is to multiplex and demultiplex incoming packets to application address spaces, but to let application address spaces perform transport level processing.

This overall architecture is depicted in Figure 10.12. The architecture is intended to support one KLP and multiple ULPs. A particular actor is then free to choose one or more ULPs to match the requirements of the encapsulated service(s). With this architecture, it is possible to provide ULPs offering standard services such as TCP or UDP alongside more specialist services, such as for multimedia communications.

As well as this inherent flexibility, the architecture has a number of additional advantages (see Section 10.2 for a fuller discussion):

- the transport protocol implementation can exploit lightweight threads and hence reduce the number of domain crossings and context switches,

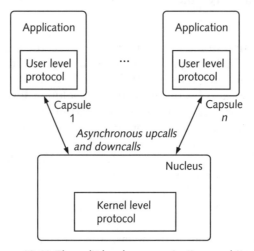

Figure 10.12 The split level communications architecture.

- we avoid the multiplexing of different transport connections through one centralized implementation, and
- transport processing and application processing can be scheduled as a single computation with a single overall deadline.

The split level implementation can also exploit the facilities offered by asynchronous upcalls and downcalls to provide lightweight domain crossings and can also exploit the feature of rt_ports which provides direct access to data, thus avoiding the cost of additional copies.

We now describe the existing implementation of the split level communications architecture in Chorus. This implementation supports one ULP: a rate-based protocol supporting continuous media streams.

Implementation of the split level architecture

We now describe in more detail the implementation of the communications architecture in Sumo-CORE. We first describe the overall structure and then consider the implementation of the user-level protocol and the kernel-level protocol. Finally, we consider some optimizations for communication both within a site and within a single address space.

Overall structure

As described in Chapter 9, the communications infrastructure in the current Chorus nucleus (v3 r5) consists of a virtual transport protocol (VTP) mapping down on to a number of specific transport protocol implementations. This functionality is then supported by a reliable data link layer (RDL) and an optional network service supporting internetworking (we do not, however, discuss internetworking further in this section). All these components reside in the microkernel. In our implementation, however, we bypass the virtual transport service and place this functionality in user space. More specifically, the kernel-level protocol is placed at the level of the RDL. The user-level protocol is then implemented in a user actor. This approach is illustrated in Figure 10.13.

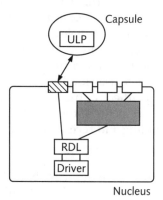

Figure 10.13 The Sumo-CORE communications architecture.

The user-level protocol has an associated rt_port for incoming and outgoing events; the user-level protocol and the kernel-level protocol then communicate using upcalls and downcalls through this rt_port. The protocol and associated application processing are implemented in the attached rt_handler and are hence scheduled according to the mechanisms described above. Note that the architecture can support further user-level protocols by having other rt_ports with other rt_handlers.

The user-level protocol
As mentioned above, the current implementation of Sumo-CORE only offers a single user-level protocol, namely a connection-oriented protocol customized for continuous media interactions. This protocol uses a rate-based scheme for flow control whereby sources and sinks negotiate a mutually acceptable transfer rate at connection setup time. This allows data to flow at a smooth rate, as required by continuous media applications. In addition, rate-based protocols are generally more lightweight and support higher levels of throughput than more traditional window-based services. They also achieve a decoupling between flow control and error control, allowing error control to be omitted for certain classes of traffic, such as uncompressed continuous media data.

The user-level protocol is based on previous research at Lancaster University in the context of the Esprit-funded OSI'95 project (Garcia, 1993; Danthine, 1994) and provides the functions of fragmentation and rate-based flow control. In our implementation, we omit error control at this level; errors are optionally notified to the consumer thread, which can then take an appropriate action if desired. The ULP supports arbitrary sized items of data, such as video frames. It is therefore necessary to fragment such data items into packets suitable for transmission over the underlying network. The precise size of the network packets is determined at connection time as part of the connection establishment protocol. Rate control is then used to determine the rate at which the network packets should be transmitted. The rate control mechanism is intended to prevent congestion in the network and overflow of the receiver's buffers. Should the latter occur, an *adaptation* mechanism can be employed to adapt the rate of transmission (see below). The receiver end must then reassemble the fragments and deliver the complete data item to the application. Note that the protocol has a further level of implicit rate control governed by the rate at which user-level data items are produced. This is determined by the period of the rt_handler execution, which is in turn determined by the QoS requirements of the associated binding.

We now consider the sending and receiving of data in more detail below.

- *Sending continuous media data*
  The sending side is initiated when the active binding places an upcall on the rt_port indicating that it wants more data. At this point, the application must insert data in the buffer provided. Following this, the rt_handler

executes the user-level protocol to perform fragmentation and rate control. In particular, the user-level protocol must release a burst of n packets of data every ω milliseconds, where n and ω are determined from the QoS requirements for the binding (see Section 10.3.1). To achieve this, the rt_handler creates a periodic worker thread with period ω. This worker thread sends a downcall to the kernel-level protocol on every execution- instructing the kernel-level protocol to release n packets to the network. This mechanism is illustrated in Figure 10.14. Note that fragmentation can be logical, as the kernel already has access to the user-provided buffer. The worker thread then informs the rt_handler when all data has been sent. At this point, the rt_handler will terminate awaiting a further invocation. A QoS violation can be detected at this stage if the rt_handler fails to complete execution before the start of the next period.

- *Receiving continuous media data*
  The receive side protocol must reassemble the incoming data fragments and then initiate application processing. To achieve this, the receiver creates an rt_port with an associated rt_handler executing on an rt_thread with period ω. Fragments are directed towards this rt_port by the kernel-level protocol. The rt_handler then has the task of collecting fragments and building the original data item. This can be achieved using the Chorus virtual memory facilities to remap data into a contiguous block, thus avoiding any data copying. When all the fragments have been collected, the rt_handler places an upcall on the rt_port for the receiver. The associated rt_handler then performs the necessary application code to consume the data. The protocol can also optionally calculate a checksum on the incoming data (indicated by a field in the QoS specification) and raise an additional event if an error is found (*error notification*). In addition, QoS violations can be detected if the receiver rt_handler does not complete execution by the end of its period or if individual fragments do not arrive by their period.

Note that the fragmentation and rate control is only required for large data items. For small data items, this mechanism can be configured out. In this case, the sender will be upcalled for data and this will immediately be transmitted. Similarly, the receiver will be upcalled on data arrival and this will immediately be consumed.

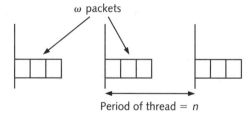

ω packets

Period of thread $= n$

Figure 10.14 Rate control using a periodic worker thread.

The adaptation mechanism operates as follows. The sender maintains a credit variable which provides an estimate of the amount of buffering available at the receiver. This is initialized at connection establishment time to the number of buffers allocated at the receiver. The value of credit is then decremented as data is transmitted and incremented by a control message from the receiver, indicating that the data has been consumed. If the value reaches zero, then transmission is temporarily suspended

Finally, as mentioned above, the protocol is connection-oriented. In particular, resources are allocated to support the interaction at connection establishment time. The nature of this allocation is determined by the quality of service requirements on the associated binding. This crucial aspect of the implementation is discussed in Section 10.5.

The kernel-level protocol

The purpose of the KLP is to form the link between the ULP and the lower-level network-specific modules. In particular, its main role is to multiplex/de-multiplex packets from/to a number of user-level connections on the same site. When a source ULP wishes to send a number of packets, it informs the KLP using an asynchronous downcall. In order to multiplex requests efficiently from a number of user-level actors, each connection has a dedicated kernel-level thread in the KLP which responds to events from that connection. This thread is created at connection time and then simply waits until an event is received from its own connection. Packet headers are then added to a queue for forwarding to the network manager.

For a sink rt_port, the kernel-level protocol must determine the destination for the incoming network packet and then upcall the corresponding rt_port with the received data. This will then be reassembled by the user-level protocol.

Note that the lower level interface between the KLP and the network manager is highly network-specific. In some cases, it may also be necessary for the KLP to perform further fragmentation and/or rate control of packets, such as the injection of cells into an ATM network.

Optimizations

The transmission of data can be considerably optimized in two important cases:

- between rt_ports in the same address space (actor), and
- between rt_ports in the same site.

We consider each case in turn below.

In the case where rt_ports reside in the *same address space*, communication proceeds as follows. The binding upcalls the sender rt_handler requesting the next item of data and provides a buffer for this data. When the next item is available, the binding raises an event in the receiver rt_port offering the same buffer for consumption. These activities can all be carried out in user space by the user-level protocol, and hence the transfer of data does not incur context switches, domain crossings or data copies.

Such local bindings are often used in the context of intra-actor pipelines (see the example in Section 10.3.2). With this approach, the address of a single buffer is passed from stage to stage as the various stages of the pipeline are executed. Finally, when the last pipeline stage in the actor has disposed of the data, the buffer can be released. If new data arrives at the actor while the previous data is being passed along the pipeline, processing of this data proceeds concurrently using a separate buffer. In this way, it is possible to implement arbitrarily long intra-actor pipelines efficiently without incurring data copying overheads.

In the case where rt_ports are on the *same site* but in different address spaces, it is possible to minimize the overheads of communication in two ways. Firstly, the event is conveyed to the rt_port using a shortcut whereby the event is placed in the area of shared memory and then delivered directly to the receiver by the KLS on inspection of this shared area. Secondly, the overhead of copying can be avoided either by re-mapping the data into the receiver address space or employing the deferred copy technique discussed in Section 9.3.3. With the former approach, no copying is required but care must be taken if the data is modified (as it is also mapped into the sender's address space). With the latter approach, no copying is performed unless particular pages of the data are written. The particular copy semantics could be specified as part of the binding process although currently this is not supported.

Discussion

The split level architecture described above exploits the modularity of the Chorus communications subsystem in providing access to the lower level aspects of the protocol stack. However, the implementation departs from the current Chorus implementation in a number of ways.

Firstly, we choose not to place reliability in the data link layer. This is not required by continuous media data, where a certain number of errors can be tolerated. We thus leave error control to the application. In terms of Chorus, we thus have a null RDL (this is actually allowed by the Chorus architecture).

Secondly, we do not place the transport protocol in the kernel (as a Chorus specialized protocol). Rather, we implement this functionality in user space. We believe this approach has significant advantages for multimedia communications in terms of performance, flexibility, schedulability and avoiding multiplexing.

Finally, we introduce an end-to-end connection-oriented service into the Chorus microkernel (that is, bindings). Previously, Chorus has been tailored towards the delivery of single messages over connectionless services. This aspect of the design is crucial to support the engineering model described in Chapter 8.

10.4.3 Buffer management

The main focus of the work on Sumo-CORE has been on scheduling and communications. Consequently, there has been less attention placed on the topic of QoS-driven buffer management. The current solution is as follows. The kernel maintains an area of memory that can be used for bindings. When a new binding is created, a fixed number of buffers are allocated to this binding with the precise number being derived from the QoS requirements of the binding (see Section 10.5.2). The buffers are then pre-mapped into the corresponding user space (as well as the kernel address space), thus avoiding copying or mapping operations once the binding is activated. Buffers can also be selectively locked in main memory to achieve a fixed access latency. Again, this is determined from examining the QoS requirements of the binding.

To illustrate the operation of buffer management, consider an incoming message from the network (similar actions are required for outgoing data). The kernel will select a buffer for this message from the pool of buffers reserved for this connection and then fill the buffer with the incoming data. The address of this buffer is then passed as part of the upcall to the associated rt_handler; the buffer will already be mapped into user space as well as kernel space and hence the rt_handler can access the data directly.

Ongoing research is examining more sophisticated strategies for buffer management in Sumo-CORE including the development of a split level approach to buffer management, the implementation of a truly zero-copy architecture (Chu, 1996; Druschel and Peterson, 1993), and the development of a QoS-driven user-level mapper (see Section 9.3.3) to manage memory allocated to communications.

10.5 QoS management

10.5.1 General approach

As mentioned previously, bindings have a unique role in Sumo-CORE in providing the unit of QoS management. More specifically, active bindings take full responsibility for the end-to-end flow of information from application thread to application thread and hence encapsulate management strategies for thread scheduling, communications and buffer allocation. QoS management can then be carried out on the whole binding rather than on individual resources thus achieving integration in the management process. This applies to both static and dynamic aspects of QoS management as discussed below:

- *Static QoS management*
  Static QoS management is applied to thread scheduling, communications and buffer management to ensure that the appropriate resources are allocated to the binding at creation time to meet the desired level of quality of service. This involves negotiating the resources required from each

component in the binding and optionally performing admission control and resource reservation functions to achieve the required guarantees.

- *Dynamic QoS management*
Dynamic QoS management is also applied to each of the components participating in a binding to ensure that the desired level of quality of service is maintained. Specific functions applied include QoS monitoring, policing, maintenance and renegotiation.

We consider each of these areas of management below. Note that the discussion centres on QoS management of stream bindings; QoS management of message bindings is not considered in detail in this book.

10.5.2 Static QoS management

Approach to static QoS management
We now consider the overall approach to static QoS management in Sumo-CORE. We first consider a crucial separation of concerns and then describe a protocol based on this separation of concerns.

Separation of concerns
The role of static QoS management is to take the necessary steps at binding creation time to ensure that the binding can meet its desired level of quality of service. This involves two distinct steps:

1. to decide on the level of resources required to support the QoS requirements for the end-to-end binding, and
2. to (optionally) carry out admission control tests and resource reservations to provide the required level of guarantees.

The first step corresponds to the QoS negotiation function. For this step, resources must be allocated for the entire end-to-end path, as shown in Figure 10.15. More specifically, the negotiation must decide on (1) the deadline to be

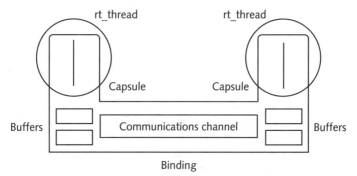

Figure 10.15 The end-to-end path associated with a binding.

Best effort $\begin{cases} - \text{isochronous } (B_I) \\ - \text{workahead } (B_W) \end{cases}$ Guaranteed $\begin{cases} - \text{isochronous } (G_I) \\ - \text{workahead } (G_W) \end{cases}$

Figure 10.16 Resource classes for QoS management.

associated with the `rt_handler` of the producer, (2) the number of buffers required by producer, (3) the quality of service for the underlying communications channel, (4) the number of buffers required by the consumer, and (5) the deadline to be associated with the `rt_handler` for the consumer.

The second step depends on the level of guarantees required by the user. In particular, we highlight four classes of binding for static QoS management, referred to as B_I, B_W, G_I and G_W. These classes are derived from the values of the commitment and delivery QoS parameters as illustrated in Figure 10.16.

The precise interpretation of each of these classes is given below:

- *The B_I class*
  The best effort isochronous class attempts to deliver data items at precisely the required rate, but does not take any actions to guarantee this level of service.
- *The B_W class*
  The best effort workahead class will deliver data items on or optionally before the required time, but again takes no actions to guarantee the level of service.
- *The G_I class*
  The guaranteed isochronous class delivers data items at precisely the required rate and performs a combination of resource reservation and admission control to guarantee this level of service.
- *The G_W class*
  The guaranteed workahead class delivers data items on or optionally before the required time and performs a combination of resource reservation and admission control to guarantee this level of service.

In addition, we introduce a third best effort class, called B_C, to refer to standard (non-real-time) Chorus threads. We also use the shorthand notation B to refer to the union of the three best effort classes.

The strategy for QoS management for each of the classes is given in Table 10.4 (the precise interpretation of the various actions will become clearer as the discussion develops).

We now describe the protocol which implements these policies.

The binding establishment protocol
The collected behaviour described above is encapsulated in a binding establishment protocol. This protocol therefore has the task of deciding on the level of resources required for each stage in the binding and then optionally carrying out the admission control tests and resource reservations depending on the class of binding. To perform this task, the protocol must interact with the scheduling, communications and buffer management components.

Table 10.4 QoS management strategy for each resource class

Commitment	Scheduling	Communications	Buffer management
Best effort	EDF policy used.	Connection established.	Buffers pre-allocated; buffers subject to swapping and preemption.
Guaranteed	Admission test on schedulability; EDF policy used.	Admission test on bandwidth, latency requirements; potential resource reservation in network.	Admission test; buffers pre-allocated; buffers locked in main memory and non-preemptible.

In implementation, the protocol passes a *flow specification* between each of the entities involved in the end-to-end binding. This flow specification contains the QoS requirements of the overall binding and also maintains a second QoS structure indicating the accumulated QoS so far. If the accumulated QoS violates the QoS requirements, the binding establishment is aborted. At the end, the flow specification is returned to the sender end. The reply message passes through all the participants in the binding and acts as a confirmation of the required level of service. The actual QoS achieved can then be notified to the user. The protocol exhibits the separation of concerns described above in that it is only concerned with passing the flow specification between the components and deciding on the overall level of quality of service (thus implementing the QoS negotiation function).

Note that this overall approach is similar to ST-II (see Section 8.4) in that the protocol is sender-initiated and connection-oriented. ST-II also relies on a flow specification and maintains the same separation of concerns. We do not, however, consider multiparty communications in our implementation (although this would be a natural extension). The other major difference is that our protocol operates on an end-to-end basis, including the allocation of end system resources whereas ST-II operates at the network level.

The interpretation of this flow specification is determined internally by each component. More specifically, the various resources managers are required to support an operation of the form:

```
typedef enum {
    RT_ACCEPT, RT_REJECT
} outcome;

outcome allocateResources (QoSVector flowSpec, *accumulatedQoS);
```

This operation takes the flow specification and attempts to allocate resources to satisfy the request. If the request can be satisfied, the accumulated QoS structure is updated to reflect the level of service supported so far in the negotiation process and an outcome of accept is returned. Otherwise, an outcome of reject is returned, resulting in the binding establishment being aborted. The implementation of this operation encapsulates the required static QoS management functions. More specifically, the following steps are carried out:

1. perform an internal translation from the QoS vector to resource specific parameters,
2. determine the resource class from the QoS vector and perform admission control and resource reservation as required by this resource class.

To populate the protocol, we therefore must provide the appropriate QoS management functions for each of the resources involved in the end-to-end path. These functions are described in detail below for scheduling, communications and, finally, buffer management.

Scheduling

We firstly consider threads management (scheduling) and consider the translation of the flow specification into thread specific parameters; we then consider the admission control test and resource reservation strategies for threads.

Translation of the flow specification

The first task is to generate thread-specific parameters from the flow specification. Note that we consider only periodic threads reflecting the decision to focus on QoS management for stream bindings (see Section 10.5.1). To aid the discussion Figure 10.17 summarizes the range of parameters associated with an earliest deadline first-based scheme for periodic threads. Individual threads have an associated *period*, with the *scheduling time* of each invocation calculated as the start of this period. They then have a *deadline* which is less than or equal to the end of this period. For continuous media data, an amount of *jitter* is tolerated and hence the thread must be scheduled by the deadline ± the permissible jitter. Finally, each invocation has an associated *quantum*, that is, the amount of processor time required to complete the execution.

For our scheme, the main values required to characterize a thread are the period, the scheduling time of the thread, the (relative) deadline, and the

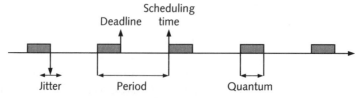

Figure 10.17 Parameters for earliest deadline first scheduling.

worst-case execution time (corresponding to the quantum above). These values are calculated as follows. The period is set to the inverse of the *buffrate*: if buffers are expected to arrive at a rate of 100 per second, then the period of the thread dealing with the buffers will be 1/100 s. Both the scheduling time and the deadline are established dynamically as execution proceeds. The standard procedure for earliest deadline first threads is for the scheduling time to be set to the start of the next period and the deadline to the end of the next period. We assume this solution for now and then present a modification of this approach below. Finally, the worst-case execution time is estimated from the expected length of protocol processing plus applications processing.

We also need to know the priority band for the particular thread (see Section 10.4.1). This is calculated directly by the scheduling subsystem based on the resource class of the particular thread:

1. G_I threads are allocated to the highest band (band$_1$),
2. G_W threads are then allocated to the next highest band (band$_2$), and
3. the B_I and B_W threads are both allocated to the lowest band (band$_3$).

Finally, as will be seen below, we need to know the permissible jitter on G_I threads to perform the admission control test. This is used to constrain the execution of such threads within a given period. The jitter is taken directly from the flow specification; that is, the tolerable jitter on threads is the same as the overall jitter allowed on the end-to-end binding.

Admission control test

We now present admission control tests for G_I and G_W threads (as mentioned earlier, tests are not required for B_I and B_W threads). In order to support the admission control tests, we must notionally reserve a portion of resource for each of the two classes. We use the notation g_i and g_w to refer to the portions of resource dedicated to the respective classes of thread, where $g_i + g_w < 1$. Other classes of thread must then compete for the remaining resources, although, if the above portions are under-exploited, lower classes will automatically be scheduled to make use of the remaining resources (see Section 10.4.1).

First consider the admission control test for G_I threads. This test is specifically designed to take into account the permissible jitter on threads. The solution exploits the concepts of deadline equivalence classes and harmonic sets (the full derivation is given in Appendix B) (Mauthe and Coulson, 1997).

The admission control test for G_I threads is as follows:

$$\forall c_i \ in \ \langle c_{min}, \ldots, c_{max} \rangle \left(\sum_{j=1}^{k} etime(j, d_i) + \sum_{h=1}^{H} E_h \right) \Big/ d_i \leqslant 1$$

The quantification expression ranges over all deadline equivalence classes. The expression E_h then represents the maximum processing time requirement over any interval d_i for the subset of threads in a harmonic set H whose deadlines are $\leqslant d_i$. The summation to H ranges over the set of harmonic sets. The other expression then deals with threads that cannot be included in a harmonic set and whose deadline is also $\leqslant d_i$; the function *etime* (j, t) gives the maximum processing time required by such a thread j in some time span t.

The corresponding admission control test for G_W threads is as follows (again, see Appendix B for the derivation of this test):

$$\sum_{i=1}^{T} \frac{e_i}{p_i} \leqslant g_w$$

where T is the number of threads in the system, e_i is the execution time of each quantum of thread i, p_i is the period of thread i and g_w is the portion of resources allocated to the G_W class.

Note that the tests described above assume that G_W threads cannot interfere with the scheduling of G_I threads and B threads cannot interfere with the scheduling of G_I or G_W threads. This condition is met by the allocation of the thread classes to the priority bands as discussed above.

Resource reservation

A thread with the required characteristics is created for both the sender and receiver `rt_ports` in the binding (see Table 10.3 for the parameters to `rt_threadCreate()`). Apart from that, there is no explicit resource reservation in the scheduling scheme. Rather, resource reservation is implicit in the admission control tests outlined above. In particular, a total amount of resources is notionally allocated to the G_I and G_W classes as described above. If the admission test is passed for a guaranteed thread, the scheduling algorithm will guarantee to find a schedule at run-time to meet the requirements of a thread. More specifically, G_I threads are guaranteed to start execution on or after the start of a period and complete execution by their deadline, where the deadline is given by the scheduling time plus the quantum plus the permissible jitter. In contrast, G_W threads are guaranteed to complete execution by the end of their period (but can start early). The best effort classes, B_I and B_W, will mirror the above behaviour if sufficient resources are available but no guarantees are given.

Communications

We now consider the same areas for communications resource.

Translation of the flow specification

For communications resources, we focus on the bandwidth, delay and error characteristics for the underlying communications connections. These are derived directly from the QoS vector as described in Section 10.3.1. In particular, the bandwidth requirement is represented by the `buffsize` and `buffrate` parameters from the QoS vector. Similarly, the maximum delay for the channel is estimated by subtracting the expected latency for end system processing (at both ends) from the overall latency given in the QoS vector.

Finally, the error requirements are derived trivially from the error and error interval fields of the QoS vector.

In addition, we consider two broad resource classes for the network:

- the guaranteed class to support both G_I and G_W bindings, and
- the best effort class to support B_I and B_W bindings.

In other words, the network is not concerned with workahead or isochronous delivery. This is purely considered at the end system. Admission control tests and resource reservations are only performed for the former class.

Admission control test
The precise admission control tests employed in the network depend greatly on the style of network in use and, more specifically, the service disciplines employed at intermediate switches. A full discussion of this topic is beyond the scope of this book (the interested reader is referred to the literature for further details (Ferrari *et al.*, 1994; Clark *et al.*, 1992, Lazar and Pacifici, 1991; Zhang, 1995)). However, as an illustration, we present one relatively simple approach. In particular, we consider simple admission control tests for throughput, latency and buffer availability in switches. The first two tests are adapted from Ferrari and Verma (1990) and assume a deadline-based scheduling discipline (in particular, Earliest Due Date).

- *Throughput test*
  The bandwidth test is required to verify that enough processing (switching) power is available at each traversed switch to accommodate an additional connection without impairing the guarantees given to other connections. The admission test must make worst-case assumptions about throughput conditions; this happens when all bindings send packets back to back at the peak rate. Note that the bandwidth test is precisely the same as the Liu/Layland test for earliest deadline first scheduling:

$$\sum_{i=1}^{C} \frac{e_i}{p_i} \leqslant g$$

  where C is the total number of connections in the system, e_i is the service time required for the connection i, p_i is the period of incoming packets for connection i, derived from the buffrate parameter, and g is the total portion of resources allocated to the guaranteed class.
- *Latency test*
  The latency test determines the minimum acceptable delay bound which does not cause scheduler saturation. To check this property, the following calculation is carried out at each switch:

$$d = \sum_{i=1}^{N_U} e_i + T$$

where d is the local delay bound incurred at the current switch by the current flow. As before, e_i refers to the service time of connection i in the current switch, but in this case the index variable i ranges over the members of a set U. The set U contains those connections supported by the current switch whose local delay bound is lower than the sum of the service times of *all* connections supported by the current switch. N_U represents the cardinality of U. T represents the largest service time of all flows in a set V, where V is the complement of set U. A full proof of the theorem underlying this formula can be found in Ferrari and Verma (1990). Following this, it is then necessary to calculate:

$$\sum_{n=1}^{N_S} d_n \leqslant delay$$

which checks that the sum of the delays at each switch is less than the delay parameter for the overall connection. N_s refers to the number of switches on the path and d_n refers to the nth value of d obtained from the first set of calculations.

- *Buffer availability test*
  Finally, it is necessary to check that there is sufficient memory available at each intermediary node in order to support the connection. The amount of memory allocated to a connection must be sufficient to buffer data for a period which is greater than the combined queuing delay and service time of the packets. Consequently, the calculation for buffer space is:

$$buffers = rate \times delay$$
$$\Rightarrow buffersize = buffers \times mtu\_size$$

where *buffersize* represents the amount of memory that must be allocated at the current switch for the current flow. The combination of the queuing delay and service time is bounded by d as derived from the delay formula above. It is then necessary to check that there is sufficient memory at each switch given the above requirements.

The above three tests are all necessary to ensure that a connection can meet its requirements.

Resource reservation
For guaranteed connections, it is necessary to reserve sufficient buffers in each node involved in that connection. The precise memory requirements are given by the value of *buffersize* as calculated above. No further resource reservation is required. As with scheduling, other aspects of reservation are implicit in passing the admission control test; that is, if a connection passes the tests for bandwidth and delay bounds, each switch will guarantee to schedule the connection correctly at run-time to meet these guarantees.

Note that no guarantees are offered for best effort classes; their behaviour is thus dependent on the overall loading on the system.

Buffer management

Finally, we consider the interpretation of the flow specification together with the admission control tests and resource reservation strategies for end system buffers.

Translation of the flow specification

For buffer management, it is simply necessary to calculate the number of buffers necessary to support a given binding. At the consumer end, the calculation is based on the `buffrate`, `jitter` and `quantum` parameters from the QoS vector for the binding. However, it is also necessary to take into account the network delay bound, *delay*, as calculated above. The network delay bound will typically permit a larger degree of jitter than the application level jitter bound and any discrepancy must be made good through the use of additional jitter smoothing buffers. Given these input parameters, the expression for the number of buffers required at the receiver is:

$$buffers = buffrate\left(delay + quantum + \frac{jitter}{2}\right)$$

$$\Rightarrow buffersize = buffers \times buffsize$$

In this formula, the expression in the brackets represents the maximum time for which any single buffer must be held. The jitter is divided by two because this parameter expresses both late and early arrival and it is only the lateness component that needs to be taken into consideration.

Only one buffer is required at the producer due to the structure of the send-side communications architecture: each buffer is assumed to be transmitted before the start of the next period.

Admission control test

An admission control test is required for guaranteed classes binding (G_I and G_W bindings) to ensure that sufficient buffers are available to support the binding. Assume that g buffers are pre-allocated to guaranteed bindings; then the admission control test is simply:

$$\sum_{i=1}^{N} buffers_i \leqslant g$$

where g is the total portion of resources allocated to guaranteed class, N is the total number of guaranteed bindings currently in the system, and *buffers_i* is the buffer requirements for the ith binding as calculated above.

Resource reservation

The strategy for resource reservation is dependent on the resource class. In particular, the required number of buffers are reserved for G_I and G_W bindings (at both ends). Guarantees are also offered on access latencies by locking the buffers in main memory. Such buffers will not be unlocked even if buffer space becomes low.

For best effort classes, however, buffers are allocated but not reserved. In addition, they are not locked in memory and are therefore subject to paging overheads. Applications can explicitly request that these buffers are locked in main memory. In this case, however, the QoS mapper can change this setting if the available main memory is becoming low.

10.5.3 Dynamic QoS management

Dynamic QoS management is much more straightforward than static QoS management. We consider the interpretation of each of the static QoS management functions below:

- *QoS monitoring function*
  QoS monitoring is supported in Sumo-CORE by providing access at
  `rt_ports` to events (compare signals). The application can then elect to
  monitor the events to ensure that a given quality of service is achieved. For
  example, an application can check the arrival times of video frames to ensure
  that the required throughput and jitter requirements are met. Such monitors
  can be written using the Esterel language described earlier (or indeed any
  other language supported by the system). The underlying infrastructure also
  generates a number of QoS violation events. The application can attach
  appropriate `rt_handlers` to the appropriate `rt_port` to deal with such
  events. Examples of such QoS violations include a thread missing its deadline
  or the detection of apparent congestion in the network.
- *QoS policing function*
  As mentioned above, active bindings do not require policing as the
  binding takes responsibility for rate of production or consumption from
  the application. This aspect of the design therefore considerably simplifies
  dynamic QoS management.
- *QoS maintenance function*
  The procedures for QoS maintenance are encapsulated within the
  resource management strategies for scheduling, communications and
  buffer management. For example, the rate-based protocol can adapt its
  behaviour at run-time to ensure the desired QoS requirements are met,
  for example by altering the rate and burst parameters. Note, however,
  that some parts of the system do not require maintenance. For example,
  the earliest deadline first-based algorithm guarantees to find appropriate
  schedules to meet the desired quality of service once the admission control
  test is passed.
- *QoS renegotiation function*
  Sumo-CORE supports renegotiation through the control `rt_port` on
  bindings. In particular, this `rt_port` accepts renegotiate messages to
  alter the resources allocated to the binding (see Section 10.4.1). This maps
  on to an invocation of the binding establishment protocol as mentioned
  above and hence is a relatively heavyweight operation.

As can be seen, the bias is towards static rather than dynamic QoS management procedures. This implies that the majority of the management overhead is incurred at binding establishment time. Most of the dynamic procedures are at the discretion of the application developer (in terms of the amount of monitoring and renegotiation required).

10.6 Performance measurements

A range of performance measurements have been carried out on the Sumo-CORE implementation to validate the architecture. A number of the key results are included below. The results compare the performance of Sumo-CORE with standard Chorus functionality. The figures recorded for Chorus are based on version 3, release 5.1 of the microkernel. Note that all the results were carried out on 486 PCs running at 60 MHz. The network used is a standard Ethernet operating at 10 Mbit/s.

Experiment 1: Cost of standard Chorus primitives
In the first experiment, we compare the cost of a range of standard Chorus calls in Chorus and in Sumo-CORE (see Table 10.5). In all cases, the Sumo-CORE equivalents are rewritten using asynchronous upcalls and downcalls. We firstly consider the relative performance of a null ipcCall() within an single actor. We then consider the relative call of semP()/semV() operations on a semaphore (within an actor in this case). In particular, we measure the cost of awakening a thread blocked on a semP() primitive by using the semV() primitive. The final figures are for the cost of performing a threadSuspend() call on lightweight threads and Chorus kernel threads respectively. All figures are in microseconds. In all three cases, the results show a performance gain of between two and four times in comparing Sumo-CORE with Chorus. This can largely be explained by the avoidance of domain crossings and context switches. For example, the ipcCall() in Chorus incurs three domain crossings and two context switches. In contrast, in Sumo-CORE, all interaction takes place in a single address space (no domain crossings) and context switches are between user-level threads and hence carry minimal overhead. Similar arguments also apply to the other measurements.

Table 10.5 Relative cost of standard Chorus primitives

Primitive	Sumo-CORE	Chorus
ipcCall()	90.5	281.0
semP()/semV()	9.4	23.0
threadSuspend()	5.7	23.0

Table 10.6 Lightweight threads vs. kernel threads

No. of elements	No. of threads	Sumo-CORE	Chorus
50	88	<1	40
100	160	20	–
400	496	60	–

Experiment 2: Kernel-level threads vs. lightweight threads

We now consider the relative overhead associated with lightweight (user-level) threads and Chorus kernel threads. The results are based on a highly concurrent quicksort algorithm consisting of large numbers of threads communicating via semaphores. The test is repeated for differing numbers of elements (larger data sets generate larger numbers of threads). The results are summarized in Table 10.6 (all timings are in milliseconds).

For 50 elements, the version based on kernel threads took 40 ms to complete. In comparison, the version using lightweight threads took less than 1 millisecond to execute (with the granularity of the system clock, it was not possible to get a more precise indication of this figure). This shows a dramatic difference in performance between kernel threads and lightweight threads. This is largely due to the much lower overheads of thread creation and context switching and partially because of the improved performance of semaphore operations in Sumo-CORE (see above). For larger data sets, the Chorus version fails, indicating that kernel implementations of threads do not scale to large levels of concurrency. In contrast, the Sumo-ORB version continues to perform well and shows no signs of degradation as the data set increases.

10.7 Summary

This chapter has considered the design and implementation of Sumo-CORE, a microkernel-based operating system designed to support the engineering model as discussed in the Chapter 8. In particular, Sumo-CORE fulfils the RM-ODP nucleus function and also provides primitive bindings for the recursive binding model. Crucially, both aspects are driven by QoS requirements. The implementation then features integrated resource management and QoS management strategies to achieve the desired level of quality of service. The most interesting aspects of the design are, firstly, the active binding model and, secondly, the split level resource management strategy. These two design choices enable integration to be achieved in QoS management and resource management respectively. The chapter also described the interface and implementation of Sumo-CORE in some depth. Key features of the implementation include:

- a split level scheduling approach based on an extended earliest deadline first policy,

- asynchronous upcalls and downcalls providing lightweight interaction between user and system space,
- a split level communications architecture with the transport service in user space,
- an implementation of a lightweight rate-based transport protocol designed to support stream interactions.

The chapter then presented the implementation of QoS management in Sumo-CORE with particular attention to static QoS management. In particular, the text highlighted an end-to-end binding establishment protocol encapsulating the QoS management functions of negotiation, admission control and resource reservation. Finally, the chapter presented some experimental results highlighting the performance improvements attained in Sumo-ORB (in comparison to the basic Chorus microkernel).

The next chapter describes a complementary microkernel-based platform which focuses more on the ODP subsystem than the underlying nucleus.

11 Sumo-ORB: an ODP subsystem for multimedia

11.1 Introduction

This chapter describes the design and implementation of Sumo-ORB, an ODP subsystem designed to support multimedia (Dang Tran and Prebaskine, 1995; Stefani *et al.*, 1995). The subsystem is based on CORBA, but with extensions to align CORBA with the programming and engineering models described earlier in this book. Briefly, the existing CORBA standard only supports operational interactions and does not have a concept of an explicit binding. Similarly, there is no support for quality of service management or real-time synchronization in the specification. Finally, most existing CORBA implementations are constructed in a rather monolithic manner and do not provide open access to internal services. Sumo-ORB rectifies these shortcomings by (1) supporting operational, signal and stream interactions, (2) supporting explicit QoS-managed bindings, (3) supporting reactive objects, (4) adoption of the recursive binding model, and (5) structuring the subsystem in a more open manner. The platform is implemented in a Chorus environment consisting of several sites connected by an FDDI network.

The implementation of Sumo-ORB also has the following additional goals:

- to retain compliance with existing CORBA implementations (the version described in this chapter is not entirely compliant with the CORBA specification; this will, however, be rectified in the next version of the software (version 3)),
- to support a range of different language bindings, including C++ and Esterel (the latter for reactive objects),
- to develop appropriate (static) QoS management functions offering deterministic guarantees on the end-to-end quality of service.

Note that operating system support is not an explicit objective of Sumo-ORB. Rather, this work relies on platforms such as Sumo-CORE to provide a QoS-driven nucleus and primitive bindings. The emphasis of Sumo-ORB is on constructing open systems on top of such facilities.

The chapter is structured as follows. Section 11.2 describes the overall approach to the design of Sumo-ORB. This section highlights three main aspects of the design: the refinements to the CORBA programming model, the binding-neutral implementation of Sumo-ORB, and the exploitation of FDDI to provide deterministic guarantees. Section 11.3 then describes in detail the extended programming interface offered by Sumo-ORB. This section describes the extensions to CORBA IDL and then discusses the C++ language mapping offered by Sumo-ORB. Some examples are also presented. The implementation of the platform is then described in Section 11.4. This section describes the structure of the Sumo-ORB platform and also considers the underlying operating system support. The specific support offered for reactive objects is then described in Section 11.5. Following this, Section 11.6 describes the quality of service management features in Sumo-ORB, discussing the approach to achieving deterministic guarantees over FDDI. Section 11.7 presents some performance figures for Sumo-ORB and Section 11.8 summarizes the major contributions of the chapter.

11.2 Overall approach

11.2.1 Refinements to CORBA

As mentioned in the introduction, Sumo-ORB is based on CORBA, but with a number of significant extensions to align CORBA with the programming and engineering models developed in this book. In this section, we examine these extensions in more detail.

Programming model extensions
The programming model of Chapter 4 describes an object model where each object can have multiple interfaces. Interfaces can then support operational, signal or stream interaction and can also have associated QoS annotations constraining the behaviour of interactions. The model also supports both implicit and explicit binding. In the latter case, the creation of bindings can encapsulate arbitrary static QoS management functions. In addition, the interface on a binding object can be used for dynamic QoS management functions. Finally, signals together with reactive objects provide the necessary support for real-time synchronization. In contrast, CORBA objects support a single interface and only support operational interactions. All bindings are implicit and no support is provided for QoS management or real-time synchronization.

Sumo-ORB addresses the deficiencies of CORBA by providing an extended programming model where (1) support is provided for operational, signal and stream interaction, (2) explicit bindings can be created between compatible interfaces, (3) QoS management is supported through binding objects, and (4) reactive objects provide support for real-time synchronization (at present, Sumo-ORB does not allow objects to have multiple interfaces, however). To retain compatibility with CORBA, it is important to support implicit binding for operational interfaces and to support standard CORBA semantics for operational interaction.

Engineering extensions

The engineering model of Chapter 8 describes a virtual machine to support the programming model. This virtual machine shares the same object model and features a recursive binding architecture. This binding architecture is supported by an abstract binding protocol together with a number of binding factories. Factories also have an important role in supporting static QoS management through the encapsulation of negotiation, admission control and resource reservation strategies. Dynamic QoS management is then supported through the concept of managed objects.

CORBA does not support any of the concepts described above. Consequently, the Sumo-ORB platform extends CORBA with (1) a recursive binding architecture, and (2) appropriate admission control techniques for static QoS management. As will be described later, dynamic QoS management is not required in the particular FDDI environment. The adoption of the recursive binding architecture has a particularly significant impact on Sumo-ORB. This aspect of the design is considered in more detail below.

11.2.2 A binding-neutral implementation

Sumo-ORB adopts the recursive binding architecture as defined in Section 8.3.2. With this architecture, bindings are arbitrary objects which can themselves contain further bindings. The recursion will eventually be resolved by mapping to primitive bindings provided by the underlying nucleus. Each binding must provide stubs for the participant interface, where the stub performs the necessary translation to the host environment. The recursive binding architecture is also supported by an abstract binding protocol which enables bindings to be initiated by a third party (again see Section 8.3.2).

In Sumo-ORB, the recursive binding architecture is supported by a micro-ORB which provides the minimal functionality required to support the binding process. This translates to the following functions:

- the management of interface references, and
- the ability to perform local bindings on adjacent interfaces.

All other functionality is built on top of the micro-ORB as open services. The overall architecture is depicted in Figure 11.1. This figure shows the micro-ORB supporting a number of binding factories. A variety of binding factories can be created. In addition, the range can be extended over time. Binding factories can also make use of reusable services in the various binding libraries; there is one binding library per style of binding (operational and signal).

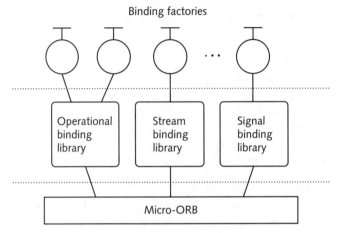

Figure 11.1 The Sumo-ORB architecture.

This approach has a number of significant benefits over more traditional implementations of ORBs. Firstly, as stated above, the binding architecture is completely *open* and can evolve over time. This approach also enables a range of *binding services* to coexist. Secondly, and most significantly, the architecture is binding-neutral in that the system does not prescribe one particular approach to binding. Bindings can be viewed as just another application. With this approach, it is possible to provide a particular ORB personality by offering particular binding factories. For example, it is possible to support a personality that can interwork with CORBA by developing an operational binding factory based on a CORBA-compliant interoperability protocol such as IIOP. It would also be possible, though, to support other operational bindings using, for example, DCE RPC. Similarly, it would be possible to enhance the environment with a range of signal or stream factories offering optimized real-time or continuous media behaviour.

Note that to fully support CORBA it is necessary to implement implicit binding. The approach to supporting implicit binding in Sumo-ORB is discussed in Section 11.3.2.

11.2.3 Exploitation of FDDI

The particular implementation of Sumo-ORB described in this book is designed to operate over FDDI and to exploit the deterministic service offered by this class of network. FDDI is a fibre optic network capable of operating at 100 Mbps (Ross, 1989). The access method is based on a token ring protocol, whereby a token is passed round the ring between stations. When holding the token, a station can transmit a number of packets. When the last packet is transmitted, the token is passed on to the next station in the ring.

The precise bandwidth allocation in FDDI is constrained by the *Timed Token Rotation Protocol*. This protocol supports two styles of traffic, namely *synchronous* and *asynchronous* traffic. Each station is allocated a guaranteed portion of the overall bandwidth for its synchronous traffic (referred to as its *synchronous capacity*). The bandwidth not used by synchronous traffic can then be used for asynchronous traffic.

To support this protocol, FDDI introduces a *Target Token Rotation Time* (TTRT). This value represents the *ideal* round-trip time for a token and is established at ring initialization time. To operate correctly, the value of TTRT must be greater than the sum of the synchronous capacities allocated to each station. Each FDDI station must also maintain a Token Rotation Timer (TRT) containing a measurement for the *actual* rotation time for the last circuit of the token. The two variables are then used to control the transmission of both synchronous and asynchronous traffic as follows.

Consider the arrival of a token at a particular node. At that point, TRT will provide a measurement of the rotational time for that token. Two cases then exist:

- *TRT < TTRT*
  In this case, some spare capacity exists in the ring. The node can therefore transmit its allocation of synchronous traffic and then any asynchronous traffic. The amount of asynchronous traffic transmitted is, however, constrained by TTRT. In particular, the total token holding time for asynchronous traffic must be less than or equal to TTRT−TRT.
- *TRT ⩾ TTRT*
  In this case, there is no spare capacity in the ring. The rules of FDDI then state that only synchronous traffic can be sent; that is, synchronous traffic is always guaranteed.

Using this approach, FDDI can provide high-priority synchronous traffic together with low-priority asynchronous traffic.

The goal of Sumo-ORB is to exploit the deterministic bandwidth offered by the synchronous service to provide guaranteed end-to-end bindings. With this style of network, it is not so necessary to perform dynamic QoS management such as monitoring and maintenance. The emphasis in Sumo-ORB is hence on static QoS management. In particular, admission control is carried out end-to-end to ensure that the overall guarantees can be met. The admission control strategies for Sumo-ORB are described in Section 11.6. Note that the admission control test is not restricted to FDDI. Rather, the test can be adapted for any network that can offer deterministic guarantees on message delay.

11.3 Programming interface and abstractions

This section describes the Sumo-ORB interface as seen by the programmer. The first subsection describes the main features of the extensions to CORBA

IDL as defined in Sumo-ORB. The second subsection then considers the particular language mapping defined for C++. Running examples are used throughout to illustrate the use of Sumo-ORB.

11.3.1 IDL extensions

The extended IDL
Sumo-ORB adopts the extended CORBA IDL as presented in Chapter 5. This extended IDL enables the description of operational, signal and stream interfaces. Rather than repeat the presentation of Chapter 5, we simply provide some examples of the use of the IDL language.

- *Example operational interfaces*
  This example illustrates the use of the extended IDL to define a bank operational interface. This interface supports three operations, namely deposit(), withdraw() and get_balance().

  ```
  interface <operational> Bank {
     void deposit (in float cash);
     void withdraw (in float cash) raises (UnderFlow);
     float get_balance ();
  };
  ```

  Note that the keyword <operational> is optional in the above declaration to retain compatibility with CORBA IDL (see Chapter 2).

- *Example signal interfaces*
  The following example is a simple clock interface. This clock receives an input signal to reset the internal time and also generates tick signals at a given granularity determined by the implementation.

  ```
  struct time_t {unsigned long seconds, unsigned long
  milliseconds;};

  interface <signal> Clock {
     signalIn      reset(time_t);
     signalOut     tick(time_t);
  };
  ```

- *Example stream interfaces*
  The first stream interface considered below is a telephone interface offering an incoming and outgoing audio flow.

  ```
  interface <stream> Telephone {
     flowIn mike(audio);
     flowOut speaker(audio);
  };
  ```

The second example then extends this interface with incoming and outgoing video flows to reflect the functionality of a videophone:

```
interface <stream> VideoPhone: Telephone {
  flowIn v_source(video);
  flowOut v_sink(video);
};
```

Note that the issue of compatibility between these two interfaces is considered below.

Signal and stream interfaces are closely related in Sumo-ORB. In particular, stream interfaces are interpreted as particular signal interactions where the history of signals is constrained by particular QoS directives, such as requiring isochronous delivery. Individual flows are also annotated by a more abstract object type whereas signal types are annotated with data structures representing the value of the signal (see the discussion in Section 5.2.2).

Representing interfaces
To enable the representation of operational, stream or signal interfaces, we introduce four predefined types into the IDL:

- the type `ClientInterface` designates a client operational interface of any type,
- the type `ServerInterface` designates a server operational interface of any type (this corresponds to the predefined type `Object` in CORBA IDL),
- the type `SignalInterface` designates a signal interface of any type, and
- the type `StreamInterface` designates a stream interface of any type,

where each type is a subclass of the general type `Interface`. This class hierarchy is illustrated in Figure 11.2. The root class encapsulates the interface reference for the given interface. This class also supports operations for binding to interfaces (see Section 11.4.2).

The introduction of interface classes enables the description of binding factory objects in the IDL. For example, the following specifications in the extended IDL define a general operational binding factory and a stream binding factory respectively.

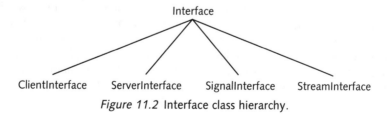

Figure 11.2 Interface class hierarchy.

- *An operational binding factory in IDL*

  A typical IDL definition for an operational binding factory is given below:

  ```
  interface <operational> BindingCtrl {
    void destroy();
  };

  interface <operational> OpBindingFactory {
    exception{BindFailure};
    BindingCtrl Bind(in ClientInterface client,
                     in ServerInterface server)
      raises(BindFailure);
  };
  ```

  where `client` and `server` designate the operational interfaces to be bound, and `BindingCtrl` is a standard operational interface representing the control interface of the established binding object.

- *A stream binding factory in IDL*

  The following IDL defines a binding factory to connect two telephones (with the type signatures as given above):

  ```
  interface <operational> BindingCtrl {
    void destroy();
  };

  interface TelecomOperator {
    exception{ConnectionFailure};
    BindingCtrl connect(in Telephone tel1, in Telephone tel2)
      raises (ConnectionFailure);
  };
  ```

  where `tel1` and `tel2` designate the stream interfaces of the two telephones to be bound together, and `BindingCtrl` is a standard operational interface representing the control interface of the established binding object.

Note that, in performing a binding, it is necessary to determine compatibility between the component interfaces. This is relatively straightforward for operational interfaces, where the rules of compatibility are well known. However, this is more difficult for stream or signal interfaces. For example, consider a binding between a telephone interface and a videophone interface (as defined above). This could be legitimate but introduces the possibility of *dangling* flows or signals. Some action would be required to deal with this possibility, such as informing the producer not to emit certain flows. The approach in Sumo-ORB is to delegate responsibility for type checking to each binding factory. Different binding factories can thus implement their own policies. In this way, some will be able to deal with problems such as dangling signals whereas others would reject the binding.

Supporting QoS specification

Finally, Sumo-ORB IDL provides support for quality of service specification. This is achieved by optionally associating a QoS clause with each signal or flow declaration (QoS specification is not currently supported on operational interfaces). The extended rule for a signal or flow declaration is therefore:

```
<signal_dcl>              ::= <signal_direction> <identifier>
                             "(" [<signal_values>] ")" [<qos_dcl>]
<flow_dcl>               ::= <flow_direction> <identifier>
                             "(" [<flow_type>] ")" [<qos_dcl>]
```

where a <qos_dcl> is given by the following grammar:

```
<qos_dcl>                 ::= <required_qos_dcl>
                          |  <provided_qos_dcl>
<required_qos_dcl>        ::= "requires" <qos_param_list_dcls>
<offered_qos_dcl>         ::= "provides" <qos_param_list_dcls>
<qos_param_list_dcls>     ::= <qos_param_list_dcl>
                             { "|" <qos_param_list_dcl> }*
<qos_param_list_dcl>      ::= "QoS" "(" <qos_param_dcl>
                             { "," <qos_param_dcl> }* ")"
<qos_param_dcl>           ::= <string_literal>
```

In defining an interface, input signals or flows can have an associated *required* QoS declaration list and output signals or flows can have a *provided* QoS declaration list (see Chapter 4). The former corresponds to QoS requirements placed on the environment for the delivery of signals/flows, whereas the latter are constraints on the object for the emission of signals/flows. A given QoS declaration list can then consist of one or more specific QoS declarations. Each declaration corresponds to a level of service that can be supported by the interface. In a particular binding, it is necessary to select one of these levels.

Each QoS declaration is composed of a set of strings, with each string defining a particular QoS attribute. These strings can be accessed and interpreted by the Sumo-ORB platform. In particular, factories can use this information to check compatibility of interfaces (as discussed above) and to perform QoS management functions. Currently two sets of attributes are defined: generic attributes and media-specific attributes. Table 11.1(a) defines a selection of generic attributes defined in Sumo-ORB and Table 11.1(b) provides some media specific attributes for audio data (a similar list can be provided for video data).

Some examples of signal and flow interfaces with QoS attributes are given below (these are extensions of flow and signal interfaces introduced in Section 11.3.1). In each case, the QoS declarations are fairly straightforward and do not require any further explanation.

Table 11.1 (a) Example generic attributes in Sumo-ORB

Attribute	Type	Description
period	Time	Nominal period of the signal
jitter_max	Time	Maximum jitter of the periodic signal
rate_min	Frequency	Minimum occurence rate of the signal
rate_max	Frequency	Maximum occurence rate of the signal
size_min	Bytes	Minimum size of the signal
size_max	Bytes	Maximum size of the signal

Table 11.1 (b) Example media-specific attributes in Sumo-ORB

Attribute	Type	Description
audio_encoding	ULAW, LINEAR, ALAW	Encoding format
audio_frequency	Frequency	Sampling frequency
audio_channels	1, 2, ...	Mono, stereo, ...
audio_precision	Bits	Sampling precision

Example 1 *QoS declarations for the clock interface*
This example extends the clock signal interface introduced earlier with a
provided clause on the outgoing signal:

```
struct time_t {unsigned long seconds, unsigned long
milliseconds;};
interface <signal>Clock {
   signalIn reset(time_t);
   signalOut tick(Time_t)
   provides QoS("period=100ms", "jitter_max=2ms");
};
```

Note that this now ascertains that the tick will be emitted every millisecond
(see above).

Example 2 *QoS declarations for the telephone interface*
This example extends the telephone signal interface with both required
and provided clauses:

```
interface <stream> Telephone {
   flowIn mike(audio);
     requires
       QoS(
           "audio_encoding=LINEAR",
           "audio_frequency=22050 hz,
           "audio_precision=16",
           "audio_channels=2")
       |
```

```
            QoS(
                "audio_encoding=ULAW",
                "audio_frequency=8000 hz,
                "audio_precision=8",
                "audio_channels=1")
            ;
        flowOut speaker(audio);
          provides
            QoS(
                "audio_encoding=ULAW",
                "audio_frequency=8000 hz,
                "audio_precision=8",
                "audio_channels=1")
            ;
    };
```

In this example, the incoming flow can be either LINEAR or ULAW encoding but the outgoing flow is always ULAW encoding.

Note that the language for QoS specification is considerably simpler than the equivalent language described in Chapter 5. This is for pragmatic reasons and may be extended in future releases of the platform.

11.3.2 The C++ mapping

The IDL defined above is language-independent. However, to program in Sumo-ORB, it is necessary to define a language mapping to a particular host language. This language mapping must define the interpretation of the various IDL features in the chosen language. In this subsection we define a mapping to C++. Note that a C++ mapping for IDL is defined in the CORBA 2 specification (Object Management Group, 1995a). We do not repeat this in detail, but instead focus on the features specific to Sumo-ORB. In particular, we consider the interpretation of operational, signal and stream interfaces. Some knowledge of C++ and CORBA is assumed, although key features are explained in the text.

  Note that Sumo-ORB also supports a language mapping for Esterel; discussion of this mapping is, however, deferred until Section 11.5.

The C++ mapping for operational interfaces

To understand the treatment of operational interfaces, it is necessary to consider both the client and server sides separately. To simplify the discussion, we first assume that interfaces support *explicit third-party bindings* and then consider the more specific cases of client-initiated bindings and implicit bindings.

Client C++ mapping

On the client side, Sumo-ORB generates a client stub from the IDL declaration. Consider the following IDL declaration:

```
interface <operational> dummy {
    long op(in string s1, out string s2) raises (Oops);
};
```

The corresponding client stub has the following form:

```
class dummy : public virtual Interface {
  public:
    virtual long op(char * s1, char * &s2, Environment &);
};
```

The stub is a C++ class with a virtual function for each of the IDL operations. The types of parameters and results are transformed into equivalent C++ types according to the CORBA C++ mapping.

Note that the (strongly typed) client stub classes are organized in an inheritance graph which mimics the one for the corresponding IDL interface declarations. For example, the IDL declaration:

```
interface <operational> A : B, C {....}
```

is mapped to

```
class A : public virtual B, public virtual C {....}
```

The stub class can then be used to create a client interface. This is achieved using the _create_ClientInterface class as defined in the underlying operational binding library. The public interface for this class is given below:

```
template <class T> class _create_ClientInterface :
    public ClientInterface {
  public:
    _create_ClientInterface();
    virtual ~_create_ClientInterface();
    T *acceptBind();
};
```

This class is a template class in C++ terminology. Such classes are generic in that they can be instantiated with different types, as given in the <> brackets. In this case, the class T refers to the appropriate stub class as introduced above. The _create_ClientInterface() function is the constructor for the class (indicated in C++ by the function having the same name as the class).

This constructor is called when a new instance is created from the class. The class also has a corresponding destructor function (indicated by the ~ syntax in C++). This is virtual to ensure that the correct implementation is invoked at run-time (to deal with the potential polymorphism in C++). Finally, the class has an `acceptBind()` function. This function blocks until a binding is established (it is assumed that this will be established by a third party). The function then returns a client stub to this binding of the required type (as given by the parameter to the template class). This ensures type-safe access to the binding.

As an example, the following code fragment creates a client interface of type dummy (assumed to have at least one operation, called op ( )).

```
_create_ClientInterface <dummy> *ic;
ic = new _create_ClientInterface <dummy>;

...

dummy *stub = ic->acceptBind();

try {
   char *string;
   long result = stub->op("hello", string);
}
catch (TORB::SystemException::StaleStub&)
   {...}
```

This program initially creates a new client operational interface of type dummy. The program then blocks awaiting a binding, using the `acceptBind()` method. This will return after a third party has created a binding between this client and an appropriate server (or servers). (The third-party code is not shown for brevity. Briefly, however, the third party will obtain interfaces for the client and server, will initiate a bind action, and will then obtain a control interface for the binding object.) Following this, the program invokes the operation op() from the interface. This will be delivered by the associated binding to the corresponding server interface and then the results returned to the client. The stub performs the necessary marshalling and unmarshalling of the parameters and results. The program also uses the C++ exception handling mechanism (`try ... catch`) to deal with any exceptions raised by the program. More specifically, the invocation of an operation can cause a StaleStub exception to be raised. This indicates that the underlying binding has been destroyed. It is assumed that the user programmer takes an appropriate action on catching this exception. In particular, the application should no longer use this binding.

Server C++ mapping
On the server side, Sumo-ORB generates a template class to provide a delegation mechanism to forward incoming invocations to a corresponding

implementation class. This is one approach advocated by the CORBA C++ mapping (the alternative is to use inheritance) (Object Management Group, 1995a). (The advantage of using the delegation mechanism is that it provides a complete separation between the C++ class hierarchy used by the ORB and the C++ class hierarchy used by the application programmer for implementing the IDL interfaces.) Consider the IDL for the dummy interface as defined above. Sumo-ORB will generate a template class _tie_dummy as follows:

```
template <class T> class _tie_dummy : public dummy {
public:
  _tie_dummy(T *t);
  virtual ~_tie_dummy();
  virtual T *_deref();
};
```

This class has a constructor operation, _tie_dummy(), which takes as parameter an implementation class of the required type. This implementation class must support all the operations defined in dummy. The effect of the constructor is to create a new interface and then forward incoming invocations to the implementation class. The template class also has a destructor operation, ~_tie_dummy(), which destroys the interface. The class also has a _deref() function which returns a pointer to the implementation class attached to the _tie_ class.

To illustrate the use of this mechanism, consider the fragment of code below:

```
class dummy_i {
public:
  virtual long op(char * s1, char * &s2, Environment &);
};

long dummy_i::op(char * s1, char * &s2, Environment &)
{
  ...
}

main()
{
  _tie_dummy<dummy_i> *dummy =
    new _tie_dummy<dummy_i>(new dummy_i);
  ...
}
```

The class dummy_i is the implementation class for the interface. The call of _tie_dummy() then creates a new interface and links this interface to the implementation class. Arriving invocations on the interface will then be dispatched to the appropriate method in the implementation class, dummy_i.

Special cases
As mentioned earlier, the above text assumes that bindings are created explicitly by a third party. We now consider the special cases of client-initiated (explicit) bindings and then implicit bindings.

The explicit creation of client interfaces is required to support third-party binding, where a separate object is responsible for creating the binding between the client and server. This can happen, for example, when a separate configuration manager is responsible for constructing configurations of objects. In many cases, however, the client will initiate the binding to a server. In this case, the interface will not be visible. Rather, the client will be directly returned a stub on to the binding.

To illustrate *client-initiated bindings*, consider the following example, based on the bank interface defined earlier.

```
class BindingCtrl {
  void destroy();
};
class BankAccountBindingFactory {
public:
  BindingCtrl *Bind(Bank *&stub, Interface *target)
throw (BindFailure&);
};
```

This example shows a binding factory for a bank. The bind() operation takes a target interface as parameter and returns a pointer to a local stub representing the binding (it is assumed that the interface, target, has been previously obtained, for example from a trading service). The operation also returns a binding control interface to enable the destruction of the binding. Note that this binding factory is provided by a local class rather than through a Sumo-ORB interface, as used previously. On completion of the binding, the client can access the bank by calling operations as follows:

```
stub -> deposit (1000);
```

Sumo-ORB also supports *implicit binding* (as required, for example, by CORBA). Suppose a client receives an interface reference for a (potentially) remote server, for example from an out parameter of an operation such as an import operation on a trader. In this case, Sumo-ORB will allocate a surrogate interface on the local site. This interface will support an *implicit stub* of the appropriate type. The implicit stub then acts as a proxy for the remote interface. All operations on the remote interface are interpreted by the stub and then forwarded on to the appropriate interface for execution. Thus, in explicit binding, the stub provides access to the binding object whereas, in implicit binding, the stub provides a proxy for the remote interface. The mechanism to support the creation of implicit stubs is described in Section 11.4.2.

To support implicit binding, it is also necessary for Sumo-ORB to generate a binding to the appropriate server interface. This binding is hidden from the programmer. This binding must then be destroyed at an appropriate point in time. The approach in Sumo-ORB is to create a binding on an operation invocation and to maintain a cache of recently used bindings. If a binding has not been used for a while, it is destroyed. Subsequent invocations of the associated binding will therefore incur the cost of a new binding creation.

The C++ mapping for signal interfaces

The handling of signal interfaces in Sumo-ORB is more straightforward. Sumo-ORB transforms the IDL for a signal interface into a corresponding stub. This stub can then be used to instantiate type-safe interfaces for the interface type. The two steps are described in more detail below.

Creating a signal stub

As above, the creation of signal stubs is illustrated by example. Consider the clock signal interface defined above:

```
struct time_t {unsigned long seconds, unsigned long milliseconds;};

interface <signal> Clock {
  signalIn      reset(time_t);
  signalOut     tick(time_t);
};
```

Sumo-ORB transforms this interface signature into a corresponding C++ class as follows:

```
class Clock : public SignalStub {
  InSignal<time_t>   reset;
  OutSignal<time_t>  tick;
};
```

This transformation creates a class `Clock` which contains an instance of a template class `InSignal` for each input signal and an instance of template class `OutSignal` for each output signal. Each template class is instantiated with the C type corresponding to the IDL signal type. In addition, each signal instance is named after the name of the signal in the IDL definition.

The template classes `InSignal` and `OutSignal` are supplied by the underlying signal binding library. They offer the following public interfaces:

```
template <class T> class InSignal {
public:
  InSignal<T> &operator>>(T&)
    throw (TORB::SystemException::StaleStub&);
  unsigned char is_active();
  QoSsignal qos();
};

template <class T> class OutSignal {
public:
  OutSignal<T> &operator<<(T&)
    throw (TORB::SystemException::StaleStub&);
  unsigned char is_active();
  QoSsignal qos();
};
```

As mentioned above, the InSignal and OutSignal classes are templated by the input and output signal types respectively (for this example, time_t in both cases). The classes then overload the C stream operators to support the emission and reception of signals, thus supporting passive bindings (active bindings are currently not supported in Sumo-ORB). The emission operator on OutSignal (<<) is non-blocking. In contrast the reception operator on InSignal (>>) will block until a signal is received at the interface. These operators can cause a StaleStub exception to be raised. As discussed above, this implies that the underlying binding has been destroyed. The is_active() operation can be used to detect whether the corresponding signal is active or dangling (see the discussion in Section 11.3.1). Finally, the qos() operation returns the current QoS attributes of the signal (again refer to the discussion above).

Instantiating a signal interface
The Sumo-ORB platform provides a template class called _create_ SignalInterface <> to support the creation of a signal interface and the subsequent type-safe access to its incoming and outgoing signals. This template class offers the following public interface:

```
template <class T> class _create_SignalInterface :
    public SignalInterface {
public:
  _create_SignalInterface(unsigned long max_binding=1);
  virtual ~_create_SignalInterface();
  T *acceptBind();
};
```

The _create_SignalInterface() operation is the constructor for the class; this is called when a new instance is created from the class. This operation takes as parameter the maximum number of simultaneous bindings that the interface can handle (which defaults to one). The `~_create_SignalInterface()` function is the destructor for the class. Finally, the class supports an `acceptBind()` function which blocks until a binding is established (as above). The function then returns a signal stub to this binding of the required type (as given by the parameter to the template class). This ensures type-safe access to the binding. Note that the `acceptBind` function must encapsulate the policy to determine whether a binding can be established. For signals, this is currently constrained by the parameter specified at the creation time of the interface. Clearly, however, more sophisticated policies could be required, such as for multimedia. We return to this issue below.

The following example illustrates the creation and use of a signal interface.

```
_create_SignalInterface <clock> *it;
it = new _create_SignalInterface <clock>(1);

Clock *stub = it->acceptBind();

try {
    stub->reset >> current_time;

    while(1) {
       time_t current_time=...;
        stub->tick << current_time;
       ...
    }
}
catch(TORB::SystemException::StaleStub&) {...}
```

This program initially creates a new signal interface of type `Clock` which can support one binding at a given time. The program then blocks awaiting a binding (assumed to be created by a third party). Following this, the program blocks awaiting a `reset` signal providing an update on the current time and then repeatedly emits ticks with an update on the time. The program also uses the C++ try facility to catch the signal corresponding to the `StaleStub` exception as discussed above.

Note that only explicit binding is supported on signal interfaces: implicit binding is disallowed.

The C++ mapping for stream interfaces

The C++ mapping for stream interfaces is similar to that for signal interfaces (the view taken in Sumo-ORB is that stream interfaces *are* signal interfaces but with a particular semantics relating to the production, transmission and consumption of continuous media). The main differences are that entries in stubs are instances of classes `InFlow` and `OutFlow` rather than `InSignal` and `OutSignal`. The types offered to the two template classes are also more specific and are related to the incoming or outgoing continuous media data. The set of types is currently restricted to `audio_packet` and `video_packet` in Sumo-ORB.

The public interfaces of these two classes are given below.

```
template <class T> class InFlow {
public:
  InFlow<T> &operator>>(T&)
    throw (TORB::SystemException::StaleStub&);
  unsigned char is_active();
  QoSsignal qos();
};

template <class T> class OutFlow {
public:
  OutFlow<T> &operator<<(T&)
    throw (TORB::SystemException::StaleStub&);
  unsigned char is_active();
  QoSsignal qos();
};
```

The underlying stream binding library also provides a template class `_create_StreamInterface <>`. This class supports the creation of stream interfaces and is identical in structure to `_create_SignalInterface <>` as described above. Again, stream interfaces only allow explicit binding.

To further illustrate the treatment of stream interactions, we present a code fragment which processes incoming audio packets to an audio device. We first present the IDL for the audio device and then provide the related code fragment:

```
// IDL
  interface <signal> AudioSink {
  {
      signalIn sink(audio);
  };

// C++

audio_packet nextFrame;
_create_StreamInterface <AudioSink> *it =
    new _create_StreamInterface <AudioSink>(1);
...
AudioSink *stub = it->acceptBind();
...
InFlow &input = stub->mike;
...
```

```
while(1) {
   try {
      input >> nextFrame;
   }
   catch(TORB::SystemException::StaleStub&) {
      // cleanup ...
      break;
   }
   // decode the audio packet
   // and submit it to the audio device driver interface....
   // some buffering might be needed to cushion delay-jitter...
   ...
}
```

This first step in this program is to instantiate an interface of the appropriate type: `AudioStub`. The program then blocks awaiting the completion of a binding to this audio device and then returns a correctly typed stub for the interface. Following this, the program sets the variable input to represent the `InFlow` element of the stub representing the audio device. The program then repeatedly loops performing the following steps:

1. use `input >> nextFrame` to consume the next incoming signal and to return the data associated with the audio packet,
2. decode the audio packet, and
3. present the decoded data to the appropriate audio device.

The precise code for the later two stages is omitted for clarity. Note that the try facility in C++ is used to trap exceptions generated by the read.

11.3.3 Examples of use

This section has presented a number of small examples throughout to illustrate the concepts. In this subsection, we now present some larger, more complete examples to illustrate the C++ mapping in Sumo-ORB.

Establishing a secure binding

The first example provides a further illustration of client-initiated operational binding using a local class. The example is an expanded version of the bank example presented above offering additional security on bindings. The program to achieve the binding is given below.

We first consider the class description for a secure binding factory.

```
class SecureBindingCtrl {
   void unbind();
};
```

```
template <class T> class SecureBindingFactory {
public:
  SecureBindingCtrl *bind(
    Interface *target,
    char      *id,
    long      *public_key,
    T         *&stub)
    throw (AccessDenied&);
};
```

This binding factory is generic in that it is a template class with the template defining the type of the participant interfaces. The bind() operation provided by the factory interface takes as input parameters an object of type interface representing the bank, a string representing the identity of the client and a public key providing authentication for the transaction. The operation also has an out parameter to return the stub for the remote interface. Finally, the operation returns a control interface to the binding. The binding can fail if the public key is invalid.

A client can then use this binding factory as shown in the fragment of code given below:

```
1   Interface *target;
2   SecureBindingFactory fty;
3   Bank *bank;
4   SecureBindingCtrl *ctrl;
5
6   trader->importOffer(bank::type_id,"name=Barclays",target);
7
8   try {
9      ctrl=fty.bind(target,"Gordon Blair",my_public_key,bank);
10  } catch (AccessDenied&) {...}
11
12  bank->deposit(1000);
13
14  ctrl->unbind();
```

The first step of the program is to create the appropriate objects. The program creates in turn (1) an object of type Interface to later store the interface of the bank (line 1), (2) an instance of SecureBindingFactory templated by bank (line 2), (3) a handle for the stub (line 3), and (4) a control interface for the secure binding (line 4). The next step is to perform an importOffer() request on a trader object (line 6). This import operation searches for an interface of type bank with name Barclays and returns the result in the target parameter. Following this, the program attempts to bind to this interface using the secure binding factory (lines

8–10). Note that this is a local class rather than a remote server accessed through an interface. This `bind()` operation takes as parameter the `target` interface, the name of the account and a public key for authentication. We assume that the latter has previously been obtained from an appropriate authority. The bind operation also has, as an output parameter, a pointer to a local stub object (providing access to the service). Finally, the operation returns a control interface to the program. Note that this binding action can generate an exception `AccessDenied`; appropriate code must be provided to deal with this case. The penultimate step is to use the stub to perform a `deposit()` operation on the account (line 12). Finally, the binding is destroyed by invoking the `unbind()` operation on the control interface (line 14).

Creating an audio binding

The second example illustrates the creation and use of a QoS-constrained audio binding factory. The IDL for the factory is given below.

```
struct QoSAudio {
unsigned long audio_encoding;
unsigned long audio_frequency;
unsigned long audio_channels;
unsigned long audio_precision;
string    proto_id;
};

interface AudioCtrl {
  void destroy();
};

interface AudioStreamFactory {
  AudioCtrl bind(
    in StreamInterface i1,
    in StreamInterface i2,
    in QoSAudio qos)
    raises (TypeMismatch,QoSMismatch,BindFailure);
};
```

The `bind()` operation takes as arguments the interface references of the two audio devices which are to participate in the binding together with the QoS requirements on this binding. The QoS requirements structure contains a number of media-specific attributes and a protocol identifier specifying the preferred communications protocol (if null, the factory will select its default protocol).

To illustrate the use of this factory, consider the following program which creates an audio binding between two phone instances, called Blair and Stefani. We assume that phones are declared of type `Telephone` as above.

```
1   Interface *i;
2   trader->importOffer(AudioStreamFactory::type_id,"",i);
3   AudioStreamFactory *fty=AudioStreamFactory::narrow(i);
4
5   SignalInterface *it1,*it2;
6
7   trader->importOffer(Phone::type_id,"host=Blair",it1);
8   trader->importOffer(Phone::type_id,"host=Stefani",it2);
9   QoSaudio qos;
10  qos.audio_encoding=ULAW;
11  ...
12  AudioCtrl *ctrl=fty->bind(it1,it2,qos);
```

First, an AudioStreamFactory interface is imported from a trader object (lines 1–3). Note that the CORBA narrow operation is used to specialize the type of returned object from Interface to AudioStreamFactory. (This narrow operation is generated automatically by the CORBA IDL compiler). Following this, Interface references for the two phones are imported (lines 5–8). A QoS structure is then initialized with appropriate values (lines 9–11) and finally the binding is attempted (line 12). Note that the factory will perform a number of checks on the interfaces it1 and it2. The binding can be rejected at this stage for one of the following reasons:

- the types of the two interfaces are not compatible (as determined by the factory policy for type checking),
- the QoS provided and required do not match,
- sufficient resources are not available to support the binding.

This would be indicated to the programmer through the raising of the appropriate exception.

11.4 Implementation

11.4.1 Overall approach

The overall Sumo-ORB architecture has already been described (Section 11.2.2). In particular, Sumo-ORB consists of three main components:

- the *micro-ORB* offering the minimal functionality necessary to support a comprehensive ODP subsystem,
- a set of *binding libraries* (one per style of interaction) offering generic support for the construction of binding factories, and
- an open set of *binding factories* supporting operational, stream and signal interactions.

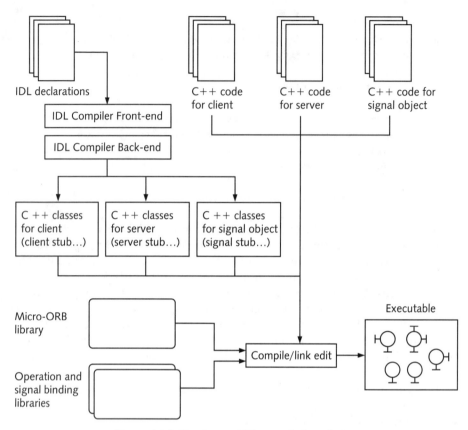

IDL declarations   C++ code   C++ code   C++ code for
                        for client   for server   signal object

Figure 11.3 The Sumo-ORB compilation chain.

The first two components are both organized as libraries which are linked into application programs at compile time. The result of the compilation process is the production of a set of RM-ODP compliant objects, including binding factory objects. The overall compilation process is shown in Figure 11.3 (omitting stream interfaces for simplicity).

The programmer provides a set of IDL declarations together with C++ code for client objects, server objects, signal objects or stream objects. The IDL declarations are compiled using an extended CORBA compiler producing the following outputs:

- a set of stub classes (operational, signal and stream stubs), one per IDL declaration, and
- a set of _tie_ classes for server operational interfaces, one per operational IDL declaration.

The IDL compiler is a modified version of a public domain compiler produced by Sun (at the time of writing, this compiler was available from ftp.omg.org). The stubs and _tie_ classes are then passed on to the compiler together with the applications code for associated objects. These objects can either be application objects providing operational, signal or stream interaction or can be user-defined binding classes. The combined C++ programs are then compiled and linked to the binding libraries and the micro-ORB library.

The binding libraries provides access to a range of calls including:

- `_create_ClientInterface <>`, `_create_SignalInterface <>` and `_create_StreamInterface <>`, supporting the creation of object interfaces of the appropriate type,
- `InSignal()` and `OutSignal()`, supporting the production and consumption of signals, and
- `InStream()` and `OutStream()`, supporting the production and consumption of stream flows.

The functionality of each of these classes was described in detail above. The binding libraries also provide access to lower level functionality not normally accessed by applications programs. This functionality can be exploited, however, by binding factories (see Section 11.4.2 for details).

The micro-ORB library provides a set of classes supporting interface reference management and local binding on adjacent interfaces (again discussed in more detail below). As above, this functionality is not normally seen by application objects.

Sumo-ORB is implemented on top of Chorus/ClassiX (release 2) partly as a Chorus subsystem and partly by modifying the microkernel. The platform has also been implemented on top of Solaris version 2.4. The discussion below focuses on the Chorus implementation.

11.4.2 The Sumo-ORB platform

This section provides further implementation details on each of the components in the Sumo-ORB architecture, namely the micro-ORB, the binding libraries and binding factories.

The micro-ORB

The micro-ORB provides the minimal functionality required to support Sumo-ORB (and more generally the binding model defined in the engineering model). The main functions supported by the micro-ORB are:

- interface reference management, and
- local bindings between adjacent interfaces.

We consider each in turn below.

Interface reference management

The functionality of the micro-ORB centres on one particular object type, namely the *interface reference*. The interface reference represents an object interface and contains sufficient data to identify the interface and to establish bindings between interfaces. The IDL structure for an interface reference is given below:

```
struct InterfaceType {
  InterfaceKind kind;
  string type;
};
struct ProtocolEntry {
  ProtocolId    tag;
  sequence<octet> data;
};

struct IfRefData {
sequence<octet>           key;
InterfaceType             type_info;
sequence<ProtocolEntry> protocols;
};
```

The key field is a (globally) unique identifier for the interface. The type_info field provides typing information on the interface. This consists of a kind field, which is one of (operational) client, (operational) server, stream or signal, and a type field, which in the current implementation is given by the name of the IDL declaration. Finally, the protocols field contains protocol-specific data associated with an interface. This is organized as a sequence of protocol entries, where each entry consists of a tag, giving the name of the protocol, and data, which is interpreted by the specific protocol. For example, the tag could be TCP and the data field could be an associated IP address, such as 148.88.8.9.

The micro-ORB supports the *creation* of interface references and also maintains an *association* between Sumo-ORB interfaces and interface references. The latter function is supported by an interface table in each capsule (see Figure 11.4).

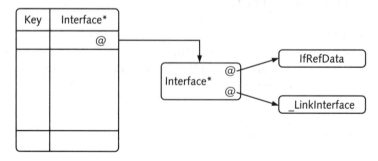

Figure 11.4 Micro-ORB interface table.

This table is organized as a series of entries of the form `<key, Interface*>` where `key` is the unique identifier of the interface (copied from the `IfRefData` field) and `Interface*` is a pointer to an instance of type `Interface`. This type is at the root of the Sumo-ORB C++ class hierarchy for interfaces (subclasses include `ClientInterface`, `ServerInterface`, `SignalInterface` and `StreamInterface`). Crucially, this root class contains functions to access interface reference data. The key functions are summarized below:

```
class Interface {
public:
  Interface(IfRefData *ir=0);
  IfRefData *getIfRef();
  _LinkInterface *getLinkInterface();
  ...
};
```

The first function is a constructor for the interface. This function takes an interface reference structure as parameter. As well as creating the interface, this constructor will add a new entry to the interface table. The second function, `getIfRef()`, returns the interface reference structure (of type `IfRefData`) for a given interface. Finally, the function `getLinkInterface()` provides access to the link interface associated to the interface (see below).

Note that special actions are required to deal with implicit binding (as discussed in Section 11.3.2). Each time Sumo-ORB unmarshalls an interface reference from a remote site, it checks the interface table for an appropriate entry. If an entry is not found, Sumo-ORB creates a correctly typed interface instance to act as a surrogate of the remote interface and then updates the table accordingly. Sumo-ORB returns the stub for the interface to the application (an *implicit stub* as defined above). On marshalling a surrogate interface, it is then necessary to retrieve the associated interface reference and marshall this instead.

Local binding

To support the generic binding protocol, the micro-ORB must provide the ability to perform local binding between adjacent interfaces. All other binding functionality is then encapsulated in binding factories. Full details on local bindings can be found in Chapter 8. Briefly, however, a local binding is a binding whereby signals are visible instantaneously to all parties participating in the binding. Furthermore, signals cannot be lost or corrupted in such bindings. They are required in order to link an object interface with the stub offered by the binding object. The required semantics can be achieved because stubs in Sumo-ORB are normally colocated with the object interface (that is, in the same address space).

To support local bindings, every interface must support a *link interface*. This link interface has the following class description:

```
class _LinkInterface {
public:
  virtual void localBind(Interface *stub)
    throw (NotLocal, BindingDenied, InvalidStub);
  virtual void localUnbind(Interface *stub)
    throw (NotLocal, InvalidStub);
};
```

The `localBind()` and `localUnbind()` functions are normally upcalled by the newly created (distributed) binding to establish the local binding between the interface and the corresponding stub. Note that the interface and the stub will be of a common type because of the semantics of stub creation (as discussed above).

The binding libraries

The binding libraries provide generic support for both the application programmers interface and for the construction of factory objects. Currently, three distinct binding libraries are implemented (corresponding to the three styles of interaction supported by Sumo-ORB):

- the operational binding library,
- the signal binding library, and
- the stream binding library.

We consider each in turn below (with particular focus on the support provided for factory objects).

The operational binding library

The operational binding library supports the application programmers interface by providing an implementation of the `_create_ClientInterface <>` operation. As stated above, this operation creates an interface of the appropriate type. In implementation, this operation will call the constructor for the `Interface` root class which will update the local interface table.

Support for bindings is more complex. The library relies on the overall model of a binding as illustrated in Figure 11.5.

In order to support bindings, therefore, the operational binding library must provide the following functionality:

- protocol channel objects, and
- client and server stub objects.

In all cases, the appropriate objects are created using factory objects provided by the library.

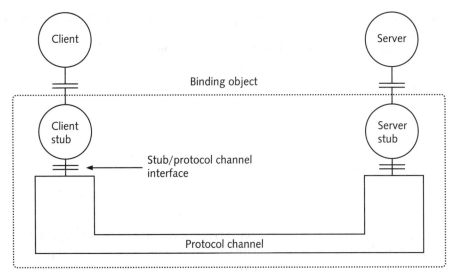

Figure 11.5 Model of an operational binding object.

Protocol channel objects are equivalent to primitive bindings in the recursive binding architecture. They implement the following functionality:

- the underlying communications protocol stack to support the communication,
- buffer management for the communication,
- appropriate transparency functions such as location and access transparency, and
- marshalling rules for requests.

The Sumo-ORB provides an abstract class called RPCProtocolChannel representing protocol channels for operational interaction. The system also currently supports a number of different factories for the creation of RPCProtocolChannel objects. These factories are either based on the CORBA interoperability protocol GIOP or a proprietary intra-ORB protocol. More specifically, one factory implements the GIOP protocol using TCP/IP (thus offering IIOP – see Section 2.3.3). Other factories implement the proprietary protocol using TCP/IP or Chorus IPC.

Each protocol channel factory has its own distinct interface. As an example, though, we present the interface of the IIOP protocol channel factory:

```
class IIOPBindingFactory {
  virtual RPCProtocolChannel *Bind(Interface *target);
};
```

The bind() operation defined on this factory simply creates a binding to the appropriate interface. Note that the binding factories can either establish a new communications channel per binding or can multiplex several bindings on to one channel.

The factory for *stub objects* has the following interface:

```
class StubFactory {
  static Interface *BuildClientStub(char *type,
                                    RPCProtocolChannel *chan)
     throw (UnknownType);
  static Dispatcher *GetDispatcher(Interface *it_server)
     throw(NotLocal, UnknownType);
  ...
};
```

The BuildClientStub() function creates a client stub of the required type (as given by the first parameter). The stub is also connected to the appropriate protocol channel (as specified in the second parameter). The stub is then returned as the result of the function. In the implementation, the stub factory relies on utility classes generated by the IDL compiler in order to create stubs for a given interface type.

The second function is used to create server stubs. Server stubs fulfil the role of a dispatcher in Sumo-ORB, receiving an incoming message, decoding the message and unmarshalling the parameters, and finally calling the appropriate local operation. The function GetDispatcher() returns a dispatcher with the required functionality. The type information is derived from the interface parameter. This information is then used to establish the necessary marshalling and unmarshalling code. The dispatcher is also linked to the appropriate implementation class for the interface (as provided by the programmer using the appropriate _tie_() operation). Note that, as the dispatcher functionality is stateless in Sumo-ORB, one implementation can be multiplexed between a number of interfaces.

The *interaction* between stubs and protocol channel objects uses a well-defined interface as discussed below:

- *On the client side*
  Client stubs interact with the protocol channel by calling a NewRequest() operation on the protocol channel object. This creates an object of type ClientRequest which in turn inherits from a marshaller abstract class. This latter class contains the appropriate operations to marshall and unmarshall all the basic data types. A given operational binding factory must provide a concrete implementation of the marshaller class; for example, the IIOPBindingFactory implements UNO CDR (Common Data Representation) marshalling rules (Object Management Group, 1995a). The client request can be sent to the receiver using an invoke() operation defined on ClientRequest.

- *On the server side*
  The dispatcher then interacts with the protocol channel by the protocol channel issuing a `dispatch()` upcall when a message arrives. This upcall is given a server request object as parameter. As above, this request object inherits from the `marshaller` class to provide the necessary operations to unmarshall the incoming data. Again, the server side must provide a concrete implementation of `marshaller`.

This interaction between stubs and protocol channels is summarized in Figure 11.6.

The signal binding library

The signal binding library provides similar functionality to the operational binding library but specialized for signals. Firstly, the signal binding library supports the application programmers interface by providing an implementation of the `_create_SignalInterface <>` operation. Again, this operation will call the constructor for the `Interface` root class, which will update the local interface table. Secondly, the library supports the creation of communication channels and signal stubs through the provision of appropriate factories as discussed below.

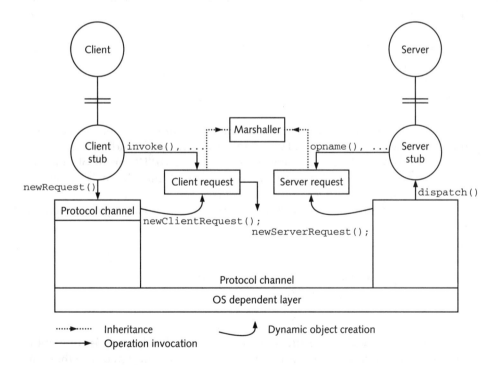

Figure 11.6 Interaction between protocol channels and stubs.

The library defines an abstract class, `SignalProtocolChannel`, as a generic communications interface for signals. The interface for `SignalProtocolChannel` is as follows:

```
class SignalProtocolChannel {
public:
  virtual commBuffer *get_commBuffer(
                unsigned char *ptr=0, unsigned long length=0);
  virtual void Send(commBuffer*)
    throw (TORB::SystemException::StaleStub&);
  virtual void Receive(
    commBuffer *&,
    unsigned char *ptr=0,
    unsigned long length=0)
    throw (TORB::SystemException::StaleStub&);
};
```

The first function provides an interface to buffer management for signals. In particular, the function supports the allocation of an area of memory of a given size. The buffer also encapsulates marshalling to and unmarshalling from this buffer by inheriting from the `Marshaller` class described above for operational interactions:

```
class commBuffer : public Marshaller
{
  virtual ~commBuffer();
};
```

The Sumo-ORB signal binding library then provides a number of concrete implementations of `SignalProtocolChannel` including a `UDP_ SignalProtocolChannel` mapping to the UDP/IP protocol and an `rt__SignalProtocolChannel` mapping to real-time channels as defined in the underlying operating system support (see Section 11.4.3).

The library also supports a factory for creating *signal stub* objects as defined below:

```
class StubFactory {
  static SignalStub *BuildSignalStub(SignalInterface *it)
    throw(UnknownType); ...
};
```

The `BuildSignalStub()` function creates a signal stub which is compatible with the signal interface given as parameter. The resultant signal stub then has the following interface:

```
class _SignalBase {
public:
  int is_active();
  QoSsignal &qos();
  void attach_SignalProtocolChannel(SignalProtocolChannel*);
}
class SignalStub : public SignalInterface {
public:
  virtual _SignalBase *operator[](unsigned long)=0;
};
```

From this, it can be seen that a signal stub is an array of objects of type
_SignalBase, where each object represents a particular signal defined on
the interface. The SignalStub class also inherits from SignalInterface
which provides access to, for example, the narrowing functions defined in the
root class Interface. Each _SignalBase object supports three functions:
(1) is_active() which determines if the signal is activated or not, (2)
qos() which returns the quality of service associated with the signal, and (3)
attach_SignalProtocolChannel() which enables a protocol channel
to be attached to that signal. The latter operation has the effect of setting the
corresponding signal to active. Note that protocol channels are attached to
individual signals. This does not, however, prevent multiplexing in the
underlying implementation.

The library also provides access to the InSignal and OutSignal classes as
required by the application programmers interface. These classes are derived
from the underlying _SignalBase class (thus providing the is_active()
and qos() functions).

Finally, the signal binding library provides a *signal interface repository*. This
repository can be used by factories at run-time to perform type and quality of
service compatibility checks. This service is necessary to support the approach
in Sumo-ORB where each factory can implement its own policies for checking
compatibility: signals.

The interface to the signal interface repository is as follows:

```
enum SignalDirection {
  SIGNAL_OUT,
  SIGNAL_IN
};
struct SignalDescription {
  SignalDirection sig_dir;
  string sig_type;
  QoSlist sig_qos;
};
```

```
typedef sequence<SignalDescription> SignalInterfaceDescription;

interface SignalInterfaceLocalRepository
{
  exception NotALocalInterface{};
  SignalInterfaceDescription
  get_interface_description(in SignalInterface it)
    raises (NotALocalInterface);
};
```

This service resides in each capsule with each service providing information about signals defined locally in that capsule. Information can be obtained on remote signals by contacting the signal interface repository in the host capsule for that particular signal.

The stream binding library
In implementation, the stream binding library is closely related to the signal library. Indeed, incoming flows are signals in Sumo-ORB. The main difference is that the underlying implementation must be designed to meet the demands of continuous media. We present a brief description of the stream binding library below, focusing on the major differences to the signal library:

- *Creating stream interfaces*
  The stream binding library provides a `_create_StreamInterface <>` template class. The implementation of this class is very similar to the corresponding `_create_SignalInterface <>` class described above.
- *Creating protocol channels and stubs*
  The library also supports protocol channels and flow stubs. Protocol channels are defined by an abstract class `StreamProtocolChannel` (which is very similar to the `SignalProtocolChannel` discussed above). The concrete implementation of this class is based on real-time channels and is designed to provide isochronous delivery of data. The associated `commBuffer` class is also specialized to avoid data copying (the implementation passes a pointer to the data). Stream stubs are based directly on signal stubs and the signal base class. The library however provides alternative classes for the application programmers interface (`InFlow` and `OutFlow` as described above).
- *Accessing the interface repository*
  The stream binding library also provides access to the signal interface repository to gain type and QoS information on the underlying signals.

The stream binding library is therefore best interpreted as a specialization of the signal binding library.

Binding factories
The task of each binding factory is to support the creation of bindings with a given functionality and a given quality of service. This is realized by providing

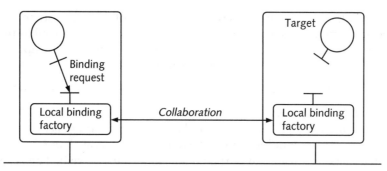

Figure 11.7 Distributed implementation of a binding factory.

concrete implementations of the abstract binding protocol described previously (see Section 8.3.2). The concrete implementation is supported by functions provided by the micro-ORB (interface reference management and local binding) and the appropriate binding library (stub and protocol channel creation).

The implementation of a binding factory in Sumo-ORB is normally distributed as shown in Figure 11.7. In particular, a particular binding factory normally consists of a number of cooperating local binding factories. The appropriate local binding factories must cooperate to create a binding between two sites.

We now present two simple examples of how binding factories exploit the underlying micro-ORB and binding libraries in their implementation. The two examples are fragments of code taken from an operational binding factory and a signal binding factory respectively:

- *An operational binding factory*
  The first example shows the client-side actions of an operational binding factory in implementing the bind() function (similar actions are, of course, also required at the server end but using the GetDispatcher() function). The factory uses the IIOP implementation of the RPC protocol channel abstract class to establish the binding. The relevant code fragment is given below.

```
1 T* IIOPBindingFactory<T>::bind(Interface *target)
2 {
3   IIOP_RPCProtocolChannel *channel;
4
5   channel = new IIOP_RPCProtocolChannel(target);
6   Interface *stub=TORB::BuildClientStub(T::type_id, channel);
7   return T::narrow(stub);
8 }
```

The bind function takes the target interface as parameter and returns a stub of type T (line 1). The first step in implementing the bind() function is to create a new IIOP protocol channel connected to target (line 5).

Following this, the program creates a new stub of the appropriate type. The second parameter defines the protocol channel to be connected to the stub (line 6). Finally, the function returns the stub, narrowed to the appropriate type (line 7). This function would be called as follows:

```
foobar *f = IIOPBindingFactory<foobar>::bind (serverInterface);
```

- *A signal binding factory*
  The second example shows the local actions of a binding factory in creating a signal binding using a UDP communication channel (again, similar actions must be undertaken at remote sites as well). The relevant code fragment is given below:

```
1  SignalStub *stub;
2  SignalInterface *it;
3  ...
4  stub=TORB::StubFactory.BuildSignalStub(it);
5
6  stub[0]->attach_SignalProtocolChannel(
7    new UDP_SignalProtocolChannel("procyon.hub.ck",1200));
8
9  try {
10   it->LocalBind(it,stub);
11 }
12 catch(BindingDenied&) {...}
```

This program first creates a properly typed signal stub for signal interface it (line 4) and then calls `attach_SignalProtocolChannel()` on this stub to attach a new instance of a `UDP_SignalProtocolChannel` (lines 6–7). The stub is then locally bound to the interface using the function offered by the micro-ORB (lines 9–12).

Note that a stream binding factory would be very similar to the second example, but would (1) call `BuildStreamStub()` rather than `BuildSignalStub()`, (2) replace `attach_SignalProtocolChannel()` with `attach_StreamProtocolChannel()`, and (3) replace the `UDP_SignalProtocolChannel()` with an instance of `rt__StreamProtocolChannel()`.

Binding factories can also encapsulate arbitrary behaviour. For example, they can invoke other binding factories mirroring the recursive binding protocol. They can also instantiate arbitrary objects such as additional transparency functions for operational bindings or filters for stream bindings.

11.4.3 Operating system support

This section describes the underlying operating system support for Sumo-ORB. We focus exclusively on the Chorus implementation where Sumo-ORB is implemented as a particular Chorus subsystem. Although efficient operating system support is not a major goal of the Sumo-ORB platform, some steps have been taken to ensure efficient operation in the Chorus environment. The issue of operating system support is considered in more depth in the design of Sumo-CORE (see Chapter 10).

We consider operating system support for Sumo-ORB under the headings of scheduling and communications (discussion of buffer management is included in the communications section in this chapter).

Scheduling

Sumo-ORB provides the programmer with real-time threads. In contrast to Sumo-CORE, the threads are kernel threads, scheduled and managed entirely by the kernel. These threads are allocated to a particular scheduling class in Chorus (see Chapter 9). This scheduling class defines a number of scheduling parameters as defined in the following data structure:

```
typedef struct {
    timeValue schedTime;
    timeValue relDeadline;
    int criticality;
    timeValue worstCaseExecution;
    timeValue period;
} KnSchedParams;
```

The scheduling parameters can be used to define two styles of thread, namely earliest deadline first threads and priority-based threads. This is determined by the value of the criticality field and by a kernel-managed constant called *threshold*:

- threads with criticality above the threshold are managed as (high) priority threads,
- thread with criticality equal to the threshold are managed as earliest deadline first threads, and
- threads with criticality below the threshold are managed as (low) priority threads.

For priority threads, all other fields in the scheduling parameter are ignored. For earliest deadline first threads, the schedTime field specifies the earliest (relative) time at which the thread can be scheduled. The relDeadline field then specifies the relative deadline of the thread. The worstCaseExecution time places a worst case of the amount of processing required by the thread. Finally, the period field specifies the period for periodic threads.

The scheduling class implementation of the kernel maps all priority-based threads on to the corresponding priority list in the kernel scheduler

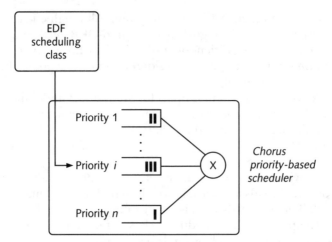

Figure 11.8 Scheduling class for real-time threads.

(remember that Chorus maintain a set of lists, one per priority level). Deadline-based threads are mapped on to a single priority level determined by the threshold value. The scheduling class must sort this list at run-time to reflect the deadlines of this set of threads. This overall approach is depicted in Figure 11.8.

The Sumo-ORB implementation also addresses the problem of *priority inversion* between threads; that is, where a lower priority thread blocks a higher priority thread. This is solved by an appropriate *priority inheritance protocol* on interprocess communication services as discussed below.

Communication
Sumo-ORB offers specialized services for semaphores, local messaging and remote channels which are discussed below.

Semaphores
The Chorus microkernel is extended with the concept of real-time semaphores as defined by the primitives given in Table 11.2. The create primitive is parametrized by two policies, a *queuing policy* and a *priority inversion control (PIC) policy*. The first policy determines how threads blocked on a semaphore are queued; the choices are either FIFO or priority ordered. The second policy determines actions on priority inversion. In particular, this parameter determines whether priority inheritance should be enforced. If selected then, if the priority of the calling thread is higher than the priority of the thread in the critical section, the priority of the thread in the critical section is raised to that of the calling thread. The only other difference is that the blocking primitive rt_semP() is given a timeout parameter.

Table 11.2 Primitives defined on real-time semaphores

Primitive	Parameters
rt_semCreate()	queuing policy, PIC policy
rt_semDestroy()	semID
rt_semP()	semID, timeout
rt_semV()	semID

Local messaging

The extended microkernel also supports a local real-time messaging service (again incorporating priority inheritance). The primitives for this service are given in Table 11.3. These primitives support the creation of rt_ports. rt_ports are based on Chorus ports, but also support the following policies (defined as parameters):

- *A queuing policy*
  This policy determines how incoming messages are queued: in FIFO order or in priority order. The priority information is carried in real-time messages as discussed below.
- *A priority propagation policy*
  This policy determines how a priority should be propagated to a receiving thread. There are three choices: (1) no propagation, (2) the priority is inherited by the receiving thread, and (3) the calling thread explicitly specifies a priority to be propagated to the receiving thread.
- *A priority inheritance policy*
  This policy is required where the number of server threads is not sufficient to handle an incoming request. This can lead to priority inversions where an executing thread has a lower priority than an incoming message. The goal of this policy is to bound this delay. If this option is selected, a server thread inherits the priority of the pending message if the priority of the message is higher.

In addition, it is possible to send real-time messages between rt_ports using either rt_send() or rt_call(). The underlying messaging carries priority information to the appropriate rt_port, which is then interpreted

Table 11.3 Primitives defined on real-time messaging

Primitive	Parameters
rt_portCreate()	queuing policy, propagation policy, PIC policy
rt_portDestroy()	rt_portID
rt_send()	target rt_portID, outgoing message, sender rt_portID
rt_call()	target rt_portID, outgoing message, sender rt_portID, return message, timeout

according to the policies defined above. Message passing can also be optimized using shared memory mapped into each actor (thus avoiding data copying). This must be established explicitly in Sumo-ORB by firstly allocating the area of shared memory and secondly mapping this into the appropriate actors. Finally, the blocking rt_call() primitive is given a timeout parameter specifying the maximum blocking time.

Remote channels
Remote channels can be created between rt_ports using a real-time transport service (RTTS). This transport service is designed to support continuous media traffic. The service is connection-oriented and minimal in nature, offering fragmentation and flow control. The service also enables buffers to be allocated to a connection based on quality of service directives. There is no error control as this is not a priority for continuous media interaction. Like the local messaging service, the RTTS propagates priority information to the receiver rt_port.

The RTTS is implemented in the kernel as a multi-threaded system actor. The implementation of the transport protocol is therefore a traditional multiplexed design with different connections managed by the same system entity (see the discussion on multiplexed implementations in the previous chapter). The actor is independent of the existing Chorus communications subsystem. Hence the service is not accessed through the standard Chorus primitives (ipcSend() and so on). Rather, the service is provided through an rt_port defined on the actor.

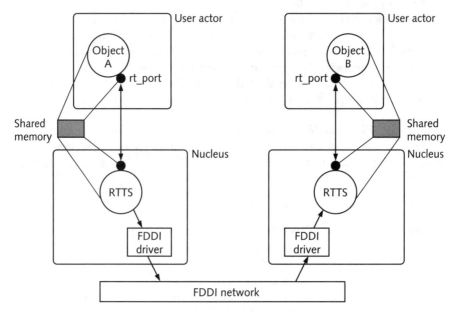

Figure 11.9 A real-time protocol channel in Sumo-ORB.

The RTTS maps down on to a device driver for the FDDI driver. This driver provides access to the synchronous bandwidth offered by the network (the asynchronous bandwidth is not used by the protocol). This enables the RTTS to offer guarantees on throughput, jitter and latency for the communications portion of a binding.

A complete real-time protocol channel consists of local communication between the producer actor and the RTTS using the real-time messaging service described above. The RTTS will then transport the data to a receiver `rt_port`. This data is then forwarded to the receiver actor using the local messaging service. The local messaging can exploit shared buffers to optimize the performance of the local transmissions. The structure of a real-time protocol channel is summarized in Figure 11.9. Note that scheduling information can be propagated from the sender thread to the receiver thread using the combined facilities of local real-time messaging and the RTTS as described above.

11.5 Supporting reactive objects

The above discussion has focused on the support provided in Sumo-ORB for asynchronous objects written in C++. Sumo-ORB, however, also supports synchronous reactive objects written in Esterel. In supporting synchronous objects, it is important however to:

- map asynchronous incoming and outgoing signals to synchronous executions, and
- ensure the synchrony hypothesis is met.

This is achieved through a specialization of the concepts defined above for asynchronous objects. We consider this support in more detail below.

The compilation process for Esterel objects is illustrated in Figure 11.10.

Reactive objects interface to the outside world through signal interfaces (which can be connected by signal bindings to other objects). These signal interfaces are described in IDL. The IDL definitions are compiled to produce stubs, as for asynchronous objects. The stubs perform their normal role of mapping to the host language. They must also, however, perform the additional mapping from asynchronous to synchronous execution models. In other words, they must collate input signals and present them to the execution automaton and then, on output, collate signals for transmission. In Sumo-ORB, the collation of input signals is achieved as follows. When a signal arrives, the signal is registered and a transition is requested. Should other (distinct) signals arrive before the transition is carried out, they are also registered and hence the automaton is presented with multiple signals. Note, however, that a second occurrence of the same signal would be an error (violating the synchrony hypothesis). This results in a warning from the underlying infrastructure. The

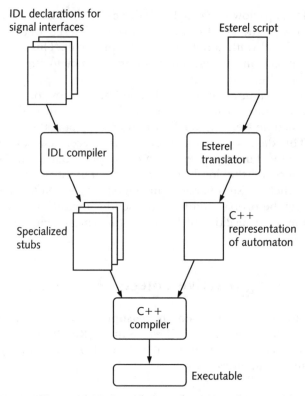

Figure 11.10 Compilation of reactive objects.

collation of output signals in contrast is straightforward and is not discussed further.

The Esterel automaton is translated using a tool which produces a C++ representation of the automaton (Boulanger, 1993). This can then be compiled and linked with the stubs and a reactive object library producing a full reactive object. The structure of the complete reactive object is shown in Figure 11.11. This figure shows the reactive object offering a number of signal interfaces (which are templated by the appropriate stubs). These can be created in the normal manner using the Sumo-ORB `_create_SignalInterface <>` operation. The precise number will vary depending on the number of incoming and outgoing signals for the reactive object. The automaton is the direct translation of the Esterel script as produced by the translation tool mentioned above. The reactive object also has a control module which presents an operational interface to the external environment. This control module has the task of controlling the execution of the reactive object and ensuring that the synchrony hypotheses is met. In the current implementation, this is achieved by having a single thread of control which repeatedly performs the following steps as signals become available:

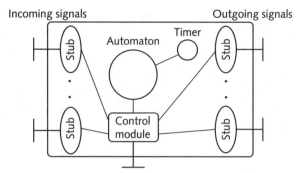

Figure 11.11 The structure of a reactive object.

1. collect a set of signals from the signal interfaces (according to the collation rules described above),
2. execute the synchronous automaton, and
3. disseminate the output signals to the appropriate interfaces for transmission.

This simple approach ensures the synchrony hypothesis is met by avoiding concurrent execution.

The control interface offered by the reactive object supports operations to configure the reactive object by stating which input signals should be checked in Step (1) above and also to start the overall execution sequence. Finally, the reactive object supports a special timer object which can be accessed by the Esterel automaton. This timer object offers the following interface:

```
interface <signal> timer {
    signalIn timerStart (delay);
    signalOut timerEnd ();
}
```

If the timer receives a timerStart signal, this object will emit a timerEnd signal in the number of milliseconds designated by delay. This facility can be used to optimize the behaviour of reactive objects by removing the need to execute at the granularity of every clock tick from an external clock. An illustration of the use of the timer was given in Section 6.3.2.

11.6 QoS management

11.6.1 Preliminaries

In this section, we describe the QoS management functions associated with Sumo-ORB. As mentioned in Section 11.1, the main aim of QoS management in Sumo-ORB is to offer end-to-end QoS guarantees exploiting the particular characteristics of the FDDI network. The same techniques are also applicable, however, to other deterministic networks. The approach is to define an admission control test for end-to-end bindings (Leboucher and Stefani, 1995a). By passing this admission control test, the required quality of service is guaranteed.

The work focuses on placing deterministic bounds on end-to-end delay. Other dimensions, such as jitter or throughput, are more straightforward, as they can more easily be decomposed into local constraints. In performing the admission control test, we consider a binding as consisting of a succession of three elementary tasks:

1. *The emission task*
   This task consists of the production of a message *m* and the periodic copying of this message to the network adapter card.
2. *The transmission task*
   This task periodically selects a new message *m* and sends it in the form of FDDI packets to the receiver. This task ends with the arrival of the last packet at the receiver.
3. *The receiving task*
   This task processes the newly arrived packets corresponding to one message and processes them. This task starts with the termination of the previous task.

The admission control test must therefore guarantee end-to-end delays over the three steps.

The admission control test is based on fixed priority scheduling. In fixed priority scheduling, threads are scheduled at run-time according to a priority assigned to the thread at thread creation time (where the priority is calculated from the scheduling parameters associated with threads). This approach is in contrast to more dynamic schemes where priority is determined at run-time (again according to the scheduling parameters).

As mentioned in Chapter 9, there has been considerable debate in the real-time and multimedia communities over the most appropriate scheduling approach. The previous chapter reported on an earliest deadline first algorithm. The fixed priority approach is adopted in this chapter principally because of the ability to analyze and compute worst-case response times and to extend this analysis to distributed sets of tasks (such as defined in the binding model above).

We are specifically concerned with rate monotonic scheduling which assigns static priorities on the basis of the task periods whereby the task with the shortest period gets the highest static priority and the task with the longest period gets the lowest static priority. The algorithm then selects the runnable task with the highest static priority. Rate monotonic scheduling is also preemptive to ensure the highest priority task is always running.

We now describe the derivation of the admission control test. This presentation uses classic scheduling notation (for example, as defined in

Tilborg and Koob (1991)). This notation is summarized below:

C_i	execution time of task i
T_i	period of task i
J_i	release jitter of task i
d_i	relative deadline of task i
B_i	blocking time of task i caused by priority inversion
$w_{i,q}$	busy period of level i starting qT_i before the current task i release time
r_i	response time of task i

11.6.2 The admission control algorithm

Background to the algorithm

The starting point for the admission control test is the classic Liu/Layland test for periodic tasks as reported in Section 10.5.2. In this model, however, the deadline of a task is treated as equal to the period. For multimedia we need to decouple the period and deadline (to compensate for jitter). In this respect, the analysis in this chapter is closely related to the analysis of Chapter 10 for earliest deadline first tasks.

Accommodating jitter in fixed priority scheduling

Joseph and Pandya (1986) present an extension of the Liu/Layland model which accommodates deadlines which are less than the period. Their analysis is captured in the following recursive equation, which places a bound on the end-to-end delay of a distributed binding:

$$r_i = C_i + \sum_{j \in hp(i)} \left\lceil \frac{r_i}{T_j} \right\rceil C_j \tag{1}$$

where r_i is the worst response time of a task i and $hp(i)$ denotes the set of tasks of higher priority than task i.

These recursive equations can be solved by successive iterations starting from $r_i = 0$. Indeed, it is easy to show that the r_i^n series is increasing. Consequently, the series either converges or exceeds T_i. In the latter case, task i is not schedulable.

The Joseph and Pandya analysis, however, is still not sufficient as it does not consider periods which are smaller than the deadline. This limitation is however overcome by Lehoczky (1990). The analysis of Lehoczky is based on the concept of a *busy period*:

Definition *Busy period*
A busy period of level i is defined as the maximum interval of time during which a processor runs tasks of higher or equal priorities than task i priority.

Lehoczky shows that to determine the worst response time of a task, it is possible to look successively at several busy periods, each one starting at a particular arrival of task i. If $w_{i,q}$ denotes the width of the busy period starting qT_i before the current activation of task i, the analysis can be performed by the following equation:

$$w_{i,q} = (q+1)C_i + \sum_{j \in hp(i)} \left\lceil \frac{w_{i,q}}{T_j} \right\rceil C_j \qquad (2)$$

These equations can also be solved by successive iterations and the worst-case response time of task i is given by:

$$r_i = \max_q (w_{i,q} - qT_i) \qquad (3)$$

Note, however, that the number of busy periods that need to be examined is bounded by the lowest common multiple of the tasks' periods. In practice, this translates to:

$$\frac{\sum_{j \leqslant i} C_j}{T_i - C_i} \qquad (4)$$

Dependencies between tasks in fixed priority scheduling
The above analyses assume that all tasks are independent; that is, they don't share common data structures or have precedence constraints. In Sumo-ORB, however, this need not be the case. We must therefore extend the analysis to deal with dependencies between tasks. Furthermore, the extensions must deal with the priority inversion problem when dealing with dependencies.

Sha *et al.* (1990) present a fixed priority algorithm which solves the problem of priority inversion (the Priority Ceiling Protocol). The priority ceiling of a semaphore is defined as the priority of the highest priority task that may lock that semaphore. A task T is then only allowed to enter a critical section if its priority is higher than the ceiling priorities of all the semaphores locked by tasks other than T. The task will run at its assigned priority unless it is in a critical section and blocks higher priority tasks. In the latter case, it must inherit the highest priority of the tasks it blocks, but will resume at its assigned priority on leaving the critical section.

Sha *et al.* have also defined a sufficient condition for schedulability for the Priority Ceiling Protocol for $D_i = T_i$:

$$\frac{C_1}{T_1} + \ldots + \frac{C_n}{T_n} + \frac{B_i}{T_i} \leqslant i\,(2^{1/i} - 1), 1 \leqslant i \leqslant n \qquad (5)$$

where B_i denotes the longest blocking time of task i by a lower priority task.

The same enhancement can also be applied to the Lehoczky busy period analysis. According to Tindell (Tindell, 1994; Tindell and Clark, 1994), this results in the introduction of a new term B_i in equation (2) above. Tindell, however, extends this analysis further by considering the notion of *release jitter*. In many cases, a task cannot be scheduled as soon as it arrives. In some cases, for instance, the exact release time of a task depends on the reception of a specific message. This can take a bounded but unknown time. Introducing release jitter into the analysis results in the following final equation:

$$r_i = \max_q (w_{i,q} + J_i - qT_i)$$

where

$$w_{i,q} = (q+1)C_i + B_i + \sum_{j \in hp(i)} \left\lceil \frac{w_{i,q} + J_j}{T_j} \right\rceil C_j$$

Worst-case analysis for distributed bindings

We now apply the final result given above to derive a worst-case bound on end-to-end delay for distributed binding objects. This discussion will exploit the concept of release jitter to relate several periodic tasks belonging to the same chain of tasks. For example, in our binding model, let us suppose the emitting task is periodic. Then the release jitter of the next task (the transmission task) is equal to the response time of the emitting task. Note that the analysis assumes that the buffering available in the network adapter card is sufficient to deal with the incoming data. This analysis is extended later in Section 11.6.3. We now consider the worst-case delay for each of the elementary tasks defined above.

The emission task

We firstly apply Tindell's analysis to the emission task E. In this analysis, we suppose that the emission task can be preempted by other periodic local tasks. However, for simplicity, we do not consider other interfering tasks such as interruptions caused by reception of packets on the network card (the analysis is extended in Section 11.6.3 to deal with this condition). The response time for task E is calculated by examining the busy periods starting before its current release time. This is given directly by Tindell's equation as follows:

$$r_i^E = \max_q (w_{i,q} + J_i - qT_i)$$

where

$$w_{i,q} = (q+1)C_i + B_i + \sum_{j \in hp(i)} \left\lceil \frac{w_{i,q} + J_j}{T_j} \right\rceil C_j$$

where $hp(i)$ denotes the set of local tasks of higher priority than i on the station p that supports the emission task E.

The transmission task

The transmission task, T, is responsible for transmitting tasks across the FDDI network. From the point of view of the workstation, the FDDI network can be seen as a processor running a set of tasks consisting of packets awaiting transmission together with a higher priority task, P, representing the rotating token when the token is away from the workstation. This latter task interferes in the computation of the transmission response time.

Let SA_p be the synchronous allocation of station p. During a period of time w, a property of the FDDI protocol is that the token will visit station p at least:

$$\left\lfloor \frac{w}{TTRT} \right\rfloor \ times \tag{6}$$

where TTRT (target token rotation time) is the target rotation time determined during the FDDI loop initialization (see Section 11.2.3).

For a task transmitting a packet, being preempted by P means that the workstation has finished its allocated synchronous time and thus the token stayed at least SA_p on station p. Therefore, the time needed by the network to serve the other workstations is bounded by:

$$CI(P,w) = w - \left\lfloor \frac{w}{TTRT} \right\rfloor SA_p \tag{7}$$

where CI denotes the computing interference of task P on the current transmission task.

During the same busy period w, the interference due to the other higher priority emitted messages is given by:

$$\left(\sum_{j \in hp(i) \cap out(p)} \left\lceil \frac{w_{i,q} + J_j^T}{T_j} \right\rceil m_j \right) \rho \tag{8}$$

where ρ stands for the duration of a packet emission, m_j denotes the number of packets of message j, and $out(p)$ denotes the set of all other emitting tasks on workstation p.

The transmission task, T, can be modelled as a periodic task of period T_i inherited from the emitting task and jitter corresponding to the response time of the emitting task. This highlights the power of the release jitter concept. In particular, this approach enables us to chain tasks and compute their response times incrementally. Once the transmission of a packet has started, it cannot be preempted. Therefore, the priority inversion duration is bounded by ρ. From all this, the response time of the transmission task can be derived as follows:

$$r_i^T = \max_q (J_i^T + w_{i,q} - qT_i) + \psi + \tau$$

where:

$$w_{i,q} = (q + 1)m_i\rho + \rho + \sum_{j \in hp(i) \cap out(p)} \left\lceil \frac{w_{i,q} + J_j^T}{T_j} \right\rceil \rho + CI(P, w_{i,q})$$

and:

$$J_i^T = r_i^E$$

where ψ denotes the optical and electrical propagation time on the network and τ denotes the worst time taken by the network adapter at the other end to recognize the packet arrival and raise the corresponding interrupt.

The receiving task

The third of the three elementary tasks, the receiving task R, can be modelled as a periodic task inheriting the period from the emitting task. Its release jitter is equal to the difference between the biggest and smallest response times of the transmission task, as follows:

$$J_i^B = r_i^T - \rho - \psi$$

Finally, a bound on the end-to-end delay is equal to the highest response time of the receiving task plus the smallest response time of the transmission task.

To find the response time of the receiving task, we can apply the same Tindell's analysis. We need to bound the computing interference due to the raising of interrupts corresponding to the arriving packets. This can be done by modelling the arriving packets by a pseudo sporadically periodic task. According to Tindell, a sporadically periodic task is a periodic burst with an outer period corresponding to the burst period and an inner period corresponding to the packet's period within a burst.

Applying this analysis, the response time of the receiving task is then given by the following formula:

$$r_i^R = \max_q (J_i^R + w_{i,q} - qT_i)$$

where:

$$w_{i,q} = (q+1)C_i^R + \sum_{j \in hp(i)} \left\lceil \frac{w_{i,q} + J_j}{T_j} \right\rceil C_j + CI(pt(i), w_{i,q})$$

where $hp(i)$ denotes the set of tasks on the receiving site which are of higher priority than the receiving task i. In addition, $CI(pt(i), w_{i,q})$ denotes the computing interference of a sporadically periodic task (this complex formula can be found in Tindell (1994)). (Note that this test is not applicable where the network adapter card uses direct memory access (without preempting the workstation processor). In particular, a solution for direct memory access would require a completely different model of the underlying resources. Such a test is not presented in this chapter.)

This formula provides the final figure for the overall end-to-end delay for the binding. The complexity of this elementary admission control test for n threads is bounded by $O(n^3)$ when the processor load and dispersion are kept bounded. Note, however, that this result is only valid for local periodic tasks. The full derivation of this result can be found in the literature (Hermant *et al.*, 1997).

The distributed algorithm

We are now in a position to define an admission control algorithm for binding objects. This algorithm is intended to be executed by binding object factories in Sumo-ORB to determine whether to proceed with the instantiation.

We assume that the algorithm is triggered by a request to the binding object factory to create a new binding between two remote interfaces located on sites E (supporting the emission task) and R (supporting the receiving task) respectively, with a guaranteed end-to-end delay no worse than r_i. Let us assume that the emission task E has fixed priority i. The algorithm can be succinctly described as follows:

1. Site E computes r_i^E and r_i^T, assuming that the priority of the new binding is lower than that of all already established ones supported by E (bindings for which E is either the emission site or a receiving site).
2. Site E sends r, r_i^E and r_i^T to site R, together with the lowest priority of its existing bindings.
3. Site R computes r_i^R, assuming that the priority of the new binding is lower than that of all already established ones supported by R.
4. If $(r_i^R + m_i\rho + \psi + \tau) \leqslant r_i$, then site R sends back to E an indication of success (the new binding can be established), together with the priority assigned to the new binding, chosen to be lower than that of any of the existing bindings in E and R. If $(r_i^R + m_i\rho + \psi + \tau) > r_i$, R sends to E an indication of failure (the new binding cannot be established).

The above message interaction must be executed as an atomic transaction to avoid conflicts between concurrent binding creations.

11.6.3 Extensions

In this section, we extend the analysis by considering the question of the bounded network adapter card memory (as raised in Section 11.6.2). To tackle this problem, we introduce a new task in our binding model, the *network adapting task*, which is responsible for periodically copying a sample of the messages already placed by the emitting tasks in the workstation memory. The sample is determined as follows. Each time the adapting task is activated, it examines a succession of queues, one for each binding object, and moves a specific quota to the network adapter card. The quotas are chosen so that their sum does not exceed the adapter card size. Only already filled queues are moved; this is indicated by a flag being set to *on*. When a queue is completely moved, its flag is set to *off* by the adapter task. The adapter task is modelled by a periodic task, ending by a token request. A token request means that the adapter card is no longer writable and that next time the token arrives, the adapter card sends its frames. The adapter task period needs to be chosen so that it is bigger than the total copy time of the card. Its release jitter is bounded by $2 \times$ TTRT since, once the token is requested, it will arrive in less than

$2 \times$ TTRT. Finally, the task's priority must be chosen to be larger than all other priorities.

Strictly speaking, it is also necessary to deal with *system interference* in our analysis. System interference relates to high-priority behaviour associated with the underlying operating system. This problem is in principle straightforward to deal with but would require a detailed analysis of the run-time behaviour of the Chorus microkernel. This issue is therefore not considered further in this book.

11.7 Performance measurements

In this section, we present some comparative measurements of Sumo-ORB against two alternative Object Request Broker implementations, namely COOL version 3.1 from Chorus Systèmes and Orbix version 2.0 from Iona. The experiments are carried out on Solaris implementations of each platform (running on a SUN Ultra 1 at 140 MHz).

More specifically, we measure the latencies of one-way announcements and two-way interrogations. In both cases, we consider the latencies for different parameter types (giving a measure of the marshalling overheads of the various types). The different cases are summarized in Table 11.4.

In the first experiment, we measure the time to achieve invocation emission. In the second experiment, we consider the time from invocation emission to the equivalent termination reception. In both experiments, the measurements are carried out between interfaces in two distinct capsules but on a single site. The relative results of the three platforms are summarized in Table 11.5 for announcements and interrogations (all figures in milliseconds).

The figures for announcements indicate that Sumo-ORB performs considerably better than COOL and Orbix (by factors of approximately 2 and 3 respectively). This can largely be explained by the optimizations that are made possible by explicit (operational) bindings. For example, it is possible to maintain mappings to the underlying transport connections. The figures for interrogations are less conclusive but still show that Sumo-ORB performs well in comparison with the two other systems. The slightly poor performance for cases 4–6 can be explained by a rather unoptimized implementation of

Table 11.4 Different cases for experiment 1

Case	Parameters	Size (bytes)
1	No parameters	0
2	Primitive arguments	25
3	Structure argument	25
4	Primitive sequence	2500
5	Sequence of structures	2500
6	Array of structures	2500

Table 11.5 (a) Performance measurements for announcements

Case	Sumo-ORB	COOL	Orbix
1	0.26	0.62	0.85
2	0.31	0.69	0.65
3	0.29	0.45	0.99
4	1.72	1.46	2.50
5	1.67	1.46	5.14
6	1.63	1.60	4.96

Table 11.5 (b) Performance measurements for interrogations

Case	Sumo-ORB	COOL	Orbix
2	1.18	1.29	1.69
3	0.74	0.96	1.68
4	5.05	4.41	7.26
5	6.03	5.95	20.40
6	4.84	4.93	18.30

unmarshalling in Sumo-ORB (in these cases, the marshalling and unmarshalling overheads tend to dominate).

Figures are not available for the Chorus platform. However, some improvements can be anticipated, particularly if the Chorus IPC implementation of operational bindings is used (see Section 11.4). Further improvements can be anticipated for signal or stream bindings due to the efficient implementation of real-time channels. For example, there is much less data movement in the implementation of real-time channels due to the use of shared buffers (see Section 11.4.3). In this case, however, comparative measurements are not possible as neither COOL nor Orbix directly supports this style of interaction.

11.8 Summary

This chapter has considered the design and implementation of Sumo-ORB, an ODP subsystem designed specifically to support multimedia. The programming interface offered by Sumo-ORB is based on CORBA. Sumo-ORB, however, addresses the limitations of CORBA with respect to multimedia. In particular, Sumo-ORB supports an extended programming model where (1) support is provided for operational, signal and stream interaction, (2) explicit bindings can be created between compatible interfaces, (3) QoS management is supported through binding objects, and (4) reactive objects provide support for real-time. These extensions were inspired by the programming model described in Chapter 4.

Sumo-ORB also extends CORBA with concepts derived from the engineering model discussed in Chapter 8. In particular, Sumo-ORB also features (1) a recursive binding architecture, and (2) appropriate admission control techniques for static QoS management. This approach also led to a novel implementation architecture where the minimal functionality is contained in a micro-ORB and the remainder of the ORB is constructed as open services. The micro-ORB contains interface reference management and local binding as required by the recursive binding architecture.

The admission control techniques in Sumo-ORB are based on extensions to classical fixed priority analysis. The extensions enable an admission control test to be developed which deals with jitter constraints in periodic behaviour and also supports distributed bindings composed of a number of elementary steps. Two algorithms based on this admission control test were also presented.

The chapter concluded with some comparative performance figures for Sumo-ORB against two other ORB implementations. Although not the main goal of the work, the figures indicate that efficient open platforms can be created using the proposed approach. Overall, we believe that this chapter together with the previous chapter indicates that open platforms can be developed using the concepts developed in this book which can provide the required functionality and real-time guarantees required by multimedia applications.

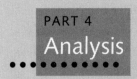

PART 4

Analysis

Chapter 12   Results, generalization and oustanding issues

12 Results, generalization and outstanding issues

12.1 Introduction

This book has considered the impact of multimedia on standards and platforms for open distributed processing. This is a crucial topic given the economic and strategic importance of both supporting multimedia applications and also providing open solutions to distributed processing. The resultant study was divided into four main parts:

- Part 1 considered the problem domain of multimedia in open distributed processing. This part firstly examined the field of open distributed processing in some depth. An important decision was made to *focus on RM-ODP* as a general framework enabling the emergence and evolution of specific open platforms. The part then presented a detailed examination of multimedia, highlighting a particular set of *requirements* for open distributed multimedia systems.
- Part 2 developed an object-oriented *programming model*, providing a framework for the development of distributed multimedia applications. This model is based on the Computational Model defined in RM-ODP but with a number of key extensions to meet the requirements of multimedia. Specific *notations* were also introduced to populate the programming model.
- Part 3 developed both an *engineering model* for multimedia and also a specific *technological approach* based on *microkernels*. Again, the engineering model is based on the Engineering Model defined in RM-ODP. In this case, however, significant alterations were required to meet the requirements of multimedia.

This part (Part 4) now concludes the book by presenting the major results of the study, applying the results to important standards and platforms such as CORBA and DCE, and highlighting some key outstanding issues.

The part consists of one chapter, which is structured as follows. The major results are summarized in Section 12.2. More specifically, this section describes our general framework for supporting multimedia in open distributed processing and also considers the main features of our specific approach based on microkernels. The section also considers the solutions proposed in the book against the requirements identified in Part 1. Section 12.3 then considers applying the results to other standards and platforms. In essence, the solutions presented in this book present the general framework or meta-standard (compare RM-ODP). This framework can then be used to guide the required modifications to specific standards and platforms. Following this, Section 12.4 considers some important areas requiring further study. Three key topics are identified, namely further population of the framework with specific notations and functions, the need for a reassessment of viewpoints, and the need to consider more sophisticated techniques for adaptation. Finally, Section 12.5 presents some concluding remarks for the book.

12.2 Results of the study

12.2.1 A general framework for open distributed processing

Overall approach

The most significant result of the book is the presentation of a general framework for open distributed processing which features explicit support for multimedia. This framework is based on RM-ODP, with specific focus on the Computational and Engineering Viewpoints. The RM-ODP standard defines two object-oriented models corresponding to the two viewpoints. We take a slightly different approach. We define a common object model for the two viewpoints. In the engineering viewpoint, however, it is important to be able to express additional concerns relating to the distribution of objects.

The difference between the two viewpoints is one of perspective. The computational specification describes a system from the application perspective and describes a set of interacting application level objects. In contrast, the engineering specification describes the system in terms of engineering components which are grounded in actual computer and communications resources. The engineering objects then define a virtual machine and the computational specification is refined towards this virtual machine. The one crucial difference, however, is that the engineering specification must identify the placement of objects in terms of nodes, capsules and clusters. It is important to realize that the boundary between the two viewpoints is fluid, and can vary from platform to platform and also in a given platform over time.

This general approach is captured in Figure 12.1 (copied from Chapter 8).

We now summarize the key features of the object model and then consider the refinements in the engineering model.

The object model

We describe the main features of the object model below. The descriptions are kept to a minimum. Full details can be found by referring back to Parts 2 and 3.

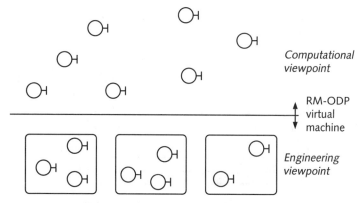

Computational
viewpoint

RM-ODP
virtual
machine

Engineering
viewpoint

Figure 12.1 The distinction between computational and engineering viewpoints.

The core object model

All entities in the distributed environment are represented by *objects*, where objects are accessed by one or more *interfaces*. Three styles of interface are supported, namely *operational, stream* and *signal interfaces* (corresponding to the three styles of interaction required for distributed applications including multimedia applications). Furthermore, interfaces are *strongly typed*. The object model does not prescribe a particular type system, but rather describes an abstract syntax and associated semantics which a compliant type system must adhere to. The type system is polymorphic, enabling *subtypes* to be determined.

A complete object is defined in terms of a *template* for that object. This template describes the object in terms of the following:

- a set of *interface templates* which fully define each interface offered by the object,
- a *behaviour specification* giving sufficient detail of the encapsulated behaviour to enable instantiation, and
- an *environmental contract* placing constraints on the distributed implementation.

Templates can then be used to *instantiate* objects in the distributed environment. This process is supported by a particular type of object referred to as a *factory*. Finally, the object model assumes the existence of a *trading* function to locate appropriate objects. Trading can also be extended across multiple domains through a process of *linkage*.

Explicit binding

Before interaction can take place, it is necessary to create a binding between participant objects. In our approach, bindings can either be created *implicitly* or *explicitly*. It is, however, explicit binding which provides support for multimedia. We therefore restrict the discussion below to this particular style of binding.

Explicit bindings are bindings that are created explicitly by the programmer. Such bindings can be created between compatible interfaces resulting in the

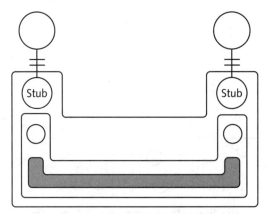

Figure 12.2 The recursive binding architecture.

creation of a binding object. Bindings are first-class objects in the environment. In particular, they are created in the same way as other objects, through the use of appropriate *binding factories*. Each factory defines its own rules to determine compatibility between interfaces based on type and quality of service information; in doing so, they can rely on generic services offered by the environment.

Different styles of binding can be created. For example, the object model supports *operational*, *stream* and *signal bindings*. Bindings can also be either *point-to-point* or *multiparty*. Furthermore, particular binding classes can *encapsulate arbitrary behaviour*, for example in terms of QoS management (see below) or filtering. Finally, bindings can be either passive or active. In *passive bindings*, the producer(s) sends data to the binding and the consumer(s) receives data from the binding. In *active bindings*, however, the binding is responsible for initiating interaction; the producer(s) and consumer(s) must provide handlers to deal with the appropriate event.

Crucially, our object model features a *recursive binding architecture*. This architecture spans both computational and engineering viewpoints and replaces the distinction between computational bindings and engineering channels in RM-ODP. With this approach, the same techniques can be used to create bindings in the application domain and in the system infrastructure.

In this approach, binding objects can be constructed using arbitrary object configurations which might contain further binding objects. The internal binding objects might themselves contain further binding objects, with this recursion ending with *primitive binding objects* offered by the underlying nucleus. The one constraint on binding objects is that they must contain *stubs*. The role of a stub is to support an interface which is connected to the binding and to perform the necessary transformations to support the binding (such as language translations or encoding). This view of a recursive binding is illustrated in Figure 12.2. The architecture is supported by an *abstract binding protocol* which is assumed to be encapsulated in binding factories.

QoS management

The object model has a number of features to support QoS management. Firstly, *QoS annotations* can be attached to interfaces (operational, stream or signal interfaces). A *contractual approach* is adopted for the definition of annotations. In particular, a given annotation can include two clauses defining (1) the QoS *provided* by the interface to the environment, and (2) the QoS *required* from other objects and the environment. Such QoS annotations form part of the environmental contract and can be used to determine compatibility between interfaces (see above). In addition, it is possible to specify the *class of commitment* for each contract; this can be, for example, guaranteed or best effort.

The object model also supports both static and dynamic QoS management as discussed below:

- *Static QoS management*
  Factories have the crucial role of performing static QoS management functions as objects are instantiated. In particular, the creator can specify the desired level of QoS for the object. This can then be *negotiated* with the participant objects. In addition, *admission control* and *resource reservation* can be carried out as required by the object class. The precise details will vary from factory to factory.
- *Dynamic QoS management*
  The object model supports dynamic QoS management functions including monitoring, policing, maintenance and renegotiation (this list is open and can be extended as new functions are identified). Dynamic QoS management is carried out by introducing managed objects. This approach assumes the existence of a management interface offering access to QoS-related events and (optionally) enabling adaptation of the object's behaviour. Again, different classes of binding object can support different levels of QoS management.

The above management techniques apply particularly to binding objects, but can also be applied to other classes of object.

Real-time control

The object model supports the concept of *reactive objects* to implement real-time control. The approach relies on access to signals through, for example, signal interfaces. The object model also supports access to underlying signals related to stream and operational interaction. Reactive objects maintain a permanent interaction with their environment, accepting signals from the environment, reacting, and consequently emitting signals to the environment. In execution, they adhere to the *synchrony hypothesis*, which states that reactions should be instantaneous; that is, atomic with respect to the environment. The class of languages capable of supporting this hypothesis are referred to as *synchronous languages*.

The resultant object model is therefore a *hybrid model* where an activity consists of a number of interacting objects some of which are reactive, and take zero time, and others of which are non-reactive, and take a finite amount of time (perhaps constrained by QoS annotations). This hybrid object model offers a clean *separation of concerns* between the synchronous world, where execution can be considered to be instantaneous, and the asynchronous world, where object execution and interaction take a finite amount of time. This approach has a number of significant advantages for the development of multimedia applications, including the explicit identification of all real-time assumptions, the increased portability of applications, and support for formal reasoning about real-time behaviour.

The role of reactive objects is to implement all aspects of real-time control, including real-time synchronization and also (potentially) the realization of dynamic QoS management functions.

Refinements for the engineering model

As mentioned above, the hybrid object model is shared by both the programming and engineering models. However, the engineering model has a number of refinements to reflect the distribution of objects. The programming model describes a computation as a group of interacting objects with distribution constraints described through the environmental contract. The engineering model must then describe an actual realization of this logical structure in terms of objects provided by the underlying virtual machine and placement of these objects on end systems in such a way that the environmental contract can be sustained. Finally, the engineering model must support the management of end system resources.

Supporting the virtual machine

The engineering model introduces the concept of a *nucleus* as an abstraction over the underlying operating system. This nucleus enables the creation of physical resources in a given end system. In terms of multimedia, the nucleus must support the creation of resources according to a given *quality of service* specification. For example, the nucleus must support the creation of threads and virtual memory with real-time guarantees. To support bindings, the nucleus must also support a set of *primitive bindings* and the `localBind` functionality as required by the abstract binding protocol (the latter creates a local binding between adjacent interfaces as defined in Section 8.3.2). Finally, the nucleus must support the creation of unique *interface references* as a means of identifying interfaces in a global distributed environment. A given platform can build on this minimal support and provide higher level abstractions from the underlying virtual machine. As the engineering infrastructure is open, this can also be extended or modified over time.

End system resources

To enable object configurations to be described, the engineering model then provides an abstract means of specifying system resources in terms of *nodes*,

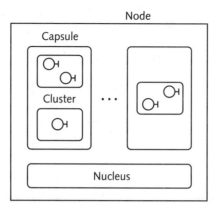

Figure 12.3 Nodes, capsules and clusters.

capsules and *clusters* (as depicted in Figure 12.3). The node is a representation of a given processing entity in a distributed configuration. There is a one-to-one mapping between a node and a nucleus (the nucleus manages the resources in a given node). Each node can contain a number of capsules where each capsule provides an encapsulation of the resources necessary to perform a computation. They provide the unit of protection in the system and also the smallest unit of independent failure. A particular capsule can contain one or more objects. Objects within a capsule must be grouped into clusters. Therefore a particular capsule will contain one or more clusters with each cluster containing one or more objects. Clusters provide the smallest unit of management for objects in terms of checkpointing, recovery, reactivation or migration.

Resource management
The engineering model also defines a management structure for nodes, capsules and clusters. *Node management* is encapsulated within the nucleus and supports the creation of resources on a given node (in terms of capsules, threads and primitive bindings). Crucially, node management must also implement appropriate strategies for multiplexing to ensure that the QoS guarantees of a given resource can be met given the limited physical resources at its disposal. *Capsule management* then supports the creation of clusters within capsules and also checkpointing, deactivation or deletion of complete capsules. In performing this task, it is necessary to communicate with *cluster managers*, which support these tasks on individual clusters. Cluster managers also support functionality for the migration of clusters between capsules. Cluster managers assume the existence of an *object management interface* on each object under its control. This overall management structure is depicted in Figure 12.4.

Finally, the various management functions are also potentially under the control of higher level managers implementing *coordination functions* (see Section 2.2.2).

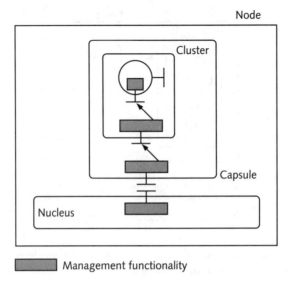

Management functionality

Figure 12.4 Management structure for system resources.

12.2.2 A technological approach based on microkernels

Rationale for a microkernel approach

The book also defines a particular approach to supporting multimedia in open distributed processing platforms. This approach is based on the use of microkernels. Multimedia imposes a number of strong requirements on the underlying operating system in terms of predictable real-time behaviour, efficiency in implementation, a diversity of QoS requirements and levels of guarantees, and support for graceful degradation on overload. Existing operating systems generally do not meet these requirements. The arguments are summarized in Table 12.1 (taken from Section 9.2.2).

Table 12.1 Summary of problems with existing operating systems

Requirement	Analysis of existing systems
Predictable real-time behaviour	Unpredictable real-time responses; lack of integration between different components; problems of priority inversion
Efficiency	Expensive and excessive domain crossings and context switches; unnecessary data copies
Diversity in terms of QoS	Bias towards interactive applications; lack of mechanisms to specify alternative styles of traffic
Diversity in terms of guarantees	Best effort only
Dealing with overload	Lack of admission control tests or resource reservations; do not offer graceful degradation

In contrast, the microkernel approach has the *potential* to overcome these problems. In particular, microkernels have the following distinct advantages:

- the lightweight nature of microkernels provides a more supportive environment for attaining real-time performance,
- the inherent flexibility of microkernels encourages specialization of various operating system components for a particular application domain, such as multimedia.

The subsystem approach inherent in many microkernels can also be used to provide a real-time, multimedia personality in *coexistence* with a traditional operating system personality (for example supporting offering a standard Unix interface). However, this approach assumes that the underlying resource management strategies (node management in the engineering model) can implement appropriate strategies to satisfy the requirements of both subsystems. This is a major technical challenge for this approach.

Note that this approach goes beyond the scope of the (modified) ODP framework as described in this book. In particular, in this work we prescribe one particular approach to realizing an ODP platform; other approaches can also be developed assuming the resultant platforms conform to the standard. This part of the book should therefore be viewed as guidelines on how such platforms can be constructed.

Experimental implementations

The book also described two complementary experimental implementations based on the microkernel approach. We summarize the main features of the two platforms below. Firstly, though, we must describe the overall architecture shared by the two systems.

The microkernel-based architecture

The overall architecture is shown in Figure 12.5. This figure shows an underlying *nucleus* supporting a number of subsystems. In particular, the figure shows an *ODP subsystem* coexisting with other subsystems (in this case, a Unix subsystem). The role of the ODP subsystem is to provide an RM-ODP compliant virtual machine. The ODP subsystem is shown spanning other subsystems, indicating that the ODP environment can be used to provide open access to services offered by other subsystems. Finally, the top layer is a set of RM-ODP compliant *applications and services*. The ODP subsystem corresponds to the Engineering Viewpoint and the applications and services to the Computational Viewpoint (with a fluid boundary between the two concerns).

The two platforms described below are complementary in that they address different parts of this architecture:

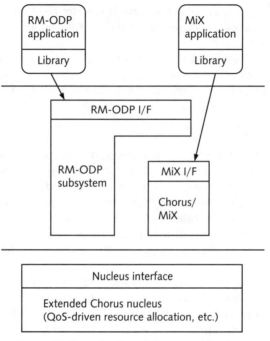

Figure 12.5 A microkernel-based architecture.

- *The Sumo-CORE platform*
  The first platform, Sumo-CORE, focuses on the underlying nucleus and, in particular, on providing the specialized real-time support for multimedia applications. The emphasis of the work is therefore to develop specialized resource management strategies (communications, scheduling and memory management) to meet the demands of multimedia. Specific attention is given to achieving integration between the various aspects of resource management to enable end-to-end bindings to be achieved. Consideration is also given to underlying support for QoS management in heterogeneous environments.
- *The Sumo-ORB platform*
  The second platform, Sumo-ORB, aims to provide an open distributed processing environment for telecommunications services and applications. The platform adopts CORBA as a basic technology but extends CORBA with support for real-time and multimedia applications, following the programming and engineering models developed in this book. The current implementation of Sumo-ORB operates over an FDDI network which offers deterministic guarantees on the underlying quality of service. This implementation therefore features more specialized QoS management services designed for this deterministic environment.

We summarize the main features of the two platforms below.

The Sumo-CORE platform

The Sumo-CORE platform is a refined version of the Chorus microkernel intended to provide the real-time QoS guarantees required by multimedia. More specifically, the platform is intended to provide explicit support for the engineering model described above. The major refinements are summarized below:

- *QoS-driven resource allocation*
  Sumo-CORE introduces two new abstractions, namely `rt-ports` and `rt-threads`. These abstractions extend the Chorus concepts of ports and threads with QoS management capabilities. For example, `rt-threads` can be defined in terms of a number of scheduling parameters, including a deadline and period. This is then supported by a modified earliest deadline first policy.
- *Explicit QoS-managed bindings*
  Sumo-CORE supports QoS-driven explicit bindings between `rt-ports` through an `rt-portBind()` primitive. The creation of the binding encapsulates static resource management functions. In addition, a control port on the binding supports dynamic QoS management functions. Crucially, bindings in Sumo-CORE are *active* rather than the more traditional passive model of interaction. This approach has significant benefits in terms of locating QoS management entirely within bindings hence achieving a higher level of *integration*. The implementation of active bindings also achieves a *separation between control and data* in the delivery of communications events. Finally, we contend that active bindings provide a *natural and effective* (event-driven) model for the development of multimedia applications.
- *Specialized resource management*
  Sumo-CORE also features specialized resource management strategies for scheduling, communications and memory management (with particular emphasis on the first two areas). The approach to scheduling is based on a modified earliest deadline first policy which ensures that deadlines for both periodic and aperiodic tasks can be met. Similarly, the communications architecture features specialized strategies for multimedia, including rate-based flow control and minimal error control. Finally, the buffer management architecture allows the creation of a pool of buffers to support the required level of quality of service on bindings. In each case, these policies can coexist with other policies, for example as required by the Unix subsystem (MiX).

Note that the implementation of each of the resource management components features a *split level approach* where management is split between the nucleus and user space. Communication between the two areas is supported by a combination of shared memory (the *bulletin board*) and *asynchronous upcalls* and *downcalls*. Again, split level management has a

Table 12.2 Static QoS management strategies

Commitment	Scheduling	Communications	Buffer management
Best Effort	EDF policy used	Connection established	Buffers pre-allocated; buffers subject to swapping and preemption
Guaranteed	Admission test on schedulability; EDF policy used	Admission test on bandwidth, latency requirements; potential resource reservation in network	Admission test; buffers pre-allocated; buffers locked in main memory and non-preemptive

number of significant advantages for multimedia. For example, user-level management can exploit lightweight user-level concurrency (avoiding expensive context switches). The split level approach also achieves a level of *integration* between communications and scheduling in that the execution of the transport protocol and the subsequent application processing are both carried out in user space and hence can be carried out by a single user-level thread with a single deadline (avoiding multiplexing). Similarly, by having transport processing and application processing in the same address space, we do not incur any context switches or domain crossings in their interaction. The split level approach is also inherently *flexible* in that user space management can be specialized to meet the needs of the particular application.

Sumo-CORE also features a *QoS management architecture* supporting both static and dynamic QoS management functions. In terms of static QoS management, Sumo-CORE supports a *binding establishment protocol* encapsulating appropriate QoS management functions for negotiation, admission control and resource reservation. Appropriate functions are then defined for threads, communications and virtual memory. The admission control test for threads is noteworthy in that it considers jitter in an earliest deadline first environment. Note that the binding establishment protocol supports the creation of a number of classes of resource. The different classes and the corresponding QoS management strategies are summarized in Table 12.2.

Dynamic QoS management is supported in Sumo-CORE by the concepts of signals and reactive objects. In particular, these facilities support the creation of managed objects as required by the engineering model. Note that active bindings, as employed in Sumo-CORE, do not require QoS policing functions.

Performance figures for Sumo-CORE indicate that considerable asynchronous system calls and lightweight threads perform well in comparison to their Chorus equivalents. In addition, the system provides improved performance in dealing with continuous media streams.

The Sumo-ORB platform

Sumo-ORB is an ODP subsystem designed to support the development of multimedia applications. Again, the platform is based on the Chorus microkernel. The programming interface offered by Sumo-ORB is based on CORBA. Sumo-ORB, however, addresses the limitations of CORBA with respect to multimedia. In particular, Sumo-ORB supports an extended programming model where (1) objects can have multiple interfaces, (2) support is provided for operational, signal and stream interaction, (3) explicit bindings can be created between compatible interfaces, (4) QoS management is supported through binding objects, and (5) reactive objects provide support for real-time.

The implementation of Sumo-ORB is inspired by the engineering model discussed in Chapter 8. In particular, Sumo-ORB features a recursive binding architecture. This approach led to a novel implementation architecture where the minimal functionality is contained in a micro-ORB and the remainder of the ORB is constructed as open services. The micro-ORB contains interface reference management and local binding as required by the recursive binding architecture. This architecture is summarized in Figure 12.6. This figure shows the micro-ORB supporting a number of binding factories. A variety of binding factories can be created. In addition, the range can be extended over time. Binding factories can also make use of reusable services in the various binding libraries; there is one binding library per style of binding (operational and signal).

This approach has a number of significant benefits over more traditional implementations of ORBs. Firstly, as stated above, the binding architecture is completely *open* and can evolve over time. This approach also enables a range of binding services to *coexist*. Secondly, and most significantly, the architecture is *binding-neutral* in that the system does not prescribe one particular approach to binding. Bindings can be viewed as just another application. With this

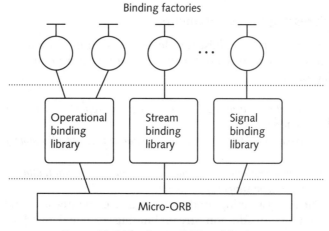

Figure 12.6 The Sumo-ORB architecture.

approach, it is possible to provide a particular ORB personality by offering particular binding factories.

Although efficient operating system support is not one of the main goals of Sumo-ORB, some work has been carried out in modifying the Chorus microkernel to support the Sumo-ORB platform. In particular, Chorus has been extended to support real-time variants of threads, ports, semaphores and messages. The microkernel also supports a new service, namely continuous media *channels*. Priority inheritance and propagation protocols are also introduced to prevent problems of priority inversion. The microkernel has also been modified to include an earliest deadline first scheduler and a communications stack supporting real-time messages and channels.

The particular implementation of Sumo-ORB described in the book operates over FDDI. One of the goals of the research is to exploit the deterministic nature of FDDI and to provide end-to-end QoS guarantees on bindings. This is achieved through the use of appropriate static QoS management techniques (dynamic QoS management is not required given the deterministic nature of the underlying environment). More specifically, Sumo-ORB defines an *admission control technique* for bindings. By passing this admission control test, the required quality of service is guaranteed. The work focuses on placing deterministic bounds on end-to-end delay. Other dimensions such as jitter or throughput are more straightforward, as they can more easily be decomposed into local constraints.

The admission control test is based on extensions to classical fixed priority analysis. The extensions enable an admission control test to be developed which deals with jitter constraints in periodic behaviour and also supports distributed bindings composed of a number of elementary steps. An algorithm based on this admission control test is defined. Note that, although the work is specific to FDDI, the admission control test can also be applied to other styles of deterministic network.

12.2.3 Addressing the requirements

We now return to the checklist developed in Section 3.3 and argue that the approach described in this book can meet our requirements for distributed multimedia computing.

1. *Does my standard or platform offer comprehensive support for continuous media interactions in terms of:*
    (a) *a programming model for stream interaction covering both simple and complex streams,*
    (b) *the ability to access and manipulate continuous media data, and*
    (c) *underlying system support for streams?*
        The programming model supports stream interfaces and stream bindings. In addition, stream bindings can be defined in terms of one or more flows. Stream interfaces also provide access to continuous

media data in the same way that operational interfaces provide access to operations or signal interfaces provide access to signals. The engineering model defines a recursive binding architecture for streams (and other styles of interaction). This provides an open approach to the development of systems support. This approach can build on primitive bindings based on technologies such as the rate-based transport protocols CMTP or RTP. Finally, the design of Sumo-CORE shows how continuous media interaction can be efficiently supported in a microkernel environment (such as minimizing data copying, context switches and domain crossings).

2. *Does my standard or platform offer comprehensive support for quality of service management in terms of:*
   (a) *the ability to specify deterministic, probabilistic or stochastic QoS requirements over both discrete and stream interactions,*
   (b) *the ability to specify classes of service such as best effort and guaranteed,*
   (c) *the ability to specify QoS contracts featuring the identification of QoS dependencies,*
   (d) *support for the static QoS management functions of QoS specification, negotiation, admission control and resource reservation, and*
   (e) *support for the dynamic QoS management functions of QoS monitoring, policing, maintenance and renegotiation?*

   The programming model enables the expression of QoS annotations as part of the environmental contract. For example, the formal language QL can be used to describe a range of (deterministic) QoS requirements including timeliness and volume properties. This approach also enables the description of QoS contracts in terms of required and provided clauses. This enables dependencies to be expressed. This approach can also be extended to enable the expression of the class of service (such as best effort or guaranteed). Static QoS management functions are included in factory objects. The particular actions will depend on whether QoS requirements are best effort or guaranteed. Dynamic QoS management functions are then realized as managed objects. This management process is supported through access to signals and can be implemented using reactive objects. Two specific approaches to QoS management are described in the book. Sumo-CORE defines specific static and dynamic QoS management functions for heterogeneous networks. Static QoS management is supported by a binding establishment protocol. In contrast, Sumo-ORB defines static QoS management functions to offer deterministic guarantees over FDDI (in this case, dynamic QoS management is not required).

3. *Does my standard or platform offer comprehensive support for real-time synchronization in terms of:*
   (a) *support for real-time intra-media synchronization,*
   (b) *support for real-time inter-media synchronization,*

(c) *the ability to operate in an arbitrary distributed configuration, and*

(d) *the ability to specify arbitrary actions potentially determined at run-time?*

Intra-media synchronization is assumed to be encapsulated within particular classes of stream or signal bindings. In addition, the primitive concepts of signals and reactive objects provide a flexible approach for the specification of arbitrary inter-media real-time synchronization policies. Furthermore, the programming model specifies the configuration of objects in a location-independent manner. The distribution of objects is however constrained by the QoS specified on objects (and particularly on bindings). As long as the QoS constraints can be met, the configuration will meet its requirements. Finally, languages such as Esterel can be used to describe reactive objects exhibiting arbitrary behaviour. Furthermore, the precise behaviour can be determined at run-time using the imperative programming constructs offered by Esterel.

4. *Does my standard or platform offer comprehensive support for multiparty communication in terms of:*

(a) *a programming model for multiparty communications enabling the establishment and management of both discrete and stream group interactions,*

(b) *systems support for the establishment and management of multiparty communications,*

(c) *support for multiparty communications where the participants may have different and potentially changing quality of service requirements, and*

(d) *the ability to specify a wide range of synchronization policies for multiparty communications?*

Bindings can either be point-to-point or multiparty. Both styles are managed in the same way through binding interfaces. Multiparty bindings will however provide additional operations to manage the group interaction. The recursive binding architecture can be used to construct multiparty bindings building on primitive bindings based, for example, on multiparty resource reservation protocols such as RSVP or ST-II. With bindings, there is no assumption that the QoS annotations for all participants will be the same. For example, the binding architecture can be used to construct classes of binding which feature filters to deal with heterogeneous levels of QoS. Finally, bindings are a general concept and it is feasible to provide a range of binding classes supporting different synchronization policies. Furthermore, some classes could support a range of synchronization policies with the precise choice specified in the environmental contract.

Overall, then, we believe the approach described in this book provides a general and flexible framework to meet the requirements of distributed multimedia applications.

12.3 Extending the results to other standards and platforms

Creating compliant standards and platforms

The approach defined in this book provides a framework, based on RM-ODP, for the development of specific standards and platforms for distributed multimedia computing. The programming and engineering models should therefore be correctly viewed as a general framework. Specific platforms and standards can then be generated by instantiating the framework with specific notations and functions. This process is illustrated in Figure 12.7.

The process of instantiation involves the following specific steps:

1. define a language for the description of interface type signatures (covering operational, stream and signal interfaces),
2. define a language for the description of behaviour specification (optional),
3. define a language for the description of environmental contracts (including QoS annotations involving required and provided clauses),
4. define a language for the expression of reactive objects,
5. provide a set of binding classes offering operational, stream and signal interaction and different levels of QoS management, and
6. provide a set of factories, including factories supporting the creation of reactive objects (with an appropriate support environment).

Some standards and platforms also require support for implicit binding (as well as explicit binding) for reasons of backward compatibility.

Analysis of existing platforms and standards

The framework can also be used to analyze existing standards and platforms, evaluating their potential contribution to open multimedia systems and also highlighting weaknesses in their support for multimedia. We look at each standard/platform identified in Chapter 2 in turn below.

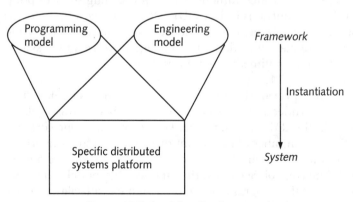

Figure 12.7 Applying the framework.

- *CORBA and MSS*

  The most important contribution of CORBA is in providing a *de facto* standard Interface Definition Language. However, as identified above, CORBA objects are restricted to a single interface and only support operational interactions. In addition, all bindings are implicit and no support is provided for QoS management or real-time synchronization. CORBA also focuses on the Computational Viewpoint and hence does not consider the engineering framework (with the exception of the interoperability architecture). This can have an impact on the level of openness of the resultant architecture. The Sumo-ORB platform described in Chapter 11, however, illustrates how the CORBA standard can be enhanced to produce platforms compliant with the programming and engineering models defined in this book. The goal of MSS is also to enhance CORBA for multimedia. MSS has some useful contributions in terms of prescribing class hierarchies for virtual devices (thus adding value to the programming model defined in this book). As discussed in Chapter 2, however, MSS focuses exclusively on the Computational Viewpoint and hence the engineering infrastructure is completely closed. In addition, MSS has a number of deficiencies in terms of support for QoS dependencies, support for different qualities of service in multiparty communication and the ability to specify the required synchronization policy for multiparty communications. Overall, we feel that Sumo-ORB provides a more comprehensive solution to multimedia by applying the framework presented in this book. (A further analysis of the requirements of a real-time ORB is given below.)

- *DCE*

  DCE is based on the client–server architecture and does not yet provide an object-oriented programming model. Such a model can be defined on top of DCE, however, with DCE providing a set of appropriate technologies and functions. For example, DCE provides a *de facto* standard remote procedure call protocol supporting operational interaction. In addition, DCE provides authentication and naming services populating two of the key functions in RM-ODP. DCE, however, does not yet provide any support for multimedia and hence extensions are required to support stream and signal interaction, QoS management, real-time synchronization and multiparty multimedia communications.

- *RM-ODP and TINA*

  As mentioned previously, the work presented in this book is closely related to RM-ODP. Indeed, many of the ideas described in this book are now included in the RM-ODP standard. However, our framework goes beyond RM-ODP in a number of significant directions. Firstly, the programming model includes the concept of reactive objects introducing a mechanism for real-time control. Secondly, the engineering model is interpreted as a refinement of the programming model with extra facilities to describe the distribution of objects. Thirdly, we define a recursive binding architecture spanning both viewpoints and replacing the distinction between bindings and channels in the RM-ODP standard. We believe that these refinements provide a more complete and consistent solution for the development of distributed systems standards and platforms. TINA can be viewed as a specialization of RM-ODP for the telecommunications domain. Hence, the criticisms of RM-ODP also apply to TINA. TINA, however, has a number of important contributions to make in the areas of defining specific binding classes and service/management architectures for the telecommunications domain.

Requirements of a real-time ORB

To conclude this section, we consider some general requirements for a real-time ORB. These requirements are derived from the experiences gained from the research described in this book. A more detailed statement of these requirements can be found in CNET (1996).

The main requirements of a real-time ORB are as follows:

- *Flexibility*
  The architecture of a real-time ORB should be minimal, modular and flexible enough to allow the introduction of new binding and communications mechanisms, and also additional transparency services (security, transaction, and so on). The architecture should also support configurability to a range of hardware platforms, including more limited platforms such as embedded systems, set-top boxes and personal digital assistants.
- *Generic binding framework*
  A real-time ORB should feature a generic binding framework supporting both implicit and explicit binding, supporting QoS-constrained bindings, enabling the creation of additional binding classes, supporting arbitrary binding scenarios (including multiparty bindings and third-party bindings), and allowing application level control over established bindings. Three different styles of bindings are required, namely operational, stream and signal bindings. All styles should enable application level processing of data.
- *Objects and interfaces*
  An ORB should enable the specification of objects consisting of multiple interfaces. In addition, we believe that three styles of interface should be supported corresponding to the three styles of binding discussed above. All interfaces should be strongly typed, enabling the creation of type-safe bindings. It is also important that the ORB supports large numbers of objects with widely different granularities.
- *Generic communications infrastructure*
  The binding framework must be supported by a generic communications infrastructure, supporting, for example, protocol decomposition and configuration. The communications infrastructure should also allow the

coexistence of multiple protocol stacks and the ability to dynamically select a protocol stack depending on application requirements.

• *Generic scheduling infrastructure*
A real-time ORB should offer a generic scheduling infrastructure with a clear separation between application-selectable scheduling policy modules and a shared set of scheduling mechanisms. Support for both priority and deadline-based policies is required. The scheduling infrastructure should support multithreading with QoS requirements stated on individual threads. The implementation should avoid problems of priority inversion.

• *QoS support*
A real-time ORB should provide minimal support for QoS management in terms of the ability to observe timed event occurrences including computational events (such as operation invocation and termination) and engineering events (such as thread creation and destruction). Such facilities should be optional and should not incur a performance penalty if not used.

In addition, a real-time ORB should support a number of specific services, including a time service, offering access to timers of a given precision, and a node management service, supporting the configuration of objects and capsules on a given node.

12.4 Outstanding issues

In this section, we highlight a number of outstanding issues in the support of multimedia in open distributed processing requirements. Note that a number of ongoing projects are addressing these concerns, including Sumo II, ReTINA and ANSA Phase 3. World Wide Web addresses for these activities can be found in Appendix A.

12.4.1 Linguistic notations

In the previous section, we considered the steps required to populate the framework defined in this book with appropriate linguistic notations. In our opinion, however, further research is required before this can be achieved. Some work is required to achieve a consensus on a language for the description of *interface type signatures*. It is clear that CORBA IDL will be a major influence in this work. However, important differences remain between this particular IDL and the Computational Model of RM-ODP (for example, on the issue of single vs. multiple interfaces per object).

More significantly, there is a lack of consensus on appropriate notations to define *environmental contracts*. In particular, there are no mature techniques for the expression of *quality of service contracts*. The language QL provides guidance on how this can be achieved. However, in some respects, QL is overly expressive and too complex for standard usage, but this language does have the advantage that it supports formal analysis and synthesis. In contrast, the notation currently employed in Sumo-ORB is too simple to support comprehensive QoS management. Further research is required to identify a compromise between these two positions.

Finally, further research is required to identify languages to populate the other RM-ODP viewpoints, in particular the *enterprise* and *information viewpoints*. Some work has been carried on languages for these two areas. However, there has been very little research on identifying the impact of real-time or multimedia systems on such notations. This topic has not been addressed at all in this book.

12.4.2 Algorithms

The previous section also highlighted the need to populate the framework with a set of binding classes and factories (including factories for reactive objects). In our opinion, further research is required before a comprehensive set of binding classes and factories can be supported. Crucially, further research is required on algorithms to support the development of binding classes and factories.

One crucial area of study is the development of appropriate QoS management functions. Particular attention is required to provide appropriate *admission control* and *resource reservation* strategies for end-to-end bindings. It is interesting to note that most existing techniques in this area either provide best effort or guaranteed services. One interesting avenue is therefore to identify *probabilistic techniques* which are better suited to the soft real-time nature of most multimedia traffic.

The development of end-to-end bindings also requires more specific research on algorithms for scheduling, memory management and communications protocols. The development of appropriate scheduling policies and associated admission control tests is a particularly important area for study. The most crucial requirement is coexistence with existing policies. The area of memory management policies supporting multimedia communications has been a rather neglected area of study and requires further research. Finally, in the network, research is required on scheduling disciplines and associated resource reservation and admission control tests to support the requirements of multimedia and real-time traffic. Support for multiparty bindings is a particularly important concern.

Further research is also required to support reactive objects. Chapter 11 described one approach to providing a support environment for reactive objects. However, further research is required to address the problems of meeting the synchrony hypothesis in an asynchronous environment and also mapping asynchronous events to signals in synchronous execution. Research is also required on languages supporting the development of reactive objects, particularly in supporting composition of reactive scripts.

12.4.3 Structures

The work described in this book has provided some insight into the architecture for future open distributed systems. In particular, the research has provided insights into the role of *viewpoints* in developing complex systems. From our experience, the Computational and Engineering Viewpoints require a shared object model. Such an approach considerably simplifies the relationship between the two viewpoints. The Computational Viewpoint represents the logical design of the application or service, whereas the Engineering Viewpoint describes the virtual machine required to support the design. The system description at the engineering level can also be seen as a refinement of the description at the computational level. This approach also simplifies the definition of consistency between viewpoints (a crucial outstanding issue in RM-ODP). However, further research is required to appreciate the broader implications of this approach. For example, consideration must be given to the interpretation of other viewpoint models.

In general, it is crucial that architectures for open distributed processing are responsive to new technological developments. Currently, one of the most important trends is towards *heterogeneous networking*, where computers can be interconnected by networks ranging from high-speed, reliable multi-service networks, such as ATM, through to low-speed and rather unreliable wireless networks, such as GSM. Crucially, the level of connectivity may *vary over time*. For example, in the office, a user will have strong connectivity. While travelling, the user may obtain partial connectivity through services such as GSM. He or she may even experience periods of complete disconnection. Such dramatic changes impose considerable demands on the underlying distributed systems platform.

Researchers working in the area of mobile computing are investigating the use of *adaptation* to overcome this problem (Katz, 1994; Satyanarayanan *et al.*, 1995). For example, in terms of multimedia, researchers are also considering the dynamic application of filtering to enable streams to adapt to the available bandwidth (Amir *et al.*, 1995). Further research is, however, required to identify the impact of this work on standards and platforms for open distributed processing. This can partially be achieved through the use of appropriate *QoS management functions* (offering feedback on the quality of service of underlying components). It is interesting, however, to consider complementary techniques which support adaptation in services. One interesting approach is to adopt *reflection* as a means of achieving adaptation throughout an open environment. In reflective systems, the meta-environment can be modified in precisely the same way as the environment (Maes, 1987; Kiczales *et al.*, 1991). This can be used, for example, to dynamically alter management strategies to meet new requirements. As such, this approach appears promising as a general solution to adaptation in open distributed processing standards and platforms.

Note that the interpretation of the programming and engineering models as described above provides a strong basis for a more reflective open distributed processing architecture.

12.5 Concluding remarks

This book has addressed the support for multimedia in standards and platforms for open distributed processing. This is a particularly difficult problem, dealing with the heterogeneity in the underlying distributed environment and also dealing with heterogeneity in the media types as used by applications. Significantly, there is a potential conflict between these two concerns. The solution to open distributed processing generally involves creating abstractions over existing resources. This can introduce a performance overhead. However, many media types impose stringent real-time requirements on the underlying platform.

We believe that this apparent conflict can be overcome. Indeed, the solutions presented in this book enable lightweight support for multimedia computing. This, however, required careful consideration of all aspects of the platform design including the programming model, the engineering support and the available underlying technology. We believe that the *viewpoint* approach of RM-ODP was crucial in supporting such a holistic approach to the design of distributed system platforms.

13.5 Concluding remarks

Appendix A
Useful WWW addresses

A.1 Open distributed processing

A.1.1 Standards organizations

Name	URL	Description
ISO	http://www.iso.ch/index.html	The official web site of the International Organization for Standardization (ISO)
ITU	http://www.itu.ch/	The official web site of the International Telecommunication Union (ITU)
OMG	http://www.omg.org/	The official web site of the Object Management Group (OMG)
Open Group	http://www.opengroup.org/	The official web site of the Open Group
IMA	http://www.ima.org/index.html	The official web site of the International Multimedia Association (IMA)

A.1.2 Specific standards

Name	URL	Description
ISO RM-ODP	http://www.iso.ch:8000/RM-ODP/	The official web site for the ISO RM-ODP standard
	http://www.dstc.edu.au/AU/research_news/odp/ref_model/ref_model.html	An unofficial site containing many items pertaining to RM-ODP (including the standard on-line)
ISO QoS Framework	ftp://ftp.comp.lancs.ac.uk/pub/ISO_QOSF/	An official site containing working papers relating to this work item
IMA MSS	http://www.ima.org/forums/imf/mss/	The official web site for the IMA Multimedia System Services (MSS)
OMG CORBA	http://www.omg.org/corba.htm	The official web site for OMG CORBA

A.1.2 Specific standards (*continued*)

Name	URL	Description
	http://www.acl.lanl.gov/CORBA/	An unofficial site containing many items pertaining to CORBA
DCE	http://www.opengroup.org/tech/dce	The official web site for the Open Group's Distributed Computing Environment (DCE)
TINA	http://www.tinac.com/	The official web site maintained by the Telecommunication Information Networking Architecture (TINA) consortium
PREMO	http://www.cwi.nl/cwi/projects/premo.html	The official web site relating to the ISO graphics standard, PREMO
DAVIC	http://www.davic.org/INTRO.htm	The official web site relating to the Digital Audio Visual Council (DAVIC).

A.2 Multimedia

A.2.1 General sources of information

Name	URL	Description
Multimedia information	http://viswiz.gmd.de/MultimediaInfo/	A web site maintained by Simon Gibbs containing pointers to a large number of other sites relating to multimedia

A.2.2 Specific technologies

Networking

Name	URL	Description
ATM Forum	http://www.atmforum.com/	The official web site of ATM Forum (a group dedicated to the acceleration in the use of ATM products and standards)
Internet	ftp://nis.nsf.net/internet/documents	A good source of documents pertaining to the Internet
OPENSIG	http://www.ctr.columbia.edu/opensig/opensig.html	A web site dedicated to the development of open signalling approaches in future broadband networks
NII	http://sunsite.unc.edu/nii/NII-Table-of-Contents.html	A web page dedicated to the development of the National Information Infrastructure (NII) in the USA

Communication protocols

Name	URL	Description
IETF	http://www.ietf.cnri.reston.va.us/	The home page of the Internet Engineering Task Force
RSVP	http://www.isi.edu/div7/rsvp/rsvp-home.html	A web page focusing on the development of the RSVP resource reservation protocol
	ftp://ftp.isi.edu/rsvp/docs/rsvpspec.ID13.txt	The current RSVP specification
MBONE	http://www.eit.com/techinfo/mbone/mbone.html	The official web site of the Object Management Group (OMG)
RTP	http://www.cs.columbia.edu/~hgs/rtp/	A web page about the real-time Internet protocol RTP
Tenet	http://tenet.berkeley.edu/	A web page maintained by the Tenet Group at Berkeley
COST 237	http://cps.cps.na.cnr.it/cost.html	A web page maintained by the European COST 237 Project (looking at development of multimedia transport and teleservices)
Video gateway	http://http.cs.berkeley.edu/~elan/vgw/README.html#intro	The home page of the Application Level Video Gateway developed at Berkeley

Compression and filters

Name	URL	Description
MPEG	http://www.vol.it/MPEG/	A web site dedicated to the various MPEG standards (MPEG-1, MPEG-2 and so on)
	http://www.mpeg.org/	A further site with pointers to MPEG-related resources
JPEG	http://www.cis.ohio-state.edu/hypertext/faq/usenet/jpeg-faq/top.html	A set of frequently asked questions (FAQ) about JPEG
Filtering	http://www.comp.lancs.ac.uk/computing/users/njy/	A page with information relating to filtering

End systems technologies

Name	URL	Description
OS Research	http://www.cs.arizona.edu/people/bridges/oses.html	A page containing pointers to many operating systems projects (including real-time and multimedia projects)
Pegasus	http://www.pegasus.esprit.ec.org	A page maintained by the ESPRIT Project Pegasus (investigating operating system support for multimedia)

A.3 Open distributed processing and multimedia

A.3.1 The Sumo project

Name	URL	Description
The Sumo Project	http://www.comp.lancs.ac.uk/computing/research/sumo/	The home site of the Sumo Project containing information and current reports
This book	http://www.awl-he.com/computing	A web page for this book, including the two reports on the formalization of the programming model (as mentioned in Chapter 4)
Chorus	http://www.chorus.com/	The official web site of Chorus Systèmes (the operating system used by Sumo)
	http://www.comp.lancs.ac.uk/computing/users/pr/www/chorus/faq.html	A set of frequently asked questions (FAQ) about Chorus
Esterel	http://cma.cma.fr:80/Esterel/esterel-eng.html	A page dedicated to the Esterel synchronous programming language (as used in Sumo)
Python	http://www.python.org/	A page dedicated to the Python programming language (as used in Sumo)

A.3.2 Other relevant projects

Name	URL	Description
IMA MSS	http://www.ima.org/forums/imf/mss/	See A.1.2 above
ReTINA	http://www.ansa.co.uk/ReTINA/index.html	A web site about the ACTS ReTINA project

A.3.2 Other relevant projects (*continued*)

Name	URL	Description
ANSA Phase 3	http://www.ansa.co.uk/	A web site describing the current activities of ANSA
OMG Task Force	http://www.dstc.edu.au/AU/ projects/mmcf/	A page dedicated to the activities of the OMG Task Force on Multimedia Common Facilities
Pegasus II	http://www.cl.cam.ac.uk/Research/ SRG/pegasus/peg2-overview/ overview.html	A web site for the Pegasus II project; this project is a follow-up to the Pegasus project (see Section A.2.2) but now broadened to consider middleware issues

Notes

1. At the time of writing, the addresses given above were correct. URLs are however liable to change over time.
2. The above list is not intended to be exhaustive. Rather, the list is intended to give selected pointers to important standards and technologies in the areas of open distributed processing and multimedia.

An admission control test for jitter-constrained periodic threads

B.1 Introduction

In this appendix, we derive admission control tests for guaranteed threads as required by the Sumo-CORE platform described in Chapter 10. More specifically, the appendix presents a full derivation of the tests for the G_I and G_W classes of threads presented in chapter 10, Section 10.5.2 (see this chapter for a definition of the G_I and G_W classes).

In the following discussion, let g_i and g_w refer to the portions of resource dedicated to the respective classes of thread, where $g_i + g_w < 1$.

B.2 Admission control test for G_I threads

B.2.1 Overall aim

Our aim for G_I threads is to develop a more constrained admission control test to take into account the permissible jitter on threads. Standard earliest deadline first schemes will schedule threads at any point between the start and end of the period. The normal admission control test for this behaviour is given below (the Liu/Layland test (Liu and Layland, 1973)):

$$\sum_{i=1}^{T} \frac{e_i}{p_i} \leqslant 1$$

where T is the number of threads in the system, e_i is the execution time of each quantum of thread i, and p_i is the period of thread i.

We, however, seek a solution where G_I threads are scheduled according to the following formula:

deadline = schedulingtime + quantum + jitter

In other words, we would like to schedule threads so that they are constrained to execute before the end of the period. At the most extreme, when jitter is zero, threads are constrained to execute purely isochronously (at a precise time every period).

We consider three solutions to this problem with each solution increasing in sophistication.

B.2.2 A first solution (adapting the Liu/Layland test)

The simplest admission control test to support the desired behaviour is given below:

$$\sum_{i=1}^{T} \frac{e_i}{d_i} \leqslant 1$$

$$\sum_{i=1}^{T} \frac{e_i}{p_i} \leqslant g_i$$

In this test, the first equation ensures that all threads will execute within the maximum allowable jitter by substituting the deadline, d_i, for the period, p_i, in the Liu/Layland formula. The second equation checks the overall resource usage for the class is less than or equal to the portion allocated to G_I threads.

This is a correct admission control test for G_I threads, but the test is rather conservative: the test will reject threads where a valid schedule can be found. For example, consider the following thread set (where p is the period, d is the deadline and e is the quantum):

$$t_1 : p = 3, d = 1, e = 1$$

$$t_2 : p = 5, d = 4, e = 2$$

This set will not pass the above admission test even though a valid schedule can easily be found that will honour the deadlines of both threads (see Figure B.1).

We have therefore developed a second, less conservative, test based on the observation that a candidate thread can be accepted if, in the *active span* of each of its quanta (the time between the start of the period and the deadline), there is sufficient spare resource to schedule the required number of quanta of all other threads with an earlier or equal deadline, even when the scheduling times of all threads concerned happen to coincide.

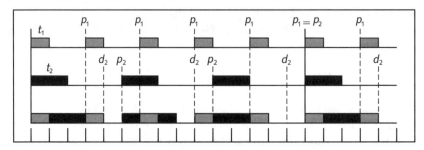

Figure B.1 An example schedule exploiting periods and deadlines.

Relating this to Figure B.1, we can see that, in a system currently supporting only t_1, it should also be possible to support t_2. This is because, in the active span of each of the quanta of t_2 (4 time units), it is possible to fit the required number of quanta of t_1 (2 quanta of 1 time unit each) and the quantum of t_2 itself (2 time units), even when the scheduling times of quanta of t_1 and t_2 coincide.

This general insight leads us directly to the solution given below.

B.2.2 A second solution (exploiting deadlines and periods)

The above argument is formally captured in the following admission test.

$$\forall c_i \ in \ \langle c_{\min}, \ldots, c_{\max} \rangle, \sum_{j=1}^{k} \frac{etime\,(j, d_i)}{d_i} \leqslant 1$$

where

$$etime(j,t) = e_j \lfloor t/p_j \rfloor + \begin{cases} e_j, & if \ t \geqslant p_j \lfloor t/p_j \rfloor + d_j \\ \dfrac{e_j}{d_j}\,(t - p_j \lfloor t/p_j \rfloor), & otherwise \end{cases}$$

In the above formula, the inequality is applied iteratively over an ordered sequence of *deadline equivalence classes* and must hold for all these classes. Each deadline equivalence class c_i contains all threads in the system that have a deadline d_i, and the sequence of classes as a whole is ordered smallest deadline first to largest deadline last. The function $etime(j,t)$ gives the maximum processing time required by a thread j in some time span t. The first subterm of *etime* considers any execution time incurred during all full periods of thread j that can occur during t. The second subterm considers the execution time to be taken into account where a period overlaps the end of t. The top condition of the second subterm is applicable where the whole active span of j falls within interval t. The bottom condition is applicable where only a portion of the active span falls within t. Given this definition of *etime*, it can be seen that the numerator of (1) sums the required execution times of some number of threads within the period d_i. More specifically, the summation ranges over $(1 \ldots k)$ which is defined to contain all threads in deadline classes up to and including the current class c_i. The numerator as a whole thus evaluates to the total CPU time required, in the worst case, in the time interval d_i by all threads with a deadline $\leqslant d_i$. To ensure that over-utilization does not take place, this quantity, when divided by d_i itself, must be less than or equal to 1. Since EDF will always find a valid and optimal schedule in these circumstances, all threads of deadline $\leqslant d_i$ will be executed according to their jitter constraints.

The reason why this admission test is less conservative than solution 1 is that it uses more information on which to base its decision. More specifically, it exploits knowledge of the *periods* of the threads in addition to knowledge of *deadlines*. Note that this distinction is not recognized by the run-time scheduler which continues to operate as before.

This second solution does, however, have the limitation that it pessimistically assumes that all threads can (in the worst case) reach their scheduling times at the same instant. Where it can be demonstrated that this cannot occur, a further degree of freedom in admission testing is possible. In particular, we can exploit the concept of *harmonic sets* (Kuo and Mok, 1991), where a harmonic set is a thread set in which the constituent threads can be ordered such that the period of each thread integrally divides its successor.

To illustrate the use of harmonic sets, consider the following thread set:

$$t_1 : p = 3, d = 1, e = 1$$

$$t_2 : p = 6, d = 1, e = 1$$

$$t_3 : p = 12, d = 1, e = 1$$

This set would be rejected by the second admission test as the maximum utilization is 3 (as required when the scheduling times of all three threads coincide). However, if we stipulate that the scheduling times of quanta of t_2 will always follow deadlines of quanta of t_1, and that the scheduling times of quanta of t_3 will always follow deadlines of quanta of t_2, then the valid schedule illustrated in Figure B.2 can be derived. This reorganization is always possible within a harmonic set. Note that this process does, however, require manipulation of scheduling times for threads belonging to a harmonic set.

B.2.3 A final solution (exploiting harmonic sets)

We now present our final admission test (as given in Chapter 10), exploiting the concept of harmonic sets. This test is a relatively straightforward extension of solution 2:

$$\forall c_i \ in \ \langle c_{\min}, \ldots, c_{\max} \rangle \left(\sum_{j=1}^{k} etime(j, d_i) + \sum_{h=1}^{H} E_h \right) \Big/ d_i \leqslant 1$$

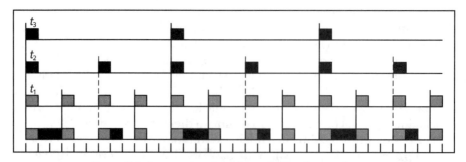

Figure B.2 A example schedule exploiting harmonic sets.

The differences from solution 2 are, first, that the original term in the numerator now only considers those threads that are *not* placed in a harmonic set, and, second, that a new term is added to express the maximum required processing time of any harmonic sets in the thread set. The expression E_h represents the maximum processing time requirement over any interval d_i for the subset of threads in a harmonic set H whose deadlines are $\leqslant d_i$. The summation to H ranges over the set of harmonic sets. To understand the derivation of E_H, refer to Figure B.3 which illustrates a harmonic set containing three threads with deadlines $\leqslant d_i$. The double arrowed lines in Figure B.3 represent the active spans of the quanta of the associated threads. Intuitively, to find E_H, the strategy is to slide the interval d_i along the time line, repeatedly calculating the processing time requirement of the subset of the harmonic set whose deadlines fall within the current d_i interval. We then take the maximum of the required processing times of all these intervals to obtain E_H.

When sliding the interval d_i along the time line, it is sufficient to consider those intervals of length d_i which either start at the beginning of an active span or end at the end of an active span (it is not necessary to consider time spans starting at other times because the actual utilization only changes at the start and end of an active span). We shall refer to the set of instants at which active spans *start* ($\{A, B, C, \ldots, G\}$ in Figure B.3) as S, and refer to the members of this set as S_i. Similarly, we shall refer to the set of instants at which active spans *end* ($\{T, U, \ldots, Z\}$) as the set D with members D_i. Given these definitions, we denote by E_S the set of processing times required over the interval d_i starting at instants in S. Similarly, we denote by E_D the set of processing times required over the interval d_i ending at instants in D. Given these definitions, we can obtain E_H by taking the maximum of the union of sets E_S and E_D to calculate the worst-case processing time of members of the harmonic set H with deadlines $\leqslant d_i$ in any interval d_i. Thus:

$$E_H = \max\{E_S \cup E_D\}$$

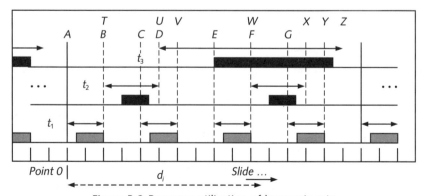

Figure B.3 Resource utilization of harmonic sets.

Further detail of the procedures to evaluate the sets E_S and E_D for a given value of d_i are given in the literature (Mauthe and Coulson, 1997).

B.3 Admission control test for G_W threads

The admission control test for G_W threads is more straightforward. For such threads, the jitter parameter is ignored. Threads can also be scheduled ahead of their scheduling time.

Given the above conditions, the admission control test for G_W threads is as follows:

$$\sum_{i=1}^{T} \frac{e_i}{p_i} \leqslant g_w$$

where T is the number of threads in the system, e_i is the execution time of each quantum of thread i, p_i is the period of thread i and g_w is the portion of resources allocated to the G_W class.

Glossary

Acronyms

ATM	Asynchronous Transfer Mode
B-ISDN	Broadband Integrated Services Digital Network
CBR	Constant Bit Rate
CORBA	Common Object Request Broker Architecture
DAVIC	Digital Audio Visual Council
DCE	Distributed Computing Environment
DQDB	Distributed Queues Dual Bus
ECFF	Enhanced Communication Functions and Facilities
EDF	Earliest Deadline First
FDDI	Fibre Digital Data Interface
GIOP	General Inter-ORB Protocol
HDTV	High Definition Television
IDL	Interface Definition Language
IIOP	Internet Inter-ORB Protocol
IMA	International Multimedia Association
IP	Internet Protocol
ISDN	Integrated Services Digital Network
ISO	International Organization for Standardization
ITU	International Telecommunication Union
JPEG	Joint Photographic Experts Group
MBONE	Multicast Backbone
MPEG	Motion Pictures Experts Group
MSS	Multimedia System Services
ODL	Object Definition Language
OMG	Object Management Group
ORB	Object Request Broker
OSF	Open Software Foundation
QoS	Quality of Service
RAID	Redundant Arrays of Inexpensive Disks
RM-ODP	Reference Model for Open Distributed Processing
RPC	Remote Procedure Call
RTP	Real-time Transport Protocol
TCP	Transport Control Protocol
TINA	Telecommunication Information Networking Architecture
TINA-C	Telecommunication Information Networking Architecture Consortium
UDP	User Datagram Protocol
VBR	Variable Bit Rate
XTP	Express Transport Protocol

Important terms

RM-ODP specific terms

binder	An *object* which is responsible for maintaining a *binding*
binding	The establishment of an association between objects as a precursor to interaction
explicit binding	The act of requesting a *binding* between objects
implicit binding	The automatic creation of a *binding* by the system infrastructure as a precursor to interaction
binding factory	An object which supports the creation of a *binding* object between interacting objects
capsule	An encapsulation of the resources (virtual memory and so on) required to support object execution (compare a process)
channel	An abstraction over the underlying communications infrastructure
class	The set of objects which adhere to a given *type*
cluster	A group of objects within a *capsule* acting as a single unit for migration, activation and so on
composite object	A configuration of interacting objects offering a composite behaviour
distribution transparency	The property of being able to hide from a user the potential behaviour of some parts of the system
environmental contract	A contract between an object and its environment (in terms of expectations and obligations)
factory	An object which supports the creation (*instantiation*) of other objects
flow	An abstraction of an ongoing sequence of interactions (generally relating to *continuous media*)
incremental inheritance	Allows a derived class to be created from a base class
instantiation	The act of creating a new object according to a given *template*
interceptor	An object which supports interactions across different management domains (for example by performing protocol translations)
interface	A point of interaction with an object, offering a subset of the object's behaviour
operational interface	An *interface* supporting interaction in terms of *operations*
signal interface	An *interface* supporting interaction in terms of *signals*
stream interface	An *interface* supporting interaction in terms of *streams*
interface reference	A globally unique denotation for an *interface*
interface type	A predicate describing the behaviour of an *interface*
node	A representation of a complete computing resource
nucleus	An abstraction over the underlying operating system
object	An entity offering a service to the environment, and hiding internal details of the implementation
operation	An interaction between a client object and a server object involving the potentially remote execution of a particular function
protocol object	An encapsulation of a communications protocol as required to support a *channel*

QoS annotation	Part of the *environmental contract* supporting the specification of QoS expectations and obligations
role	A subset of the behaviour of an object offering a given functionality
selective transparency	The ability to select the desired level of *distribution transparency*
signal	An atomic event relating to the interaction between objects
stream	An interaction involving one or more *flows*
stub	Provides the interface between an object and a particular *binding*
subclass	One class is a subclass of another if and only if the former is a subset of the latter
subtype	A type is a subtype of another if and only if the former implies the latter
template	A description of an object in sufficient detail to support *instantiation*
thread	A sequential chain of actions on objects
trader	A third-party service offering brokerage on available services in the distributed environment
type	A predicate describing the behaviour of a set of objects
viewpoint	A complete view of a system from a given perspective
enterprise viewpoint	Considers the system in terms of its scope and objectives
information viewpoint	Considers the system in terms of its information flows and processes
computational viewpoint	Considers the system in terms of a logical partitioning into interacting objects
engineering viewpoint	Considers the system in terms of its support infrastructure
technology viewpoint	Considers the system in terms of policies for procurements and installation

Multimedia-specific terms

compression	A transformation of a *media* stream to reduce the overall QoS requirements
filtering	An arbitrary transformation of a *media* type
jitter	The variability in end-to-end delay (*latency*) experienced in a *stream* interaction
latency	The end-to-end delay for a given interaction
lip synchronization	Real-time synchronization between audio and video *streams* to ensure the correct audio is heard when lips are seen to move
media	The storage, transmission, interchange, presentation, representation and perception of different information types
continuous media	A *media* type with an implied temporal dimension
discrete media	A *media* type without a temporal dimension
multimedia	Handling a variety of representation *media* in an integrated manner
quality of service (QoS)	A set of non-functional properties associated with a given service

QoS contract	A statement of QoS in terms of expectations and obligations
QoS management	Supervision and control to ensure that the desired level of QoS is sustained
static QoS management	*QoS management* functions carried out at *binding* creation time
admission control	A *static QoS management* function which performs a test to see if a given interaction can be accepted (given its desired level of QoS)
QoS negotiation	A *static QoS management* function to reach agreement on the given level of QoS to be sustained
resource reservation	A *static QoS management* function which pre-allocates resources in an attempt to guarantee a given level of QoS
dynamic QoS management	*QoS management* functions carried out during the lifetime of a *binding*
QoS monitoring	A *dynamic QoS management* function which checks that a given level of QoS is being sustained
QoS renegotiation	A *dynamic QoS management* function enabling the level of QoS to be changed
QoS policing	A *dynamic QoS management* function to ensure that an application adheres to its *QoS contract*
QoS maintenance	A *dynamic QoS management* function to ensure that a given object attains the desired level of QoS
real-time synchronization	The ability to preserve real-time constraints within or between *media* types
intra-media synchronization	Preserving temporal relationships within a given *media* type
inter-media synchronization	Preserving temporal relationships between different *media* types
throughput	The volume of information delivered in unit time for a given interaction

Others

actor	A term used in Chorus to denote an execution environment (*capsules* in RM-ODP)
conformance	A relationship between a specification and an implementation (any property that holds in the former must also hold in the latter)
distributed system	A system consisting of multiple autonomous processing elements that do not share primary memory but communicate using asynchronous messages over a communications network
engineering model	A framework to support the construction of a distributed system (compare *engineering viewpoint*)
fixed priority scheduling	A scheduling discipline where *threads* are scheduled at run-time according to priorities assigned at creation time
heterogeneity	The property of being diverse in character
homogeneity	The property of being uniform in character
implementation repository	A service in CORBA offering information on available object implementations

interface repository	A service in CORBA offering information on available *interface* descriptions
Internet	A global network of networks, the unifying factor being the *IP* protocol
interoperability	The ability to interwork with different systems
microkernel	A minimal operating system kernel
micro-ORB	A minimal *object request broker* (compare *microkernel*)
object adapter	A service in CORBA offering a range of basic functions for object management
object-oriented	A design and development methodology based on objects, class and inheritance
open distributed processing	Achieving *openness* in a distributed system
openness	Capable of supporting *interoperability* and *portability* through internationally agreed interfaces
port	An end-point for communication
portability	The ability to run software directly on a different system
programming model	A framework to support the design and development of a distributed application (compare *computational viewpoint*)
reactive object	An object maintaining a permanent interaction with the environment, accepting *signals*, reacting to signals and emitting signals
split level scheduling	A scheduling discipline where management is shared between the user level and kernel level
synchronous language	A programming language adhering to the *synchrony hypothesis*
synchrony hypothesis	A property whereby reactions to *signals* are instantaneous; that is, atomic with respect to their environment

References

Abernethy T.W. and Munday C.A. (1995). Intelligent networks, standards and services. *BT Tech. J.*, **7**(2), 9–20.

Abrossimov V., Rozier M. and Shapiro M. (1989). Generic virtual memory management for operating system kernels. In *ACM Symp. Operating Systems Principles (SOSP'89)*, Arizona, December 1989.

Alur R. and Henzinger T.A. (1990). Real-time logics: complexity and expressiveness. In *Proc. 5th Annual IEEE Symp. Logic in Computer Science*, pp. 390–401.

Amir I., McCanne S. and Zhang H. (1995). An application level video gateway. In *Proc. ACM Multimedia '95*, San Francisco CA, November 1995.

Anderson D.P., Tzou S.Y., Wahbe R., Govindan R. and Andrews M. (1990). Support for continuous media in the DASH system. In *Proc. 10th Int. Conf. Distributed Computing Systems*, Paris, May 1990.

APM Ltd (1993). ANSAware 4.1 Application programming in ANSAware. *Document RM.102.02*, APM Cambridge Limited, Poseidon House, Castle Park, Cambridge CB3 0RD, UK.

ATM Forum (1996). ATM user–network interface signalling specification v4.0. *Document Number af-sig-0061.000*.

Bacon J. (1993). Concurrent Systems. Wokingham: Addison-Wesley.

Beitz A., King P. and Raymond K. (1993). Comparing two distributed environments: DCE and ANSAware. In *DCE – The OSF Distributed Environment: Client/Server Model and Beyond* (Shill A., ed.), Lecture Notes in Computer Science, Vol. 73, pp. 21–38, London: Springer-Verlag.

Berry G. (1989). Real-time programming: special purpose of general purpose languages? In *Proc. IFIP Congress*, Amsterdam: North-Holland.

Berry G. and Gonthier G. (1988). The ESTEREL synchronous programming language: design, semantics, implementation. *INRIA Report No. 842*, INRIA, Domaine de Voluceau-Rocquencourt, BP 105, 78163 Le Chesnay Cedex, France.

Bershad B., Anderson T., Lazowska E. and Levy H. (1990). Lightweight remote procedure call. *ACM Trans. Computer Syst.*, **8**(1), 37–55.

Bershad B.N., Savage S., Przemyslaw P., Sirer E.G., Fiuczynski M.E., Becker D., Chambers C. and Eggers S. (1995). Extensibility, safety and performance in the SPIN operating system. In *Proc. 15th ACM Symp. Operating Systems Principles*, pp. 267–84, Copper Mountain CO, December 1995.

Birman K. (1993). The Process Group approach to reliable distributed computing. *Commun. ACM*, **36**(12), 36–53.

Blair G.S., Papathomas M., Coulson G., Robin P., Stefani J.B., Horn F. and Hazard L. (1994). Supporting real-time multimedia behaviour in open distributed systems: an approach based on synchronous languages. *Proc. ACM Multimedia '94*, 1994.

435

Blair G.S., Coulson G., Papathomas M., Robin P., Stefani J.B., Horn F. and Hazard L. (1996). A programming model and system infrastructure for real-time synchronisation in distributed multimedia systems. *IEEE J. Selected Area Commun. (JSAC), Special Issue on Multimedia Synchronisation*, **14**(1), 249–63.

Blair L. (1995). Formal specification and verification of distributed multimedia systems. *PhD Thesis*, Lancaster University.

Boulanger F. (1993). Integration des modules synchrones dans la programmation par objects. *Thèse no. 2977*, Ecole Supérieure d'Electricité, Université de Paris-Sud.

Boussinot F. and de Simone R. (1996). The SL synchronous language. *IEEE Trans. Software Eng.*, **22**(4).

Bowman H., Derrick J., Linington P. and Steen M.W.A. (1996). Cross viewpoint consistency in open distributed processing. *Software Eng. J.*, **11**(1), 44–57.

Bricker A., Gien M., Guillemont M., Lipkis J., Orr D., and Rozier, M. (1991). Architectural issues in microkernel-based operating systems: the CHORUS experience, *Computer Commun.*, **14**(6), 347–57.

Bulterman, D.C. and van Liere R. (1991). Multimedia synchronisation and UNIX. In *Proc. Second Int. Workshop on Network and Operating System Support for Digital Audio and Video*, Heidelberg, November 1991. Berlin: Springer Verlag.

Campbell R.H. and Tan S.M., (1995). μ-choices: an object-oriented multimedia operating system, *Proc. HotOS-V*, Washington, May 1995.

Caspi P. and Halbwachs N. (1986). A functional model for describing and reasoning about time behaviour of computing systems. *Acta Informatica*, **22**, 595–627.

Castagna G. (1995). Covariance and contravariance: conflict without a cause. *ACM Trans. Programming Languages and Systems*, **17**(3), 431–47.

Cheriton D. (1986). VMTP: a protocol for the next generation of communication systems. In *Proc. SIGCOMM'86 Symp. Communication Architectures and Protocols*, pp. 406–15.

Chesson G. (1988). XTP/PE overview. In *Proc. 13th Conf. Local Computer Networks*, pp. 292–6, Minneapolis, 1988.

Chu H.J. (1996). Zero-copy TCP in Solaris. In *Proc. 1996 Usenix Technical Conference*, pp. 253–64, San Diego, January 1996.

Clark D.D., Lambert M.L. and Zhang L. (1987). NETBLT: a high throughput transport protocol. *Computer Commun. Rev.*, **17**(5), 353–9.

Clark D., Shenker S. and Zhang L. (1992). Supporting real-time applications in an integrated services packet network: architecture and mechanism. In *Proc. ACM SIGCOMM'92*, pp. 14–26, Baltimore, August 1992.

CNET (1996). Requirements of a real-time ORB. *Technical Report, ACTS Project AC048 (RETINA)*, available from CNET, Centre Paris A, 38–40, Rue du Général Leclerc, Issy-les-Moulineaux, France.

Coulouris G., Dollimore J. and Kindberg T. (1994). *Distributed Systems: Concepts and Design* 2nd edn, Wokingham: Addison-Wesley.

Coulson G., Blair G.S., Horn F., Hazard L. and Stefani J.B. (1995). Supporting the real-time requirements of continuous media in open distributed processing. *Computer Networks and ISDN Systems (Special Issue on the ISO Reference Model for Open Distributed Processing)*, **27**(8).

Coulson G., Blair G.S. and Robin P. (1994a). Micro-kernel support for continuous media in distributed systems. *Computer Networks and ISDN Systems*, **26**, 1323–41.

Coulson G., Blair G.S. and Robin P. (1994b). Extending the Chorus microkernel to support continuous media applications. In *Proc. 4th Int. Conf. Network Support for Digital Audio and Video*, November 1993, Lecture Notes in Computer Science, Vol. 846, London: Springer-Verlag.

Cowen G., Derrick D., Gill M., Girling G., Herbert A., Linington P.F., Rayner D., Schulz F. and Soley R. (1993). *Prost Report of the Study on Testing for Open Distributed Processing*, APM Ltd.

Dang Tran F. and Perebaskine V. (1995). TORBoyau: Architecture et Implémentation. *Note Technique, NT/PAA/TSA/TLRJ4587*, CNET, Centre Paris A, 38–40, Rue du Général Leclerc, Issy-les-Moulineaux, France.

Danthine A. (ed.) (1994). The OSI95 transport service with multimedia support. *ESPRIT Research Reports*, Springer-Verlag.

Delgrossi L., Halstrick C., Hehmann D., Herrtwich R., Krone O., Sandross J. and Vogt C. (1994b). Media scaling in a multimedia communication system. *ACM Multimedia Systems*, **2**(4), 172–80.

Delgrossi L., Herrtwich R.G., Hoffmann F.O. and Schaller S. (1994a). Receiver-initiated communication with ST-II. *ACM Multimedia Systems*, **2**(4), 141–9.

Delgrossi L., Herrtwich R., Vogt C. and Wolf L.C. (1994c). Reservation protocols for internetworks: a comparison of ST-II and RSVP. In *Proc. 4th Int. Workshop on Network and Operating System Support for Digital Audio and Video*, Lancaster, November 1993, Lecture Notes in Computer Science, Vol. 846, London: Springer Verlag.

de Prycker M. (1991). *Asynchronous Transfer Mode: Solution for Broadband ISDN*. New York: Ellis Horwood.

Druschel P. and Peterson L.L. (1993). Fbufs: a high-bandwidth cross-domain transfer facility. In *Proc. 14th ACM Symp. Operating System Principles*, Asheville, December 1993 (published in Operating System Rev., **27**(5), 189–202).

Dupuy F., Nilsson G. and Inoue Y. (1995). The TINA Consortium: toward networking telecommunications information services, *IEEE Commun. Mag.*, **33**(11), 78–83.

Engler D.R., Kaashoek M.F. and O'Toole J., Jr (1995). Exokernel: an operating system architecture for application-level resource management. In *Proc. 15th ACM Symp. Operating Systems Principles*, pp. 251–66. December 1995.

Eriksson H. (1994). MBONE: the multicast backbone. *Commun. ACM*, **37**(8), 54–60.

Ferrari D. and Verma, D. (1990). A scheme for real-time channel establishment in wide area networks. *IEEE J. Selected Areas in Commun.*, **8**(3).

Ferrari D., Benerjea A. and Zhang H. (1994). Network support for multimedia: a discussion of the Tenet approach. *Computer Networks and ISDN Systems*, **26**, 1267–80.

Fluckiger F. (1995). *Understanding Networked Multimedia: Applications and Technology*, Englewood Cliffs NJ: Prentice-Hall.

García F. (1993). A continuous media transport and orchestration service, *PhD Thesis*, Lancaster University.

Gaultier O. and Metais Y.O. (1994). Mise en place d'une plate-forme Chorus, conception et implantation d'un ordannanceur a echeance au sein du noyau Chorus. *Ingenieur Diplôme*, CNAM, Paris, March.

Gibbs S.J. and Tsichritzis D. (1994). *Multimedia Programming: Objects, Environments and Frameworks*, Reading MA: ACM Press, Addison-Wesley.

Govindan R. and Anderson D.P. (1991). Scheduling and IPC mechanisms for continuous media. In *Thirteenth ACM Symp. Operating Systems Principles*, Pacific Grove CA. SIGOPS **25**, 68–80.

Gupta A., Howe W., Moran M. and Nguyen Q. (1995). Resource sharing for multi-party real-time communication. In *Proc. IEEE INFOCOM'95*, Boston MA, April 1995.

Hadzilacos V. and Toueg, S. (1994). Fault-tolerant broadcasts and related problems. In *Distributed Systems* 2nd edn (Mullender S., ed.). Reading MA: Addison-Wesley.

Halbwachs N. (1993). *Synchronous Programming of Reactive Systems*. New York: Kluwer.

Hanko J.G., Keurner E.M., Northcutt J.D. and Wall G.A. (1991). Workstation support for time critical applications, *Proc. Second Int. Workshop Network and Operating System Support for Digital Audio and Video*, Heidelberg, November 1991. Berlin: Springer Verlag.

Hansson H. (1991). Time and probability in formal design of distributed systems. *PhD Thesis*, Uppsala University.

Harel D. and Pnueli A. (1985). On the development of reactive systems. In *Logics and Models of Concurrent Systems* (Apt K., ed.), NATO ASI Series. New York: Springer-Verlag.

Hehmann D.B., Herrtwich R.G., Schulz W., Schuett T. and Steinmetz, R. (1991). Implementing HeiTS: architecture and implementation strategy of the Heidelberg high speed transport system. In *Proc. Second Int. Workshop on Network and Operating System Support for Digital Audio and Video*, Heidelberg, November 1991. Berlin: Springer Verlag.

Hehmann D.B., Salmony M.G. and Stuttgen H.J. (1990). Transport services for multimedia applications on broadband networks. *Computer Commun.*, **13**(4), 197–203.

Hermant J.F., Leboucher L. and Rivierre N. (1997). On comparing fixed/dynamic priority driven scheduling algorithms, *Research Report NT/DTL/ASR/5007*, CNET, Centre Paris A, 38–40, Rue du Général Leclerc, Issy-les-Moulineaux, France.

Hoffman D., Speer M. and Fernando G. (1994). Network support for dynamically scaled multimedia data streams. In *Proc. 4th Int. Workshop on Network and Operating System Support for Digital Audio and Video*, Lancaster, November 1993. Lecture Notes in Computer Science, Vol. 846, London: Springer Verlag.

Horn F. and Stefani J.B. (1993). On programming and supporting multimedia object synchronisation, *Computer J.*, **36**(1).

Hutchison D., Coulson G., Campbell A. and Blair G.S. (1994). Quality of service management in distributed systems. In *Network and Distributed Systems Management* (Sloman M. ed.), pp. 273–302. Wokingham: Addison-Wesley.

Interactive Multimedia Association (1994a). Multimedia system services – Part 1: Functional specification (2nd draft), *IMA Recommended Practice*, September 1994.

Interactive Multimedia Association (1994b). Multimedia system services – Part 2: Multimedia devices and formats (2nd draft), *IMA Recommended Practice*, September 1994.

ISO/IEC (1992). IS 10744, *Hypermedia/Time-based Document Structuring Language (HyTime)*.

ISO/IEC (1995a). CD 10746-1 | ITU Recommendation X.901, *Open Distributed Processing – Reference Model – Part 1: Overview*.

ISO/IEC (1995b). 10746-2 | ITU Recommendation X.902, *Open Distributed Processing – Reference Model – Part 2: Foundations*.

ISO/IEC (1995c). 10746-3 | ITU Recommendation X.903, *Open Distributed Processing – Reference Model – Part 3: Architecture*.

ISO/IEC (1995d). CD 10746-4 | ITU Recommendation X.904, *Open Distributed Processing – Reference Model – Part 4: Architectural Semantics*.

ISO/IEC (1995e). CD 13236.2, *Quality of Service Framework*.

ISO/IEC (1996). CD 14478-1, *Presentation Environments for Multimedia Objects (PREMO), Part 1: Fundamentals of PREMO*.

ISO/IEC (1997). 13235-1 | ITU Recommendation X.950, *Open Distributed Processing – Trading Function: Specification*.

ITU-T (1991). ITU-T Recommendations M.3010, Principles for a telecommunications management network. *Working Party IV, Report 28*, December 1991.

Jahanian F. and Mok A.K. (1986). Safety analysis of timing properties in real-time systems. *IEEE Trans. Software Eng.*, **12**(9).

Jeffay K., Stone D. and Donelson Smith F. (1991). Kernel support for live digital audio and video. In *Proc. Second Int. Workshop on Network and Operating System Support for Digital Audio and Video*, Heidelberg, November 1991. Berlin: Springer Verlag.

Jensen E.D. and Northcutt J.D. (1990). Alpha: a non-proprietary operating system for large, complex, distributed real-time systems. *Proc. IEEE Workshop on Experimental Distributed Systems*, Huntsville AL, pp. 35–41.

Joseph M. and Pandya P. (1986). Finding response times in a real-time system. *Computer J.*, **29**(5), 390–5.

Kafura D.G. and Lee K.H. (1989). Inheritance in actor based concurrent object-oriented languages. In *Proc. ECOOP'89*, pp. 131–45. Cambridge: Cambridge University Press.

Katz R.H. (1994). Adaptation and mobility in wireless information systems. *IEEE Pers. Commun.*, **1**(1), 6–17.

Kiczales G., des Rivières J. and Bowbrow D.G. (1991). *The Art of the Metaobject Protocol*. Cambridge: MIT Press.

Kopetz H. (1994). Scheduling. In *Distributed Systems* 2nd edn (Mullender S., ed.). Reading MA: Addison-Wesley, 1994.

Kopetz H., Damm A., Koza C., Mulazzani M., Schwabl W., Senft, C. and Zainlinger R. (1989). Distributed fault-tolerant real-time systems: the Mars approach. *IEEE Micro*, 25–41.

Koren G. and Shasha D. (1992). D^{over}: an optimal on-line scheduling algorithm for overloaded real-time systems. In *Proc. 13th Real-Time Systems Symp. (R-TSS'92)*, Phoenix, Arizona, 1992.

Kretz F. (1990). Multimedia and hypermedia information objects coding. In *Proc. 3rd IEEE Comsoc Int. Workshop on Multimedia Communication (Multimedia'90)*, Bordeaux, November 1990.

Kuo T.W. and Mok A.K. (1991). Load adjustment in adaptive real-time systems. In *Proc. 12th IEEE Real Time System Symp.*, San Antonio, 1991.

Lakas A., Blair G.S. and Chetwynd A. (1996). A formal approach to the design of QoS parameters in multimedia systems. In *Proc. 4th Int. Workshop on Quality of Service*, Paris, March, 1996.

Lamport L. (1994). The temporal logic of actions. *ACM TOPLAS*, **16**(3), 872–923.

Lazar A. and Pacifici C. (1991). Control of resources in broadband networks with quality of service guarantees. *IEEE Commun. Mag.*, October, 66–73.

Leboucher L. and Stefani J.B. (1995a). Admission control for end-to-end distributed bindings. In *Proc. 2nd Int. COST 237 Workshop*, Copenhagen, November 1995. Lecture Notes in Computer Science, Vol. 1052. London: Springer-Verlag.

Leboucher L. and Stefani J.B. (1995b). An axiomatic definition of the ODP computational model with QoS declarations. *Technical Report*, CNET, Centre Paris A., 38–40, Rue du Général Leclerc, Issy-les-Moulineaux, France.

Lehoczky J.P. (1990). Fixed priority scheduling of periodic task sets with arbitrary deadlines. In *Proc. 11th IEEE Real-Time Systems Symp.*, December, 201–9.

Leslie I.M., McAuley D. and Mullender S.J. (1993). Pegasus operating system support for distributed multimedia applications. *Operating Syst. Rev.*, **27**(1), 69–78.

Levy E. and Silbershatz A. (1990). Distributed file systems: concepts and examples. *ACM Computing Surv.*, **22**(4).

Linington P. (1991). Introduction to the ODP basic reference model. In *Proc. 1st Int. IFIP Conf. Open Distributed Processing*, Berlin, Germany, October 1991.

Linington P.F., Derrick J. and Bowman, H. (1996). The specification and testing of conformance in ODP systems. In *9th Int. IFIP TC6/WG6.1 Workshop on Testing of Communicating Systems (IWTCS'96)*, Darmstadt, Germany, September 1996.

Liu C.L. and Layland J.W. (1973). Scheduling algorithms for multiprogramming in a hard real-time environment. *J. ACM*, **20**(1), 46–61.

Locke C.D. (1986). Best effort decision making for real-time scheduling, *Doctoral Dissertation*, Carnegie-Mellon University.

Maes P. (1987). Concepts and experiments in computational reflection. In *Proc. OOPSLA'87, ACM SIGPLAN Notices*, **22**(12), 147–55.

Marsh B.D., Scott M.L., LeBlanc T.J. and Markatos E.P. (1991). First class user-level threads. In *Proc. Symp. Operating Systems Principles (SOSP)*, ACM, October 1991, pp. 110–21.

Matsuoka S., Taura K. and Yonezawa A. (1983). Highly efficient and encapsulated re-use of synchronisation code in concurrent object-oriented languages. In *Proc. OOPSLA'93, ACM SIGPLAN Notices*, **28**(10), 109–29.

Mauthe A. and Coulson G. (1997). Scheduling and admission control for jitter constrained periodic threads. *Multimedia Systems*, **5**(5).

Meyer-Boudnik T. and Effelsberg T. (1995). MHEG explained. *IEEE Multimedia*, **2**(1), 26–38.

Miloucheva I., Bonnesz O. and Buschermohle, H. (1993). XTPX based multimedia transport system for flexible QoS support. *Internal Report*, Technical University of Berlin.

Mishra S., Peterson L.L. and Schlichting R.D. (1993). Experience with modularity in Consul. *Software Practice and Experience*, **23**(10), 1050–75.

Mitchell J.G., Gibbons J.J., Hamilton G., Kessler P.B., Khalidi Y.A., Kougiouris P., Madany P.W., Nelson M.N., Powell M.L. and Radia S.R. (1994). An overview of the Spring System. In *Proc. IEEE 1994 Computer Conference (COMPCON '94)*, February 1994.

Montz A.B., Mosberger D., O'Malley S.W., Peterson L.L., Proebsting T.A. and Hartman J.H. (1994). Scout: a communications-oriented operating system. *Technical Report 94-20*, Department of Computer Science, University of Arizona.

Mowbray T.J. and Zahavi R. (1995). *The Essential CORBA: System Integration using Distributed Objects*, New York: John Wiley & Sons/Object Management Group.

Mullender S. (ed.) (1993). *Distributed Systems* 2nd edn. New York: ACM Press and Reading MA: Addison-Wesley.

Najm E. and Stefani J.B. (1995a). A formal semantics for the ODP computational model. *Computer Networks and ISDN Systems*, **27**(8), 1305–29.

Najm E. and Stefani J.B. (1995b). A formal operational semantics for the ODP computational model with signals, explicit binding, and reactive objects. *Research Report NT/PA/TSA/ TLRJ4187*, CNET, Centre Paris A, 38–40, Rue du Général Leclerc, Issy-les-Moulineaux, France.

Nieh J. and Lam M.S. (1995). Integrated processor scheduling for multimedia. In *Proc. Fifth Int. Workshop on Network and Operating System Support for Digital Audio and Video*, Durham NH, April 1995.

Nieh J., Northcutt J.N. and Hanko J.G. (1993). SVR4 UNIX scheduler unacceptable for multimedia applications. In *Proc. Fourth Int. Workshop on Network and Operating System Support for Digital Audio and Video*, Lancaster, November 1993. Lecture Notes in Computer Science, Vol. 846, London: Springer-Verlag.

Open Group (1990a). DCE overview. *Report Number OSF-DCE-PD-1090-5*, The Open Group, 11 Cambridge Center, Cambridge, MA 02142, USA.

Open Group (1990b). Security in a DCE: White Paper. *Report Number OSF-O-WP11-1090-3*, The Open Group, 11 Cambridge Center, Cambridge, MA 02142, USA.

Open Group (1994a). *OSF DCE Application Development Guide*, The Open Group, 11 Cambridge Center, Cambridge, MA 02142, USA.

Open Group (1994b). DME overview. *Report Number OSF-DME-PD-0394-2*, The Open Group, 11 Cambridge Center, Cambridge, MA 02142, USA.

Object Management Group (1995a). *The Common Object Request Broker: Architecture and Specification (Release 2.0)*, The Object Management Group, Framington Corporate Center, 492 Old Connecticut Path, Framington, MA 01701-4568, USA.

Object Management Group (1995b). *CORBAservices: Common Object Services Specification* revised edn, The Object Management Group, Framington Corporate Center, 492 Old Connecticut Path, Framington, MA 01701-4568, USA.

Papathomas M. (1995). Concurrency in object-oriented programming languages. In *Object-Oriented Software Composition* (Nierstrasz O.M. and Tsichritzis D., eds.). Englewood Cliffs NJ: Prentice-Hall.

Papathomas M. (1996). ATOM: an active object model for enhancing re-use in the development of concurrent software. *Research Report 963-I-LSR-2*, IMAG-LSR, Grenoble, France.

Papathomas M., Blair G.S. and Coulson G. (1995a). A model for active object coordination and its use for distributed multimedia applications. In *Proc. ECOOP Workshop on Coordination Models and Languages for Parallelism and Distribution*, Bologna, Italy, July 1994. Published as *Object-Based Models and Languages for Concurrent Systems* (Yonezawa A., Nierstrasz O. and Ciararini P. eds.). Lecture Notes in Computer Science, Vol. 924. Berlin: Springer-Verlag.

Papathomas M., Blair G.S., Coulson G. and Robin, P. (1995b). Addressing the real-time synchronisation requirements of multimedia in an object-oriented framework. In *Proc. IS&T/SPIE High Speed Networking and Multimedia Computing '95*, San Jose, California, 1995.

Partridge C. (1994). *Gigabit Networking*. Reading MA: Addison-Wesley.

Pasquale J., Polyzos G., Anderson E. and Kompella V. (1994). Filter propagation in dissemination trees: trading off bandwidth and processing in continuous media networks. In *Proc. 4th Int. Conf. Network Support for Digital Audio and Video*, Lancaster, November 1993. Lecture Notes in Computer Science, Vol. 846. London: Springer-Verlag.

Peterson L.L., Buchholz N. and Schlichting R.D. (1989). Preserving and using context information in interprocess communication. *ACM Trans. Computer Syst.*, **7**(3), 217–46.

Pierce B.C. (1994). Bounded quantification is undecidable. *Information and Computation*, **112**(1), July.

Powell D. (ed.) (1991). *Delta-4: A Generic Architecture for Dependable Distributed Computing*. ESPRIT Research Reports. London: Springer-Verlag.

Rashid R., Baron R., Forin A., Golub D., Jones M., Julin D., Orr D. and Sanzi, R. (1989). Mach: a foundation for open systems. In *Proc. 2nd Workshop on Workstation Operating Systems (WWOS2)*, September 1989.

Raymond K. (1993). Reference model of open distributed processing: a tutorial. In *Proc. 2nd Int. IFIP Conf. Open Distributed Processing*, Berlin, Germany, September 1993, pp. 3–14.

Ross F. (1989). An overview of FDDI: the Fiber Distributed Data Interface. *IEEE J. Selected Areas in Commun. (JSAC)*, **7**(7).

Rudkin S. (1993). Templates, types and classes in open distributed processing. *BT Technol. J.*, **11**(3), 32–40.

Satyanarayanan M., Noble B., Kumar P. and Price M. (1995). Application-aware adaptation for mobile computing. *Operating Systems Rev.*, **29**(1), 52–5.

Sha L., Rajkumar R. and Lehoczky J.P. (1990). Priority inheritance protocols: an approach to real-time synchronization. *IEEE Trans. Computers*, **39**(9), 1175–85.

Stankovic J.A. and Ramamrithan K. (1991). The Spring kernel: a new paradigm for real-time systems. *IEEE Software*, **8**(3), 62–72.

Stankovic J., Spuri M., Natale M.D. and Buttazzo G.C. (1995). Implications of classical scheduling results for real-time systems. *IEEE Computer*, **28**(6), 16–26.

Stefani J.B. (1993). A small real-time logic and an improved procedure for checking the validity of RTL formulas, *Esprit Project No. 2267 (ISA), Report CNET/RC.V01.ENJBS.006.*

Stefani J.B., Hazard L., Perebaskine V., Horn F., Auzimour P., Dang Tran F. (1995). A real-time DPE on top of Chorus. *Note Technique, NT/PAA/TSA/TLR/4179,* CNET, Centre Paris A, 38–40, Rue du Général Leclerc, Issy-les-Moulineaux, France.

Steinmetz R. (1994). Data compression in multimedia computing standards and systems. *ACM Multimedia Syst.,* **1**(5), 187–204.

Steinmetz R. (1995). Analyzing the multimedia operating system. *IEEE Multimedia,* **2**(1), 68–84.

Steinmetz R. and Nahrstedt K. (1995). *Multimedia: Computing Communications and Applications.* Englewood Cliffs NJ: Prentice-Hall.

Tanenbaum A.S., van Renesse R., van Staveren H, Sharp G.J., Mullender S.J., Jansen A.J. and van Rossum, G. (1990). Experiences with the Amoeba distributed operating system. *Commun. ACM,* **33**, 4663.

Tennenhouse D.L. (1990). Layered multiplexing considered harmful. In *Protocols for High-Speed Networks.* Amsterdam: Elsevier Science Publishers.

Tilborg A. and Koob G.M. (1991). *Foundations of Real-Time Computing: Scheduling and Resource Management.* New York: Kluwer.

Tindell K. (1994). Fixed priority scheduling for hard real-time systems. *PhD Thesis,* University of York.

Tindell K. and Clark J. (1994). Holistic schedulability analysis for distributed hard real-time systems. *Microprocessing and Microprogramming,* **40**(23), 117–34.

Tiuryn J. and Urzyczyn P. (1996). The subtyping problem for second-order types is undecidable. In *11th IEEE Symp. Logic in Computer Science,* New Brunswick NJ, July 1996.

Tokuda H. and Mercer C.W. (1989). ARTS: a distributed real-time kernel. *ACM Operating Syst. Rev.,* **23**(3).

Tokuda H., Nakajima T. and Rao P. (1990). Real-time Mach: towards a predictable real-time system. In *Proc. Usenix 1990 Mach Workshop,* Usenix, October 1990.

van der Linden R. (1993). An overview of ANSA. *Document APM.1000.01,* APM Cambridge Limited, Poseidon House, Castle Park, Cambridge CB3 0RD, UK.

van Renesse R., Birman K.P. and Maffeis S. (1996). Horus, a flexible group communication system. *Commun. ACM,* **39**(4), 76–83.

Watters A., van Rossum G. and Ahlstrom J. (1996). *Internet Programming with Python.* Henry Holt (MIS/M&T Books).

Wegner P. (1987). Dimensions of object-based language design. In Proc. Conf. Object-Oriented Programming Systems, Languages, and Applications (OOPSLA '87). *ACM SIGPLAN Notices Special Issue,* **22**, 168–82.

Wolfinger B. and Moran M. (1991). A continuous media data transport service and protocol for real-time communication in high speed networks. In *Second Int. Workshop on Network and Operating System Support for Digital Audio and Video,* Heidelberg, November 1991. Berlin: Springer Verlag.

Yang Z. and Duddy K. (1996). CORBA: a platform for distributed object computing. *ACM Operating Syst. Rev.,* **30**(2), 4–31.

Yeadon N., Garcia F., Shepherd D. and Hutchison D. (1996). Filters: QoS support mechanisms for multipeer communications, *IEEE J. Selected Areas in Commun., Special Issue on Distributed Multimedia Systems and Technology,* in press.

Zhang H. (1995). Service disciplines for guaranteed performance service in packet switching networks. *Proc. IEEE,* **83**(10), 1374–96.

Zhang L., Deering S., Estrin D., Shenker S. and Zappala D. (1993). RSVP: a new resource ReSerVation Protocol. *IEEE Network,* September.

Index